Modern Comparative Politics Series
edited by
Peter H. Merkl
University of California,
Santa Barbara

Modern
Comparative
Politics

990

MODERN COMPARATIVE POLITICS

Peter H. Merkl
University of California,
Santa Barbara

HOLT, RINEHART AND WINSTON, INC.
New York   Chicago   San Francisco   Atlanta
Dallas   Montreal   Toronto   London   Sydney

Copyright © 1970 by Holt, Rinehart and Winston, Inc.

Library of Congress Catalog Card Number: 70–118656

SBN: 03–078510–3

Printed in the United States of America

9 8 7 6 5 4 3 2 1

FOREWORD
TO THE SERIES

This new series in comparative politics was undertaken in response to the special needs of students, teachers, and scholars
that have arisen in the last few years, needs that are no longer
being satisfied by most of the materials now available. In an age
when our students seem to be getting brighter and more politically aware, the teaching of comparative politics should present
a greater challenge than ever before. We have seen the field come
of age with numerous comparative monographs and case studies
breaking new ground, and the Committee on Comparative
Politics of the Social Science Research Council can look back
proudly on nearly a decade of important spade work. But teaching materials have lagged behind these changing approaches to
the field. Most comparative government series are either too little
coordinated to make systematic use of any common methodology or too conventional in approach. Others are so restricted
in scope and space as to make little more than a programmatic
statement about what should be studied, thus suggesting a new
scholasticism of systems theory that omits the idiosyncratic richness of the material available and tends to ignore important elements of a system for fear of being regarded too traditional in
approach.

In contrast to these two extremes, the Modern Comparative Politics Series attempts to find a happy combination of rigorous, systematic methodology and the rich sources of data available to area and country specialists. The series consists of a core volume, *Modern Comparative Politics,* by Peter H. Merkl, country volumes covering one or more nations, and comparative topical volumes.

Rather than narrowing the approach to only one "right" method, the core volume leaves it to the teacher to choose any of several approaches he may prefer. The authors of the country volumes are partly bound by a framework common to these volumes and the core volume, and are partly free to tailor their approaches to the idiosyncrasies of their respective countries. The emphasis in the common framework is on achieving a balance between such elements as theory and application, as well as among developmental perspectives, sociocultural aspects, the group processes, and the decision-making processes of government. It is hoped that the resulting tension between comparative approaches and politicocultural realities will enrich the teaching of comparative politics and provoke discussion at all levels from undergraduate to graduate.

The group of country volumes is supplemented by a group of analytical comparative studies. Each of these comparative volumes takes an important topic and explores it cross-nationally. Some of these topics are covered in a more limited way in the country volumes, but many find their first expanded treatment in the comparative volumes—and all can be expected to break new scholarly ground.

The ideas embodied in the series owe much to the many persons whose names are cited in the footnotes of the core volume. Although they are far too numerous to mention here, a special debt of spiritual paternity is acknowledged to Harry Eckstein, Gabriel A. Almond, Carl J. Friedrich, Sidney Verba, Lucian W. Pye, Erik H. Erikson, Eric C. Bellquist, R. Taylor Cole, Otto Kirchheimer, Seymour M. Lipset, Joseph La Palombara, Samuel P. Huntington, Cyril E. Black, and many others, most of whom are probably quite unaware of their contribution.

P. H. M.

Santa Barbara, California

PREFACE

This book is meant to serve a dual purpose. First, it was written as the core book of the Holt, Rinehart and Winston Modern Comparative Politics Series, to be used together with a flexible selection of country studies in the series. For this purpose, the core book and all the country monographs follow a common outline for the convenience of instructors and students who emphasize topical comparison. With minor deviations to accommodate multiple-country studies and special exceptions to political uniformity, parallel chapters in the core book and the country studies can be assigned and compared with ease. This is no small feat considering the great differences among political systems around the globe, and the reader should not expect the uniformity to be carried out in every detail.

The second purpose of the book is to serve independently as a comprehensive introduction to comparative politics for undergraduates and beginning graduate students. The subjects have been treated in such a way that the book is not dependent on the country studies. It could be used as the main textbook at various levels and supplemented with topical or case studies just as easily as with country monographs. It would be particularly suitable for introductory courses on comparative politics such as many departments now recommend prior to their upper division or graduate offerings in country or area studies.

There has long been a need at all levels for a book that would draw together the varied contributions from brilliant minds in many topical and geographic areas of comparative politics. Because there is so much to cover, and because so many new studies are forever coming out, this book should reduce to manageable proportions the student's need to consult a vast literature, for it summarizes much that appears scattered elsewhere. The book also attempts a synthesis rather than a mere accumulation, such as is already being offered in the form of many books of readings in the field, but without trying to offer anything like an exclusive road to salvation and ultimate truth. The discipline of comparative politics is still too much in a state of transition and upheaval, and there are far too many new, authentic voices clamoring for attention to impose closure on the many open questions before us. Finally, it seems high time for a book in comparative politics to integrate the older, more conventional approaches with the new psychocultural and sociocultural knowledge and with the emphasis on political development. This book was written with obvious commitment to both the new and the old and in awareness of the needs mentioned earlier. Whether it succeeds in combining and balancing all these facets in one framework for the use of students and instructors is a question for the users to decide.

P. H. M.

Santa Barbara, California
February 1970

CONTENTS

INTRODUCTION

WHY WE COMPARE

Millions of Americans every year spend some time abroad, encountering alien cultures, foreign tongues, and different ways of life, customs, and attitudes they cannot readily understand. Their reactions range from emphatic rejection to "going native." Most of them gain a new awareness of many things characteristic of their own country that they had taken for granted. No other experience can so teach a person to appreciate the privileges, comforts, and conditions at home as an extended stay abroad. Few other experiences, by the same token, will as much awaken his critical sense for things he need not have accepted at home to begin with or for his country's role and responsibility in the world.

As a means for thorough understanding of politics at home, abroad, and international, sophisticated comparison has always been unsurpassed. From Aristotle's *Politics* to some of the quantitative research of contemporary behavioral political scientists, the comparative study of politics has preoccupied many of the finest analytical minds. Without going into the history of the discipline,[1] it is worth the time of the beginning student to

[1] For a brief historical sketch, see Harry Eckstein's essay in David E. Apter and Eckstein, eds., *Comparative Politics: A Reader*. New York: Free Press, 1963, pp. 3–42.

ponder some of the prominent motives and purposes of comparative political analysis.

Philosophical goals

The most personal and perhaps also the loftiest goal of comparative political study has been philosophical self-knowledge and, by implication, personal growth and maturity. Since an important aspect of our human nature finds its fulfillment in political understanding and participation, anything that deepens our insight into the nature of politics will make us more complete and mature human beings. Since the times of Plato and Aristotle, political philosophers have told us that man can fully realize his quest for human freedom only by being an active and intelligent participant with others in joint political action as a good citizen of his community, his country, and his world. If an American abroad begins to understand his own personal and cultural identity better as a result of his encounter with an alien people, he will become a better American citizen at home. If he learns to appreciate and tolerate cultures and ways of life different from his own, he will be a better citizen of the world and a better human being.

Scientific goals

On a more empirical, scientific level, comparative political analysis has a primary commitment to the collection, ordering, and broadening of our empirical and theoretical knowledge of the world in which we live, simply for the sake of knowledge. This was a major motive of Aristotle, the father of a political science based on comparative study and philosophical reflection. The basic steps this famous Greek philosopher appears to have followed in his comparative political research more than two thousand years ago are worth noting, because their logic is still compelling today. Aristotle addressed his study to the causes of the many revolutions that made the politics of Greek city-states turbulent and unstable. By implication, he also wanted to learn what constitution, or form of political system, showed the greatest stability in this setting. So he sent out his students to collect 158 case histories of Greek city-state constitutions (all but one of these, that of Athens, have since been lost).

Aristotle's method   The first step of Aristotle's comparative research was to conceive of a problem, a question capable of being answered by the comparative method. His second step was the collection of descriptive data, a step not unlike the collection of case histories in medicine or of plant samples in botany. The third step consisted in classifying his constitutional histories by the use of several meaningful criteria. First, using the conventional criterion of the number of formal rulers, he divided political systems into oligarchic-aristocratic rule by a few and mobocratic-democratic rule by the masses, there being no monarchies (rule by one) in his sample. Then he added a classification by actual mode of operation, which might be oligarchic or democratic. This was followed by a classification of social systems according to whether the citizenry of a city-state was composed of only a small upper class and a large, poor lower class, or whether it also had a significant middle class. The fourth step of the research operation consisted in correlating the established categories with one another and with the incidence of revolution, in order to determine, as the fifth step, which combinations were the most stable and which were the least stable. To recapitulate, Aristotle's method of comparison can be outlined as follows:

1. Formulation of problem (causes of political stability and instability)
2. Collection of cases
3. Classification of cases
   3a. by number of rulers: monarchy, oligarchy, democracy
   3b. by mode of operation: oligarchic or democratic
   3c. by class structure and distribution of power among classes
4. Correlation of *3a–c* with relative stability or instability
5. Analysis—which types are most stable and why

As far as can be gathered from his *Politics,*[2] which contains the final research report, so to speak, Aristotle found two least stable forms of city-state government: pure democracies and pure oligarchies. In pure democracies the poor masses tended to

[2] Aristotle's *Politics* consists of the lecture notes taken by some of his students. The relevant passages are so generously laced with his philosophical conclusions that it is difficult to separate them from his empirical findings.

"soak the rich," thereby inciting the latter to conspire against the government. In pure oligarchies the few rich would incite the masses to revolt by their selfishness and privileges. The most stable city-states were those in which power was either held by a strong middle class, if there was one, or shared between the upper and lower class, as in democratically functioning oligarchies or oligarchic democracies.

Contemporary method   Comparative political analysis today still follows basically the same logical sequence, although with a considerable increase in the diversity of systems considered and in the sophistication of tools and concepts. The conception of a project, the collection and classification of data, and correlation and analysis are still the basic steps for exploring the empirical world around us.

The comparative method need not be used only across national borders. It can be used very profitably among subunits of the same country, just as Aristotle preferred comparing Greek city-states to one another rather than to the great empires rising and declining in his age. Comparison can also be used over distances in time rather than in space—for example, in a comparative study of the American presidency of the 1950s with the same institution in the 1850s. The more similar the political settings under comparison are, the more precise the comparative method can be. Broader, more inclusive comparison, on the other hand, leads to conclusions of more general validity.

The empirical, scientific nature of many studies has earned the comparative method a reputation as *the only truly scientific approach to politics,* as distinguished, for example, from partisan bias or philosophic speculation. Some comparison, indeed, is implicit in all scientific conceptualization and definition. To define a thing one must, at least subconsciously, compare it to something from which it differs. Consequently, all political-science terms and concepts agreed upon by the members of the discipline and appearing in textbooks carry within them the fruit of comparison, even when they seem to be used in a noncomparative context. Such a broad interpretation of the "comparative" method, however, goes considerably beyond the customary usage in political science, where "comparative politics" refers chiefly to the study of foreign political systems.

Practical applications

The search for empirical knowledge about the political world around us is often accompanied by the goal of practical application. Just as the physical sciences have advanced the goal of harnessing the energies and regularities of the physical environment for human use, much comparative political study has aimed at the development of more adequate forms of government or better solutions for various practical political problems. This motive can be traced down through the centuries, from Aristotle to the recent burgeoning of studies of the politics of the developing areas, studies motivated at least in part by a sincere desire to discover among the great diversity of social and political patterns the kinds of processes and forms of government that would contribute to a country's optimal development.

The goal of practical application of comparative analysis is rarely divorced from that of expanding the range of empirical political knowledge. As party systems or the impact of different social systems on the patterns of politics are compared—with a view, perhaps, toward solving problems of stability or better design—new thories and theoretical models emerge that help to order or reclassify the existing knowledge of politics. A new view of the world of political processes, relationships, and institutions may in turn influence the current attempts at designing constitutions or changing political processes. No student of comparative politics can fail to notice the extraordinary frequency with which institutional patterns and whole legal systems spread from country to country simply by imitation. Constitutional assemblies and policy makers frequently use comparison in order to design better constitutions or policies. And although imitation across national boundaries may often have its pitfalls and unwanted side effects, it is an undeniable tribute to the practical relevance of comparative study.

For the student who seeks a broad empirical grasp of the world of politics, the imitation of institutions or policies creates something like a series of experiments with a set of working hypotheses. To the extent that British parliamentary institutions and executive-legislative relations have been copied by many other countries or that Roman legal and judicial systems have been widely imitated, for example, a contemporary Aristotle could easily analyze them comparatively and thereby learn much about the elements of design and the environmental factors that make for viable representative institutions, executive branches, and courts. For purposes of theory building, cases of faulty imitation or poor results are just as enlightening as perfect working copies of the best models of parliamentary, executive, or judicial organization in that they highlight the specific causes of failure or success. And this is no less true, say, of the comparison of various democratic electoral systems and their effects or of any particular kind of public policy or procedure of policy making in several countries.

Applications for policy

Comparative study also has such mundane goals as grow from political activity itself. Often, for example, observers of foreign politics use their comparisons for large-scale and sweeping prediction of trends, such as "creeping socialism" in the West or "creeping capitalism" in the Soviet Union. A famous example of such prediction was the book *Democracy in America* by the French aristocrat Alexis de Tocqueville, whose extended visit to the United States in the 1830s led him to speculate perceptively on what the eventual coming of democracy might bring to his country and to the rest of Europe. International revolutionary movements, such as nationalism, communism, or fascism, also frequently derive detailed predictions of trends in their own favor from comparative political observation and experience. Predictions of the "inevitable triumph" of a movement's own creed often accompany an elaborate theory of stages of social and economic development lying at the core of its ideology. In practice, however, the victories of such movements are more often the result of revolutionary efforts than of careful comparative study of trends of development.

Similarly interested in manipulation rather than detached observation are the ministries and legislative committees of foreign affairs the world over, not to mention the larger espionage and secret services. A secretary of state or other maker of foreign or defense policy needs to know a great deal about the strengths and weaknesses of foreign countries in order to plot his strategies. For this purpose he may rely on elaborate research operations that closely resemble and often partly depend on academic research. Yet his chief interest remains the manipulation of other countries by diplomacy, military policy, foreign aid, or subversion, as the case may be, and the anticipation of their attempts to manipulate his own country.

There is an obvious borderline to be drawn between legitimate academic research in comparative politics, whether applied research or basic theory building, and the power-oriented purposes of governments, political parties or groups, and ideological movements. There is no escaping the awesome responsibility of the "policy scientist" for the policies pursued on his authority or with his support. The integrity of political-science research as an academic discipline depends on its ability to remain free from entanglements with actual policy making. This is not to say that political scientists should refrain from holding and expressing opinions, values, and preferences regarding their subject. In comparative politics, as in other social-science disciplines, it is the privilege and moral obligation of the well-informed student of foreign systems to tell the public what he believes to be true.

RECENT TRENDS IN COMPARATIVE POLITICS

Although the study of comparative politics is a venerable discipline dating back at least twenty-three hundred years, chiefly in the last several decades has it progressed at an ever-accelerating pace to its present state. To appreciate the more prominent trends of comparative study today, one need not review the many schools and landmarks of its development during the last hundred years. Suffice it to say that political scientists and related social scientists before the 1950s were preoccupied largely with exploring and explaining the many aspects of the political transformation of Western Europe and North America in the century and a half since the French and American revolutions of 1789 and 1776. Although much of the great transformation of European traditional societies had started considerably earlier, it was chiefly in the decades before and after 1900 that significant numbers of social scientists began to observe and compare, to search for antecedents and speculate upon the direction of trends.

Effect of the Industrial Revolution

After nearly a thousand years of monarchy and aristocracy in Europe, these venerable institutions had begun to totter before the onslaught of a new age of masses and machines. The Industrial Revolution had set the whole social order in motion, moving masses of long-dormant peasant populations to cities and industrial centers, and offering enterprising young men unheard-of opportunities of acquiring wealth and social status. Entire new social classes were born and united by common views (ideologies), which they opposed to the old aristocratic ruling classes. The rise of a new politics of mass participation and the threat of popular revolt against reluctant old elites translated the social upheaval into an inexorable trend toward new political patterns and institutions. As old empires fell and new nation-states were formed in Europe and North America, the task for political scientists seemed clear: they had to catalog and classify, to compare and analyze the momentous changes before them.

Many students of comparative government in Europe and America rose to the challenge by constructing elaborate institutional taxonomies that allowed the comparison of different Western systems in significant detail. Constitutional lawyers, parliamentarians writing the new constitutions, and erudite politicians and administrators watching one another across national boundaries helped to create a distinctive Western pattern of government with plenty of legal definitions and relationships. This school of comparative political study was soon developed to a fine point of perfection that is still evident in many of the older textbooks and treatises in use today.[3] A second school developed simultaneously along the lines of political sociology, concerning itself chiefly with the nature of the social upheaval and the new elites, urbanization, the bureaucratization of government and economic life, and the nature of the new political groups (both parties and interest groups) that characterized the political transformation. Even though members of this second school were first regarded as sociologists rather than political scientists, their contribution to an understanding of European politics was substantial from the beginning and soon influenced the practical researches of political scientists.

The rise, malfunctioning, and breakdown of many of the

[3] See, for example, Karl Loewenstein, *Political Power and the Governmental Process*. Chicago: University of Chicago Press, 1957; or Herman Finer, *The Major Governments of Modern Europe*. New York: Harper & Row, 1960.

new republican governments in Europe during the 1920s and 1930s intensified the concern of students of comparative politics with questions of institutional design and with the sociological substructure and the political group life that had failed to sustain the institutions formerly considered so important. It brought many an innovation in the ways of looking at politics, especially a greater emphasis on the psychological dimension, as with the "new school" of political science advanced by such men as Charles E. Merriam and Harold D. Lasswell or with the extensive literature on totalitarian forms of government.[4] Nevertheless, the standard coverage of textbooks in comparative government remained the major European powers—including the Soviet Union—and, by implication, the United States.[5]

The revolution in comparative politics

At this point the great change came over the study of comparative politics. Basic approaches and techniques were revolutionized and the older methods subjected to scathing criticism.[6] Much of the innovation consisted in deliberate attempts to base the rather crude empiricism of single-case studies and narrow topical comparsions on a body of well-founded systematic theory. Important impulses for methodological reform came from the new *behavioral approaches,* which simultaneously made inroads in most other political-science fields with their incisive quest for quantitative measurement and scientific precision.[7] Other im-

[4] See, for example, Sigmund Neumann, *Permanent Revolution.* New York: Harper & Row, 1942; and Carl J. Friedrich and Zbigniew K. Brzezinski, *Totalitarian Dictatorship and Autocracy,* 2d rev. ed. Cambridge, Mass.: Harvard University Press, 1965, and the bibliographies included there.

[5] This was true even of such ingenious combinations of political philosophy, institutional theory, and sociology as C. J. Friedrich's *Constitutional Government and Democracy* (Boston: Ginn & Co., 1946; reissued by Blaisdell, 1968) and Herman Finer's *Theory and Practice of Modern Government* (New York: British Book Center, 1949; reissued London: Methuen, 1961), two classics well worth a careful reading by the beginning student today.

[6] See especially Roy C. Macridis, *The Study of Comparative Government.* New York: Doubleday, 1955.

[7] For a convenient summary of the behavioral approach see, for example, Heinz Eulau, *The Behavioral Persuasion in Politics.* New York: Random House, Inc., 1963.

pulses came from the interdisciplinary emphasis of area studies, which consistently called on economics, geography, history, social psychology, and cultural anthropology to help illuminate the politics of an area or a group of countries.[8]

The politics of developing areas   The most momentous single factor for the current transformation of the study of comparative politics, however, was the rising importance of the politics of the developing areas. With the great rush of former colonies to independence and nationhood, and with their increasing importance in world politics, they simply could no longer be ignored. Legions of social scientists visited developing countries in Asia, Africa, the Middle East, and Latin America, and their research reports and theorizing had a revolutionary impact on the study of comparative politics.

To understand the full significance of the inclusion of the politics of developing areas, we need only reflect on Aristotle's failure to include in his comparative study the phenomenon of the great empires, such as the one with which his own pupil Alexander the Great soon took over all the democratic and oligarchic city-states of Greece, thus putting an ironic end to Aristotle's research problem of the causes of revolution and political stability. Had Aristotle attempted to consider empires along with his city-states, he would have had to change his whole frame of reference and also his conclusions.[9] Perhaps he too would have used a broadly inclusive term such as "political system" and the broad functional prerequisites that both empires and city-state governments have in common. Inevitably, Aristotle would also have had to account in some fashion for the intimate relationship between Greek political institutions and procedures and the ways and values of the Greek way of life. Since the great empires of antiquity each represented values and mores rooted

[8] See, for example, the reflections of Merle Kling, "Area Studies and Comparative Politics," *American Behavioral Scientist,* September 1964, pp. 7–10.

[9] To give an illustration, Aristotle's rejection of "pure democracy" as a viable form of government is closely related to the size of the political unit he was describing. Had he been forced to consider larger units comparable to modern nation-states, he might even have discovered representative government, an institution unknown in his time.

in their cultures and social systems, he might well have had to supplement his research design with an explicit account of the *sociocultural matrix* underlying each political system. And last, but not least important, he might have wished to classify his societies and their politics by empirically defined *stages of development* that would clearly distinguish the earlier phases of Athenian monarchy from the democratic era [10] or the primitive empires from their refined bureaucratic forms.[11] Equipped with these conceptual tools, Aristotle's comparative research of twenty-three centuries ago would fit well into the current modes of study of comparative politics.

GENERALIZING ABOUT THE POLITICAL SYSTEM

The beginning student of comparative politics needs a thorough understanding of what the term "political system" has come to mean to political scientists. This term was designed in part to accommodate the extreme variations in political patterns that threatened to break up the narrow definitions of an earlier, less diverse universe of political comparison. The "political system" is the lowest common denominator among empires and city-states or even among local politics and international politics of a global scale. In fact, one could describe the politics of the world as one huge international system made up of the varying relationships among more or less independent "national systems" [12] of variable size and groupings. The independent systems constitute the level with which we will be most concerned in this book. Each independent system is in turn made up of numerous subsystems, even sub-subsystems, which have a way of acting and interacting rather autonomously within the system. Such subsystems can be groups, however defined, or cultural patterns or organized patterns of human interaction, such as institutions and processes. The smallest moving part of any political system is the

[10] See also the perceptive comments of Eric A. Havelock, *The Liberal Temper in Greek Politics.* New Haven, Conn.: Yale University Press, 1956, chap. 13.

[11] See S. N. Eisenstadt, *The Political Systems of Empires.* New York: Free Press, 1963.

[12] The word "national" here only designates the level of the units in the global system. The presence of a "nation" needs to be demonstrated empirically from case to case.

individual who makes up groups and institutions and who feels and behaves in cultural and other organized patterns.

System elements and structure

To make up a minimal definition of the political system, a great many sophisticated concepts and theories have been added with the help of sociological and anthropological systems theories [13] and from the practice of political research.[14] The term "system" generally implies a certain kind of order among its elements, and a regularity among the patterns of relationships present. The elements and relationships making up the system need to be specified. Figure 1 presents a composite diagram of the various systems to be discussed. Some political scientists follow the sociologist Talcott Parsons, who described a "social system" as a system of "processes of interaction" among the "actors" that constitute the units of the system.[15] The more stable or recurrent relationships and processes form the *structure* of the system, which in turn defines the interactive *role* of each actor. The political system is a major subsystem of the social system. It is distinguished by its exercise of authoritative control over the whole system, or the function of goal attainment (Parsons), and it interacts frequently with other nonpolitical subsystems, such

[13] See, for example, A. R. Radcliffe-Brown, *Structure and Function in Primitive Society*. New York: Free Press, 1952; Robert K. Merton, *Social Theory and Social Structure*. New York: Free Press, 1957; the survey by F. X. Sutton included in Apter and Eckstein, *Comparative Politics*, pp. 67–79; and the contributions by Marion J. Levy, Jr., and Talcott Parsons to Roland Young, ed., *Approaches to the Study of Politics*. Evanston, Ill.: Northwestern University Press, 1957.

[14] Behaviorally oriented political-science research generally needs to spell out systemic theories before it can go to work. See, for example, Austin Ranney, ed., *Essays on the Behavioral Study of Politics*. Urbana, Ill.: University of Illinois Press, 1962.

[15] For a brief sketch, see Parsons' study in Young, *Approaches to the Study of Politics*, pp. 282–301; Parsons and Edward Shils, *Toward a General Theory of Action*. Cambridge, Mass.: Harvard University Press, 1951; and Parsons, *The Social System*. London: Routledge, 1951. Parsons is often criticized, however, for stressing the equilibrium, or pattern-maintaining, qualities of society at the expense of change and conflict. See, for example, Walter Buckley, *Sociology and Modern Systems Theory*. Englewood Cliffs, N.J.: Prentice-Hall, 1967; and, for a change-oriented systems theory, George C. Homans, *The Human Group*. New York: Harcourt, 1950.

Figure 1 A composite diagram of the political system

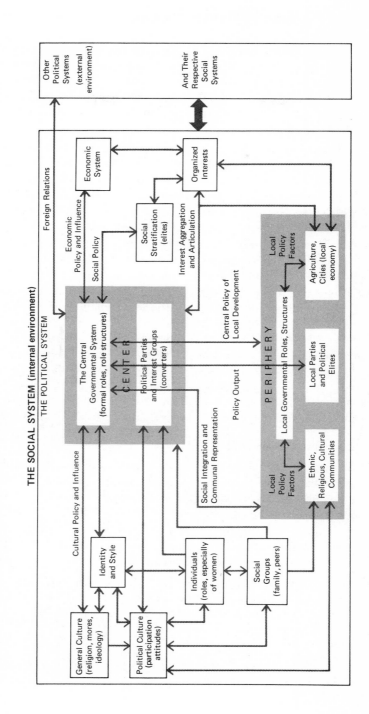

as the economic system. Typical elements of the structure of the political system are formal political institutions, such as legislatures, or informal institutions, such as political parties and interest groups. Some of the processes of political interaction are the bargaining or persuasion going on during election campaigns, the nomination of candidates for public office, or group lobbying with public agencies. Typical political roles are the individual roles of the legislator, of the voter, of the campaign manager, or of the administrator. They could also be group roles, such as the formal role of a legislative committee or the informal one of a rioting mob. Since the roles are defined by the structure of the system, they generally persist beyond the presence or activity of their occupants at any one time.[16]

Understanding a given political system, subsystem (such as a political party), process, or case study, then, involves as a first step the identification of the various elements present and, as a second step, the charting of their significant interrelations and interactions. To speak of significance, however, raises further problems of definition. To note as "significant" the presence of a particular combination of elements or a particular relationship between elements is to give political understanding a sense of direction in the middle of an enormous ocean of potentially significant items of political information, an ocean so large, in fact, that no single systems theory can hope to encompass it all.

Conceptual frameworks

Several conceptual frameworks have been designed, each with a particular research interest in mind. One important school of systematic theory, for example, stresses models of decision making by entire political systems or parts thereof. Political scientists with this focus of interest may be interested in how political problems are resolved [17] or how different elements of a system

---

[16] One of the foremost attempts in political science to develop a broadly applicable theory of the political system is by David Easton, whose model stresses the behavior of the political system vis-à-vis its environment in terms of analyzing inputs (demands and supports) and outputs (authoritative allocation of values or policy decisions and actions). See his *A Systems Analysis of Political Life.* New York: Wiley, 1966; and his earlier *The Political System.* New York: Knopf, 1953.

[17] See, for example, Herbert J. Spiro's *Government by Constitution.* New York: Random House, Inc., 1959.

enter into the making of a policy decision or perhaps in the content of the policies.[18] Another kind of systems theory uses communications theory and models of communication systems to conceptualize the process of political integration among several countries or ethnic communities making up a new system. Since many of the so-called new nations are really polycommunal (that is, made up of several ethnic communities) and have not yet become nations, such an approach is as timely for today's problems as for an understanding of Eastern European nationalism fifty or a hundred years ago.[19] A third type of systems theory that deserves a more detailed discussion here is the *structural-functional approach,* although it should be made clear from the beginning that this approach is a matter of considerable controversy.[20]

The structural-functional approach   In a sense, the functional approach to political science is as old as Plato and Aristotle, who were the first to speak of particular functions they wanted the political system to perform in order to maintain and order the political community. Despite the teleological overtones sometimes carried over from these ancient philosophical antecedents, functionalism has been revived with impressive scientific credentials in such fields as anthropology and sociology.[21] It is hardly surprising that political scientists studying government in primitive societies or the processes of political modernization should have been tempted to follow the footsteps of anthropol-

[18] For a sample of the huge literature, which is often related to psychological, economic, and sociological decision-making research, see the contributions of Richard C. Snyder and James G. March in Ranney, *Essays on the Behavioral Study of Politics.*

[19] See especially the many writings of Karl W. Deutsch on political integration, beginning with his *Nationalism and Social Communication.* Cambridge, Mass.: M.I.T. Press, 1953; and his *The Nerves of Government.* New York: Free Press, 1963; and Easton's cybernetic model, *A Systems Analysis of Political Life* and *The Political System.*

[20] For a broad survey, see *Functionalism in the Social Sciences,* Monograph No. 5, Annals of the American Academy of Political and Social Science, February 1965.

[21] In social anthropology, the prevalent tendency has been to evolve idiographic models of functions for each primitive society studied, whereas sociologists such as Parsons and Robert K. Merton have attempted rather to develop nomothetic, generally applicable functional approaches.

ogists such as A. R. Radcliffe-Brown or Bronislaw Malinowski in using a functional approach.[22] At the same time the considerable influence of Talcott Parsons and other functionally oriented sociologists on the recent development of comparative politics also reintroduced functionalism as a conceptual tool capable of organizing great masses of political research data and relating them to the needs of the entire system. This latter feature—the relating of single phenomena to the whole system—is the great virtue of functionalism, allowing a range of generalization and inclusiveness unequaled by any other theory. And yet, the very generality of the functional approach also contains its pitfalls.

Examples of current functional theories illustrate this point. Talcott Parsons and Neil Smelser [23] proposed four major functions that any social system must meet in order to survive, much as a biological organism must satisfy certain basic needs for its survival: (1) pattern maintenance and tension management, (2) goal attainment (including mobilization of resources), (3) adaptation, and (4) integration. Each of these major functions involves several more specific functional requisites, such as (a) the passing on of cultural norms and social mores from one generation to the next (socialization and enculturation) and (b) control of deviations from the rules of behavior prescribed by the system. Each functional need must be met by structures performing this function for the whole system. Upon reflection, the student can easily see the political relevance of these major functions and their functional requisites. Almost all major political processes, roles, and institutions that we can observe fulfill important functions for the whole social system.

A classic attempt to spell out specifically "political functions" is that of Gabriel Almond,[24] who, in addition to such

[22] See, for example, Robert T. Holt and John E. Turner, *The Political Basis of Economic Development.* New York: Van Nostrand, 1966.

[23] Talcott Parsons and Neil Smelser, *Economy and Society.* New York: Free Press, 1956. Often the term "functional requisites" may also be applied to numerous smaller elements such as roles, institutional patterns, cultural norms, devices for social control, and so on. Such use of the functional approach generally increases its practical usefulness while reducing its value for systematic comparison.

[24] See his brilliant introductory essay in Almond and James S. Coleman, eds., *The Politics of the Developing Areas.* Princeton, N.J.: Princeton University Press, 1960. For a survey of other political struc-

age-old governmental functions as rule making, rule application, and rule adjudication,[25] posited five more functional activities as worthy of comparative investigation: (1) political socialization, or the induction of the individual into the role of a citizen of the system; (2) political recruitment, or the processes of selection for membership in political parties, public office, or political leadership positions; (3) interest articulation, or the processes by which specific societal interests are formulated and represented by groups in the political system; (4) interest aggregation, or the aggregation of several such organized interests by representative devices, such as political parties or bargaining with public officials and agencies; and (5) political communications, or the channels and processes through which political information is transmitted among the different groups and between the governed and their rulers. This list of political functions is said to be universal to all societies though not necessarily exhaustive. And the political structures of any given society [26] are usually multifunctional or at best only in small part functionally specific.

Both Almond's and Parsons' functional approaches have been highly influential among students of comparative politics. They seemed particularly useful to attempts to describe any political system as a whole or to relate its various major activities or processes to one another. Some political scientists even felt they could base a general theory of politics on them. On the other hand, Almond's approach was criticized for not going far enough in the direction of a complete, systematic theory, and it has since been modified considerably.[27] The most important modifi-

---

tural-functional literature, see also the political-science parts of *Functionalism in the Social Sciences,* pp. 84–126.

[25] These functions correspond not only to such familiar institutional structures as legislatures, administrations, and courts. They can also be found in some of the oldest literature of political thought and down through the ages as logical derivatives from the basic function of government, the authoritative control over the system.

[26] According to Almond, in *The Politics of the Developing Areas,* p. 11, no society maintaining its order is without such a structure. Political structure is defined as "legitimate patterns of interaction by means of which this order is maintained." See also the list of "structural requisites" proposed by Apter in Eckstein and Apter, *Comparative Politics,* pp. 84–85.

[27] See especially Gabriel Almond and G. Bingham Powell, Jr.,

cation appears to be an attempt to systematize and reorder the original elements of the theory under new headings, subsuming political socialization and recruitment under the "system maintenance and adaptation" function (as in Parsons) and the other six (interest articulation, interest aggregation, political communication, rule making, rule application, and rule adjudication) as "conversion functions" (as in Easton), converting "demands and supports" into a flow of policies. The "capabilities" of a system to interact effectively with its environment, both domestic and international, also form an important part of Almond's remodeled approach,[28] along with greater detailing of the developmental aspects and the role of the cultural systems in politics.

THE OPEN DOOR OF EMPATHY

To the beginning student who is barely becoming aware of the elements and processes that conditioned his own outlook on politics, even a thorough grasp of systems theory still leaves a long way to go toward an understanding of, say, French or Indian politics. Each system tends to deviate in major ways, not to mention the countless little idiosyncrasies, from the nomothetic model of the political system. To understand the politics of France or India, a student must look for the basic elements present and try to piece them together, using perhaps the functional way of thinking, but better not a preconceived model of any sort. Otherwise, he risks forcing the living political realities into a Procrustean bed of theory, stretching a limb here or cutting off the feet there, just as the legendary Greek giant used to do to his hapless visitors.

Systems theory and political disorder

Of particular importance is the recognition that most models of political systems presuppose an orderly, if not rational, pattern.

Comparative Politics: A Developmental Approach. Boston: Little, Brown, 1966, pp. 12–15. Note also the more systematic emphasis on political culture that began to crystallize with Almond and Sidney Verba's classic *The Civic Culture.* Princeton, N.J.: Princeton University Press, 1963.

[28] Capabilities analysis is of great importance also in the current theories of international relations and of obvious utility in distinguishing the more highly developed from the developing countries. Being "devel-

Systems theorists often speak of "pattern maintenance" and "stable equilibrium," and functionalists assume too readily that basic functions are being met and complement one another. But the truth is that in most systems of our age, political order is frequently disrupted by major breakdowns or permanent crises, ranging from domestic upheavals to the overshadowing presence of international conflict. Patterns are not being maintained but are subjected to rapid change. Instead of stability and equilibrium, instability and disequilibrium [29] are far more typical of contemporary societies, whether they be developing or already highly developed. Basic functions that might be fulfilled in a more stable setting are sometimes completely in abeyance. Normally complementary functions may be exercised so as to conflict with each other or to be dysfunctional to the system.

The resort to intuitive perceptions

To cite a classic example, Lucian W. Pye's study of personality and modern nation building in Burma proposed at one point that "the ultimate test of development is the capacity of a people to maintain large, complex but flexible organizational forms." Pye further concluded that the effectiveness of organizational life presupposed a measure of mutual trust and "associational sentiments" not present in Burmese political culture because of the isolative qualities—fear, shame, and ridicule—of childhood socialization in the Burmese family.[30] There are many such systems, in which isolative childhood socialization appears to inhibit adult cooperation in voluntary political groups—as, for example, in parts of France. Elsewhere, Pye describes the insufficient political acculturation of many Burmese politicians in terms of the sharp distinction between their "private feelings and public postures and actions." In almost exactly the same words, the sociologist Rolf Dahrendorf speaks of the yawning gap in

---

oped," in itself, could be defined as a greatly increased capacity to extract, mobilize, and distribute a country's resources.

[29] For a perceptive analysis of the prevalence of disequilibrium and its contribution to revolutionary change, see Chalmers Johnson, *Revolutionary Change*. Boston: Little, Brown, 1966, chaps. 4 and 6.

[30] Lucian W. Pye, *Politics, Personality, and Nation-Building*. New Haven, Conn.: Yale University Press, 1962, pp. 51–52, 125–126, chaps. 9 and 12, pp. 227–230.

modern Germany between the "cult of the private virtues" nur-
tured by family life and the neglected "public virtues" required
to sustain Western-style democracy.[31] Finally, Pye also shares
the view of the eminent psychologist Erik H. Erikson [32] that new
nations emerging from traditional societies undergo a major
identity crisis not unlike that of an adolescent emerging from
childhood and straining toward an adult identity. In many such
societies, the adoption of a charismatic leader who struggles
through a major identity crisis himself is another cogent example
of the richness of political pathology, which seems to call for
empathy and intuitive grasp at the individual level rather than
for systems analysis.

Empathy and intuition can be hazardous tools if they are
used to glimpse the inner rationale of entire political systems.
As used frequently in the past for a kind of "*Gestalt* political
science" or configurative analysis, they have often reinforced
grossly distorted caricatures of alien systems, as systems analysis
never would. The instances of how politically well-informed
Englishmen or Americans have misunderstood French politics—
not to mention those of more exotic lands—and vice versa would
fill many books. But using empathy to build up an understanding
of an alien system from the basic elements offers unique advantages to the student of comparative politics. Every student,
regardless of his present age, was once a child and can grasp
intuitively what may be different about the childhood socialization experiences of Frenchmen, Congolese, Indonesians, or
Venezuelans. Every person interested in politics has at least some
idea of how he himself became politically involved and will
understand how the young of other countries were "politically
socialized" or "politically acculturated." He also understands
most basic political sentiments, attitudes, and ideological rationalizations and should have no difficulty empathizing with the novel
elements of "political culture" he may encounter.

Once the political attitudes of individual Frenchmen or
Russians in all their diversity are well understood, the student is

[31] Pye, *Politics, Personality, and Nation-Building*, pp. 227–228.
Rolf Dahrendorf, *Gesellschaft und Demokratie in Deutschland*. Munich:
Piper, 1964, chap. 20.
[32] See Erik H. Erikson, *Childhood and Society*. New York: Norton,
1950; and *Young Man Luther*. New York: Norton, 1958.

a giant step closer to an understanding of the dynamics and weaknesses of the group life of these countries and of its cleavages between city and countryside, the old and new generations, and different social classes, traditions, and religions. With the individuals and groups in their cultural system thus accounted for, the patterns and uses or abuses of political institutions become a variable item in a relatively stable setting. Institutions can be changed or modified at will. They can break down at a time of crisis or perform their assigned tasks well or poorly, depending on attitudes and habits understandable from the patterns of political socialization and culture. Where forms of government come and go, sometimes overnight, or turbulence is more prevalent than any recognizable structure, as in many developing countries, the people and their attitudes are far more constant than anything else. In the setting of a modern or modernizing country, unlike traditional cultures, few structures will remain unchanged for as long as a generation of citizens and political elites set in their political ways.

1
CATEGORIES OF HISTORICAL DEVELOPMENT

With the general recognition that the study of developing areas must be included, the developmental classification of political systems has become a cornerstone of comparative analysis. There had always been some awareness among social philosophers and social scientists of the significance of development.[1] The easily observable effects of industrialization and urbanization on society, however, have dominated contemporary theories of development.

"AGRARIA" AND "INDUSTRIA" SYSTEMS

As F. X. Sutton characterized it, an "agricultural society" is distinguished by:

> *1.* The predominance of ascriptive, particularistic, diffuse patterns [2]

[1] Early examples are the charts of "ages of human progress" of the Marquis de Condorcet (1743–1794) and Auguste Comte (1798–1857), and the speculations of Karl Marx (1818–1883) about the dialectic evolution of economy and society under the impact of industrialism.

[2] This characterization refers to some of Parsons' pairs of *pattern variables:* (1) affectivity—affective neutrality, (2) collectivity—orientation—self-orientation, (3) particularism—universalism, (4) ascription—

2. Stable local groups and limited spatial mobility
3. Relatively simple and stable "occupational" differentiation
4. A "deferential" stratification system of diffuse impact, such as a landowners' class, or "estates"

Even agricultural societies often have a few cities, but the great bulk of the population is rural.

A modern, urban-industrial society is characterized by:

1. The predominance of universalistic, specific, and achievement norms
2. A high degree of social mobility
3. A well-developed occupational system insulated from other social structures
4. An "egalitarian" class system based on generalized patterns of occupational achievement
5. Prevalence of functionally specific associations [3]

The distinction between "agraria" and "industria" types of social systems has many readily apparent implications even though it is only a beginning in the understanding of development and calls for further refinement. The political processes and institutions of "industria," for example, tend to be *functionally specific*. There are parties to help formulate the will of the people and to select and support candidates for public office. Interest groups will pursue specific policies for the benefit of their clients. The making of laws, their application, and their adjudication are likely to be in the hands of differentiated institutions, each carefully designed to perform its own function. Administrators and elective officials are recruited on the basis of proven ability and promise of achievement. The criteria of selection and

---

achievement, and (5) diffuseness—specificity. Of each pair, the first-mentioned pattern characterizes less-developed societies. See Talcott Parsons and Edward Shils, *Toward a General Theory of Action.* Cambridge, Mass.: Harvard University Press, 1951.

[3] F. X. Sutton, in Harry Eckstein and David Apter, *Comparative Politics.* New York: Free Press, 1963, p. 71. By ascription, sociologists mean the assignment of rank or role on the basis of birth, age, or sex rather than achievement. Particularism refers to an emphasis on kinship and local relations, whereas universalism denotes the prevalence of generally applicable norms, such as laws and principles. Thus, ascription is particularistic, ranking by achievement universalistic.

promotion in the public service, as in a large part of private economy, will be *universalistic* in character. And so will be the governing of the body politic, by means of laws and fair procedure.

"Agraria," on the other hand, is likely to have political institutions and processes in which *symbolism* and *diffuse patterns of deference* outweigh recognizable purposes. It will probably be ruled by a monarch and an aristocracy who owe their positions to *ascription* and their authority to *particularistic* norms. And there will be very little, if any, of the differentiated role structure of bureaucracy and associations typical of a highly developed system.

STAGES OF SOCIAL DEVELOPMENT

The political development of a people is closely tied to its social development. A particular political system may encourage, even hasten, the growth of social development, or it may limp behind it; however, a truly modern political system could hardly be sustained for any length of time by a traditional society or vice versa. And since the social system is a far more complex and encompassing phenomenon than the political system, social development deserves to be examined in considerable detail and with a view toward identifying categories and stages of development.

Any attempt at periodizing the history of a country is likely to stir up controversy. There is no reason to expect less than the same from the present attempt. Analyzing social development by segments or major topics, on the other hand, may lend concreteness and clarity to this undertaking. Given the great variety of cultures and of social systems, this approach allows us to pinpoint differences and regularities without having to arrive at summary judgments. In fact, segmental analysis of social development should be considered a way of looking at the resisting facts to be learned rather than a new set of sweeping generalizations with overtones of a philosophy of history.

Analysis in six segments

The segments of social development to be discussed here are (1) the economic system, (2) the social structure, (3) the family,

(4) the role of the individual, (5) the cultural system, and (6) the political system. We begin with the economic system, chiefly because there have been many specific attempts to conceptualize stages of economic development, but none of these segments should be considered more fundamental than the others. The first five, and others not regarded as relevant here, are closely interrelated and mutually dependent. Yet they also seem autonomous enough to be examined separately or to have developed at different rates. At a later point, the political system will be appropriately related to these five segments and discussed in greater detail.

Three basic social stages   The basic stages discussed with respect to each segment will be the customary three: traditional societies, modern societies, and the transitional stage in between. Traditional and modern societies presumably each form a fairly harmonious system with internal forces and processes that maintain their patterns.[4] Transitionalism, on the other hand, begins with the breakdown of traditional society for reasons of internal disequilibrium or external pressures. It is sometimes described as a mixture of traditional and modern elements, sometimes as a very unhappy time of confusion and conflict.[5]

The three stages indicate a continuum of social development and differentiation, and so they will have to be taken with a grain of salt. The few observable uniformities of traditional societies should not make us forget their extraordinary diversity nor the fact that they, too, evolved from earlier antecedents. Nor should modern societies as presently exemplified in Europe, North America, and other isolated instances be mistaken for the goal of social evolution, after which nothing different can be expected. The process of development itself should not be interpreted in a quasi-Marxist fashion as inexorable progress toward a final stage

[4] For an attempt to explain pattern maintenance in traditional societies in terms of personality types and their interaction, see Everett E. Hagen, *On the Theory of Social Change.* Homewood, Ill.: Dorsey Press, 1962, chaps. 4–8.

[5] Since almost all contemporary developing societies are at the transitional stage, a huge literature could be cited to illustrate different versions of transitional conflict. See, for example, Kalman H. Silvert, ed., *The Conflict Society: Reaction and Revolution in Latin America.* New York: American Universities Field Service, 1965.

of salvation. There have been too many regressions of highly developed civilizations to more primitive stages to let us believe that such lapses could no longer happen.[6] Finally, the threefold periodization appears to be much too crude to shed a great deal of light on the many in-between stages of transitionalism and modernity that explain the particular problems and crises of contemporary politics. Suggestions on further periodization will be offered, therefore, where it seems appropriate.

THE ECONOMICS OF DEVELOPMENT

From the viewpoint of members of highly developed countries such as the United States, much of the interest in the process of development focuses on economics. Misled by the announced goals of foreign aid policy and by Cold War competition for the loyalty of the new nations, the American public hears of "rich" and "poor" or "underprivileged" nations and sees the difference largely as one of levels of living standards and per capita income. Planners of foreign policy international aid suggest, not inaccurately, that if we could only transform the stagnant economies of developing countries into economies of steady, self-sustaining growth, the countries concerned would move directly on toward modernity.

Limitations of traditional societies

However, we must guard against projecting our own modern, achievement-oriented attitudes upon societies that are barely emerging from traditional ways of life. Economic growth in such a society in the early phases of transition is not responsive to economic incentives or foreign aid boosts by themselves. It requires basic changes in attitude among masses of people and a favorable and stable political climate. It is only at a rather advanced phase of transitionalism, for example, when substantial numbers of people have begun to produce for markets, that

[6] The most likely causes of such a regression today would be the misuse of nuclear technology in war between the great powers or social disorganization in and among the more developed nations. But see also the sophisticated theory of political decay in Samuel P. Huntington, *Political Order in Changing Societies*. New Haven, Conn.: Yale University Press, 1968, chaps. 1 and 4.

developing societies begin to see their salvation in economic development. Only at that point can they be expected to make a commitment to economic growth as such, and only then is foreign aid likely to produce immediate results.[7]

By way of contrast, the market economies of typical traditional societies are not likely to be of prime concern. The vast majority of the population is probably living in rather isolated village or tribal communities or both. Their methods of growing or otherwise producing food[8] are of very simple technology, and their production rarely exceeds the very modest demands of subsistence. Owing to the basic set of traditional peasant attitudes, they not only lack incentives for improving the technology of production but may even have profound fears of innovation. The aristocratic military, landowning, or priestly elites, including frequently a reigning monarchic family, will likewise have little incentive for economic improvement as long as they receive their tribute in the form of symbolic deference and material sustenance.

Traditional societies usually possess also a small class of traders in small cities, among which a relatively more modern life style prevails. But neither trade nor urbanism touch the life of the peasants to an appreciable degree until the stable patterns of traditional society begin to break up.[9] The disintegration could originate with natural catastrophes of direct economic impact, such as famine or flood, or with cultural crises, such as a breakdown of established religion or the challenge of new faiths. Often the causes are exogenous: contact with or conquest by a more advanced civilization threatens the traditional pattern and produces a strong reaction in any one of the five segments or in the political sphere.

The process of transition

Once the process has begun, changes in one segment easily touch off major changes in the others. Thus, the exploitation of natural

[7] For a glimpse of the voluminous literature of economic development see, for example, Albert O. Hirschmann, *The Strategy of Economic Development*. New Haven, Conn.. Yale University Press, 1958.

[8] Many traditional societies still include nomadic herdsmen, hunters, and collectors. There are also great differences in productive methods and land tenure among agrarian societies.

[9] See especially Max F. Millikan and Donald L. M. Blackmer, eds., *The Emerging Nations*. Boston: Little, Brown, 1961, chap. 2.

resources by a new colonial master may not only have long-range effects for economic production, but it may also cause migration to cities, which in turn would break up tribal or village communities, weaken the traditional family structure, emancipate individuals, and effect cultural changes. Given sufficient time, the cumulative effect of accelerating social change will tend to touch the lives of so many people that the great transition finally ushers in modernity.

By definition, traditional societies see very little change and innovation, whereas modern societies are characterized by constant, fairly rapid, and noticeable change touching the life of nearly everyone. The transitional period, economically speaking, begins with the creation of what W. W. Rostow has called the "preconditions for the takeoff" of modern economic growth, such as the insights of modern science into more rational agricultural and industrial production, the lateral expansion of world markets, and the appearance of entrepreneurial elites, such as those that began the industrial and commercial revolution in many Western countries during the eighteenth and nineteenth centuries. Other preconditions for the takeoff appear to be the political consolidation (or independence) and the "social overhead" in transport and communications indispensable for economic growth. The takeoff stage is characterized as the point where the forces making for economic progress become dominant over the remaining barriers of traditional society. About two generations later, under optimal conditions, industrializing countries tend to reach urban-industrial maturity, the economic equivalent of the beginning of modernity.[10]

At this point a highly differentiated economy is ready to produce and manipulate nearly anything it wishes, although industrially mature nations have shown a high propensity to external power struggles and empire building. The reasons behind this propensity are probably largely noneconomic, Marxist specu-

---

[10] See W. W. Rostow, *The Stages of Economic Growth*. New York: Cambridge University Press, 1960, chaps. 2–5. Rostow places the beginning of the takeoff in Great Britain in the 1780s, in France, the United States, and Germany between 1830 and 1850, and in such developing countries as China and India in the 1950s. Maturity was reached first by Great Britain in the 1850s and by France, the United States, and Germany about 1910.

lation notwithstanding. The "drive toward economic maturity" invariably causes such social dislocations and cultural strains that an explosive potential for external aggression results. A supporting observation is that the following "stage of mass consumption" generally brings about the end of the explosive potential in its most chauvinistic form. One might conjecture that the spread of individual satisfactions on a mass level dissipates the pent-up collective energies into harmless, private channels—or that the promise of affluence that industrialism holds out to the man in the street is finally fulfilled after generations of painful deprivations and frustration.[11] Since only the stage of mass consumption truly involves the vast majority of the people as participants in the urban-industrial system, it is the consumer-oriented, full-employment economy that fully represents the advent of economic modernity.

SOCIAL STRUCTURE

The social structure of a given traditional society is central to an understanding of its nature. By social structure we mean essentially two kinds of patterns, a spatially arranged system of village, tribal, and/or ethnic or other social communities and the horizontal stratification that separates social classes or the elites from the masses.

The traditional society

The division of a traditional society into relatively self-contained and more or less isolated villages, tribes, ethnically distinct communities, or feudal fiefs rests on low spatial mobility as well as on the importance of face-to-face contacts in traditional life. The typical traditional villager, tribesman, or feudal serf lives within a parochially circumscribed small circle that requires no outside contact, and he rarely encounters any.[12] Consequently,

---

[11] Mass consumption also helps to stabilize the economic system by creating a huge and growing internal market for most of the goods produced, thus reducing the dependence of an industrialized country on markets abroad. See also Rostow, *The Stages of Economic Growth,* chap. 5 and the conclusions drawn in later chaps.

[12] The literature describing traditional villages is very large. See, for example, the writings of Oscar Handlin on Eastern Europe, S. R. Srinivas on India, or Oscar Lewis on Mexico, or the remarks of Samuel Huntington, *Political Order in Changing Societies,* pp. 72–78.

regional and village-to-village differences in culture, customs, language, and religious observances can develop or increase without check within the same society. The problems of poly-communalism, multinationality, and minority discrimination or persecution begin to arise chiefly when modernization brings about greater contact and competition among the disparate elements.

Another aspect of traditional social structure in some societies are rigid occupational-social communities, such as the European medieval guilds or the Indian caste system. Caste membership completely and inescapably defines a person's social and cultural identity and severely restricts his choice of occupation, way of life, and marriage partner.[13] Neither the tribal, village, and ethnic communities nor the different castes of traditional societies ever implies an equal start or equal status for the individual.

Politically, the most significant feature of traditional society is the authority relationship between the aristocratic, landowning or military elites and the vast peasant masses. In the Middle Ages, for example, centralized patrimonial and the more decentralized feudal rule were both based on the rule of a small elite by ascriptive authority, by dint of the privilege of the elite person as a member of a particular group over the masses of the non-privileged.[14] Many traditional, hierarchic systems comparable to European feudalism, in spite of an extraordinary range of variety, could also be found among African tribal kingdoms, among Indonesian princes, and in Saudi Arabia or Yemen. The equivalent to the traditional religious authority of medieval bishops also existed in Islamic countries and among certain other religions.[15] Religious sanction, heredity, and the ownership of land or cattle make the traditional elite status nearly impervious to change or

[13] See, for example, Lloyd I. and Susanne H. Rudolph, "The Political Role of India's Caste Associations," *Pacific Affairs,* 33 (1960), 5–22.

[14] See esp. Reinhard Bendix, *Nation-Building and Citizenship.* New York: Wiley, 1966, pp. 33–40.

[15] See, for example, David E. Apter, *The Politics of Modernization.* Chicago: University of Chicago Press, 1965, pp. 88–106; L. Fallers, "The Predicament of the Modern African Chief," in Immanuel Wallerstein, *Social Change: The Colonial Situation.* New York: Wiley, 1966, pp. 232–248; and Fred von der Mehden, *Politics of the Developing Nations.* Englewood Cliffs, N.J.: Prentice-Hall, 1964, pp. 78–86.

to newcomers, except by military conflict. A defeated king may indeed lose throne and kingdom, and a minor elite figure in charge of a victorious army may become the new king; otherwise, dreams of major social advancement are confined to the swineherds in fairy tales.

Breakup of traditional strata

When traditional societies break up, their systems of social stratification only show the most dramatic changes. Frequently, a favorable maritime location or trading opportunities nourish the power and prestige of a new merchant class, emerging from the rather small and insignificant role of the traders and artisans in traditional societies. Sometimes, the middle classes arise upon the acute need of princes and kings for their moneymaking and banking skills. Not infrequently, also, the needs of the state [16] for administrators or professional military men, or the needs of organized religion for administrators and priests, open channels for the social advancement of the middle and lower classes that in the long run revolutionize the traditional social structure.

In Western European societies, for example, the middle classes began to emerge for the first time as the rise of cities, art, and commerce disrupted the traditional feudal society in about the eleventh century. In the most advanced areas, such as northern Italy, this development led to the flowering of an entirely new civilization, the Renaissance, although political anarchy, invasions, and the old aristocratic elites tended to limit severely the fruition of its revolutionary consequences. Elsewhere in Europe, the progress of the rising middle classes took a more circuitous, if ultimately more decisive, course as a result of a long-range collusion between the monarchic dynasties and the urban middle classes [17] against aristocratic resistance. In France and England it still took centuries of development, including bloody revolution and industrialization, until the middle classes actually became dominant late in the nineteenth century. Yet their influence was

---

[16] Traditional societies vary considerably in the extent to which they have a strong political organization. Some incline toward setting up a strong monarchic or even theocratic authority, while others have been called stateless, or politically decentralized, or localized.

[17] The urban middle classes are called the *bourgeoisie* after the French word for "town," *bourge,* in other words, city dwellers who were neither of the peasantry nor of the feudal aristocracy of traditional society.

pervasive enough to liberalize large portions of British and French society and even to recruit prominent aristocrats for the cause of bourgeois revolution.

The rise of a distinct working class, which followed industrialization and the mobilization of the countryside for "parity" with the urban worker, complete the familiar system of modern society. The long struggle of workers and peasants for equality and a share of power is evidently the last phase of transitionalism in the social structure. When all the new classes have won their share of power and the class barriers are waning, along with barriers based on ethnic origin or religious creed, the modern stage can be said to have begun, at least in Western societies.

However, for the many transitional societies at various stages today, still struggling with the centripetal effects of polycommunal composition and ethnic and religious friction, it is difficult to lay down a model of modern social structure. Not only must we account for the impact of Western colonialism, or exogenous modernizations, but the importance of technology and industrialization as the catalysts in the known Western examples does not seem to apply equally to many developing nations.[18] Countries such as the Soviet Union, where coerced industrialization helped a semitraditional society leap over many stages without entirely arriving at modernity, further complicate the picture. The effect of communist rule on the vestiges of traditional Russian social structure has been, perhaps, the most dramatic feature of the system, even if we concede that some inequalities may still be found among nationalities and creeds or between urban workers and the rural population.

The individual and the family

The question of the role of the individual in traditional or in modern society should be aimed chiefly at individuals of the lower and most numerous classes. Kings, high priests, and other members of the traditional ruling elites may actually be character-

---

[18] See, for example, Wallerstein, *Social Change,* pt. V, or the discussion of India in Bendix, *Nation-Building and Citizenship,* chap. 7, where education, community development, and representative institutions at all levels are seen as more crucial than technology. See also John H. Kautsky's essay in Kautsky, ed., *Political Change in Underdeveloped Countries* (New York: Wiley, 1962), with its emphasis on the "intellectual class."

ized by many of the traits and orientations we associate with modernity. It is the state of mind of the traditional peasant, or even the nomad, and their extended families on which this discussion will focus.

When Daniel Lerner and his researchers examined the traditional peasants and nomads of the Middle East and the anthropological literature about their equivalent elsewhere, they found them to be living in a "constrictive world" of their own. The peasants were illiterate, rooted to their wretchedly poor village, and mortally afraid of leaving it or of knowing anything about the world outside of it. They were singularly vague about concepts of time, space, or measurement beyond their immediate needs and rather unwilling to learn anything new.[19] They could not imagine themselves doing anything other than what they were doing. Prizing physical courage above verbal skills and ingenuity, they also exhibited a propensity for violence at slight provocations. Jordanian Bedouins, although spatially more mobile, appeared to protect their constrictive world with a mixture of towering contempt for civilization and rank superstition. As with the peasants, absence of knowledge and absence of manipulated or well-understood social change reinforced one another. A substantial increase in knowledge about the outside world and in empathy toward new individual roles, economic, social, or political, denotes the breaking up of the constrictive world.[20] The advent of mass education is a major landmark of individual development, depending, of course, on its inclusiveness and content.

The traditional family   The character of the traditional family is almost universally determined by a strict hierarchy of age

[19] See *The Passing of Traditional Society*. New York: Free Press, 1958, pp. 131–135, 317–328.

[20] Mass education thrust into a traditional environment will always create a rival socialization process competing with what the family and other social agents try to impress upon the child or adolescent. It may mobilize the dormant masses or inculcate them with faith in the traditional order of things. Often it is held back at first by a lack of well-trained teachers. The extension of full educational opportunities to the lower-class peasants and workers, to minorities, or to women, moreover, is often deliberately withheld, even in otherwise highly developed societies. See also James S. Coleman, ed., *Education and Political Development*. Princeton, N.J.: Princeton University Press, 1965.

and sex. Males are considered superior to females and older persons superior to younger ones. The yoke of the constrictive world of the traditional, in other words, lies twice as heavily upon women and upon the young. The extended family is the fulcrum of most collective endeavors and values, often to the exclusion of other associations for the exercise of social, economic, or civic functions. An observer accustomed to the rich social and associational life of more developed societies may find such "familism" amoral, callous, and irredeemably sterile.[21] A young African of modern economic ambitions, by the same token, is sometimes reluctant to take on an employment career in the knowledge that all his cousins, aunts, and uncles may wish to claim their share of his modest economic betterment.

The traditional family also includes relations and processes that assure the proper socialization of the young into the prevailing social and cultural patterns. Since the relations between fathers and sons (and husbands and wives) in traditional society are invariably authoritarian, it is easy to imagine how authoritarian fathers will inculcate the appropriate fears of change and of the unknown along with authoritarianism itself in the next generation. When paternal authority breaks down as a result of external crisis or defeat—or of prolonged absence of fathers in war—the consequence may well be a breakdown of the traditional socialization patterns and the emergence of a whole generation tending toward innovation and experimentation.[22] It is conceivable also that the emancipation of women may be advanced by the "defeat" or prolonged absence of fathers and husbands; this occurred in many Western nations during World War I and was followed promptly by woman suffrage and the "roaring twenties."

Emancipation of the individual

In the final analysis, however, regardless of the accidents of psychological or economic causation, long-range changes in the status of individuals, and especially of women and young people,

---

[21] See, for example, the analysis of "amoral familism" in a poor southern Italian village by Edward and Laura Banfield, *The Moral Basis of a Backward Society.* New York: Free Press, 1967. It should be noted that Banfield's account of southern Italy raised some criticism among European sociologists.

[22] See Hagen, *On the Theory of Social Change,* chaps. 9–11.

have to be accepted by the cultural system in order to stay. Looking at the evolution of Western societies, for example, we can note the point when the more individualistic religious sects of Protestantism challenged the older, collectivity-oriented Catholic faith on a mass scale. Great thinkers such as Richard Tawney and Max Weber have even suggested a causal link between the rise of Protestantism and the individualistic ethic of capitalist enterprise. There are also other telltale landmarks of individual emancipation in Western cultures, such as the first literary and dramatic featuring of commoners, even lower-class persons, as heroes, rather than kings and noblemen. It is easy also to date the first literature dealing with the education and development of the child and the hopes and aspirations of women. Then there is the rise of popular culture and mass entertainment, indifferent to the rarefied tastes of a wellborn or highly educated elite. For the lower classes, the rise of sports and physical culture, the age of motion pictures and popular singers, and the rise of a political "man of the people," offer both the individualistic hope of a sudden meteoric rise from obscurity to stardom and intimate communing between the elite of stars and the empathetic mass audiences. For middle-class tastes, and usually antedating popular culture, the equivalent to the triumph of athletic and movie stardom is the triumph of technological invention, scientific discovery, and managerial ability. The great inventor, scientist, business executive, and government administrator symbolize the middle-class urge for individual achievement as succinctly as the movie star at a later point represents the individualistic dreams of the little man and woman.

As the great transition brings about changes in the roles of individuals on an increasingly massive scale, though not everywhere at once, their attitudes continue to change also in more fundamental ways. Transitional man harbors within his mind great potential tensions, which make him at once far more perceptive and more unpredictable than his traditional or modern cousins. He is ambivalent both toward the traditional set of attitudes and toward modernity, and he tries to reconcile the two in his own vacillating or quixotic way. The problems and reactions of migrants from a traditional rural setting to the slum areas of big cities all over the world symbolize well the ambivalence of the transition. The transitional intellectual, in particular, responds to the agonies and ambiguities of the situation with a brilliance, depth of feeling, and creativity that make his modern equivalent seem dull indeed. Illiterate rural-urban migrants and intellectuals alike, however, are prone to emotionalism, social deviation, and a faith in extremist ideologies and charismatic leadership.

Limitations of modern "freedom"

Modernity for the individual and the family is a difficult state to generalize about, except in the abstract and with due allowance for cultural differences. While the general trend from the collectivity orientation of the traditional individual toward modern individual autonomy is clear enough, there are many limitations upon the forms that individual autonomy can take without defeating itself. There are biological limits to the autonomy of children, women, and old people that are insuperable except for minor modifications.[23] There are also psychological prerequisites for child rearing and the maintenance of the institution of monogamous marriage that stand in the way of an unlimited quest for individual autonomy.

Finally, there is the logical paradox of individual freedom—the ambiguity of the word "freedom" itself. Most classical Western philosophers of liberalism lived in transitional societies that yearned for a lessening of restraints upon the individual; therefore, they defined freedom negatively as *freedom from external control*.[24] For an industrial entrepreneur in England around 1800, for example, freedom meant stopping a busybody government or traditional social forces from interfering with his economic pursuits. The negative definition of freedom, or of the individual rights of man, will always play a role wherever individuals or groups yearn to shake off the stifling control of elites, groups, the majority of the people around them, or of a hostile government.[25]

[23] The biological fetters of childhood and adolescence, of maternity, and of old age may manifest themselves also as a psychological propensity to seek moral and material support from the family.

[24] Typical representatives of classical liberalism are such thinkers as the economist Adam Smith (1723–1790) and the philosopher John Stuart Mill (1806–1873).

[25] The threat to individual freedom negatively defined is just as likely to come from the prejudices and demands for conformity of the

Objective indicators of individual progress

Of what good, however, is freedom from external control to the masses of poor, illiterate peasants who are just awakening from the age-old slumber of traditional society? When the quest for individual freedom first begins to shine in their constrictive world, their first need is to broaden the horizon and improve the economic situation for themselves and their children. Increasing their individual freedom means acquiring literacy, occupational training, and opportunities for spatial and social mobility. Hence it is not surprising that social scientists tend to choose as objective indicators of the progress of a country's individuals the literacy rate, the spread and quality of education, the circulation and use of newspapers, radios, and other mass media, and the level of per capita income and consumption.[26] These are indices of individuals' capacity to participate in social, cultural, and economic life. Effective political participation in the selection of candidates and policies completes the operational definition of what social philosophers have long called the positive concept of freedom. Individuals can maximize their freedom by effective participation in society's joint enterprise to increase everyone's mastery over the economic, social, and political circumstances of his life.[27]

Development of associations   Another important landmark in a society's development is the appearance of associations in general

---

vast majority of people in a transitional or modern society as from government, and just as likely from a government democratically elected by and responsible to such a tyrannical majority as from the bureaucrats of an autocratic government.

[26] Admittedly, the absence of restraints on individual freedom, or the effective protection of individual rights, is far more difficult to measure or to compare in quantitative terms. This should not lessen the importance of freedom from restraint in societies where the individual has developed his capacity to help himself.

[27] While the two concepts of freedom can be reconciled easily in practical life, they do clash when carried to extremes. Participation in the joint enterprise of a developed society requires a good deal of voluntary cooperation and self-restraint for the sake of the common effort. Even a democratic system may need to provide for coercive procedures against individuals who carry their liberty to the extreme, seriously disrupting the joint enterprise. It is the task of democratic theory and constitutional jurisprudence to weigh the priorities and to draw the line between the requisites of the two concepts of freedom.

and of certain kinds of associations in particular. As the guilds, estates, and castes, the ancient tribes and villages of traditional society lose their hold over the emerging individual; new ties appear desirable and useful to him. He learns soon that one of the best ways of maximizing his influence and voice in economic, social, and political life is to join or form associations with others of like mind or like interest. Thus castes may develop caste associations, and chambers of commerce may grow from the old guilds. Labor unions may sprout in order to articulate the interests of the new industrial working classes, or they may develop from journeymen's groups or mutual assistance societies. Farmers anxious to respond to the challenge of a market economy may rediscover the ancient advantages of cooperative organization. Industrial entrepreneurs and investors for the same reason hit upon the joint stock company.

Thus modern society is characterized by a vast welter of organizational forms and devices, most of which begin to be adopted at significant stages of the great transition. Political parties are, perhaps, the most important among the many associations and organizations that play a prominent role in politics. Through them, as through his other group memberships, the individual strives to maximize his freedom.

THE CULTURAL SYSTEM

The cultural system, fifth in the list of social segments, is by no means the least significant. Remember that none of the five aspects of social systems discussed here should be regarded as a prime cause of all the others, even though they obviously and deeply influence one another. Some philosophies and perspectives do imply such a causal relationship. Marxists, for example, believe that the economic and technological life of society is the prime cause and all its other manifestations mere "superstructure." Individualistic societies such as that of the United States tend to accord a central role to the position of the individual. Some schools of depth psychology, such as those of Sigmund Freud and Alfred Adler, may see a prime cause in the conditions of individual maturation. Some philosophers of history and culture, such as Oswald Spengler, have sought the primary social causation in the cultural system, which, in a sense, includes all the other aspects of society in a coherent and consistent whole.[28] Such a culture-centered view would also make the political system a mere expression of culture. Let us attempt a definition of the cultural system that avoids such misunderstandings.

Defining the cultural system

In 1952 a critical review [29] contained no less than twenty-eight pages of definitions of culture. For our present purposes, however, the American anthropologist Edward B. Tyler, whose definition is included therein, put it well enough in 1871: "Culture or civilization, taken in its wide ethnographic sense, is that complex whole which includes knowledge, belief, art, morals, law, custom, and any other capabilities and habits acquired by man as a member of society." Thus culture is a system of beliefs, moral and aesthetic values, habits of behavior, and capabilities that the individual acquires from society in the process of his socialization. It forms a socially cohesive whole, a recognizable configuration, of which the cultural elites of a society, such as the priests of primitive religions or the teachers of advanced civilizations are rationally more aware, while the masses may absorb it chiefly as preexisting ritual and habits of thinking or as symbolically learned patterns of behavior.

Culture evolves and changes in creative interaction with a society's natural and social environment.[30] The specific patterns

[28] On this point see especially the literature on cultural evolution by cultural anthropologists such as Leslie White, or the book by Marshall D. Sahlins and Elman R. Service, eds., *Evolution and Culture.* Ann Arbor, Mich.: University of Michigan Press, 1960.

[29] A. Kroeber and C. Kluckhohn, *Culture: A Critical Review of Concepts and Definitions.* Cambridge, Mass.: The Museum, 1952.

[30] The environment of nature and neighboring peoples can change dramatically, either intrinsically or as perceived by the cultural system. Not only is the natural habitat subject to change by natural catastrophe, drought, or animal and human epidemics, but the same habitat may serve a people first as hunting grounds, then as farmland, then as mining area, and finally as site for processing industries. The crucial changes here lie in the approach of a culture to the land or in the extractive capabilities of a people, rather than in the transformed land itself. The neighboring tribes likewise may change intrinsically, as when they become aggressive or take a notion to conquer or colonize the culture concerned, which would then have to adapt itself to their behavior. But the more incisive changes in the social environment are endogenous, such as evolving

of interaction are the four segments discussed earlier, plus politics. Each of these aspects represents a rather autonomous pattern of adaptation to a stable or changing environment. Thus culture mirrors both the environment and the established patterns of interacting with it. These patterns exist in the minds of the members of the collectivity and strain toward psychological consistency. Each established pattern of interaction, such as of the political system, plays a major role in shaping the culture, which in turn gives its characteristic forms and style to the pattern of interaction. The process of adaptation to the environment is not only creative but also self-limiting, in that it gives a cultural bias to the capabilities of a society in economics, social organization, individual achievement, and political functioning.

Varieties of cultural systems

When we speak of traditional cultures, we lump together a vast variety of systems—some elaborate and sophisticated, as in precolonial India and in the venerable civilizations of China, the Middle East, and ancient Greece and Rome; others primitive tribal cultures with rather simple social structures and hardly any political structures, such as some of the mountain tribes of South East Asia; some highly authoritarian, such as the Incas of Peru; others, such as the trading cultures around the Mediterranean and in Western Europe, tending toward pragmatism. David E. Apter has drawn attention also to the important difference between "instrumentalist traditional cultures" in Africa, which tend to build elaborate "pyramidal" political structures and demand performance of their officeholders, and religion-based "consummatory cultures" of high social solidarity and simple structure, such as the Ashanti.[31] Obviously different cultures will experience different strains and present different degrees of resistance to modernization in the various social sectors and in politics.

---

notions of empire, of being encircled by hostile neighbors, or of the "white man's burden," which can cause a culture to view its neighbors differently and to adapt its behavior to the changed image, regardless of any objective change in the behavior of the neighbors.

[31] *The Politics of Modernization.* Chicago: University of Chicago Press, 1965, pp. 92–106.

Cultural transition

The traditional cultural system in transition to modernity mirrors the changing patterns of economics, social structure, and individual and family roles already discussed. Technological and economic modernization, the homogenization and integration of the social structure, and the emergence of the individual produce broad patterns of cultural modernization, in which the cultural system tries to reconcile the uneven impulses and adaptive innovations occurring in each sector of social interaction with the changing environment.

Quite frequently during the great transition, however, the cultural conflicts between formerly separate ethnic communities, religious groups, social classes, or generations become too overpowering for reconciliation. Instead of achieving further general modernization, then, the conservative, pattern-maintaining tendency of cultural systems consolidates the camps on opposite sides of a cultural cleavage, thereby aggravating the conflict and producing a deep cultural malaise in the community. If the conflict remains mild, such cleavages can easily become the temporary basis of political alignments or party systems. In some European societies with deep cultural cleavages and few cross-cutting patterns of identification, there resulted what the Dutch call *verzuiling*—a formation of rigid columns of sociocultural and political identification. Each voter is born into and remains all his life in such a column, or closed little world—Catholics in Christian Democratic or Catholic Conservative parties, Protestant workingmen in Social Democratic parties, and persons of the old middle classes in Liberal parties. If the conflict is exacerbated by circumstances of crisis, the cultural malaise may well become a harbinger of revolution, civil war, or international wars. All cultural systems in transitions are likely to experience acute conflict, as traditions resist the encroachment of change and modernity. And the conflict increases with the falling of geographical and social barriers, which in the traditional state allowed different groups to live and evolve in relative isolation.[32]

[32] See also Charles W. Anderson, Fred R. von der Mehden, and Crawford Young, *Issues of Political Development*. Englewood Cliffs, N.J.: Prentice-Hall, 1967, chap. 3.

Innovation by minorities   Another aspect that deserves detailed discussion is the dynamics of modernization of a culturally fragmented traditional society, a process that can produce or aggravate cultural conflicts, as we have seen. Most traditional societies are so fragmented into innumerable geographic, ethnic, social, and religious groups, with little contact and communication among each other, that the presence of distinct ethnic or religious minorities is hardly noticeable. National consciousness, for example, not to mention nationalism, was quite alien to the Middle Ages. This is not to deny that the power structure of medieval society was in the hands of aristocratic members of the ethnic or religious majority. But a French nobleman would invariably identify with the nobility of other European countries rather than with the common people of France. The onset of modernization, however, tends to rally the cultural majority and to set off cultural minorities.

When such a traditional society begins to break up, often the ethnic or religious minority rather than the majority awakens first and begins to innovate. Thus, for example, the Protestant Huguenots in Catholic France and Protestant groups in England and on the European continent, Jews in Eastern and Central Europe, overseas Chinese in South East Asia, and Indians in East Africa or British Guiana tended to be the modernizers, far ahead of the native majorities. It is easy to speculate about the sociological and psychological motives that may stir up members of minorities to prodigious and imaginative efforts to better themselves or to ward off majority oppression by developing new forms of social or political organization (or slogans such as "Huguenot power"). It is a matter of record, in any case, that minorities such as those mentioned were pioneers in the development or adoption of new forms of production and commerce, bold new social philosophies, and novel forms of political organization, and in the application of scientific method to problems of everyday life. The majorities of their respective countries and other minorities rarely appreciated and often resented the relatively superior economic or political capabilities that cultural modernization lent the pioneering minority. But eventually they too found their way to modernization along their own characteristic lines. Evidently, cultural modernization requires a catalyst, at least at the outset. For the minorities described it may have

been their status among or their oppression by the majority.
For majority cultures, it may take prolonged socioeconomic crisis
or a foreign challenge in the form of war of a colonial con-
queror.[33]

Modernization and traditional religion   Another important ingredient in cultural modernization is the role and nature of
religion. Religion in most traditional societies is so pervasive and
intimately related to all the customs and beliefs of society that
it makes up a major part of the cultural system. The functional
requisites of living traditional roles such as that of a lowly
peasant or of a woman and the fatalism and superstitions of
traditional religion penetrate each other until it is impossible to
tell the desires of human masters from the alleged command-
ments of the gods. Kings and aristocrats and the elders and
males of the family are invested with a kind of divine authority,
while the rebel against human tyranny is branded a rebel against
the divine will.

Yet, traditional religion is not only confining and hostile to
social reform. It is also comfortable and accommodating like
an old shoe for the vast majority of people, who fit themselves
willingly into the hierarchic society and are satisfied with its
religious sanctions. Modern man finds it difficult to understand
the deep satisfactions of living in the closed world of a traditional
culture unified by religion. He may dream of the islands of the
South Pacific and yet realize that he himself could not bear the
primitive life for very long. Cultural anthropology and social
psychology have thrown some light on the extraordinary consistency of primitive cultures. We can assume that even in such
elaborate traditional societies as India or China before the
Western intrusion, life was characterized from the cradle to the
grave by a cultural consistency that modern societies have lost.
South Sea islanders and other traditional people find fulfillment
in their societies by reason of early socialization from childhood
to the rites of passage amid a harmony of religious rituals and

[33] See also Hagen, *On the Theory of Social Change,* chaps. 2, 13–
18; and Francis X. Sutton in J. Roland Pemock, ed., *Self-Government in
Modernizing Nations.* Englewood Cliffs, N.J.: Prentice-Hall, 1964, pp.
26–37. Further, Rupert Emerson, *From Empire to Nation.* Boston:
Beacon, 1959, chaps. 12–14.

symbols that will carry them through adult life to a well-understood death. Traditional religion, even though it may be otherworldly, has an answer for everything, including questions of political importance.

How then does the change begin from the easygoing, collectivity-oriented life in the traditional village or tribe? Does traditional religion just die out when its injunctions and rituals lose their social function? Does the coming of modernity imply radical secularization of all the social relationships that were once suffused with religious dogma? Although modernization often does bring attempts to separate social issues and government from religious influence, it would be rather superficial to equate modernity with secularism. The weight of the evidence suggests renovation and reform within the prevailing religions rather than their abandonment as a prime path of cultural modernization. Erik H. Erikson has emphasized the extent to which the rise of Protestantism in Europe signified a new departure over traditional Catholicism. He has also suggested that Russian communism as a spiritual movement for this worldly human "salvation by works" is a kind of Protestant movement against Russian orthodoxy, social and religious.[34] The close association of social reform movements in nineteenth- and twentieth-century Protestant countries with the missionary tradition of certain Protestant churches also indicates an identity between religious and modern ideologies that we have tended to ignore. Even the militant atheism and social activism of some radical social or nationalist leaders and movements in developing countries could be interpreted as a "Protestantism" of determined individual effort against the background of a traditional past.

[34] See Erik H. Erikson, *Young Man Luther.* New York: Norton, 1958; and *Childhood and Society.* New York: Norton, 1953, chap. 10. Cyril E. Black makes similar remarks about the Jacobins of the French Revolution in *The Dynamics of Modernization.* New York: Harper & Row, 1967, p. 107. See also Fred R. von der Mehden, *Religion and Nationalism in South East Asia.* Madison, Wisc.: University of Wisconsin Press, 1963, chaps. 1–3, 5, and 9; and the contributions of Robert N. Bellah, *Religion and Progress in Modern Asia.* New York: Free Press, 1965. Further, S. N. Eisenstadt, ed., *Religious Transformation and Modernity: The Protestant Ethic in Comparative Perspective.* New York: Basic Books, 1967.

Insecurity and crises of identity The emergence of a new cultural sense of identity from the varied, fragmented, particularistic traditional society often presents enormous personal problems of inner uncertainty and open cultural conflict. The new sense of identity is attached to secular enterprises, such as political independence and economic success, and hence is painfully vulnerable to their failure. Lucian W. Pye tellingly described the fear of failure in Burmese administrators as a major obstacle to further modernization,[35] and similar attitudes may be expected in other countries at this stage. Under the fear of failure lurks personal insecurity and the conflict between traditional and modern motives in many transitional persons, who may be only a generation or less removed from their traditional antecedents.[36]

Like young adults setting out on strange and more ambitious careers than their parents ever conceived, young nations envision their future identity as fanciful mixtures of old images and new capabilities. They will eventually settle down with a new sense of identity only if they succeed in attaining modern capabilities —a triumph that seems to soothe the cultural insecurities and latent conflicts as if by a magic wand. If they fail, however, their fears and uncertainties return with a vengeance, and they are likely to respond with despair or infantile rage against their real or imaginary enemies. What may have been a mild cultural conflict, for example, may turn into fratricidal war or ethnic-religious persecution. (We shall return to this theme of cultural identity in the next chapter.)

Modernizing of communications Cultural harmony in a traditional society also implies a system of communications of sorts and, perhaps, relatively small communities in which cultural consistency can in time be established or restored. In a modernizing society, however, where increasingly rapid social changes must be explained and harmonized for increasingly large masses

[35] Lucian W. Pye, *Politics, Personality, and Nation-Building.* New Haven, Conn.: Yale University Press, 1962, chap. 15.
[36] See again the description of Martin Luther's identity crisis by Erikson. See also the discussion of nationalism and Islamic religion in Manfred Halpern, *The Politics of Social Change in the Middle East and North Africa.* Princeton, N.J.: Princeton University Press, 1963, chaps. 7–11.

of uprooted individuals, the old mouth-to-mouth communications system and its transmission of symbols become hopelessly inadequate. To satisfy the instant communication needs of masses of individuals as well as the new groups and organizations of a modernizing society, entirely new communications structures and media are developed.[37] Individuals acquire literacy, radio sets, telephones, television, and other facilities for receiving messages regularly. Organizations and corporations—including government agencies—develop news handouts, informational gazettes, and a public relations staff. Independent news agencies and media begin to specialize in the gathering and distribution of information in the form of newspapers, pamphlets, leaflets, radio, films, and television. The arrival of mass media and their technical capability or actual use is another prime indicator of the stage of modernization reached in a developing society.

Once a society is fully literate and ready to "receive," and once it has available and actually uses the mass media to their full extent, its cultural system can complete the task of social reintegration to the point of the homogenization of tastes and judgments typical of television-owning civilizations. Apart from the aesthetic effects, there can be little doubt about the effectiveness of modern mass media in diffusing cultural innovations and in broadcasting to everyone an understanding of his or her economic capabilities and desires or of individual social and political rights. American blacks and other poverty-stricken groups in this wealthy society, as social scientists have pointed out, became far more aware of the material life denied them once they began in larger numbers to see it on television. Thus expectations may be awakened that help to develop capabilities or to arouse revolutionary sentiment. In any event, and even at their most sensational, the mass media will cater to and increase the sense of empathy that to Daniel Lerner signified the greatest change that had come over his Anatollan peasants.[38]

[37] On this point, see especially Wilbur Schramm in Lucian W. Pye, *Communications and Political Development.* Princeton, N.J.: Princeton University Press, 1963; and S. N. Eisenstadt, *Essays on Comparative Institutions.* New York: Wiley, 1965, pp. 349–357.

[38] See above, pp. 33–37, and his *The Passing of Traditional Society* (New York: Free Press, 1968), as well as his article in Pye, *Communications and Political Development.* Princeton, N.J.: Princeton University Press, 1962.

THE SPONTANEITY OF POLITICAL DEVELOPMENT

A sixth sector of social development is the political system. We have noted that the level of political development is not likely to be far behind, nor can it for very long be far ahead of, the other sectors of social development. It can hardly be imagined that politics would be completely independent of such essential elements of a society as the economics, the social composition and stratification, the role of families and individuals, and the culture. In fact, we saved the discussion of political development until now precisely in order to avoid the impression that the small tail of political development is wagging the large dog of social evolution.

Ponderous momentum of social change

There is a notable difference between the usual course of development in the other sectors and the development in the political system. Economic systems, social structure, culture, and the role of individuals in a given society are more apt to change gradually and over several generations. Even violent political intervention cannot change them overnight. Moreover, once major changes in these sectors begin to occur on a mass scale, the momentum of change seems to be largely self-generating and self-sustaining, making it practically impossible to stop or reverse the trend. Barring a major catastrophe, for example, it seems so unlikely that urbanization could ever be reversed, the accumulation of skills and hardware of advanced industry scattered, and the emancipated individual reencapsulated in ancient culture that even persuasive prophets of the cultural decay of the modern world sound hollow to the sober mind. Thus major social change takes on the appearance of an automatic process of development, and people assume, not always rightly, that one stage will automatically lead to the next higher one. What is worse, they naïvely assume that political development is similarly automatic, given sufficient time—when in fact nothing could be further from the truth.

Uncertainties of political development

Politics is the realm of free choice, the master science of control over the other social functions of man. A fully developed, well-functioning political system is a great achievement, a skillful work of art. To begin political development and to sustain it requires good planning, enormous effort, and rather favorable circumstances, if not sheer luck. As we shall see shortly, many "developing" countries never reach the politically developed stage or are sidetracked along the way by foreign intervention, anarchy, civil war, dictatorship, or simply a general inability to achieve political consensus. Politically developed countries, for that matter, can very easily backslide and fall victim to the same transitional ailments. If the word "political development" is to have any analytic meaning, as Samuel P. Huntington has argued, it must be held up against the possibility of political stagnation and decay.[39] Institutions and procedures as well as the quality of political life can quite easily deteriorate and disintegrate.

At the heart of politics and of political development, though it may sound truistic, are *people*—not gross national products or literacy rates. And although objective indices may help us measure changes in the people's way of life, we must never forget that the foremost object of our study is the people's political state of mind. This is why we so diligently study the *political culture* of a given people, the processes of *political socialization* and *recruitment* by which various groups acquire their roles in the subcultures of the political system, and the group processes of *parties, interest groups, institutionalization,* and *governmental decision making.* If we can understand how a given people thinks and functions politically at a particular time in its history, we can also grasp whether, how, and why its political system is developing, stagnating, or decaying.

What then is political development? What would constitute a fully developed, well-functioning, modern political system? How does political development correlate with the stages of social development from traditional to modern? Could a traditional or transitional society be politically "fully developed"? How can one study political development at its various current stages in different countries? These and related questions will be discussed in the sections that follow.

[39] See his article "Political Development and Political Decay," *World Politics,* April 1965. Rupert Emerson coined the phrase "erosion of democracy in the new states" to pinpoint one of the more obvious current problems of political decay. See his *From Empire to Nation.* Boston: Beacon, 1959, chap. 15.

THE FIVE BASIC PHASES OF POLITICAL DEVELOPMENT

The term "political development," as used by native politicians and social scientists alike, has taken on such mystical qualities that the student does well to look at it with suspicion. If he believed all the rhetoric of Independence Day speeches in various countries or dissected the enormous literature on the subject, he might well picture political development as a growth process like that of a redwood tree, adding another layer every year, or perhaps as a manifestation of a national collective soul in the context of history. What is really needed is a rather cautious, analytical definition. Let us begin by carefully restricting the term to actions, changes, and policies of development that are purely, or at least largely, political and that are deliberately undertaken by their originators and their supporters (see Fig. 2). This is not to deny, only to demystify, the social context of politics and such political changes as come about without deliberate intention.

Political development in the advanced as well as the developing countries has been above all a *state-building process* aimed at a particular kind of state, which we must seek to describe. It takes place in five basic phases, which are not necessarily everywhere equally complete, separate, consecutive, or in the same order.

1. The first step achieves the unification and external autonomy of a common territory.

2. This is followed or accompanied by the development and differentiation of political institutions and roles.

3. The third phase involves the transfer of power from ascriptive elites to individuals and groups chosen by criteria of achievement.

4. Then there occurs an enormous growth and interpenetration of organized social interests and governmental functions, which could also be called democratization, accompanied by both social integration and further institutional and political role differentiation.

5. The fifth step is the enormous rise of governmental capability in molding the human environment, extracting resources, and marshaling power in dealing with other nations.

These five steps will be discussed in some detail. They are all related to a certain amount of simultaneous social develop-

Figure 2 A segmental view of development

SUBSYSTEM	Antecedents	Tradition	Transition	Modernity	Future
ECONOMIC	Preagricultural economies; nomadism	Primitive economy; little urbanization or industry and commerce; mostly agricultural; rural isolation	Major dislocation; released man-power; new technology; industry; urbanization; building of communications	Industrial maturity; high urbanization; mass consumption; high technology; specialized skills	→
SOCIAL STRUCTURE	Isolated and small communities	Hierarchic social status; ascription; ethnic and cultural communities; tiny middle class	Migrations; ethnic and cultural conflict; formation of classes, especially bourgeoisie and proletariat	Increasing social mobility and equality; universal and maximal education; mass communications	→
INDIVIDUAL AND FAMILY		Collectivity-oriented; kinship; clan; hierarchy of age and sex (role of women, children)	Social mobilization in groups and/or as individuals; increasing emancipation from family; status	Individual autonomy; high participation, also "escape from freedom" and "escape from authority"	→
CULTURE	Stateless societies	Highly diverse local and communal village cultures; immobility; pervasive religion; fatalism	Increasing cultural amalgamation, but also conflicts; religious conflict, including church versus state	Secularization and religious reformism; individualism; sociocultural integration	→
POLITICAL		Traditional government; sacred monarchy; oligarchy; god-emperors; particularism	Bureaucratic empires; benevolent despotism (output-oriented)	Popular government; democracy; mobilization regimes; high participation (input-oriented)	→

PHASES OF POLITICAL DEVELOPMENT

1. Territorial unification and/or autonomy
2. Structural and role differentiation; constitutional development
3. Transfer of power from ascriptive to achievement elites
4. Interpenetration of organized interest and governmental functions (democracy or totalitarian bureaucracy)
5. High capability stage (environment, resources, power)

—State building

ment, and yet clearly they have been the object and goal of deliberate political action in all the countries under consideration. Once the basic steps are recognizable, we can discuss in-between stages as well as alternative routes to political development.

Territorial unification and autonomy

Unification and external autonomy are both aspects of the same process of establishing an independent, self-contained political community. Because of the precedent of the older Western states, we tend to speak of *national independence* and *national unification*. But we should not think of nations as preexisting, unmistakable entities prior to their modern emergence. The *grande nation* of France was unrecognizable in the Middle Ages and could easily have turned into two or more national communities, judging from such indicators as language and earlier political units. Great Britain still shows the seams of the political amalgamation of the English, Scots, Welsh, and Northern Irish within its geographical confines. There is, then, no other difference but the effect of time between the obvious polycommunalism of the "new nations" and the relative homogeneity of their older predecessors. The great problems that developing nations such as India or the former Belgian Congo have with their diverse regional components may well be aggravated, however, by another factor: they are struggling to achieve at the same time several other basic steps, which the older nations tackled one by one at considerable time intervals.[40]

In our day, the first step most commonly involves the struggle of colonies for independence from the British, French, Dutch, or Belgian colonial empires. Native regimes then take over new political "communities" that have little in common but their former colonial masters and the arbitrary borders they happened to draw at the time of the original conquest. These borders often cut larger tribal or other potential national communities in two or enclose several tribes or parts of tribes that cannot seem to get along with each other in the long run, as in Nigeria. But at the same time it should be noted that the challenge of polycommunalism to the political ingenuity and statesmanship of the

---

[40] On the genesis of an ethnic sense of identity that can grow into nationalism, see also Anderson *et al.*, *Issues of Political Development*, chap. 2.

emerging native elites can make a valuable contribution to the political culture that more homogeneous communities will miss.

The experience with the "new nations" of the last hundred years is very instructive in this respect. When the Russian, German, Austro-Hungarian, and Turkish empires collapsed in 1918, releasing captive national minorities by the dozen, many small new "nation-states" were founded in Eastern Europe. Individually they soon fell prey to native dictators, and collectively they were so divided and weak as to invite the territorial aggrandizement first of the Axis powers and then of the Soviet Union. There, as in contemporary Africa, South East Asia, or Latin America, the creation of larger political unions would have avoided the bane of Balkanization. The peoples involved, and especially their political leaders, could have profited from the experience of building a more inclusive community rather than learning to hate and distrust each other to the point of total segregation.

The importance of considering the international setting is also evident in the unification of Germany and Italy in the 1860s. In both cases, it was not lack of size or capacity but failure to reconcile national ambitions with the established international order that defeated the nation-building enterprise. Aggression, war, and defeat brought both nations down and split Germany once more. Only in the embrace of such larger communities as the Common Market or the Warsaw Bloc do the restless national ambitions, particularly of the Germans, appear to have found at least temporary repose.

The growth of national unity among the European states varies widely from country to country as soon as we look beyond France and Great Britain, where the obstacles to unity were few. Consider, for example, the history of Italy, in whose city-states modern economics, art, science, and social and political life dawned earlier than in France, England, or anywhere else in Europe. Notwithstanding its cultural headstart in the Renaissance and its heritage of Roman law and statecraft, Italy fell far behind France and England over the centuries, and to this day, Italians rather lack a sense of nationhood.[41] During the centuries

[41] See Joseph La Palombara in Lucian W. Pye and Sidney Verba, *Political Culture and Political Development.* Princeton, N.J.: Princeton University Press, 1966, chap. 8.

when the royal dynasties of England (with the help of the great lords) and France (with the help of the emerging bourgeoisie) unified and consolidated their hold on their respective countries, Italy possessed neither a "national" monarchy nor nation-building lords or commoners to overcome the particularism of its independent city-states and other components. On the contrary, the major supraregional political forces in Italy—the Catholic Church, the Germanic Holy Roman Empire, and the foreign powers that continually invaded or occupied parts of the country —favored political identification beyond the nation-state and were rather hostile to the idea of national unification. Thus Italian political development was held up decisively while modern France and England emerged. And when at last a national movement arose in the nineteenth century to unify the country, it does not appear to have stirred up the area to the south of Rome, not to mention Sicily; the Italian South still is not *quite* a part of the nation. The new nations now grappling with national unification need not develop toward England or France rather than Italy. In many new nation-states in Latin America and elsewhere the lack of national pride and sense of identity exceeds that of southern Italians.

Attention should also be drawn to the difference between unification from above and unification by a popular movement. The relative effectiveness and long-range success of unification in past centuries owed much to its autocratic procedure. A royal dynasty of legitimate authority and even the armed might of a usurper could unify a territory once they had overcome the resistance of regional centers of power and of foreign enemies of national unification. In this age of popular government, however, a national movement must also overcome the tribal, religious, and other divisions among the people it seeks to unite. This is a nearly impossible task, considering that national movements are fueled by a heightened awareness of cultural identities and exclusiveness, which can be at least as divisive as it can be unifying.

A good example is the distintegration of the nation-building thrust of Nnamdi Azikiwe's National Convention of Nigeria and the Cameroons (NCNP) party before the jealousies of Hauss-Fulani (north) and Yoruba (west) tribesmen, who suspected it to be an instrument of Ibo (east) tribal ambition. Looking back upon bloody civil war and tribal massacres in Nigeria, we will recognize the hazards of the sense of ethnic identity awakened by social modernization.[42] He may also begin to understand why modern nonethnic ideologies, such as African socialism or communism, not to mention anti-Americanism in Latin America or anti-British and anti-Israel propaganda in the Middle East, recommend themselves to the nation-building politician. Nigerians who distrusted Azikiwe and his NCNP as Ibo instruments might have accepted them as socialists, just as many Arabs who suspect Egyptian ambitions may support President Nasser as a foe of Israel and Great Britain.

Differentiation of political institutions and roles

The second basic step of political development involves the differentiation of political institutions and roles. By this process, for example, specifically political institutions, procedures, and individual roles are conceptually separated from religious headship, economic influence, or social prestige. Even though religious leaders or prestigious landowners may continue to play political roles, their specifically political functions are recognized as such and their performance in them critically judged. In the advanced countries this process has produced whole systems of specifically political institutions and roles [43] for the performance of political functions.

The emergence of political institutions ushered in an extended era of institutional experimentation and refinement, which is still going on intermittently in all countries. As later chapters will show, the Western European countries and the United States evolved traditions of constitutional law, specific governmental structures and functions, and substantive and procedural safeguards that have been widely admired and have been adopted among newer nations. Imitation and adaptation are standard procedures in institutional development. Of course, no analysis can rest content with the examination of legal forms or the pious promises of paper constitutions; rather, we must assess the living realities of a given country's political life.

[42] See especially Frederick R. O. Schwartz, Jr., *Nigeria: The Tribes, the Nation, or the Race.* Cambridge, Mass.: M.I.T. Press, 1965.

[43] On the crystallization of roles, see Eisenstadt, *Essays on Comparative Institutions,* pp. 30–38, and the sources cited there.

In-between stages of political development The milestones of the institutional tradition of the West mark the in-between steps of phase two of political development. One can note in a country's history, for example, at what point purely political institutions and roles emerge, when they become autonomous, and when their autonomy is submerged by other social forces. There is also a recognizable point in the history of Western monarchies, say in England, when the magic of monarchic authority gives way to the recognition of distinct functions, of which the specifically political ones, such as executive decision making, are eventually vested in a cabinet responsible to Parliament. The monarchy may endure but its functions have changed, and the quasi-religious, symbolic overtones are separated from the political executive. There is also a point in the history of Western parliaments when their representative and legislative functions emerge clearly and their earlier judicial functions are left to a carefully separated hierarch of courts of law. And there is a point also, which some advanced nations still have not reached, when a system of effective safeguards guarantees the public rights and liberties of individual citizens—especially their right to vote, to be adequately represented, to exercise free speech, and to enjoy equal access to public office and opportunity. Finally, all the other nations have had to develop and maintain a well-trained and impartial public service to administer the manifold concerns of the modern state.

The standards drawn from Western precedents deserve to be applied rigorously to many of the new and old nations as long as their governments and intellectuals profess an ardent commitment to representative democracy, public liberties, and even much of the legal language employed in Western constitutional law. A presidential system in Latin America that features executive omnipotence, a rubber-stamp legislature, and spineless judges—despite what its constitution says about the separation of powers—clearly shows backsliding in political development. Soviet citizens cannot really enjoy the rights and liberties enumerated in their constitution; the gap between promise and performance, whatever may be its reasons, is an undeniable indication that the Soviet political system cannot or will not perform at the level of political development it has solemnly proclaimed to its citizens and to the world. And the same is true whenever the practice of constitutional rights in the United States fails to measure up to their promise or when the freedom of the press in France or West Germany falls below the standards proclaimed.

The goal of any attempt to gauge the in-between stages of political development according to the differentiation of institutions and roles is not just to create dichotomies of democratic-undemocratic, constitutional-authoritarian, or politically sincere versus sham constitutional, not to mention more ethnocentric dichotomies. We should aim at a continuous, multidimensional scale, ranging from undeveloped and poorly developed states of political institutions and roles over stages of increasing differentiation and institutional systematization toward an open-ended peak of the possible. The tricky questions of alternative routes will be discussed later in this chapter. Because of the complexity and variety of modern political institutions and roles the scale has to measure several dimensions at once. For example, it is necessary to consider the superior qualities of the French civil service along with the restrictions imposed on the freedom of the press under de Gaulle in comparison to countries with a freer press and a poorer civil service.

A good example of this second step of political development is the constitutional history of Great Britain, although it should not be taken as a model that others are expected to follow. We see very clearly the emergence of modern political functions and their appropriate structures from the context of traditional monarchy and Parliament, their integration with the rise of ministerial responsibility to Parliament, the development of public service and local government, and the evolution and safeguarding of political roles such as citizenship, suffrage, and free speech.

The first two phases are so basic to political development as to make a country without unity, independence, and a specifically political structure a nonentity among states. Three further steps are required to complete development, although one would hesitate to call a country that had not yet undergone them entirely undeveloped. Great Britain, for example, had reached a rather admirable level of political development with the unfolding of much of its constitutional edifice prior to any of the later phases.

The same can be said about the early United States, which actually started out with phase three, and about many of the older states.

Transfer of power

The third of the five basic steps of political development is the transfer of power from traditional elites to new leaders who base their authority on recognized achievement, though not necessarily on popular election. In a Western European context, this can be largely equated with the passing of aristocracy, or rather of its political significance. Dating the stages of this process in any particular country can be a difficult undertaking in itself.

Great Britain   In Great Britain, for example, the beginnings of the process reach far back into British history, when new urban elites began to emerge. But the British monarchy and aristocracy were astute enough not to draw the class lines too sharply, to confer peerages on large numbers of deserving commoners, and to adopt many of the modernizing concerns of the rising new elites. Thus the battle was never clearly joined, although many historians see in the electoral reforms of 1832 and 1867 or in the repeal of the Corn Laws [44] in 1846 the beginning of the end of aristocratic rule. The Victorian Age witnessed a good deal of bourgeoisification of British politics and even of the life style of English aristocrats, although it also reaffirmed such aristocratic values as the glories of monarchy and empire. In 1911, finally, the House of Lords was demoted from the equal status with the House of Commons it had enjoyed for so long; and after World War I, the custom evolved that no peer could become prime minister unless he first dropped his title. Nevertheless, most prime ministers or cabinet members of whatever social origin are still willing today to accept a peerage upon retirement from active politics.

France and Germany   Let us compare the British case to those of France and Germany. The French Revolution of the 1700s had as one of its prime objectives the forceful elimination of

[44] The Corn Laws were protective tariffs on grain; the landed interests strove to preserve them, while the entrepreneurial classes wished to eliminate them to reduce the cost of industrial production.

aristocratic privilege and political power, which had been in gradual decline since the rise of royal absolutism in the seventeenth century. The defeat of Napoleon at the hands of the allies, however, put an end to a quarter century of rule by the new elites and led to the restoration of ascriptive authority and autocracy throughout much of the nineteenth century. Nevertheless, the bourgeois evolution took its course underneath the official forms of real and make-believe nobility and during the revolutionary interludes of 1830, 1848, and 1871.[45] The Third Republic was born with a monarchistic majority loyal to various dynastic lines and yet, within the first decade of its life, unmistakably became the permanent beginning of rule by the new elites. As in Great Britain, the final transfer was only in small part related to the expanding suffrage. Both Napoleon I and III had actually used universal manhood suffrage as their key to the imperial crown, and the voters of the early Third Republic had elected their monarchists and noblemen deputies as willingly as they voted for their bourgeois and proletarian successors.

The passing of aristocracy in Germany took place long after its equivalent in England and France. After the first attempted takeover by the bourgeoisie in the abortive revolution of 1848, the Bismarckian empire of 1871 was founded on the joint rules of the Prussian Junkers and the reigning monarchs of the other German states. The German military defeat in 1918 toppled the old ruling classes, and the constitution of the Weimar Republic even abolished all aristocratic titles. Nevertheless, republican politics still accorded aristocratic names undue reverence, and one of its last cabinets was known as the "cabinet of the barons." It was only after the totalitarian interlude and World War II that the German aristocracy could be said to be politically dead. In East Germany, in particular, where most Prussian Junkers had their estates, the Soviet occupation and the German Communists made a clean sweep of all remainders.

The less-developed countries   What about the transfer of power in the less-developed countries? In some countries in Europe, such as Spain and Portugal, the nobility is still in possession of considerable power, and this was also true of Eastern European

[45] See, for example, Roger L. Williams, *The World of Napoleon III.* New York: Free Press, 1965.

countries until the communist takeover after World War II. In many parts of Africa there are tribal heads, paramount chiefs, even kings of ascriptive authority, as in the kingdoms of Morocco, Ethiopia, and Buganda and the tribes of Central Africa. British colonial policy generally preferred indirect rule, thus leaving the ascriptive elites in power, whereas the French preferred to turn them into civil administrators or to oust them. The Dutch in Indonesia vacillated between utilizing and ignoring the local aristocracy. Elsewhere in South East Asia and in Nepal and Sikkim kings and princes still hold real power; such rulers could also be found in India and Ceylon before independence, as well as in the Middle East today.

Colonial governments   Two questions arise from the study of systems in which the passing of aristocracy has not even begun or where colonialism has obscured the basic issues. One question is how colonial governments, whether of the Western variety or of Russian or Chinese Communists, fit into the picture. A colonial government, possibly together with a colonial ruling class from the mother country, is not a "new elite," even though it may be modern and may have replaced or subordinated the old ascriptive elites. Colonial governments and their residents are an ascriptive elite in the sense that they derive their status and power from their ethnicity and association with the might of the motherland. They may, of course, raise and train a "new elite" of natives, or the latter may take over by themselves after independence. The new eliteness may be based on any conceivable achievement in the public eye, such as a prominent role in the national movement, a record of persecution and imprisonment by the colonial government, military or other technical training, leadership in guerrilla warfare, or organizational leadership of political parties or trade unions.

Costs of violent overthrow   The second question is whether a country would not be better off if it could avoid adding the violent overthrow of the old ascriptive elites to all the other difficulties and disruptions of modernization. At first glance, the bloody business of the French Revolution and the Russian Revolution of 1917 in killing off or driving into exile the old ruling classes has the appearance of a horrifying excess. A country such as Great Britain or Japan, where the traditional ruling classes in large part initiated or at least cooperated with the modernizing drive, until the progressing society quietly overtook them, avoids not only the horrors of the bloodbath itself, but also further generations of bitterness and recrimination that can preclude the consensus needed for continuous modernization. Whether violent revolution can be avoided, however, depends largely on the tractability of the traditional elites, which very often fight modernization with savage repression. The French and Russian aristocrats were, with rare exceptions, singularly unenlightened and hostile to modernization long before they had a violent uprising on their hands.[46]

In assessing the need for violent revolution against repressive traditional elites we should also consider cases where the traditional forces won out, as in the Iberian peninsula [47] or in Bismarckian Germany. In Germany, the Prussian Junkers favored economic and scientific development but were adamant against any political development that might undermine their privileges and power. By way of gradual political counterrevolution, they used conservative-military indoctrination to redirect social pressures from below against foreign rivals and enemies. Three decades of repeated wars and devastating defeats, from 1914 to 1945, have been far more costly than an early violent revolution could possibly have been.

Interpenetration of group pressures and government functions

The fourth step of political development is characterized by the enormous growth and interpenetration of the organized interests of society and the functions of government, changing the very character of government and politics. Before the beginning of this phase, as in countries such as Great Britain, there may be political parties, organized interests, and even popular movements,[48] and the great growth of movements and agitation for various causes

[46] Compare the posture of the French and Russian traditional elites also with that of their Japanese equivalent after 1868. Robert E. Ward and Dankwart A. Rustow, eds., *Political Modernization in Japan and Turkey*. Princeton, N.J.: Princeton University Press, 1966.

[47] See also the case studies of various Eastern European countries prior to 1945 in Eugene Weber and Hans Rogger, eds., *The European Right*. Berkeley, Calif.: University of California Press, 1965.

[48] See, for example, the account in Samuel H. Beer, *British Politics in the Collectivist Age*. New York: Knopf, 1965, pp. 16, 43–48 and *passim*.

around the middle of the nineteenth century still forms a transition to phase four rather than part of it. The actual beginning in Great Britain was the massive growth of extraparliamentary party organization in the 1870s, so that "the people at large should be taken into the counsels of the party and . . . have a share in its control and management," to quote the Liberal party leader of the Birmingham Caucus, Joseph Chamberlain.[49] Samuel Beer speaks of the ensuing National Liberal Federation as a fusion of numerous separate pressure groups into a national reformist party. The rise of broad traders', manufacturers', and the agriculturalists' associations against the railway monopoly in the 1880s and of trade unions and cooperatives in the 1890s finally ushered in the "collectivist age" of Tory and socialist democracy, characterized by government intervention in economy and society "as a whole." [50] Obviously, the full development of the associational aspects of society takes time, although expanding government activity and the organization of functional interests greatly spur on each other's growth, as shown by the development of the United States.

The full development and interpenetration of interest organizations and governmental functions can also be broken down into in-between steps, which might help to classify relative stages of political development. We begin with political systems of a largely undifferentiated, tribal or agricultural village society, showing hardly a trace of modern organization of parties, public opinion, or associational interest groups. Next come systems with rudimentary organizations, such as the early parliaments of Western countries, whose legislative factions were composed of local notables, large landlords, or, as in England, men in the pay of a patron or of the government. At this stage there is hardly any permanent extraparliamentary organization, and organizing efforts and political communications are intermittent, occurring at the time of elections or on special occasions. After this, we find systems that show great discontinuity among regions or between cities and countryside. This stage is that of the chief periods of urbanization in the older countries as well as a great many new nations in Asia, Africa, and Latin America today.

[49] Quoted by Beer, *British Politics in the Collectivist Age,* p. 52.
[50] Beer, *British Politics in the Collectivist Age,* p. 80.

Italian and French politics still reflect marked discontinuities between industrialized or urbanized areas and the intense localism of rural areas.[51] Outside the cities in Africa and Asia, tribal or village chiefs and communities often provide a traditional framework that swallows up such new-fangled devices as popular elections in the traditional ties of community and ascription. In Latin America, where parties and associations have long been far more developed, they rarely possess a fully developed extra-parliamentary structure, and large areas have indigenous populations and traditional structures only.[52]

For the more developed societies, and increasingly the new nations as well, the rise and penetration of labor has been a good indicator of a certain degree of development of political organization, closely related, of course, to the stage of industrialization and communications and to the demands of the lower classes for economic and political participation. Mass labor organizations, both trade unions and socialist parties, rose in such countries as Great Britain, France, Germany, and Italy during the last decades of the nineteenth century.[53] In spite of the considerable differences in the politics, the organizational forms, and the role of these early labor movements, there are striking similarities. The early movements were characterized by what a recent book has called "political unionism." The process of development, among other effects, brings about considerable functional change in such movements, forcing them, for example, to make up their minds whether to become a trade union or a political party.[54]

The early labor movements also had the potential to become what Sigmund Neumann called "mass parties of integrating." The masses of individuals uprooted by the urbanization and

[51] See also Joseph La Palombara and Myron Weiner, *Political Parties and Political Development*. Princeton, N.J.: Princeton University Press, 1966, pp. 19–22, 24–33; and Hans Daalder in the same work, pp. 52–58.

[52] See William J. M. McKenzie and Kenneth E. Robinson, *Five Elections in Africa*. New York: Oxford, 1960; and La Palombara and Weiner, *Political Parties and Political Development*, chaps. 10, 12, 13.

[53] See especially Walter Galenson, ed., *Comparative Labor Movements*. Englewood Cliffs, N.J.; Prentice-Hall, 1952; and Seymour M. Lipset, *Political Man*. New York: Doubleday, 1960, chap. 2.

[54] See Bruce H. Millen, *The Political Role of Labor in Developing Countries*. Washington, D.C.: Brookings, 1963.

industrialization of the modernizing progress were gathered up and socially integrated by the intensive group life of the large European socialist parties and trade unions. As the uprooted transitionals from rural to industrial life form new communities, and as new generations issue forth and grow up, safe in the security of the newly integrated society at the labor level, the labor movement itself will mature. Its early militancy will wane, and it is more likely to become an equal partner in the common enterprise, because traditional class barriers and hostilities fade and industrial productivity can be shared equitably between capital and labor.

As a last point about the organizational phase, we still need to consider whether and to what extent organizational development and social reintegration bear a relationship to democratization. There can be little doubt that the coming of mass parties and of associational development does signify the end of the traditional forms of political oligarchy. Instead of the tribal chief, village *jefe* (elders), landowners, notables, government officials, or captains of industry, the new masters are likely to be large, anonymous organizations and their elected officials. The individual in his labor union or other mass organization—or even more the nonjoiner—can usually increase his effectiveness and influence by active participation, up to a point. He can run for an office in his organization and come to wield a good deal of power. Supposing, however, that he fails to use fully his opportunities for active participation, does the organizational revolution still denote democratization for him? Or is there, as the sociologist Robert Michels claimed more than half a century ago, an "iron law of oligarchy" inherent in all mass organizations? Is democracy to be defined as a mere framework of opportunities for individual participation that must be used and developed by most people in a society in order to make it a desirable system? These are still unresolved questions,[55] although most observers would answer them in the affirmative.

[55] The controversy actually dates back to Alexis de Tocqueville's theory of the mass society, which could be secured against anarchy and dictatorship only by a multitude of associations and widespread membership in them. As a case in point, the student might compare the 40 to 50 percent of associational members in the American, French, British, German, and Swedish populations to the nearly total absence of such

Level of capabilities

The fifth step of political development again is rather indefinite in its outlines and, in particular, open-ended; we cannot know today in which direction modern political development may yet take us. The fifth step deals with the full development of the capabilities of political systems and is, for that reason, easily quantifiable, though not with reference to any fixed potential. If we speak of the capability of political systems for the extraction of natural resources, for example, there may be, perhaps, a limit to the extraction of any one resource, such as the depletion of coal or of iron in the territory of the country in question. But there is no limit to natural resources as such or to the human imagination for their use, except for the deplorable habit of some nations shortsightedly to despoil, pollute, and destroy the best features of their natural habitat. Yet even under industrial wasteland and in polluted water and air lie great potential uses that a more careful husbanding can make available.

The role of government and politics in the extraction and husbanding of resources consists not so much in the extracting itself as in deciding what shall be extracted, to what use, and for whose benefit. Comparative study reveals deeply felt convictions and beliefs that may limit or spur on extractive activity. In the American political tradition, for example, faith in the right of the public to determine matters of conservation and pollution has often run a poor second to the conviction that the rights of private property transcend even the most flagrant and obnoxious abuses of resources in private hands. Comparable ideologies or systems of belief of one sort or another are present in all systems at all times as one of the significant variables. Comparative study must seek nonideological standards by which to measure more-developed against less-developed systems.

---

memberships in underdeveloped southern Italy as described in Edward and Laura Banfield, *The Moral Basis of a Backward Society*. However, the functioning of highly organized societies such as those of the advanced West rarely gives the individual such complete personal satisfaction as to assure his participation. In the seemingly perfect mechanism of modern mass-participational politics there lurk plenty of causes for personal despair and alienation. In the last analysis, it is also a matter of personality and cultural tradition whether individuals find it more fulfilling to join the game or to spurn it.

Exploitation of resources   From this point of view, then, the scale of measurement of the fifth phase begins with countries that are not yet aware of the resources they could tap and the technology and skills by which to exploit them, followed closely by developing countries or colonies that must leave such exploitation entirely to others. Then come countries that make poor, wasteful, and disorganized use of resources or do not use them to the benefit of all the inhabitants, possibly for lack of basic public control or because of extremes in oligarchy, as in parts of Latin America. The more developed systems in this respect often have their industrialization and democratization behind them and, consequently, allow all the adult members of their society a role in determining, as voters and as consumers, what shall be produced and how.

Since technology develops rapidly and the capabilities of modern societies change within a few years from one fuel to another, say from coal to oil or nuclear energy, and from one means of transportation to the next, say from canals and railroads to buses and private automobiles and then to supersonic jet planes and whatnot, developing newcomers often adopt the latest technological wrinkle of production or communication. It is not sufficient, therefore, to look only at the superficial appearances; rather one must analyze how the extractive capabilities of whole populations are organized.[56]

Molding of the environment   Another notable capability of political systems is to change and mold the human environment. Traditional societies accept most of the human predicament as immutable. They rationalize that it is willed by the gods, the law of nature, or human nature and cannot be changed for the better, if indeed they admit that it is bad. Man's intelligence can just as easily be used for elaborate, defensive excuses as for the exploration of paths of betterment. But in increasingly large areas, such as technology and economic production, social legislation, and mass education, a belief in the possibility of improvement has

---

[56] See also Gabriel Almond and G. Bingham Powell, *Comparative Politics: A Developmental Approach*. Boston: Little, Brown, 1966, chap. 8; and Bruce M. Russett *et al.*, *The World Handbook of Political and Social Indicators*. New Haven, Conn.: Yale University Press, 1964, pp. 60, 215.

evidently taken hold. As the transitional stage approaches the doorstep of modernity, moreover, a burgeoning system of communications will spread both the belief and the knowledge of the means of change to a country's farthest corners.

Even modern societies, as we know them today, still cling to some beliefs in the immutability, for example, of violence and war as recurring forms of human behavior or of criminality or ethnic prejudices. Nevertheless, modern societies are characterized by habituation to change and to constant attempts to mold the human environment from the cradle to the grave. One might cite how extraordinary to the average American of a mere thirty or forty years ago are such things as mass higher education, public measures to eliminate racial discrimination, and a host of standard contemporary habits of preventive medicine, personal hygiene, and food technology. Young Americans are considerably taller, slimmer, healthier, brighter, and more knowledgeable today, and they face incomparably better economic and cultural opportunities thanks to these now-routinized changes than did their predecessors of the 1920s. And there are further changes just around the corner, such as permanent solutions to the problems of population expansion, of the diminishing food supply,[57] and of childhood retardation, that hardly anyone thought possible ten years ago and many still do not today.

Like those discussed previously, the capability to change and mold the human environment rests on the state of development of the political system at least as much as on technology. The technical solution to a given problem may be figured out long before there is a willingness to adopt it. Means of birth control, chemical substitutes for our customary foods, and medical insights into the causes of retardation have been available for a long time, although they may have needed considerable improvement for routine use by masses of people. Cost also can be a major obstacle. But the core of such changes remains a matter of political decision, just as opposition to them on whatever grounds will have to use political means such as organization, propaganda, or legislation to stop them.

The governments of new nations are often more than eager

[57] According to current scientific predictions, the need for food may be satisfied within a few decades largely by chemically produced substitutes for many of the "natural foods" we now eat.

to introduce innovations they consider beneficial to their countries. But the capability of their political systems for inducing change is severely limited by inadequate communications, political strife, and an already pressing overload of desired changes, not to mention technology, trained personnel, and funds. Hence very little can be accomplished overnight in spite of the best intentions. The reception of American grain shipments by starving Indians several years ago was quite typical of the cultural obstacles change can encounter. Not even famine and hunger could make grains other than the customary rice an acceptable food staple. By contrast, several absolutist regimes in eighteenth-century Europe introduced the potato to their lower classes as a new food staple at a point in their social development considerably less modern than India and succeeded almost immediately.

Political capabilities, in other words, like other indicators of political development can outpace or lag behind the social development. The capability of changing and molding the human environment may also regress significantly in the midst of a highly urbanized and industrialized environment. In some of the most highly developed states and cities of America, for example, a loss of civic-mindedness and of concern for improving the human environment has at times led to wholesale retrenchment and neglect of social services, urban improvement, and quality education for the mass of the people. Just as political development may signify bringing a better life to wider circles of the people, and especially to the less fortunate, political decay may take the form of a progressive withdrawal of help and guidance from these wider circles.

Assertion of national power A third capability arising from political development is that of a given system to assert itself in the international world. Since states are often hostile or at least competitive toward one another, the development of this capability is frequently a matter of survival or of freedom and independence. International competition, both economic and military, and especially the threat of war and conquest have always been a major spur to modernization in general and to the breakup of traditional patterns. The establishment of great empires, and of colonial empires in particular, reflects significant differences in this capability between an imperial power and its colonial conquests. At the time of conquest, evidently, Ghana was no match for the British, or Algeria for the French, or Indonesia for the Dutch. Conversely, the disintegration of empires does indicate that the gap in development has narrowed, even though other factors may play a role. The end of the Austro-Hungarian Empire in 1918 confirmed the inability of the Austro-German and Hungarian regimes to maintain their rule and the readiness of the subject nationalities for independence and self-government, if not for democracy.

International economic power is, of course, intimately related to the internal state of economic development. When nineteenth-century Great Britain commanded an empire that took up one sixth of the solid parts of the globe, controlled the seven seas, and dominated international trade and finance, she was no larger than today, a tight little island. But she was ahead of everyone else by fifty to one hundred years in industrialization. Today she is on about the same level as a dozen other economically advanced countries and often barely able to compete with them. At present the United States exercises economic hegemony over Latin America, and the short-range trends indicate, if anything, a widening gap in economic prowess and in their growth rates. But, as in the case of Great Britain, who can tell what the relationship will be one hundred years from now!

Economic and political capability in the international world are, of course, also related to certain resources of fixed amount, such as geographic size, population size and skills, natural resources, and location. For example, we can see very clearly the superior present capabilities of Japan over the People's Republic of China, which has twenty-five times the territory and over seven times the population of Japan. Although handicapped by her past international exploits, Japan is the third greatest industrial power in the world today. But who is to doubt that the sleeping giant of mainland China will eventually pull herself up to become one of the world's superpowers? Another example may be found in the repeated confrontations of tiny Israel and her hostile Arab neighbors, who with at least twenty times her population have suffered crushing defeats in spite of very substantial Soviet military aid. As in the story of David and Goliath, it is not size by itself but ability to marshal one's resources that counts most toward survival.

Since the Middle Ages, the rising capabilities of political systems to make their presence felt in the international world have created ever-widening international systems, such as the competition for colonial empires during the "age of imperialism" (1850–1945) or the European concert of powers of the preceding centuries. From about the 1890s on, we can even speak of a *world politics,* whose dangerous mechanisms of international conflict have demonstrated their reality in two world wars and the continual threat of a third. In spite of collective efforts to control rampant conflict by international organization and peace-keeping devices, the power competition has raised combative capabilities among the great powers to the awesome level of hydrogen bombs that can destroy the civilized world many times over. And although the very destructiveness of the bombs, among other factors, seems to have kept the hostility between the communist states and the Western countries from erupting into World War III, there have been ominous confrontations, brush-fire wars, and internal struggles between communist revolutionaries and Western-supported native governments.

The United States had enjoyed a hundred years of relative isolation from international power politics up to the turn of the century, when international politics became a worldwide system. Thereafter, the changing international setting as well as the rising international capabilities of the United States thrust upon this reluctant nation staggering involvements and responsibilities all over the globe. Unlike the French, the British, or other Europeans who have been accustomed for centuries to the harness of power politics, Americans still vacillate between the illusion of omnipotence and a desire to withdraw from the world and to concentrate on internal improvements. But there is no real choice between a country's using its international capacity or disdaining its role in power politics. Withdrawal by a great power that could stabilize and pacify the international chaos can have disastrous consequences for itself and the whole world. All that is necessary for evil to triumph, to paraphrase Edmund Burke, is for good men to do nothing to resist it. American policy following World

War I provides a telling example of the price of isolationism. Even if we grant the hazards of reconstructing the course of history, it is a fair guess that the Axis powers would not have precipitated World War II if the United States had not abandoned the League of Nations and its international role. World War II, with its estimated sixty million dead and untold human suffering, not to mention the enormous material waste and destruction, could have been headed off by a strong international organization led by American power at such historical turning points as the peace settlement of 1919 and the first aggressions of the Axis challengers in Manchuria, Ethiopia, and the Rhineland.

Nevertheless, the capability to wield power in international affairs poses a moral dilemma, as do the other capabilities mentioned. The many instances where international might has seemingly made right, and the example of developing countries such as Nasser's Egypt, Sukarno's Indonesia, or Nkrumah's Ghana, which squandered on foreign ventures the funds and energies needed for internal development, lend persuasiveness to those who criticize the pursuit of greater capabilities as such. Who needs higher production levels, manned flights to the moon, supersonic transport planes, greater control over the human environment, and a greater nuclear overkill capacity, they say, when even the most developed nations seem unable to use their present capabilities with the proper sense of responsibility? Such a plea, however, has two major flaws. To a poor and developing country, it sounds like a rich man's dilemma. The countries of Latin America, for example, may well agree that the capabilities and living standards of the United States are already too high to be conducive to nonmaterial, humanistic concerns. But they are most unlikely to apply similar strictures to their development. For the real issue in long-range perspective is not at all whether an increase of capabilities is desirable, but rather *which* capabilities should be increased *how much* in relation to other capabilities and *what use* is to be made of the heightened power. To deny the desirability of increasing capabilities in general would be mere romantic nostalgia for the "good old days," which upon closer examination invariably reveal themselves to have been not all that good. In the same way, the use of a country's international capability is always a question of good foreign policies versus ill-considered, bad ones. The nonuse of international power is as likely to be bad policy as is a flagrant abuse of power.

ALTERNATIVE PATHS OF POLITICAL DEVELOPMENT

It is a notion common to all developing peoples and deeply ingrained in the thinking of their leaders that each country wants to follow its own developmental path. Contemporary new nations may admire various aspects of more developed countries such as France, the Soviet Union, Great Britain, the United States, or Red China, but they never intend a slavish imitation of any foreign pattern. Intentions aside, the different patterns of actual development are also divergent enough to suggest various distinct types, although scholars disagree about any one morphology of political development. Let us take a closer look at some of the basic problems of definition, as well as the typologies proposed by different scholars.

Approach to "world culture"

"East is East and West is West" wrote Rudyard Kipling, polarizing the cultural differences between Asia and Western Europe. Since most political values and their institutionalization are culture-bound, it is very hazardous to attempt to lay down universal standards. A way out of this dilemma has been proposed by Lucian W. Pye, who speaks of the progressive diffusion of a "world culture" of state and nation building throughout the Third World, amounting to a nearly universal adoption of modern Western industrial urban practices, standards, and values.[58] Politically, this cosmopolitan culture envisions an ideal regime of *civilian rule through representative institutions in the matrix of public liberties.*[59] Military dictators and their supporters among the new states, and even pro-Soviet or pro-Chinese leaders, see in dictatorship or totalitarianism at best a temporary expedient toward this long-range goal—a commendable view though no guarantee against abuse. The native elites of former

---

[58] See Lucian W. Pye, *Aspects of Political Development.* Boston: Little, Brown, 1966, pp. 9–11. See also Emerson, *From Empire to Nation.*

[59] See the formulation of Edward Shils, *Political Development in the New States.* Mouton & Co., 1962, pp. 47–48.

colonies, moreover, tend to approach political development largely within the political traditions of their erstwhile colonial masters. Nevertheless, the cultural differences arising from the traditional antecedents of the societies concerned, as well as from their particular problems of socioeconomic modernization, still make for considerable differences.

The cultural problem of defining standards applies with particular force to the historical antecedents of the spreading "world culture." Perhaps, there is a certain convergence of political ideals today. But is it appropriate to measure ancient Greece and Rome or the great bureaucratic empires or the cities of Renaissance Italy against exactly the same standards as contemporary states? It would appear that ancient Athens during her celebrated democratic age reached a pinnacle of political development comparing favorably with all contemporary non-Greek states, indeed with present-day Greek politics. To be sure, the Athenian record shows some major flaws, such as slavery and the failure to achieve a larger union. Ancient Rome too, though in very different ways, reached a pinnacle of political development, boasting a liberal constitution and the impressive edifice of Roman Law. Rome, too, suffered flaws and eventual political decay. The early Middle Ages were generally marked by political chaos and regression, and yet they produced notable breakthroughs for long-range political development such as representative government and the beginnings of the British constitutional tradition, comparable perhaps to the Renaissance experiments in urban self-government amid rampant feudal oppression and anarchic strife. Also deserving of a high rating are the development of sophisticated public finance and administration by such disparate autocracies as Byzantium, the court of Frederick II in thirteenth-century Sicily, or the absolute monarchy of France.[60]

On one dimension or another, we can account for the spotty political development of earlier ages, giving special credit

---

[60] It is only fair to accord similar credit to the enormous organizing efforts of "hydraulic societies," such as the ancient Near Eastern, Indian, Chinese, and pre-Columbian civilizations, whose need for large-scale irrigation and flood control is said to have produced "agrarian despotism" of a centralized nature. See Karl Wittfogel, *Oriental Despotism*. New Haven, Conn.: Yale University Press, 1957, and L. Robert Sinai, *The Challenge of Modernization*. New York: Norton, 1964, p. 304.

for the invention or independent reinvention of complex concepts, procedures, and institutions. More significant still, we must measure the political development of a particular country at a particular time against its own values and those of its age. Even contemporary societies such as Athens and Sparta should not be compared without consideration of their differing value systems, although this need not stop us from proclaiming Sparta unnecessarily crude and brutal or Athens politically unstable and fickle. Nor should contemporary democratic and totalitarian systems be compared without consideration of their respective ideologies and the extent to which they may sincerely strive to live up to them. It is an open secret that fascist regimes violated their own standards as well as many others, that no communist system has quite lived up to its own Marxist theories, and that democratic governments rarely have much reason for smug self-satisfaction in this respect either. The attempt to consider each system on its merits, moreover, need not prevent us from adjudging fascist totalitarianism incredibly primitive and barbarous and its communist equivalent a form of government hardly fit for backward, undifferentiated peasant societies. The disdain of Marxist theorists for the complexities of constitutional law and the procedures of individual and public liberties in no way protects them against a charge of extreme naïvete and political primitivism, if nothing worse.

Some typologies of current regimes

Many eminent social scientists have proposed typologies of the different configurations of political development today, and we can select only a few of the most notable. Bear in mind that these alternatives are neither moral equivalents nor consecutive stages, even though some are obviously better developed than others. Instead, they might be called the present results of the somewhat uncertain groping of native elites against obstacles of various kinds toward essentially similar, though rather differently perceived, goals of human fulfillment.

Shils' five types   The first such typology was proposed by the sociologist Edward Shils, who contributed extraordinary insights to our present understanding of political development. Shils distinguishes five types of regimes, beginning with *political democracy,* which he describes as centered around a legislature elected by universal adult (or male) suffrage. Both parliamentary and presidential regimes are included, provided they feature a constitutional order, a competitive party system, and effective legislative, popular, and judicial checks on executive power. A second type, *tutelary democracy,* is defined as an attempt "to retain as much of the institutions of civilian rule, representative government, and public liberties as they can" in spite of an insufficiently developed political system, while assuring stable and effective government and unhindered economic and social development. In this category Shils included Bismarckian Germany (1871–1918) and Sukarno's "guided democracy" as well as other benign developmental dictatorships or certain emergency regimes of a military nature. To differentiate tutelary democracy from oligarchic dictatorships, he specified that its leadership must be genuinely attached to the idea of democracy and must minimize the use of coercive means of achieving consensus. De Gaulle's France may fit this category, too, as do some Latin-American or Asian societies in which a "democratic military" intervenes in order to restore democracy and good government and to substitute its authority for the lack of popular consensus.

A third type, *modernizing oligarchies,* is typical of countries that are considerably removed from the social and economic development that makes tutelary democracy feasible. Shils cites the Sudan, Iraq, Egypt, and Pakistan as countries whose elites consider oligarchy the only way to modernize society and to provide unity and a centralized, honest administration. They are too impatient with their "modernization gap," with the dead weight of tradition, and with political opponents to let progress depend on popular participation or consent. The oligarchs are generally military men or members of the traditional elite and have no more tolerance for an independent legislative or judiciary than for opposition parties. Although they clothe themselves in the mantle of national service and moral righteousness, they rarely command the administrative efficiency to accomplish much.

Totalitarian oligarchy is "oligarchy with democratic airs"— manipulated with mass participation and with an elaborate ideology.[61] As intolerant of opposition and governmental checks and balances as the modernizing oligarchs, the totalitarians go considerably further in seeking to dominate every sphere of public and private life. Fascism, nazism, communism, and pre-1945 Japanese nationalism are examples of totalitarian oligarchy.

Shils' fifth type is *traditional oligarchy,* which is said to rest on a firm dynastic constitution buttressed by traditional religion. It is long on legitimacy but short on modern political institutions, such as legislative processes or an effective administrative apparatus. Local traditional elites must wield power independently, because the central oligarchy is unwilling and unable to do so. No popular participation is expected, nor are there any channels for it. Traditional oligarchies are incompatible with any considerable social or economic modernization, such as mass education or urbanization, which would soon destroy them.[62]

Black's seven patterns   Another typology of global scope is proposed by Cyril E. Black, an outstanding scholar of Russian history,[63] who attempts to capture the historical and geographical dynamics of political and general modernization in seven patterns. After discussing the enormous variety of the 175 societies under consideration, Black concludes that the evident convergence of social functions among such countries as Japan and France, the United States and the Soviet Union,[64] and Mexico and Poland has not led to a comparable convergence in institutional structure.[65] His seven patterns emerged when he analyzed

[61] On the "democratic" mass-participation character of totalitarian government, see also the classics Hannah Arendt, *The Origins of Totalitarianism.* New York: Harcourt, new ed., 1966, chap. 13; and Carl J. Friedrich and Zbigniew Brzezinski, *Totalitarian Dictatorship and Autocracy.* New York: Praeger, 2d ed., 1965, chap. 1.

[62] For details see Shils, *Political Development in the New States,* pp. 47–84.

[63] See also his symposium *The Transformation of Russian Society: Aspects of Social Change since 1861.* Cambridge, Mass.: Harvard University Press, 1960.

[64] On this pair see also Zbigniew Brzezinski and Samuel P. Huntington, *Political Power: USA/USSR.* New York: Viking, 1963.

[65] Cyril E. Black, *The Dynamics of Modernization.* New York: Harper & Row, 1966, pp. 49, 90–94; see also his excellent survey of the literature of modernization, at the end of the book.

and tabulated for all his societies their style of modernization and (1) the period during which their modernizing leadership consolidated itself, (2) the period when they underwent their economic and social transformation, and (3) the period of their social integration—processes which the societies to varying degrees have not yet completed.

The first pattern of political modernization is formed by Great Britain and France, the earliest countries to modernize, becoming models widely followed. The consolidation of the British modernizing leadership, for example, runs from the Puritan revolutionaries of 1649 to the electoral reform of 1832, that of the French from the Jacobin revolutionaries of 1789 to the revolution of 1848, followed in both countries by the socioeconomic transformation until 1945, when the integration of their societies begins. The second pattern is the modernization of Great Britain's overseas offspring nations, the United States, Canada, Australia, and New Zealand, whose starting dates vary considerably. The British constitutional heritage also affected many former British colonies, though far less deeply.

The third pattern was the reception of the ideology and the institutions of the French Revolution by all of continental Europe except Russia. Directly introduced by Napoleon's armies, the French republican heritage found lasting favor with native elites throughout southern, northern, central, and eastern Europe and cast a powerful spell on African, South East Asian, and Middle Eastern societies temporarily under French control. Black calls Jacobinism as a generalized ideology "the leading alternative revolutionary doctrine to Marxism-Leninism" and an inspiration to such leaders of developing nations as Kemal Ataturk, Nasser, Ben Bella, Sun Yat-sen, Nehru, Sukarno, Cárdenas, and the early Castro. Through its influence on Spain, Portugal, Belgium, and the Netherlands, it has also helped to mold in its image native attitudes in the former colonial empires of these countries. Except for Scandinavia, Germany, and the Benelux countries, however, the European countries of the French pattern have not yet completed their socioeconomic transformation.

The fourth pattern consists of Latin-American societies formed by European states of the third pattern but greatly delayed in their modernization by their peculiar composition and agricultural wealth, by foreign control, and by the lagging in socioeconomic development of their chief colonizers, Spain and Portugal. Nevertheless, an increasing number of these countries are today well on their way to modernity.

Black's fifth pattern is a grab bag of countries distinguished by the ability of their traditional governments to resist colonial conquest; hence these countries have experienced largely endogenous modernization. They include Russia, Japan, China, Iran, Turkey, Afghanistan, Ethiopia, and Thailand, the first two being particularly successful in their socioeconomic development. Their development, unlike that of many other societies, was relatively undisturbed by problems of cultural identity, territorial unity, and, at least in the earlier phases, crises of legitimacy of constituted authority. Consequently, their patterns of political development are distinctively their own except for minor currents from other traditions.

The sixth and seventh patterns of Black's morphology embrace the more than a hundred states of Asia, the Near East, Africa, South America, and Oceania, including some not yet independent. Members of this group are characterized by well-developed traditional cultures and by their interaction with the cultures of the tutelary societies that were their colonial masters or overlords. The interaction of cultures also includes the adaptation of traditional forms of Near Eastern and Asian government to modern political functions, a process comparable to the political modernization of European feudalism of the bureaucratic systems of old Russia, China, Japan, and the Ottoman Empire. The seventh pattern, chiefly in sub-Saharan Africa and Oceania, lacked, according to Black, the developed religions, language, and political institutions for amalgamated development and therefore adopted modern ideas and institutions directly.[66]

Apter's analysis   Another important set of distinctions and types of modernizing systems is by David E. Apter. Apter's analysis begins with a basic distinction between two kinds of value systems underlying different paths of development. One, the

---

[66] Black, *The Dynamics of Modernization,* chap. 4.

secular-libertarian model, consists of units (individuals and groups) capable of reason and aware of their self-interest. This value system underlies our modern notions of individualistic democracy, a marketplace economy, and a mechanistic system of government. The other value system is that of the *sacred-collectivity model,* in which the political community lends to its individual members a sense of moral purpose, and a feeling of individual self-realization in playing a role in the community. These contrasting models are not only reminiscent of the philosophies of John Locke and Plato, or of the sociological distinction between *Gesellschaft* and *Gemeinschaft,* but they also stand at opposite poles of a continuum of subtypes of actual political systems.

The first such system is characterized by the limited governmental function of reconciling, mediating, and coordinating, rather than organizing or mobilizing, the diverse interests and communities that make up the body politic. The values enshrined in the laws and institutions of the pure secular-libertarian model generate legitimate governmental authority in these *reconciliation systems,* which often feature the well-known devices of constitutional government from the United States and Western Europe to India and Pakistan. The basic mode of the sacred collectivity, on the other hand, appears in the religio-political unity of old monarchies and also in the modern subtype of the *mobilization system.* Mobilization regimes are characterized by a mass party of solidarity led by a charismatic leader and by an intense "political religion," an ideology that creates legitimacy for the new government, teaches new modernizing roles and instrumental values, and gives to the whole nation-to-be a sense of meaningful identity and direction. As examples, Apter mentions Touré's Guinea, Ghana, and, by implication, the Soviet Union and Red China.[67] Mobilization systems need not be totalitarian, although they have little use for political competition and opposition. They can easily turn to totalitarianism, however, if they respond to the complexity of the moderniz-

[67] See the scholarly debate regarding the Soviet system as a "movement regime": Robert C. Tucker and others in *American Political Science Review,* 55 (June 1961), 281–293, and in Donald W. Treadgold, ed., *The Development of the USSR.* Seattle, Wash.: University of Washington Press, 1964, chap. 1.

ing task with increasing coercion. In any case, they are supremely well suited to accomplishing rapid modernization, because (1) they can change traditional attitudes by ideological reinterpretation and propaganda, and (2) their mobilization creates a new dynamic social unity across traditional, polycommunally fragmented societies whose diverse interests would have to be catered to in a reconciliation system. Whether they are nationalist, socialist, or communist, mobilization movements also hold out a special, quasi-religious appeal to alienated citizens of reconciliation systems by offering them a sense of belonging to a more meaningful collectivity.

Apter also discusses three sybtypes that are combinations of the secular-libertarian and the sacred-collectivity models. One is the *modernizing autocracy,* such as Morocco, Thailand, and Ethiopia, which is headed by a monarch, although his power may be shared with a bureaucracy and other agencies. The monarch can be a very popular modernizer who uses his legitimate authority to fit innovations into the traditional framework of his society. Very similar is the nationalist *military oligarchy,* except that instead of a king it has a military leader or junta, who are often quite incompetent in their political dealings. A third mixed type is the *neomercantilist society,* which uses a mixture of private and public enterprise for its political purposes. Headed by a "presidential monarch" of ritualized authority, not a traditional king, it is often the stable product of earlier mobilization regimes whose ideological fervor has cooled or of modernizing reconciliation systems that have stepped up their use of coercion for the sake of progress.[68]

Moore's three paths   Finally, many typologies grew out of the comparative study of the role of a particular group in the modernization process. Barrington Moore, Jr., for example, has reviewed grand revolutionary theory in an analysis of three alternative paths of development among nobility, bourgeoisie, and peasantry. One is the road of bourgeois revolutions traveled

[68] See David E. Apter, *The Politics of Modernization* (Chicago: University of Chicago Press, 1965), esp. chaps. 1–2, 9–11, and his *The Political Kingdom of Uganda* (Princeton, N.J.: Princeton University Press, 1961) for an example of a modernizing autocracy.

by Great Britain, France, and the United States under different circumstances but with a similar result: parliamentary democracy. Another is that of nonrevolutionary bourgeois capitalism with "revolutions from above," which led to fascism in Germany and Japan. The third is the communist route in Russia and China, which originated chiefly in revolution by the peasants, including proletarianized or conscripted former peasants.[69] Other studies base their classifications or typologies on the role of the military,[70] political parties, the bureaucrats,[71] organized labor, the changing composition of elites,[72] or a classification of transitional situations.[73]

[69] See Barrington Moore, Jr., *Social Origins of Dictatorship and Democracy.* Boston: Beacon, 1966; also Chalmers A. Johnson, *Peasant Nationalism and Communist Power.* Stanford, Calif.: Stanford University Press, 1962; and the essay of John H. Kautsky in his *Political Change in Underdeveloped Countries.* New York: Wiley, 1962.

[70] See, for example, John J. Johnson, ed., *The Role of the Military in Underdeveloped Countries.* Princeton, N.J.: Princeton University Press, 1962; Morris Janowitz, *The Military in the Political Development of New Nations.* Chicago: University of Chicago Press, 1964; and Jason L. Finkle and Richard W. Gable, *Political Development and Social Change.* New York: Wiley, 1966, chap. 11.

[71] Finkle and Gable, *Political Development and Social Change,* chap. 15; Myron Weiner, *The Politics of Scarcity.* Chicago: University of Chicago Press, 1962; and Apter, *The Politics of Modernization,* chap 6. See also La Palombara and Weiner, *Political Parties and Political Development;* and James S. Coleman and Carl G. Rosberg, Jr., eds., *Political Parties and National Integration in Tropical Africa.* Berkeley, Calif.: University of California Press, 1964. On bureaucracy, see, for example, Joseph La Palombara, ed., *Bureaucracy and Political Development.* Princeton, N.J.: Princeton University Press, 1963; and Douglas E. Ashford in *New Nations and Political Development,* Annals of the American Academy of Political and Social Science, March 1965, pp. 89–100.

[72] See Millen, *The Political Role of Labor in Developing Countries;* Finkle and Gable, *Political Development and Social Change,* chaps. 10 and 14; and the rapidly expanding field of elite and recruitment studies.

[73] See especially Chalmers A. Johnson, *Revolutionary Change.* Boston: Little, Brown, 1966; but also the theory of crisis of legitimacy, integration, and participation in La Palombara and Weiner, *Political Parties and Political Development,* chap. 1; as well as S. N. Eisenstadt, "Breakdowns of Modernization," in *Economic Development and Cultural Change,* 12 (July 1964), 345–367.

THE CROSS-NATIONAL APPROACH

Since much information about the stages of social and political development lends itself to quantitative statements, a growing literature now suggests ways of testing broad generalizations about comparative development by the *cross-national approach*. The term "cross-national" denotes a methodological posture with special emphasis on quantitative processing, hence a preference for easily quantifiable "hard" statistical data (of the sort to be found in statistical yearbooks and annuals) over "soft" data (derived from subjective judgments or controversial generalizations). Actually, there may be no real limit to the kind of data of either sort that can be processed by computer to test appropriate hypotheses about comparative politics. There are great differences, however, in the various attempts that have been made in this direction and in the degree of sophistication they allow in comparative research. There are also definite limits to the ease with which reliable and useful cross-national data can be obtained, limiting in form the worthwhileness of cross-national research projects.

The cross-polity survey

One of the more ambitious cross-national projects to appear in recent years, the *Cross-Polity Survey,*[74] will serve as an example of very broadly gauged quantitative approaches and their uses for the study of political development. The unit of analysis in the *Cross-Polity Survey* is the independent polity. The authors have collected relevant information on 115 independent polities in the form of 57 important "raw characteristics." These attributes include hard data such as size, population, growth rate per capita, gross national product, and literacy rate; developmental categories such as stages of economic and political development; sociocultural traits such as religious, racial, and linguistic homogeneity; and a large number of variables distinguishing different types and modes of operation of the political systems of the polities.

[74] Arthur S. Banks and Robert B. Textor, *Cross-Polity Survey*. Cambridge, Mass.: M.I.T. Press, 1963. See also Bruce M. Russett *et al., World Handbook of Political and Social Indicators* (New Haven, Conn.; Yale University Press, 1946), which emphasizes hard data.

Basic technique   The basic technique in the *Cross-Polity Survey* is called "pattern search and table translation." [75] The data are put on punch cards in the form of dichotomous variables, all of which are then "crossed" with each other. Of the resulting two-by-two contingency tables, those showing a strong association between two variables are printed out in grammatical English sentences. The computer 7090 printout constitutes the bulk of the book. The concept of pattern is borrowed from the cross-cultural method of cultural anthropology [76] and defined as "concatenation of co-occurrences among attributes considered important by the observer." As the researcher scans the patterns presented, he can formulate and test meaningful hypotheses regarding, for example, what types of political systems appear to thrive in what kind of environmental or sociocultural setting.

Advantages and limitations   The advantages of this type of cross-national approach are readily apparent. The cross-polity survey is a global coverage, and so it permits a superior level of generalizations. It facilitates in particular the classification of whole polities in an infinite variety of ways. At the very least, it lays a fairly sound groundwork of objective generalizations upon which more sophisticated research can be built. Its faults and limitations, on the other hand, are just as obvious. The authors themselves acknowledge the difficulties of obtaining reliable "hard data" on many of the new nations and of applying many of the judgmental categories current in comparative politics to particular countries. With the rapid progress of comparative research on particular countries and of general comparative theory, any authoritative cross-polity survey, rather than serving as a lasting foundation for the discipline, runs the danger of being soon outdated.

For the study of social and political development, further-

[75] The data could also be subjected to other correlation, cluster, scaling, or factor-analysis methods. See Russett *et al.*, *World Handbook*, pp. 50–51; and Phillip M. Gregg and Arthur S. Banks, "Dimensions of Political Systems: Factor Analysis of Cross-Polity Survey," *American Political Science Review*, 59 (1965), 602–614.

[76] See Frank W. Moore, *Readings in Cross-Cultural Methodology*, Princeton, N.J.: Human Relations Area Files Press, 1961.

more, the cross-polity survey is singularly lacking in the kind of empirical detail on which research would thrive. The self-imposed limitation to traits of whole polities, for example, excludes automatically the partial developments and idiosyncratic phenomena that frequently initiate, expedite, or inhibit development. Development is rarely the result of a polity-wide process. An even greater shortcoming for the study of development is its cross-sectional character.[77] Since the mysteries of development are still largely unexplained, a cross-polity survey that included the time dimension would be much more helpful in the generation of hypotheses about the sequence of stages and phenomena. Such a survey, however, would probably encounter insuperable difficulties in obtaining all the relevant data on a global scale.

Finally, there are the problems of comparability and relevance, which especially bedevil quantitative comparative research. A global cross-polity survey cannot help using a set of fairly explicit assumptions about the nature of social and political systems everywhere, which thereby tend to take on a global uniformity contrary to most empirical evidence. In fact, the cross-polity researcher may quite possibly come to take uniformities for granted that still need to be demonstrated. Or he may construct a survey of such elementary generality that he adds little to our common knowledge. There is also the danger of ignoring the idiographic peculiarities that refuse to fit into the systematic framework of the comparison. This danger is greater with quantitatively oriented research because a substantial amount of crucial social, cultural, and political evidence is nonquantitative or exceedingly difficult to quantify. The quality of all comparative political analysis, nevertheless, rests on the depth of understanding of each of the systems included. Thus a global survey or a systems model claiming global applicability

[77] See also Russett *et al., The World Handbook of Political and Social Indicators,* p. 299. As the title suggests, this work carefully avoids the holistic implications of speaking of policies or systems and is content with supplying information in an atomistic framework, with little hint as to the likely relationships among the different "indicators." See also the contributions on the cross-national approach in Richard L. Merritt and Stein Rokkan, eds., *Comparing Nations* (New Haven, Conn.: Yale University Press, 1966), especially the description of the "dimensionality of nations project" by Rudolph J. Rummell.

requires an extraordinary amount of detailed knowledge such as can be expected, at best, only of a large and well-coordinated teamwork effort.

Other types of cross-national research

Other types of cross-national research have been notably more successful in meeting the objections to cross-polity studies. They are generally content with comparing only a few political systems that have something in common, such as the same region, culture, international alliance, or approximate stage of development. Their greater similarity allows a more tailormade systematic framework, and their smaller number encourages more attention to empirical detail, including nonquantifiable material and important idiosyncrasies. The resulting generalizations immediately provide a feedback of sophisticated relevance for the understanding of each of the countries compared, offering insights into the functioning of each system. Quite frequently, these less ambitious undertakings have focused on a particular process of relationship, such as party systems or elections, in the fairly safe assumption that this partial object plays largely the same role in all the countries concerned. Thus, topical specialization and a less than global scope of comparison may work together toward a higher level of sophistication in comparative research. A few representative examples will illustrate this approach.

Benefits of smaller-scale comparison. One of the immediate benefits of smaller-scale comparison is to highlight the very real difficulties of using judgmental categories for quantitative comparison. In the pioneering days of quantitative applications, two political scientists devised an imaginative scale to measure the relative democratic development over fifteen years of twenty Latin-American countries.[78] The fifteen criteria used to rank them were educational level, living standard, internal unity, political maturity,[79] national independence, freedom of press

[78] Russell H. Fitzgibbon and Kenneth F. Johnson, "Measurement of Latin American Political Change," *American Political Science Review,* 55 (1961), 515–526.

[79] Political maturity was defined as popular "belief in individual political dignity and maturity."

and speech, free elections, free party organization, judicial independence, fiscal responsibility,[80] enlightened social legislation, civilian supremacy over the military, freedom from ecclesiastical control, enlightened administrative development, and effective local government.[81] Most of these categories, such as political maturity, are obviously of the sort that political scientists, area specialists, and just about everybody else could argue for years. The judgments of ranking in each category, however, were made by consulting a large panel of American specialists on Latin America on four occasions, in 1945, 1950, 1955, and 1960, so that they represent at least a collective judgment of experts.

The resulting rankings of the twenty countries were correlated in several ways, giving groupings of relative democratic achievement and measurements of the varying degrees of democratic improvement. The consensus among the specialists involved in the collection of data cannot completely remove the question of the subjectivity of judgment. A panel composed, say, of knowledgeable Latin Americans, or of ultraconservatives, or communists, would probably have arrived at different judgments or might have wished to consider other categories for ranking. At the same time, subjective judgment can have decided advantages over the mere feeding of "hard data" into the computer, which can only do blindly what it is programmed to do. Judgmental control can allow for highly refined, selective, and sophisticated categories while guarding against misinterpretation by data-processing techniques. The human mind is still infinitely more adaptable to the needs of social research than any existing computer. But it is also far too slow in the quantitative manipulation of great masses of data to be self-sufficient in dealing with them.

There is a significant procedural difference also between using soft data based on the invisible processes of private judgment and using data arrived at by steps that anyone can see and replicate. Consider, for example, two sociological studies of

[80] Defined as "public awareness of accountability for the collection and expenditure of public funds."

[81] Defined as "intelligent and sympathetic administration of whatever local government prevails," a cautious formulation evidently suggested by the underdeveloped and uneven organization of local government in the subcontinent.

political development that differ considerably in their reliance on hard data versus political performance. The first inquired into the "social prerequisites of democracy" among stable and unstable democracies and unstable dictatorial regimes in European and English-speaking nations and unstable democracies and stable dictatorships in Latin America.[82] Countries on these dichotomous lists were compared as to their average economic development, including degree of urbanization and education. The average indices of economic development clearly separated stable democracies from unstable democracies and dictatorial regimes in Europe and in English-speaking countries, although the most developed dictatorships still outranked some of the less developed stable democracies. In Latin America, the average indices similarly related stable dictatorships to socioeconomic backwardness. The author further pointed up the importance of "cross-cutting politically relevant affiliation" for democratic stability and contrasted it to countries divided by unbridgeable ideological or other cleavages.

The second study compared the indices of education, economic development, communications development, urbanization, and labor-force distribution of seventy-seven nations against a more sensitive scale of stable democracy than the simple dichotomies of the first study.[83] Each nation was given two points for every year from 1940 to 1960 during which its lower chamber of the legislature had two or more parties and 30 percent or more of its seats were occupied by the opposition. It received only one point if the opposition had less than 30 percent and none if there was only a colonial or other "mock parliament" or none at all. A further point was granted for every year a parliamentary or presidential chief executive elected in open competition held office, half a point for noncompetitive election or

[82] Seymour M. Lipset, "Some Social Prerequisites of Democracy: Economic Development and Political Legitimacy," *American Political Science Review*, 53 (1959), 69–106. The Union of South Africa was not included. See also Seymour M. Lipset, *Political Man*. New York: Doubleday, 1960.

[83] Phillip Cutright, "National Political Development: Measurement and Analysis," *American Sociological Review*, 28 (1963), 253–264. Africa was left out for lack of appropriate data. Lipset had specified as his criterion for stable democracy that during the past twenty-five years no totalitarian movement polled more than 20 percent of the popular vote.

for colonial elective regimes, and none for years during which a chief executive and his party had banned the opposition. The procedures of this study are so overt that the student can immediately assess its merit. It evidently measures political development by the extent to which national party systems and executive-legislative relations approach the Western model of competitive national politics. The clarity of this focus also accounts for blind spots of the study, such as the heavy Western bias and the unconcern with the nature and intensity of potentially destructive cleavages or with the local and individual angles of political development.

A study of citizenship patterns   Thus far the most ambitious and rewarding cross-national study with a bearing on political development has been a study of citizenship patterns in the United States, Great Britain, West Germany, Italy, and Mexico.[84] About one thousand representative interviews were conducted in each country to ascertain the political knowledge and beliefs, the feelings toward the political system, and the judgments and opinions that link information and feelings with action. Three basic citizenship orientations were found to prevail in varying mixtures in the five countries: (1) the parochial orientation, characterized by very low awareness of and affection for the national government and the roles and functions of the political system; (2) the subject orientation, which involves a considerable level of political knowledge, feeling, and opinion, but stresses chiefly the *output* side of government activity, such as taxes, welfare, or conscription; and (3) the participant orientation, which combines high awareness and affect with an emphasis on individual participation (*input*) in politics. A pure type of parochial orientation may be found in certain African tribal societies, traditional villages, and also among large numbers of

[84] Gabriel Almond and Sidney Verba, *The Civic Culture*. Princeton, N.J.: Princeton University Press, 1963. Like all survey research, this study was vulnerable to criticisms of its sampling methods, procedures, and comparability, of which the most serious was perhaps that the Mexican survey omitted communities under 10,000 inhabitants. More consequential still was the failure to divide the national samples into significant subcultures, which meant, for example, that the survey of American attitudes completely missed the imminent Negro revolt.

women, farmers, and youths even in the more developed societies. A pure subject orientation is probably characteristic of the more mobile strata of population in the historical regimes of centralized European absolutism or the "bureaucratic empires." Participant style, finally, typifies the political activism of democratic countries or at least the sense of political efficacy and pride of civic participation of their more politically involved citizens.

The political culture of any one country represents invariably all three orientations, and the mixture can be measured and compared as to the relative quantities of each type and their relationship to particular social classes, age and sex groups, religious and partisan identifications, or other characteristics. The presence of participant orientations also allows a measurement of micropolitical development, although the progression from parochial to subject to participant orientations is by no means as clearly prevalent as our hypothetical three steps— traditional, transitional, modern—would suggest. Thus the five-nation survey found a clear progression in which the three orientations form a harmonious whole only in the British case, where the structures of local and parochial identification survived the growth of central power and, in fact, eventually became the school and vehicle for modern political participation. On the Continent, on the other hand, powerful absolutistic regimes, as in France and Germany, extirpated earlier parochial loyalties with such thoroughness that the modern participant elements have not yet quite overcome the patterns of subject orientation. Their frustration has led to a vicious circle of alienation and authoritarian lapses that interfere with the development of stable democracy.

American political culture, by contrast, registered very high in participant orientation but low in subject orientation toward government administrators and other outputs of the political system. American political history from the rebellion against the British Empire to the Progressive movement bears witness to the sources of this attitude toward governmental authority. At the same time, parochial attitudes and primary attachments are strong and often fused with the channels of political participation. The Mexican mixture of parochialism with a strong pride in the creed of the Mexican Revolution and in El Presidente, almost independent of actual government performance, finally affords a glimpse of the pattern of the better-developed new nations today.[85]

While the developmental dimension of the five-nation study is in large part conjectural or based on our knowledge of the national histories rather than on the cross sections of citizenship patterns, one secondary analysis of a part of the same data clearly pins down an aspect of sociopolitical change itself.[86] This study examines the extent to which the respondents in each of the five nations hold an authoritarian view of parent-child relationships and how they differ according to age, education, social class, and so on. Since the ages of the respondents span nearly two generations, all breakdowns by age and nation showed a progression in each country from more autocratic to more democratic family ideologies. Far from supporting the conventional national stereotypes, for example, the data showed successive stages of democratization of attitude toward parent-child relations that would place Americans born before 1900 on about the same level of permissiveness as Britons born after 1910 or Italians born after 1934 on the same stage as Germans and Mexicans born before 1910 and Britons born before 1900. Since the respective autocratic or more or less democratic family ideology is probably acquired in the first decade of a person's life, the age groups give us a glimpse of changing attitudes of a crucial nature. With due allowance for the greater autocratic tendency of respondents of rural origin or lower-class status, the measurement reveals simply the cross sections of comparable family democratization in each nation and group.[87]

---

[85] See especially Almond and Verba, *The Civic Culture,* chaps. 1, 14, and 15.

[86] Glen H. Elder, Jr., "Role Relations, Socio-Cultural Environments, and Autocratic Family Ideology," *Sociometry,* 28 (1965), 173–196. The "autocratic family ideology" appears to be frequently related to autocratic views in politics, industrial relations, education, and social life, according to the sources cited by Elder, pp. 175–181.

[87] Many further pertinent cross-national studies will be described later, such as the studies of the evolution of party systems in Seymour M. Lipset and Stein Rokkan, eds., *Party Systems and Voter Alignments.* New York: Free Press, 1967; La Palombara and Weiner, *Political Parties and Political Development;* and the cross-national comparisons of within-nation differences in Merritt and Rokkan, *Comparing Nations,* pt. III.

2
POLITICAL SOCIALIZATION, PARTICIPATION, AND RECRUITMENT

Political action always takes place among collectivities. A completely isolated hermit, no matter what his sentiments, is incapable of political action. Yet collectivities are made up of individuals, whose political attitudes and behavior in fact constitute the political system. Comparative study gains greatly by analyzing how individuals in different countries become involved in the various political roles and role structures. Often the structures of different systems seem deceptively similar systems, as in the French and the British, and it is in the individual and his attitudes that the profound differences reside.

The scientific study of the acquisition of political attitudes and behavior patterns by members of a political system or subsystem is generally called the study of *political socialization*. Some political scientists prefer to analyze this process as the way in which society transmits political orientations to newcomers, such as the young or immigrants.[1] Others stress the conservative, pattern-maintaining function of political socialization for the whole society, since by teaching and politically indoctrinating its

[1] See the definition by David Easton and Jack Dennis in Roberta Sigel, ed., *Political Socialization: Its Role in the Political Process,* Annals of the American Academy of Political and Social Science, September 1965, p. 40 (hereafter referred to as *Political Socialization* (Annals)).

young, society guards itself against the disruptive potential of "the successive invasions of barbarian hordes"—the untutored young generations.[2] Still others stress the development, growth, and attainment of individual political orientations: the learning rather than the teaching.[3] A growing literature now also inquires into the political socialization of specially selected groups, such as members of political parties, judges, or legislators,[4] in order to learn more about their special qualities and about the selection process that picks them rather than other people. Thus the study of political socialization is not always easy to keep separate from the study of recruitment or, for that matter, from the study of parties, legislatures, or public administration. Similarly, political socialization is so closely intertwined with the processes of general socialization—that is, the general process by which children and newcomers are integrated into society—that it is not advisable to try sharply separating the two.

We shall examine the processes of political socialization in a variety of ways. First, we shall consider the individual life cycle from childhood to old age and the ways in which political orientations are learned and taught at the various stages. We shall discuss not only the patterns of political involvement of different age groups, but also their varying capabilities for the different political roles as well as the mechanics of adult opinion formation under the impact of historical events.

Next we shall turn to the relations between the generations, between parents and children as well as outside the family. While there can be little doubt about the significance of the family as an agent of political socialization,[5] there have also been many

---

[2] See Gabriel A. Almond and James S. Coleman, *The Politics of Developing Areas.* Princeton, N.J.: Princeton University Press, 1960, p. 27; and especially David Easton and Jack Dennis, *Children in the Political System: Origins of Political Legitimacy.* New York: McGraw-Hill, 1969.

[3] See, for example, Jack Dennis, *A Survey and Bibliography of Contemporary Research on Political Learning and Socialization,* Occasional Paper No. 8 of Center for Cognitive Learning, Madison, Wisconsin: University of Wisconsin, March 1967, p. 2.

[4] See, for example, James D. Barber, *The Lawmakers: Recruitment and Adaptation of Legislative Life.* New Haven, Conn.: Yale University Press, 1965; or Seymour Lipset and Aldo Solari, *Elites in Latin America.* New York: Oxford University Press, 1967.

[5] See especially Herbert Hyman, *Political Socialization.* New York: Free Press, 1959, p. 69 and *passim.*

instances of generational conflict and "generation gaps." In particular, the growth of "youth cultures" in all modern societies has produced youthful political rebellion and extremist politics.

Third, we shall focus on the process of early political learning itself and on the prime agents of political socialization besides the family. The significance of formal education and the school setting, the influence of peer groups and voluntary associations in school, neighborhood, and at work, and the effect of partisan propaganda and recruitment are examples of extrafamilial political socialization with which we must deal.

The political socialization of the young also takes place amid a welter of social divisions and cleavages typical of a given society—such as social classes—and ethnic, religious, or sex differences. Our fourth concern will be to explore the depth and nature of these divisions, the presence of cross-cutting, integrating affiliations, and trends toward decreasing or increasing division.

Following this, we shall examine the socialization processes of particular governmental or political elites in connection with their recruitment and, more broadly, the patterns of political participation. There is an escalating ladder of political roles from simple, passive participation to active involvement and finally the holding of public office. There is also a range of attitudes toward participation which extends from alienation toward the whole system, over political opposition to a particular government, to strong support for both system and government; attitudes are also learned by the process of political socialization. The content of these learning processes will be deferred, as far as practical, to the next chapter. An examination of quantitative methods applied to these learning processes will conclude the discussion of political socialization.

THE AGES OF MAN

"Tall oaks from little acorns grow," wrote the poet. The student of politics has little reason to doubt that the mature political participant similarly developed a substantial part of his political attitudes and behavior patterns as a child and young adolescent. American research on political socialization has shown clear evidence of the politicizing process from the age of three. The basic pattern of general if diffuse support for government is settled very early and even partisan orientations have evolved, at least among the dominant groups of American society, by the age of thirteen. By that time identification with the symbols of the political community, and even with authority figures in the government, is pretty well established for the rest of one's life.[6] That political scientists have shied away from studying earlier phases of the socialization process is understandable. However, the existing literature of child development touches inevitably on some basic experiences of children under three that have an undeniable relevance to later political attitudes.

Infancy and social trust

A very instructive theory of child development in this respect is that of Erik H. Erikson, who speaks of "eight ages of man." Man's first age, in infancy, is characterized by internalization of the certainty that his mother will return to minister to his creature comforts. This is his first demonstration of *social trust,* in contrast to the basic mistrust that would be engendered by a lack of consistent loving care. It is also the first rudiment of a sense of ego identity, as child and mother begin to "recognize" each other and as the child thus learns to relate to an outside object. Erikson relates these basic mechanisms to breakdowns of trust and faith and the occurrence of rational hostility among adult groups. Social trust is indeed a cornerstone of government and social cooperation. When the interviewers of Almond and Verba's study, *The Civic Culture,* asked respondents whether or not they felt that "people can be trusted," they were aiming at a measurement of such social trust. Even more to the point was their asking whether respondents expected to be heard and treated fairly by government bureaucrats and politicians.[7] To be sure, a deep sense of distrust of government among adults could result from untrustworthy behavior on the part of government

---

[6] See David Easton and Robert D. Hess in S. M. Lipset and Leo Lowenthal, eds., "Youth and the Political System," *Culture and Social Character.* New York: Free Press, 1961, pp. 229–243. Also Richard E. Dawson and Kenneth Prewitt, *Political Socialization.* Boston: Little, Brown, 1969, pp. 44–52.

[7] Gabriel A. Almond and Sidney Verba, *The Civic Culture.* Princeton, N.J.: Princeton University Press, 1963, pp. 111–115 as well as on the following pages on the receptivity for political communications.

officials. But far more often, as in the case of the French peasants in Laurence Wylie's famous sociological study, mistrust is so pervasive even in the face of an honest administration that its causes must lie deeper.[8]

The sense of autonomy

Erikson's second stage is a *sense of autonomy,* demonstrated in infantile experimenting with the world of objects—having, holding, and letting go. It can be weakened by the inculcation of a sense of "shaming" a child common among many traditional cultures—a device, according to Wylie, used among his southern French villagers. A well-nurtured sense of individual autonomy, "self-control without loss of self-esteem," makes for good will and pride rather than willful or spiteful behavior, while parental overcontrol and a loss of self-control leave a lasting propensity for shame and self-doubt. Consequent fears of a "loss of face," or even of hidden conspiracy, can figure importantly in domestic and international politics. Erikson relates basic trust to the institution of religion, and a sense of autonomy and self-control to the institutional principle of *law and order,* or justice—an individualistic, adult order delineating every individual's right and duties. This stage may well coincide with the one at which children first become aware of political objects and symbols.

A third stage is that of *initiative* versus a sense of guilt, an inclination heavily involved with work identification at a time when children are in kindergarten or school and rapidly learning to get along with others of both sexes. The fourth stage is characterized by a sense of *industry* and struggle against a sense of inferiority. If the "age" of initiative gave the child an economic ethos and adult examples of economic striving, *industry* serves the development of a technological ethos and the learning of the

[8] Laurence Wylie, *Village in the Vaucluse.* Cambridge, Mass.: Harvard Press, 1951, pp. 59, 108, and chap. 10. The inhabitants of Peyrane, like those of Banfield's southern Italian town, will of course invent or embellish stories of governmental misconduct to rationalize their feelings. On southern Italy, however, see now also Joseph Lopreato, *Peasants No More.* San Francisco: Chandler Publications, 1967. Wylie has reaffirmed his thesis with minor changes in Stanley Hoffmann *et al., In Search of France* (New York: Harper Torchbooks, 1965), pp. 207–215, where Jesse R. Pitts also presents a similar theme on bourgeois life in France, pp. 250–262.

skills and techniques of adult society. These two, perhaps more relevant to political participation than to socialization, complete the period of childhood proper.

Identity crises

Puberty and adolescence begin an entirely new set of stages, which in a sense must reestablish the certainties of childhood shattered by the physiological revolution of the adolescent body and the acute need to be accepted by one's peers. The fifth age sees the birth of a new sense of ego identity; failure here raises potentially nihilistic dangers of role confusion. No other crisis of youth development supplies as useful a key to understanding the emergence of youth cultures in modernizing societies, when the older generation can no longer transmit a sense of inherent meaning in its class, occupational, sexual, political, and religious roles.[9]

The violent yearning for a sense of identity also makes youth extraordinarily avid for group discipline and ideologies such as nationalism, anticolonialism, communism or democratic socialism, or fascism. The deeper the identity crisis, one might conjecture, the more desperate the urge to merge one's self with a group (even a neighborhood gang of criminal propensity), the more likely the involvement with potentially totalitarian movements, and the more desperate the attachment to heroes and glamorous leaders. Modern political ideologies, such as nationalism, fabricate individual identities by creating whole cosmologies of history and society in which roles are supplied to the individual. The admired war hero, star of sports or entertain-

[9] See Easton and Hess, "Youth and the Political System," pp. 244–252. Erikson supplies illuminating illustrations of the identity crisis in *Young Man Luther* (New York: Norton, 1959), p. 42, when speaking of the need for devotion to new faiths and leaders and the need for repudiation of parents, accepted traditions, arbitrarily chosen other people, or oneself. See also pp. 44, 100, 115. Note also the analysis of the age patterns of American, British, French, and Italian Communists in Gabriel A. Almond, *The Appeals of Communism*. Princeton, N.J.: Princeton University Press, 1954, pp. 217–221. Almond found that as many as half of his respondents had engaged in their first radical political activity by the time they were eighteen and three-fourths before the age of twenty-three. Middle-class university students, in particular, tended to be party members only as long as they were students or until they had outgrown this youthful phase.

ment, gang leader, and popular tribune also supply role identities that can be acquired by emulation.

Intimacy, generativity, and ego integrity

Erikson's table of the ages of man includes three further stages of maturation. One is a *capacity for intimacy,* opposed to the isolation that comes from inability to give of oneself. Another is *generativity,* or productivity and creativity, which has considerable social and political significance, since it implies a relationship of guidance and support toward younger generations, a kind of broad "social parenthood." The final stage of maturity, and the eighth age, is *ego integrity,* acceptance of the world order and one's life in it. This last stage is again heavy with political overtones in that it involves also the complete integration of the individual with his political system and his full acceptance of the political roles it offers him as inherently meaningful. Applied to politics, Erikson's concept of personal maturity implies taking the game of politics seriously and accepting as meaningful its rewards and satisfactions. The lack of such political integrity may show up not only in political corruption—the misuse of the political integrity of other people for nonpolitical, personal gain —but also in a "politics of despair" or extremism, or in political indifference or strong mental reservations about the validity and meaning of political action.[10]

Individual versus societal development

The profound significance of Erikson's theories is further demonstrated by their illumination of the process of political development in the midst of the disruption of traditional community and value patterns. Premodern societies, the reader will recall, have patterns of social stratification that generally withhold the development to political maturity from all but a small social elite. The breakdown of the old oligarchy and the advent of political equality saddle the awakening masses with political responsibil-

[10] Erikson's contrast to ego integrity is despair, manifested in a fear of death. The eight ages of man are presented in detail in *Childhood and Society.* New York: Norton, 1950, chap. 7. See also the review of *Young Man Luther* by Lucian W. Pye, *"Personal Identity and Political Ideology,"* in Dwaine Marvick *et al.,* eds., *Political Decision-makers.* New York: Free Press, 1961, pp. 290–313.

ities for which their political socialization did not prepare them. As Lucian Pye has pointed out, there emerges a painful gap between private, personal identity, which understands itself as an integral part of the web of personal and social relationships within the local authority structure, and the problems of national politics. Lacking an efficient communication system comparable to the press of Western countries, inadequately socialized, and reluctant to take seriously the roles provided by national political institutions and pluralistic party politics, premodern societies are not likely to agree on the legitimate ends and means of political action. Charismatic leaders and ideological, revolutionary movements will seem far more attractive than political brokers or mediators, expressive-affective political action far more satisfying than a discussion of clearly defined issues or interests.[11]

Erikson's stages of child development can be set alongside the explorations in political socialization by David Easton, Jack Dennis, and Fred Greenstein in the United States. Robert D. Hess and Easton in a study of Chicago schoolchildren and Greenstein in a similar project in New Haven found that children learn to love and identify with their government, especially the President, long before they know anything about what the presidency and other national roles actually involve.[12] Greenstein also confirmed Herbert Hyman's earlier finding that children in the first two grades are already capable of identifying with political parties, namely those of their parents.[13] In the early stages, also, children identify political roles with those familiar from their personal world. Presidents are fathers, rival political leaders hostile adults, partisan friends the playmates, and the homeland the narrowest circle of familiar faces.[14]

[11] See Lucian Pye in Marvick, *Political Decision-makers,* pp. 309–310; and *Politics, Personality, and Nation-Building.* New Haven, Conn.: Yale University Press, 1962, pp. 16–17, 20–31. See also Robert Levine in Clifford Geertz, *Old Societies and New States.* New York: Free Press, 1963, pp. 280–283.

[12] See Robert D. Hess and David Easton, "The Child's Changing Image of the President," *Public Opinion Quarterly,* 1960, pp. 632–644.

[13] Fred Greenstein, "The Benevolent Leader: Children's Images of Political Authority," *American Political Science Review,* 1960, pp. 934–943. See also his *Children and Politics.* New Haven, Conn.: Yale University Press, 1965, chaps. 1, 2, and 4.

[14] See, for example, Jean Piaget and Anna-Marie Weil in *International Social Science Bulletin,* 1951, pp. 561–578.

Regressive effect of crises

Political maturation and the interplay between the individual life cycle and the development of the political community involve a growing perception of political objects, roles, and functions as separate and different from the earlier personal associations. As their political knowledge and interest increase, adolescents and young adults react to events, recognize their roles, and take sides. Nevertheless, as in all maturation, the later stages supersede without dissolving the earlier emotional base. The rational political behavior of the mature adult can be shattered, at least temporarily, by a shock such as the assassination of a head of state [15] or some other major crisis that evokes the emotional images and associations of childhood. Among such crises could be, for example, a great depression or sudden enemy attack or involvement in a major war. When large numbers of people find themselves challenged in what they believe to be their national honor or threatened in their survival or livelihood, they rally around their flag and their government like children around their parents and protectors. And since everyday life, domestic and international, is always beset by crises of greater or lesser import, it remains always possible for governments and political leaders to manipulate the infantile fears underlying the political rationality of their peoples.

THE SUCCESSION OF GENERATIONS

The political maturation of the individual is only one dimension of the socializing process. Another dimension universally found is the succession and interrelation of the generations. The child grows up to become a parent, the student becomes a teacher, and the conforming, unready adolescent becomes an adult who sets values and standards of behavior for the next generation. Thus society is really a collectivity of those who are still receiving primary socialization and those who are teaching them while they themselves undergo various, if slow and subtle kinds of

---

[15] See the insightful literature on the impact of the assassination of President Kennedy on American children and young adults in Bradley S. Greenberg and E. S. Parker, eds., *The Kennedy Assassination and the American Public*. Stanford, Calif.: Stanford University Press, 1965; and Martha Wolfenstein and Gilbert Kliman, eds., *Children and the Death of a President: Multi-Disciplinary Studies*. New York: Doubleday, 1965.

adult socialization. In addition, the entire collectivity should be viewed along the time dimension, which gives it an age-hetero-geneous composition, as shown in the accompanying schematic figure based on ten-year intervals and an average lifespan of seventy-five years (Fig. 3).

Characteristics of seven American generations

In Figure 3, for the sake of argument, each generation of present American society has been based on a new decade, and each should be thought of as having reached full political awareness and, hopefully, maturity, between the ages of fifteen and twenty. Their respective periods of maturation very likely molded the attitudes of these generations in a decisive manner. Thus, the generation born about 1890 would be the last pre-World War I generation, formed by an age of progressivism and the social evils progressivism sought to cure. The next would be the war generation, many of whose males were "over there" fighting the Kaiser. The following generation, today about sixty, would have grown up in the heady atmosphere of the Roaring Twenties, the first period of mass consumption and of woman suffrage any-where. Then came the "depression generation," which during its politically formative period witnessed economic collapse, gov-ernmental expansion, and political extremism of various sorts. The next was another war generation, that of World War II and its immediate aftermath, a generation which was about forty years old in 1970. The following generation, born about 1940, was formed by unprecedented prosperity at home and the Cold War and nuclear stalemate abroad. The generation born around 1950 is the last one to have completed its politically formative period, influenced mainly by the civil rights struggle and the debate over the war in Vietnam, although the next generation is already waiting in the elementary grades.

These seven generations, from the progressives to the Viet-nam war protesters, are living side by side in the same families, organizations, and economic pursuits, in proportions that one can look up in the current *Statistical Abstract of the United States*. In their voting and their discussions of current political issues they very likely show differences of opinion related to the politically formative periods of their lives. Although age is not the only determinant, their attitudes obviously were shaped to a

Figure 3   Age cohorts and contemporary United States history [1]

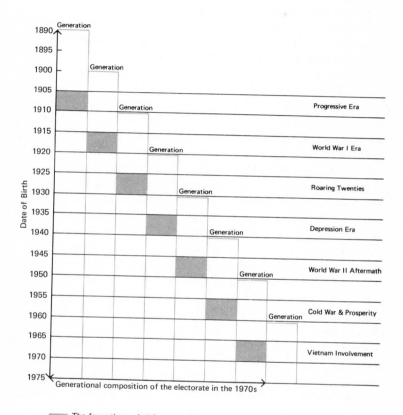

The formative period from age fifteen to twenty of each generation, during which contemporary history has the greatest socializing impact.

[1] Each generation's childhood and education is molded by parents and teachers born and socialized from thirty to fifty years earlier.

considerable degree by the encounter of their personalities at a particularly responsive time with distinctive political settings and challenges. They also differ, incidentally, in their political capabilities, since voting rights are not granted until a certain age, and active leadership positions in political parties are usually available only after many years of political apprenticeship, a specialized kind of further political socialization.

Generational inheritance and disinheritance

The succession of generations, together with the progression of individual life cycles, is a major mechanism of political change and development. Each succeeding generation grows up and learns in the setting provided by the several generations preceding it, especially that of its parents, who may have spent a lifetime rising above the conditions in which they themselves grew up. The result can be considerable progress from generation to generation. However, there can also be major lapses and regressions, since new generations invariably face new challenges and crises for which their training could not possibly have prepared them. There is as much danger as there may be safety in the allegedly pattern-maintaining functions of the socialization process. New generations that have been socialized too narrowly into patterns of the past, it would seem, are more rather than less likely to fail before the unknown challenges of the future than are rebel generations. For the latter have already become accustomed to recognizing the limitations of their parents and teachers. They are used to coping with their problems as autonomous individuals, once they have stopped spending their energies on rebellion alone.

Generally, it can be said that political attitudes and loyalties are passed on from parents to children.[16] A very substantial proportion of American Democrats and Republicans have parents of the same party loyalty. Socialist voters in European countries can often recall that not only their fathers, but even their grandfathers, identified with the same party. In many European and Latin-American parties that date back more than a generation similar relationships can be found. Young neo-Nazis in

[16] See, for example, Robert E. Lane, *Political Ideology*. New York: Free Press, 1962, pp. 268–269; or Richard Rose, *Politics in England*. Boston: Little, Brown, 1966, pp. 61–62.

Germany are often the children of ex-Nazis. Even communists in Western countries frequently are descended from communists or other left-wing revolutionaries, such as revolutionary socialists, anarchists, syndicalists, or liberal firebrands.[17] This is hardly surprising, since the children usually share with their parents such determinants as social class, local environment, friends, and public-opinion influences, especially during the formative stage of their second decade of life. The decisive influences of the first decade, moreover, will already have laid an emotional basis for the chidren's political attitudes that is likely to be further reinforced by direct parental teaching and example.

Rebellion against dependency   Nevertheless, the maturation of the young demands that at a certain point, for their own good, they must learn to become mentally independent of their parents. Thus, the universal struggle for adult autonomy has to be waged against the young person's own habits of dependency as much or more than against parental reluctance to let him go his own way. In some cultures, and at times of cultural strain more than at others, this struggle for youthful independence may manifest itself in open rebellion and in the identity crisis Erikson describes. Both effects may severely disrupt the political consensus between fathers and sons, especially if they drive sons to repudiate deliberately all their parents stand for and to dedicate themselves to movements of radical opposition or of political messianism.

America's "generation gap"   Among American youth, according to severai recent studies,[18] the pattern of out-and-out rebellion appears to be relatively weak in spite of much parental concern about a "generation gap." In comparison to other cultures, the youthful repudiation of American parents could be termed rather gentle and laced with sympathy and understanding even where the younger generation strongly disagrees with its elders. One could surmise, perhaps, that the present "generation gap"

[17] See Almond, *The Appeals of Communism*, pp. 221–224. Also Dawson and Prewitt, *Political Socialization*, chap. 7; Langton, *Political Socialization*, chaps. 2 and 3; and James C. Davies in *Political Socialization* (Annals), pp. 10–19.

[18] See especially Lane, *Political Ideology*, chap. 17.

looks much larger from the side of many middle-aged parents who are undergoing a crisis of their own amid crumbling Puritan, nationalistic, and other white-Anglo-Saxon-Protestant (WASP) values. American youth, evidently, has little to rebel against, given the permissive nature of parental control and especially the role of the father, who is said to be more of a brother and friend to his sons under the proverbial matriarchy of Mom. This is not to deny that some American adolescents have experienced severe crises of identity, in particular among second-generation immigrants during the days when massive waves of immigration and distinct ethnic communities were still commonplace. However, American child-rearing attitudes and practices place a great deal more emphasis on inculcating a sense of autonomy in children than do most of the older civilizations of Europe or Asia.[19] Accustomed as they are to autonomy, then, American adolescents are prepared for coping with adolescent crises, unless they are black, especially black males, who have to wrestle with a negative identity taken over from the stereotypes of the white world.[20]

Effect of European and Asian familism   Youth in certain European and Asian societies seem to experience different patterns. Lucian Pye has described the child-rearing setting in the Burmese family as one that by its unpredictable extremes engenders insecurity in the child. An early period when the infant is spoiled by the mother and everyone else is followed by an increasing unpredictability of the mother's affection and extensive use of shame, ridicule, and spiritual fears, which tend to destroy the basic trust in human relationships without diminishing a childlike optimism. From school age on, the demands for conformity and the authoritarian nature of traditional Asian families suppress any striving for autonomy from the family, the be-all and end-all of most traditional societies. The Burmese child is taught with particular emphasis that strangers are enemies and only the

[19] See Erikson in *Childhood and Society,* chap. 8. A certain maternal harshness so as "not to spoil the baby" is said to be the chief device of this training for autonomy, which Erikson attributes to cultural needs developed during the frontier days of America.

[20] See Erikson, *Childhood and Society,* pp. 241–245 and chap. 8.

family can be trusted. In turn, a good child is supposed to be ready to deny and sacrifice himself for the family. Pye believes that from this intense familism, together with latent hostility against the mother and perhaps also the father, spring the combination of gentleness and a propensity for violence, and especially the easily wounded, explosive ego of Burmese males. The Sharp distinction between family and outsiders makes for close cliques of friends and an inability to deal with conflict or opposition except by unrestrained hostility. The lack of trust, self-confidence, and facility of communication is particularly damaging to Burmese public administration, political parties, and parliamentary government.[21] These problems appear to be fairly representative also of India, Ceylon, and several other countries.

Familism and the distrust of strangers characterize French and Belgian child rearing, too. The French child also is taught a lifelong mistrust of anyone beyond the *foyer*. However, while French practices of disciplining also include shaming and ridiculing, there is evidently little early spoiling, and a growing sense of autonomy is fostered by rigid control by parents and teachers. Child rearing in Italy, on the other hand, may well be said to add early indulgence to the pervasive familism of society, yielding comparable results of social distrust.[22] Other Latin countries in Europe and in Latin America, furthermore, add another ingredient similar to that of the Burmese father with his domineering, volatile ego. Spanish and Latin-American males indulge in a conspicuous cult of courage and strutting masculinity, *machismo,* which evidently constitutes an overcompensation for the hidden tensions of Spanish family life. A father who is *muy macho,* like the Burmese father, is quite likely to inhibit or distort the maturation of his sons, either by his overbearing manner or by his making premature and inordinate demands on the *macho* qual-

---

[21] See *Politics, Personality, and Nation-Building,* chaps. 13–14. Burmese politics exhibits a propensity for factionalism and cliques that may well stem from these patterns of political socialization.

[22] See Wylie, *Village in the Vaucluse,* chaps. 3–5; and Margaret Mead and Rhoda Metraux, *Themes in French Culture.* Stanford, Calif.: Stanford University Press, 1954. Banfield, in *The Moral Basis of a Backward Society* (New York: Free Press, 1958), found child-rearing practices in southern Italy familistic, vacillating between extremes of harshness and affection, as well as punitive in an aimless way.

ities of the son.[23] In all of these cases, possible motives of youthful rebellion can be clearly sensed, although the isolating effect of distrust and individualism appears to relegate rebellion and the identity crisis to the obscurity of individual problems and tragedies.

Generational tension in Russia and China   In other countries, by contrast, the friction between the generations invariably moves into the public limelight. In Russia, for example, the generational tensions have tended to flare every now and then even under dictatorial regimes. Youthful rebellion in the Soviet Union is not necessarily politically motivated, except perhaps in recent protests about the repressive government action against the writers Sinyavsky and Daniel and the editors of the underground newspaper *Phoenix*. Back in the days of student conspiracies and demonstrations against the czarist regime, which had political motives, only small numbers of youths were involved; the overwhelming majority did not participate. After Stalin's death, general idealistic and romantic sentiments rather than specific political issues mobilized masses of young people for spontaneous appearances at poetry readings and other cultural affairs discouraged by the authorities.

Red China, too, has had a conspicuous demonstration of generational tensions, that got rather out of hand. Three generations were involved. The first is easily symbolized by such veteran leaders of the long March of 1934 as Mao Tse-tung and Lin Piao. The next is represented by party bureaucrats who, after the first decade and the abortive Great Leap Forward of 1958, succeeded in sidelining aging Chairman Mao. After them, the millions of teen-age Red Guards, who arose at the back of

---

[23] See also S. N. Eisenstadt, *From Generation to Generation*. New York: Free Press, 1956, pp. 52–53, 240–247, 262–263. It should be noted that there is still considerable controversy about the nature and circumstances of political socialization in all these countries. See now also Charles Roig and F. Billon-Grand, *La Socialisation Politique des Enfants* (Paris: Colin, 1968), a study of ten- to fourteen-year olds, which confirms many of the findings of low support for political parties of the classic study by Philip E. Converse and Georges Dupeux, "Politicization of the Electorate in France and the U.S.," *Public Opinion Quarterly*, 26 (1962), 1–23.

the old revolutionary leader to recapture the spirit of the Communist revolution, represent the first generation that has grown
up entirely under the Communist regime. They have fully
absorbed the Communist propaganda and lived with the immense efforts of the regime to change Chinese traditional society.
Painfully aware of the gap between communist aspiration and
achievement and impatient with the tenacious reminders of an
ageless culture, they set out to bring a "cultural revolution" regardless of the cost; their efforts plunged the country into
anarchy.[24]

Modernization and rebellious youth   There seems to be a
causal link between certain stages of modernization and the explosive emergence of youth in the political arena. Modern urban
societies separate universalistic roles and functions along such
age-related lines as mass education and large-scale industrial
employment, which for part of the day tend to break up such
age-heterogeneous groups as families, family businesses, and
neighborhoods. They not only segregate youth from their elders,
but further stratify them into age grades and groups, which then
come to associate and compete with each other, creating the
tyranny of peer groups and the social trimmings of the elaborate
youth cultures typical of many advanced industrial societies
today.[25] They also separate the traditionally more integrated
role of the father into the various functionally specific roles he is
called upon to enact in society, such as his parental role as dis-

[24] See Eisenstadt, *From Generation to Generation,* pp. 172–173.
Earlier antecedents of Chinese youth rebellion go back into the period of
the crumbling empire and the gathering of young adults in various youth
movements under the impact of contact with the alien cultures of the
West. Such youth rebellion as a result of culture contact, alien occupation, or immigration into a different culture was quite typical of many
colonial societies under Western domination, where the family structure
tended to break down and adolescents would gather in groups of acculturation to the powerful invaders, or possibly in order to fight them. The
harsh Japanese occupation of China in the 1930s or the German occupation of Eastern European countries played a major role in mobilizing
masses of traditional young peasants under the Communist flag. See
Chalmers A. Johnson, *Peasant Nationalism and Communist Power.*
Stanford, Calif.: Stanford University Press, 1962, chaps. 1, 2, and 6.
[25] Eisenstadt, *From Generation to Generation,* p. 161.

tinct from his role in industry, his role as a citizen, and so on.[26] The children's world also becomes more sharply differentiated from that of the adult world than it was in family life on the farm, and there sets in a kind of estrangement, especially between the absent father and the children. Fathers in modern society tend to respond to the challenge of alienation with confusion, resorting either to erratic displays of authoritarianism— not to be confused with the culturally determined paternal autocracy of most traditional societies—or to child-guidance books. The children above a certain age respond by creating or flocking to youth movements, agencies, and groups.

Youth movements in Germany   One of the more explosive series of youth rebellions took place during Germany's modernization after the 1890s, when rapid industrialization and urbanization first introduced strains into the patriarchal German middle-class family. Reflecting the traditional oligarchic control of Bismarckian society, the educational system reinforced the authoritarian rigidity of the old against the presumably pernicious influences of modern, achievement-oriented individualism and "materialism." Girls and women, in particular, were trained to remain submissively in their place in a world of *Kinder* (children), *Küche* (kitchen), and *Kirche* (church). Male middleclass youth responded to the strain with the romantic *Wandervogel* (migratory bird) youth movement, repudiating modern achievement-oriented society, the power-oriented Bismarckian empire, and parents, teachers, and heterosexual maturity. Beyond their cult of nature hikes, folk songs, and romantic empathy with Germany's medieval past, these Peter Pan groups were dedicated to no cause except, perhaps, glorying in youth itself and in youthful comradeship. Short-lived, as youth movements tend to be because of the age turnover, this German Youth Movement passed its zenith with World War I and the following decade.[27]

[26] The reader might compare this role organization with that on the family farm, where the father is boss over his "child employee" and at the same time his almost constant companion, both being relatively isolated from peer and community influences. See also Eisenstadt's remarks on Chinese youth, *From Generation to Generation*, p. 173.

[27] See Eisenstadt, *From Generation to Generation*, pp. 101, 316–321; also Walter Z. Laqueur, *Young Germany*. New York: Basic Books, 1962.

Meanwhile a new wave of youthful rebellion, a movement much larger than the middle classes, had arisen under the impact of the war years, German defeat, and the fall of the traditional oligarchy. Sociologists have called these the *political activist youth* because they flocked to various extremist political parties, especially to their paramilitary organizations and to militant veterans' groups, even though a large part of this generation had never seen war or military service. They constituted the hundreds of thousands of armed and uniformed fighters of the communist Red Front, other left-wing revolutionary groups, and right-wing vigilante organizations such as the Steel Helmet veterans, the Young German Order, and the Nazi storm troopers. As compared to their predecessors, they not only dedicated themselves with a vengeance to political causes, but also shifted their objects of repudiation to the parliamentary democracy of Weimar and the established older generation. They still rejected individualism and materialism, but not achievement and national power as such. Instead of the gentle ways of the guitar-and-rucksack *Wandervogel,* however, they believed in quasi-military uniforms, marching, and revolutionary violence. More ominous still, they preferred charismatic, centralized, and authoritarian leadership to the diffuse and decentralized authority structure of their predecessors. Hitler and his Third Reich lost no time in pressing this youth rebellion into service, especially to forge a powerful army to renew the military struggle stopped in 1918.

The generational conflict of the first two waves was followed, after German defeat and occupation in 1945, by the alienation of yet a third wave of German youth from its parents. The postwar generation in occupied Germany repudiated its parents precisely for their ideological commitment, their nationalism, and their support of the Nazi regime. German postwar youth not only rejected these attitudes emphatically; they remained aloof from political parties and declared in public opinion polls that they could not conceive of any cause, ideology, fatherland, or religion for which they would want to risk their lives. Sociologists called it the "skeptical" or "count-me-out" generation,[28] though it was hardly indifferent to the moral issues of politics.

[28] See, for example, Helmut Schelsky, *Die skeptische Generation.* Düsseldorf: E. Diederich, 1957; or, on Japanese postwar youth, R. J. Lifton, "Youth and History: Individual Change in Postwar Japan," *Daedalus,* Winter 1962, pp. 172–197.

In the 1960s another rebellious young generation appeared in West Germany and Berlin, especially among university students and trade union youth, who participated by the thousands in political demonstration against German rearmament, atomic weapons, the Shah of Iran, United States policy in Vietnam, their own government, and the harsh practices of German police authorities against them. They reject once more their own parents and condemn as "insincere democrats" the liberal democratic "establishment" in West German political parties, the public-opinion media, and the government. In a memorable confrontation, one of the prominent members of the skeptical generation, Rolf Hochhuth, the author of controversial plays about the World War II era,[29] once agreed to answer questions before an audience of the present student generation. To his surprise, the thirty-six-year-old author learned that the students regarded him as a part of the "establishment" and his controversial Churchill play as ancient history. They told him that he ought to be writing a polemical play against the war in Vietnam.

The current crop of German student rebels looks with admiration to American student demonstrators and identifies with some of their concerns, such as educational reform, a lively issue in Germany's archaic educational system. Their interest in politics is almost as keen as that of their predecessors of the 1920s, although lacking their violence and militancy. Such occasionally flaunted heroes as Ché Guevara or Mao Tse-tung are used chiefly for their shock value and as a foil for the romantic imagination, not as political reference points. Nevertheless, generational tensions have continued to spawn violent youth rebellion in Germany, even though the assumed original causes—the cultural strain between the old German patriarchal traditions and the achievement orientation of modern society—have long disappeared. It would appear that some youth cultures, once evolved, manifest themselves again and again in political rebellion, simply because of the inherent problems of coming of age, the need for repudiation of the existing order and for rededication in opposition to it. Since the rebellious youths of today

---

[29] His play *The Deputy* accused Pope Pius XII of complicity in the Nazi persecution of Jews. Another play, *The Soldiers,* was banned in Great Britain because it implicates wartime Prime Minister Winston Churchill in the death of a Polish exile leader.

inevitably turn into the confused parents and teachers of tomor-
row, generational conflict is a major agent of political change.

THE CHIEF AGENTS OF POLITICAL SOCIALIZATION

Family influences

If it is true that most of the fundamentals of political orientation
are learned in the first dozen years of a person's life, then the
family more than any other agent should perform most of the
teaching of politics.[30] The child, after all, spends these years
mostly in a state of physical and emotional dependence upon his
family. However, a great deal more is involved than just the
child's dependence. Even a small family, not to mention the
extended families of many traditional and transitional societies,
is a complex microcosm, in which the child is made to play a
well-defined role. The learning processes involved in socialization, as Talcott Parsons points out,[31] are an integral part of the
process of interaction between complementary roles, such as
parent-child, leader-follower, or teacher-pupil. Parents will play
the role of teacher to the child only insofar as he will play that
of a learner. Hence it is not surprising that parental teaching of
political orientations is rarely an overt, formal process. In fact,
as many parents have discovered, any attempts at indoctrination
on politics, as on other subjects involving judgment and conduct,
are more likely to fail than they are to succeed. The best teaching
of politics seems to occupy rather subtly and inadvertently, by
way of imitation and identification on the part of the child as well
as by off-hand remarks and the osmotic effect of views strongly
held by the parent or other persons of influence.[32] Few deliberately proffered gems of political wisdom seem to leave such a
lasting impression as does the force of example or of overheard
and only half-understood adult conversations.

Differing roles of family members   An analysis of the influence
of the family in political socialization should also take into ac-

---

[30] See also Hyman, *Political Socialization,* p. 69.

[31] Talcott Parsons, *The Social System.* New York: Free Press, 1951,
p. 209.

[32] See Roberta Sigel and James C. Davies in *Political Socialization*
(Annals), pp. 1–19.

count the differing roles of father, mother, older and younger brothers and sisters, and members of the extended family. The precise allocation of roles varies considerably from one culture to another. In traditional familistic societies, for example, grandfathers and uncles are a major influence as political socializers of the young and may even play more formal teaching roles than the natural parents. The nuclear family of modern societies, on the other hand, greatly restricts the influence and even the contact of the child with the extended family. Grandfathers and uncles become the harmless purveyors of candy and little adventures for the young but are no longer accorded a serious teaching role unless families break down.[33] There is, of course, always a significant percentage of children that have to be raised by relatives, adoptive parents, or even orphanages.

The teaching of political orientations by father and mother invariably involves role conceptions as different from one another as are their roles in marriage and society. Mothers presumably are much closer to the child and hence more influential in his early years when fundamental emotional patterns are established. Yet Western cultures, historically, have defined the feminine role as dependent and only very recently have accorded women equal legal status and the vote. With some exceptions, most Islamic, Asian, and African societies still stamp them as inferior and childlike, fit to be sold as brides or used as cement for political federations, as in Saudi Arabia, but hardly fit for a role involving political decision and control. Even among the supposedly emancipated women of the United States, equality in occupation or public career is tangled up in deep-seated cultural notions about the nature of masculinity and femininity.[34] Such cultural notions invariably pattern the transmission of political orientations within the family as well. Mothers in many societies are allowed to teach allegiance to an organized religion and to

---

[33] See also the remarks of Parsons on the kinship in the United States, *Essays in Sociological Theory,* rev. ed. New York: Free Press, 1954, p. 189. Family breakdown and juvenile delinquency have been explored by many social scientists. See, for example, T. R. Fyval, *The Insecure Offenders* (Baltimore, Md.: Penguin, 1963), on the problem in Great Britain. On the different roles of fathers and mothers, see also Langton, *Political Socialization,* chap. 3.

[34] Parsons, *Essays in Sociological Theory,* pp. 192–195. See also Langton, *Political Socialization,* chap. 2.

the country and its traditions. They may also have the implicit right to try to restrain their sons from dangerous or dishonorable political involvement. Their judgment on issues of everyday politics, however, no matter how sound, is rarely listened to or adopted.[35] Aunts, grandmothers, and sisters fare no better. Fathers and older brothers, by comparison, enjoy authority in matters political even if they are talking nonsense.

Divergence of girls and boys The sex differences in political socialization also pertain to the growing child, who is soon placed into a learner's role differentiated by sex. Girls are simply not given the same message as boys, a pattern repeated in the sex segregation of public schools in most countries of the world.[36] In many developing countries, and in modern countries until a mere seventy-five years ago, most girls received very little or no formal education or were especially instructed in convents and religious schools or by the older women, which was sure to make them far more traditional in cast of mind than their future husbands and sons. Latin countries in Europe and South America also are famous for their bifurcated socialization: the catholic

[35] This pattern often prevails even where mothers wield considerable authority in the home, as in the United States. This might be considered the wry undercurrent in the old American joke that Mom makes "only the little decisions," such as what house or car to buy or to what college to send the children, while Dad makes the "big decisions," such as matters of peace and war and foreign and domestic policies. Often he really does. It should be borne in mind, however, that the processes of learning from each parent to the child are extraordinarily complicated by further variables such as social class, religion, culture, and personality. See, for example, the account by David C. McClelland of the transmission of the achievement motive in *The Achieving Society*. New York: Van Nostrand-Reinhold, 1961, chap. 9.

[36] Quite apart from the patterning intended by parents and society, there are also complex psychological mechanisms at work that influence, inhibit, or reinforce the sexual identification of the child. See especially Roger Brown, *Social Psychology*. New York: Free Press, 1965, pp. 374–381. Regarding sex-related differences in political status and orientations, see *Women Around the World,* Annals of the American Academy of Political and Social Science, January 1968, pp. 52–101. On women's childhood socialization, see Fred I. Greenstein, *Children and Politics.* New Haven, Conn.: Yale University Press, 1963, chap. 6; and "Sex-Related Political Differences in Childhood," *Journal of Politics,* 1961, pp. 353–371.

women and girls devoted to the practice of religion, and the boys and men growing up alienated from the church and dedicated to some brand of anticlerical political activism. With the advent of woman suffrage, similar patterns manifest themselves also in voting habits. It is almost universally true that women vote in smaller numbers and that they join political parties and attend political rallies far less than men. Their political beliefs also differ; women are considerably more likely to vote for conservative and religiously oriented parties, such as the Catholic or Christian Democratic parties of Europe, while men turn out in larger proportion for liberal, socialist, and extremist parties.[37] We can hardly avoid the conclusion that girls must undergo a political socialization stressing a different set of values than those offered the boys. In many cultural settings they may also learn from their mothers to defer to the political judgment of their fathers and of future husbands.

Instruction by professional teachers

Formal instruction by professional teachers is probably also a profound molder of future citizens. Indeed, it was always meant to be, although the school setting and intervening factors such as the importance of peer groups may sometimes lead to unintended results.[38] From the days of Plato and Socrates, expressly or implicitly, training for good citizenship has always been a vital part of educational theory and practice.

The institutions of mass education in modern nations have been developed to increase the capabilities of all the members of a society, and of the society itself as a system. The goals are not only the acquisition of useful skills, but also the development of a literate communication system among all the members, between political leadership and dormant masses, and between the modernizing government and the traditional and transitional

---

[37] See Mattei Dogan, "Les attitudes politiques des femmes en Europe et aux États-Unis," in *Le Vocabulaire des Sciences Sociales,* ed. by Lazarsfeld and Boudon. The Hague: Mouton, 1965, pp. 283–302.

[38] The same can be said of all socializing agents, including the parents. There seems to be a definite correlation, for example, between harsh corporal punishment for children and their later deviancy or delinquency. The internalization of the mores of society in a child's conscience is evidently accomplished best by a loving atmosphere and merely psychological punishment. See Brown, *Social Psychology,* pp. 381–401.

parts of the population. The communication system is one of the functional prerequisites of a modern polity and is particularly important for continuing adult socialization. As for the political socialization of the young, formal education offers an extraordinary opportunity for (a) transmitting knowledge about the political system, (b) inculcating the young with positive feelings toward the country and its governmental system—a factor of great significance wherever geographical ethnic or religious cleavages endanger national integration, (c) inducing modern universalistic attitudes, such as achievement orientation —particularly important in developing countries, and (d) generating the sense of civic competence and participation desirable in a modern democracy.[39]

American public education   The political socialization process in the fully differentiated system of formal education—primary, secondary, vocational, professional, and adult—varies with the age levels and the amount of overt civic education intended. At the lower levels, indirect teaching aimed at inculcating loyalty to symbols may have far more lasting impact than the more advanced civics lessons. American public education has traditionally been dedicated to transforming a heterogeneous population with strong contingents of foreign immigrants into one national community; it has accomplished this goal both in specific civics lessons and by a host of indirect and symbolic means that tend to pull parents and outside organizations into the socializing process for the young. The American model could probably serve many a developing nation, given a sufficient and adequately trained staff, since the ethnic minorities and traditional parental influence there roughly correspond to the effect of the immigrant subcultures on the process of Americanization of the second generation. The strategic role of the separation of church influences from public education in the United States is particularly noteworthy, since it removed one of the most potent sources of friction between many an immigrant home and the majority tenor of the public schools.

[39] See also James S. Coleman, *Education and Political Development*. Princeton, N.J.: Princeton University Press, 1965, pp. 13–19 and the sources cited there. See also S. N. Eisenstadt, *Modernization: Protest and Change*. Englewood Cliffs, N.J.: Prentice-Hall, 1966, pp. 16–18, 27.

Divisive tensions in European schools   In continental Europe, by contrast, mass public education showed the strains of religious dissension, ethnic heterogeneity, and social class pressures from the very beginning. Countries split between Protestantism and Catholicism, or multireligious populations with an established church, witnessed bitter, never-ending struggles over the content of school curricula and teacher training. Control over the elementary school curriculum in many European countries was viewed by the Catholic church and its friends as the only way to halt the onrush of secularization, while its anticlerical, liberal, anarchist, or socialist opponents in control of the state wanted to prevent the religious indoctrination of the public schoolchildren at any price. Many continental European countries to this day live with compromise solutions, allowing local options or exempting only secondary education from church influence.

Similarly, the presence of ethnic minorities of different language and customs evoked bitter strife over who controlled the schools and what the language of instruction was to be, such as has also erupted in India since 1947. The political socialization process going on in schools under siege of such disputes is very likely to inculcate a conflict of loyalties, if not downright rebellion against the public authorities and their indoctrination attempts against the home influences. In fact, the evidence suggests a process of escalation in ethnic conflict at work in multinational countries, as mass public education brought minority children into schools where the Austro-Hungarian empire, for example, may have tried to Germanize or Magyarize them. The resulting cultural conflicts between home and school probably awakened a sharp sense of ethnicity and active nationalistic rebellion in the young, producing precisely the explosive energies that broke up these century-old empires into smaller, more homogeneous, national states.

The pressures of social class in Europe likewise left their mark on the forms and procedures of mass public education. In the traditional social order, the upper classes had shown little interest in the values of education, and the eagerness of the rising middle classes produced no particular conflict. The bourgeoisie could have its degrees and diplomas; the noblemen had their titles. The introduction of mass education for the lower classes, however, opened a Pandora's box of problems. The evolving industrial society created tensions among the social classes and rising expectations in the working populations. The upper classes, controlling both the economy and the state, had a vested interest in domestic tranquillity and the civic loyalty of the working classes. It was understandable, therefore, that they should attempt to indoctrinate and ingrain the workers' children with belief in law and order and one's proper place in society. Millitant working-class organizations such as trade unions and socialist parties just as understandably resisted the attempt to smother their class interests and egalitarian aspirations under a blanket of patriotic unity.

As a consequence of these cross-pressures, many continental European school systems tended until 1945 to neutralize their civic overtones to the point of omitting patriotic appeals altogether or of limiting them to pious symbols of a country's history and identity, by comparison with which American civics and symbolic ceremonies seem chauvinistic. Even the height of nationalistic sentiment among European nation-states, for example, produced no formal civics lessons, but only a strong ethnocentric bias in the teaching of history, geography, and literature. The teaching of patriotism, moreover, was mostly a matter of the sentiments of the teachers, who between the 1880s and 1930s were known to be among the most chauvinistic groups of their societies. Even a mathematics or biology teacher seething with ethnocentric phobias could be a powerhouse of nationalistic indoctrination within his small circle.

The process of political socialization can sometimes become utterly unpredictable when conflicting impulses in the school environment play against one another. Such a situation arose, for example, during World War I, when the celebration of national holidays and of war victories in the schools in France and Germany, not to mention the other belligerents, became feasts of youthful enthusiasm for killing and humiliating the enemy. The political socialization of millions of workers' children up to World War I had already been an irreconcilable mixture of socialist internationalism and class belligerence on the one hand and patriotism and national belligerence on the other. The contradictory motives led socialist parties in the belligerent states on a wildly vacillating course, which began with the confident hope that international solidarity among the workers would undercut any "capitalistic war" with a general strike. Once war was actually breaking out amid threats and counterthreats, however, a wave of patriotic enthusiasm in the various belligerent states swept away the internationalist element of the socialization process. Only several years later, as the terrible war dragged on amid great hardships at home and at the front, did the socialist element break through again and produce munitions workers' strikes and a wave of pacifism. In the minds of individuals, the contradictory motives were probably never completely reconciled.

Educational conflict in developing societies   The role of formal education in the context of a developing society has already been touched upon above. Here, too, strongly conflicting elements in political and, for that matter, general socialization are the rule rather than the exception. The conflict begins with the acculturating impact of the French or British colonial education on indigenous elites. Colonial education was not only self-serving and imperial-ethnocentric, but in the long run it produced the skills and personnel of the national independence movements. Whole generations of African and Asian students in colonial educational institutions and in the universities of the mother countries so earnestly strove to become French or British gentlemen that they painfully tried to bury the marks of their indigenous socialization, only to find their path blocked by lines of racial or cultural discrimination. Lucian W. Pye has described the deep-seated insecurity of the acculturated in his portraits of Burmese administrators who have difficulty reconciling their British socialization with the roles appropriate to an independent Burma.[40] The triple conflict of the native home, the British acculturation, and the roles of the new independent state may considerably reduce an individual's capacity to function. Many Asian and African intellectuals with such conflicts developed also a mental rigidity fraught with fears of intellectual or political competitors, which in some cases underlies the wave of anti-intellectualism that follows the first generation of revolutionary intellectuals in the history of many new nations.[41]

[40] Lucian W. Pye, *Politics, Personality, and Nation-Building*, chaps. 15 and 16.

[41] See also S. M. Lipset, *The First New Nation*. New York: Basic Books, 1963; Shils, "The Intellectuals in the Political Development of the New States," *World Politics*, 12 (April 1960), 329–368; and Coleman, *Education and Political Development*, pp. 35–44.

The socializing process of education in all developing countries also feels the stress of the conflict between the modern goals of education and the traditional elements passed on by the home and other structures such as organized religion. In developing countries, education is bearing the chief burden of modernization. In those we earlier referred to as totalitarian and those characterized by centralized mass-movement regimes with a "political religion," the role of the educational system is even more crucial. The "political religion" or "ideology" must be taught in the schools to the exclusion of all other beliefs, as a crusading faith that will motivate the masses of the future. This necessity usually increases the tendency of the new nations to "indigenize" and "politicize" their curricula and casts its spell over the whole school environment.[42] Teachers must be preachers of the "political religion" of the movement, and teaching methods and the teacher-child relations in the classroom must also reflect the faith—in much the same way, for example, that democratic schools should "teach democratically." Indigenization of education is an understandable part of the nationalistic drive for reestablishing native pride and national identity. It is often more passionately desired by the students than by the governments, who are concerned also about the economic cost and the effectiveness of education. In view of the cultural and even revolutionary nationalism shown by European university students only a few generations ago and by Asian and African students before and after independence, student radicalism appears to be a hallmark of a certain stage of modernization. Psychologically, moreover, there seems to be very little difference between revolutionary nationalism, communism, socialism, or mixtures of these ideologies, as far as the students are concerned. All three, of course, are anti-imperialistic and frequently opposed specifically to whatever great power seems to offer the most convenient target—the United States, as in Latin America, Great

---

[42] The African nationalist criticism of the educational policies of the former colonial empires also objects to the humanistic "impracticality" of British or French higher education, charging that "this form of education is really perpetuated so that foreigners can come to Africa and steal our minerals and other products whilst our people learn Latin and history." From a speech by Davidson Nicol before the Royal African Society and the Royal Commonwealth Society in L. Gray Cowan *et al.*, *Education and Nation-Building in Africa*. New York: Praeger, 1965, p. 287.

Britain, as in the Near East, or even Red China, as in Indonesia.[43]

Education in communist countries The most instructive example of the socializing role of education is offered by the communist countries. Red China, in particular, has amended the existing program of mass education to stress hard work as an integral part of education. It projects a future in which mass education will have filled the gap between the then-educated workers and peasants and the intellectuals trained in hard work, a "cultural revolution" as compared to the "bourgeois idea" of "education for the sake of education." [44] Soviet education, by contrast, has been aimed at creating something more than a nationalistically tinged vision of "industrial man," namely the new "Soviet man," whose belief in the official ideology and loyalty to the party and regime are actually more important than his economic prowess. The primacy of political loyalty, however, does not preclude the use of economic function, hero worship, and the leadership of a Stalin (in his day), and a rather blind and ethnocentric "Soviet patriotism" as the cement of youthful loyalty to the regime. Only at the upper levels of Soviet education does political socialization intertwine Soviet patriotism with specific elements of Marxism-Leninism and an intimate knowledge of the official history of the Communist party of the Soviet Union.[45] At no level, however, do the Soviet schools exchange the basic stress on disciplined service and sacrifice to Soviet patriotism for the internationalism that the Communist

[43] See especially Coleman, *Education and Political Development* pp. 43–48 and chaps. 3, 6, and 14; and S. M. Lipset, *Student Politics,* Special Issue of *Comparative Education Review* (1966). See also the excellent papers presented on the panel "Youth in Politics" at the sixth International Political Science Association meeting in Geneva, 1964.

[44] See John W. Lewis in Coleman, *Education and Political Development,* pp. 414–429. Thus, in practice, Chinese education now imparts to the young, from kindergarten on, the economic achievement motive that David McClelland in *The Achieving Society* suggested would have to be inculcated during the years from age five to eight in order to launch economic modernity on a mass scale—departing sharply from the educational atmosphere of classical Chinese education.

[45] See Jeremy R. Azrael in Coleman, *Education and Political Development,* pp. 234–243; and Frederick C. Barghoorn, *Politics in the USSR.* Boston: Little, Brown, 1966, chap. 3.

party (USSR) has always preached to the Communist and Socialist parties of other countries.

Outside, although working through the Soviet schools, are organizations for the political socialization of youth that have become typical of all totalitarian and some semitotalitarian dictatorships. Next to parents and formal education, peer groups constitute a very important agent and structure of political socialization. For this reason all Communist parties and the Soviet regime developed communist youth organizations, in order to control the development of the peer group throughout what, in Russian culture as in many others, can be a rebellious age. Communist youth organizations are characterized by the same basic pattern as childhood training in Soviet schools. Far from being indulged in individual spontaneity, Soviet youth from kindergarten age are raised in a spirit of strict discipline and authoritarian hierarchy. The habituation of self-discipline and conformity to the *Kollektiv*, which demands obedience reaching far into what American youngsters would consider their private sphere, is also typical of Soviet youth organizations such as the Little Octobrists and Young Pioneers (age six to fourteen) and the Young Communist League (*Komsomol*). In the lower grades, school *Kollektivs* compete in projects of "socially useful labor," such as tending public parks or collecting scrap metal. The older levels, the *Komsomol*, sign up their members for volunteer weekend or summer construction projects, which are sure to awaken in them a healthy respect for manual labor and a lively appreciation for socialist idealism.[46] *Komsomol* members are also supposed to propagandize the other students and to lean on flagrant nonconformists. The stream of propaganda and indoctrination continues to inundate the adult Russian as well, and since the death of Stalin elaborate adult programs and organizations have nourished his loyalty to ideology and regime.[47]

---

[46] Jeremy Azrael in Coleman, *Education and Political Development*, pp. 243–247, 265. To give an example, the *Komsomol* has always frowned on such manifestations of "bourgeois decadence" as youths fancying Western jazz, dances, or girls' hairdos. Its most effective weapon against such offenders is group pressure.

[47] Barghoorn, *Politics in the USSR*, chaps. 4–5. Premier Khrushchev, in particular, is credited with having broadened and popularized political indoctrination beyond its restricted use on party cadres.

The communist idea of channeling the political socialization process directly toward desired outcomes had its equivalents in the fascist dictatorships of Italy and Germany, and in Spain, Portugal, and other fascist regimes. Education in fascist Italy and Nazi Germany was made the vehicle of political indoctrination from a tender age, and the textbooks of all levels were rewritten to fit the totalitarian message. Huge, all-embracing state youth organizations, such as the Italian *Balilla* (ages eight to fourteen) or German *Jungvolk* (ages ten to fourteen), or the *Avanguardisti* and Hitler Youth (ages fourteen to eighteen), put youth in uniforms and drew them into demonstration marches and massive rallies or celebrations. Here, too, the indoctrination in the early age groups fostered obedience to hierarchic authority, peer conformity, and youthful group life, while the fascist ideology was saved for later stages of activist cadres. Nevertheless, the early political socialization was also characterized by the careful building up of heroic examples, military spirit, and belligerent patriotism.

Influence of peer groups

Even where the process is not monopolized by the political powers that be, the general influence of the peer groups in political socialization is profound. In fact, it stands to reason that the patterns of cooperation with and conformity to one's peers established at high-school age continue to cast their spell as the young, newly enfranchised adults strive to conform politically to their associates at work, to their neighbors at home, or to their crowd of friends. In practice, however, the analysis of how important peer groups are in the process of political socialization becomes a complex and difficult task requiring sophisticated research.[48] We must take into account that much peer-group socialization takes place in the school environment and that most of the "peers" involved have similar social backgrounds, reflecting parents reared in the same culture. With these and other factors of socialization interlocking, how can one tell which factor had what effect?

[48] For an example of such research, see Kenneth P. Langton, "Peer Group and School, and the Political Socialization Process," *American Political Science Review,* 61 (September 1967), and the sources cited there, or David Ziblatt in *Political Socialization* (Annals).

SOCIAL DISCONTINUITIES
AND POLITICAL SOCIALIZATION

If political socialization in a given nation-state, say France, denotes the learning process by which small children become active participants in the political system, there is a definitional danger of glossing over all kinds of gaps and incoherences in French life and politics. We erroneously take it for granted that political socialization in the little southern village of Peyrane will be the same as, say, in the villages of the Bretagne or in big cities like Paris. We assume that it will be the same among farm laborers and well-to-do peasants, among steelworkers and bourgeois shopkeepers or entrepreneurs, among practicing Catholics and anticlericals, atheists, or those of other religious faiths. Such an assumption is demonstrably false in France. And it may be less true in countries of a polycommunal, multiethnic character, such as most of the new nations today.

Influence of authority patterns

In a traditional society without the common socializing denominator of a system of public education, the differences between the socialization processes of different religious, ethnic, tribal, or simply local communities can present stark contrasts. Robert Levine has described such patterns of political socialization of two stateless societies, the Nuer of the Sudan and the Gusii of Kenya, which are in many ways similar and could easily have become part of the same colony or new nation, given the quixotic nature of colonial boundaries. The Nuer were democratic in their local affairs, inclined toward aggression, and characterized by an affectionate, nonpunitive father-son relationship. The Gusii had wealthy men of power who enjoyed deference and a dominant local position. Gusii fathers and husbands were aloof and severe toward children and wife, and physical abuse of both was a common experience. Nevertheless, Nuer parents encouraged their children to fight when attacked, while Gusii parents rewarded theirs for reporting the attack instead of responding to it. The colonial government had difficulties with the Nuer blood feuds and also with the reluctance of judges appointed from among the Nuer to pass on their fellow men, while Gusii judges and judicial procedure were easily substituted for the old blood feuds. In the old East African kingdom of Buganda, one of the most centralized, autocratic, and despotic monarchies, the learning of complete obedience and deference to superiors, elders, and especially the father was the chief goal of child rearing. The adult world obviously tends to shape the child's behavior toward other persons according to the authority pattern it believes in.[49]

A telling example of a biethnic community in which political socialization differs noticeably is that of the Flemings and Walloons of Belgium. Owing evidently to parental attitudes similar to those observed among the Dutch and the French, respectively, Flemish children seem to develop a good deal more trust in political processes and governmental authority than Walloon children, who grow up to patterns of political disaffection and alienation. From common observation of child-raising practices, it would appear that the distrust of the latter may be related to parental overprotection and the early portrayal of the world beyond the *foyer* as hostile and treacherous. The Flemish and the Dutch, by comparison, allow their youth far more freedom to interact with other children, which may well generate the social trust and political cooperativeness they show as adults.[50] It is conceivable that a comparative study of French Canadians and Anglo-Canadians or of comparable ethnic communities of Switzerland might yield similar differences, although it is hazardous to generalize. There may also be religious differences involved, which would be difficult to separate from ethnic factors of culture. Macroscopic statistical correlations, moreover, are not always very satisfactory for explaining social reality. To hazard a guess, furthermore, there seems to be some evidence that political socialization patterns high in social trust, as in Great Britain, Holland, or Protestant Germany, also exhibit a larger propensity for ethnic or religious prejudice than does French culture. It could well be that the French parental fear of open conflict, overprotection, and anxious guidance of the emotional and intellectual growth of the child has its compensations.

---

[49] Clifford Geertz, ed., *Old Societies and New States.* New York: Free Press, 1963, pp. 289–297.

[50] See also the study of French, Belgian, and Dutch students by Frank Pinner in *Political Socialization* (Annals); and Mead and Metraux, *Themes in French Culture*, pp. 27–35.

Ethnic patterns

Even in the melting-pot society of the United States, ethnic differences in political socialization patterns are probably considerable. Different ethnic communities still exist, and even in the second and third generation they seem to influence voting to such a marked degree that politicians cannot afford to ignore them. As sociological studies of Polish-Americans and Italian-Americans have shown, moreover, even the overt rebellion of the Americanized children of immigrants against the ways of their parents barely hides the fact that their interpersonal relations and group structures remain contained almost exclusively within the confines and patterns of the ethnic community.[51] Urbanization itself is no guarantee of ethnic integration or amalgamation. In fact, extended families in cities in India and Turkey have been known to inhabit the different units in apartment houses in the full splendor of its traditional social hierarchy.[52]

Differential urbanization

The differences in the process of political socialization may also express themselves as a differential in timing of social and political mobilization or of political maturity. In some of the multinational areas of Eastern Europe, for example, the chief difference and cause of friction between such awakening nationalities as Czechs, Slovaks, Poles, Germans, and Hungarians appears to have been the time and rate at which they underwent urbanization. Those who first left the agrarian villages tended to seek to dominate and exploit those who remained behind. Among the members of the same ethnic community the patterns of communication and solidarity evidently made for a rapidly growing mobilization toward a richer life, whereas between ethnic groups these sparks would not fly as readily, until the stimulus of ethnic friction or exploitation by another group might bring about the

---

[51] See Herbert J. Gans, *The Urban Villagers.* New York: Free Press, 1962; and Michael Parenti, "Ethnic Politics and the Persistence of Ethnic Identification," *American Political Science Review,* 61 (September 1967).

[52] It should be noted here that an urban setting is not always and need not be modern, though urbanization denotes a social mobility and mobilization that are conducive to rapid modernization.

mobilization in the long run. The fact that at a particular time in their common history some nationalities had already begun to move to cities and to acquire education, urban attitudes and occupations, and political power while others still lay dormant in rural villages says nothing, of course, about their "national character" or supposedly innate superiority or inferiority, even though their actual relationship at the time may have touched off seething nationality feelings and enough ethnic friction to totter whole empires.

Class differences

The German Empire   The impact of class differences on political socialization can be very dramatic in a setting characterized by rigid barriers of social class. A close reading of political biographies of men born and raised in the German Empire of 1871–1918, for example, reveals the following differences between the socialization experiences of typical working-class members and typical families of the bourgeoisie: A son born to a poor tradesman in the 1860s or 1870s would probably receive a rather conservative, patriotic formal schooling reinforced by the religious faith and cultural interest of his mother. From his father or paternal friends he might catch an attitude of bitter resentment of the upper classes but learn no overt political involvement. At the age of fourteen he would leave school, become an apprentice with a tradesman who owned his own shop, and join an association of apprentices and journeymen of his trade. From that time on he was likely to be swept into the political interests and activities of his peers and associates at work. He might receive, read, and discuss socialist literature and take an active part in electioneering—under considerable risk to health and livelihood—by the time he was fifteen or sixteen. Once he had passed his years of apprenticeship, moreover, he would become a wandering journeyman, having excellent opportunities during his travels to become aware of the condition of the working classes elsewhere and to meet active socialists all over Germany and abroad. Thus political activism and international proletarian solidarity became a living faith rather than a pallid doctrine gathered from books, although socialist newspapers, pamphlets, and books obviously helped the adolescent and young adult to formulate his *Weltan-*

schauung and would continue to support it during his mature years.

A son of the upper bourgeoisie, by contrast—at least before the days of the Youth Movement—a movement typical of bourgeois socialization of the generations born just before the turn of the century—was likely to grow up in a home that carefully sheltered him from awareness of "dirty politics." This parental attitude was evidently the reaction of the German bourgeoisie to its failure to win power and its capitulation to the Junkers of Bismarck's Empire. It was colored by classical humanism, which preferred to think of the political freedom of the ancient Greeks rather than of one's own, and may also have reflected a desire not to notice the misery and exploitation of the working classes in the factories of early industrialism. The bourgeois child and adolescent, in fact, came to associate active political participation with socialist agitation by what seemed to him unrespectable "men of questionable livelihood," just as some American middle-class parents today identify all youthful interest in politics with disreputably dressed agitators and race riots. From the age of ten, the son of the German upper bourgeoisie would go to a Latin school (*Gymnasium*) or its equivalent, where his mixture of political alienation with a vague patriotism would be deepened by like-minded teachers. He could graduate at seventeen and report for one year of reserve officer training, which would place him for the rest of his life above the salt as a part of the feudalized bourgeoisie of the Empire. Or he could complete Latin school and attend a university, in which case his education might receive its military-patriotic twist in the traditional student fraternities to which nearly everyone belonged. The ritualized conviviality and the fencing duels were enough to warp any normal personality with romantic-feudal or military ideals. It was generally only in his twenties, if ever, that the young bourgeois might become aware of political realities. By then he had probably developed set attitudes of political alienation and hostility against the lower classes and foreign countries that were unlikely to yield to a soberer vision for the rest of his life. Many a bourgeois used to admit freely in his later years that he never came to understand or to feel comfortable with everyday politics, an attitude he shared, though for reasons of traditionality rather than alienation, with the children of most German farmers and people in the small towns.

The Negro in America   In the example of German children, the political self-image of a given social class combines with the stratification of the educational system—German workers' children were, and still are, rather unlikely to go to the Latin schools or their equivalent, not to mention the universities. A differential in political socialization of somewhat similar dimensions but different results is found between whites and blacks in America, especially if we look beyond the ethnic angle to compare the old German class society with the classlike barriers between the vast middle class of whites and the similarly proponderant lower-class element among the Negroes of the south and the urban ghettoes of the north. Except for a minority of Negro youth, blacks are still far from the political mobilization and activism or the militant "class consciousness" of German workers around the turn of the century. The political socialization of middle-class whites, at least outside the south, is also far from the alienation and distorted perception of the old German bourgeoisie. But there can be little doubt that the political socialization of the American black has run along very different lines than that of whites, even where they go to the same schools. The vast majority of southern blacks are still in segregated schools, many of which until rather recently simply left civics out of the curriculum, while many northern black children are also subject to *de facto* school segregation related to patterns of housing and other discrimination. At the core of the differential in political socialization lies a lack of faith in the democratic roles of voter and citizen, in equal treatment from government officials and especially from the police, to which are added all kinds of personal experiences of discrimination and rejection.[53] Since the experiences and settings are highly diverse, the outcome varies a great deal and appears to rest on cycles of protest, alienation, reconciliation, and, where the environment permits it, resocialization.

[53] See especially the article by Dwaine Marvick, "The Political Socialization of the American Negro," *Political Socialization* (Annals). For purposes of studying the patterns of political socialization, the "class angle" is more significant than ethnicity, since the vast majority have taken on the majority culture rather than developed their own.

European social classes   The differential in political socialization among social classes in other European countries and in West Germany today is probably less dramatic but nevertheless pronounced. The political equality implied by the principle of one man (one woman), one vote, is still at variance with pronounced social and economic inequalities that are passed on in the family and often reinforced by an educational system restratifying society along class lines. From this disparity result working-class attitudes of distrust and disaffection toward government and frequently against their own party leaders, who are seen as failing to break down the barriers when in power. A typical example of such lower-class discontent was the controversy at a British Labour party convention about the requested abolition of the "public schools" (prestigious private schools), which failed to be adopted, many a prominent Labour leader being himself an alumnus of one of these holdouts of the old class society. On the other hand, the well-educated social elites of France or Germany, for example, are quite likely to inculcate in their children and through their *lycées* and *Gymnasien* an ill-concealed contempt for the *hoi polloi* and the political processes and elective officials of democratic politics.

Egalitarian societies   In more egalitarian societies, such as the United States or Australia, the differences of political socialization among various strata of society are rather mild and may well differ more among other groups and regions and according to the state of social ascent or decline than among the strata as such. Downward mobility generally tends to create a socialization pattern of disaffection at home. More noteworthy than social class differences in an egalitarian society that lacks other major cleavages is the difference between urban and more rural settings. Youth in rural and small communities is socialized into preexisting and well-understood role structures, while the amorphous and highly mobile context of rapid urbanization makes for unpredictable patterns of political socialization.[54] This is not to deny that there are certain pockets in American society, espe-

[54] See also Kurt B. Mayer, "Social Stratification in Two Equalitarian Societies, Australia and the United States," in Reinhard Bendix and Seymour M. Lipset, *Class, Status, and Power,* 2d ed. New York: Free Press, 1966, pp. 149–161.

cially certain ethnic minorities—blacks, Puerto Ricans, Indians, and Chicanos (Mexican-Americans)—and several economically marginal groups, such as migratory farm labor and welfare families, where children receive a distinctively different and probably quite stunted political education.

Intergroup communication gaps

If we picture the socializing processes of political society separated by the various social divisions discussed above, we can also attempt to grasp the larger social mechanisms at work, and their political consequences. Each separated group in its process of socializing its young or new members is a communication system passing a stream of information from the old to the new generation. Parents and teachers within a group, so to speak, tell their dependent charges about the character of the political outside world, especially passing on attitudes toward the other groups. They also communicate their own experiences, their hurt pride or resentment, and their own ways of coping with the outside world by ignoring it, withdrawal from it, trusting it, cooperating with it, or trying to dominate it. Youth rarely forget these lessons, although further perceptions and feelings may be fed into its socialization and help to produce the final result. What is clear, however, is that there is very little communication between the groups, and this noncommunication is a major source of potential misunderstanding and friction.

The depth and political salience of social divisions seem to vary widely. Not every group communication gap is bound to produce a significant political cleavage, nor would it do so with every generation. Sometimes, also, the discontinuity of one kind of division, say social class, is bridged by voluntary organizations, churches, or the public schools, which attempt to teach a uniform message of political socialization to all their charges. If the workers in different communities of a polycommunal society discover, for example, that their respective trade unions have a great deal in common, then there is a cross-cutting cleavage that modifies the divisive effect of polycommunalism.[55] Cleavages of a political nature can also increase or decrease, depending on the dynamic

[55] See, for example, M. Freedman, "The Growth of a Plural Society in Malaya," in Wallerstein, *Social Changes: The Colonial Situation.* New York: Wiley, 1967, pp. 278–289 and *passim.*

development of political socialization on either side of the discontinuity. The new generation of members of a given group, for example, while growing up or afterward, may develop new feelings or apprehensions toward another group. If the feelings are hostile or apprehensive, a new political cleavage may be born. If the feelings are more positive than with the preceding generation, the ground may be prepared for integrating the groups with each other.

Thus the study of political socialization within the matrix of social divisions can help us understand basic social change, or the evolution of the matrix of social divisions itself. It may also reveal important mechanisms of nation building and national integration via the decline of the traditional cleavages under the impact of urbanization, industrialization, major crisis, or involvement in war.[56]

POLITICAL SOCIALIZATION AND RECRUITMENT

Electioneering

One of the most immediate and effective agents of the political socialization of children and adults is the spectacle of politics itself. As group games and sports help to socialize children, so the game of politics, especially the competition, may get adolescents and adults involved. Experiencing an election campaign in a modern political system means the activation of all kinds of agents that are otherwise not particularly political, such as the family, the work environment, friends, or voluntary associations. But above all, being addressed by candidates, volunteers, and political parties and being drawn into temporary participation form a major socializing experience. Whether we reconstruct this crucial moment in a person's life with the benefit of hindsight from the biography of a prominent politician or observe people being drawn into active politics during an election, we thereby encounter a point where political socialization may become a spur

[56] See the excellent analysis by Lester Seligman in *Leadership in a New Nation* (New York: Atherton Press, 1964) of the processes of socialization and recruitment in Israel, a nation of immigrants from many backgrounds.

to active participation or even recruitment for a political party and, perhaps, for leadership roles in this party.

Political parties, trade unions, and peer groups at work or at school can become recruitment mechanisms for some people, while their effect on most amounts merely to politically socializing them. Whole educational systems, such as the French *École Normale Supérieure* or *École Polytechnique,* the British "public schools," certain military academies, and—unintended and unwillingly—colonial higher education, can be structures for the recruitment of governmental elites or political movements, such as the independence movements of former colonies. Even the parents can become agents of recruitment if they motivate their children to join the same political party or to begin a political or administrative career.

Recruitment and socialization compared

To put it another way, the study of political recruitment and that of political socialization are concerned with different aspects of substantially the same process, though not the same function. They differ in two respects: the level of participation and the definition of the group to be examined. The study of political socialization is content to examine the learning process by which a child, immigrant, or other nonparticipant becomes an active citizen and voter; thus this study is interested in all members of a given community. The study of political recruitment singles out a small elite of varying definition—but always of greater involvement, influence, or formal authority—than the average citizen, such as members or officials of parties, governmental officials, or other association or communication elites. Essentially, then, it studies the selection processes by which a given elite, however defined, is recruited from among larger numbers. A recruitment study could, of course, also look into the socialization process by which its elite members first became introduced to politics, into their adult socialization, or into their socialization process into the elite as a group. There are interesting studies, for example, that attempt to chart over a period of time the process by which a new member of a given group, such as a political party or a given legislature, progressively adopts the language, opinions, and moves of the group, subtly changing his earlier habits and views.

Focus of recruitment studies

The definition of groups whose recruitment is to be determined is highly arbitrary.[57] It could be practically any politically relevant group or even the membership of a trade union or the priesthood of a church. Most current recruitment studies, however, like to consider a fairly narrow political elite group, either mixed of various group elements or one group alone. One of the more ambitious early political elite studies, the Hoover Institute studies of Harold D. Lasswell, Daniel Lerner, and C. Easton Rothwell, for example, examined the membership of the Soviet Politbureau from 1917 to 1951, select Italian fascist officials prior to 1934, the Nazi elite listed in a Nazi Who's Who of 1934, and the Kuomintang and the Chinese Communist elites of the 1920s and 1930s. These varying samples of political leadership were investigated statistically as to their social and geographic origins, occupation, education, personal history, and political career, and compared to nonelite groups of the same societies, in the hope that the comparison would lay bare the motivation or inner rationale behind the rise of these revolutionary movements.[58] The Politbureau study concluded, for example, that this body has been not at all representative of the groups of Soviet society, including few workers, not a single woman, or a single peasant among the topmost elite of the "workers' and peasants' state." Its membership began with the brilliant middle-class intellectuals of the revolution and slowly picked up less colorful but efficient administrators, remaining very stable in its composition except for increasing age, a noticeable contrast to the rapid change in the leadership of Western countries.

The Italian study stressed the rise of elements of the lesser bourgeoisie and the number of political careers based on skills in violence or in party organization or propaganda. The Nazi study

[57] For a sampling of the diverse definitions and theories in the literature, see especially Lewis J. Edinger, ed., *Political Leadership in Industrialized Societies.* New York: Wiley, 1967, pp. 5–9 and chap. 12.

[58] See Harold D. Lasswell and Daniel Lerner, *World Revolutionary Elites* (Cambridge, Mass.: M.I.T. Press, 1965), where the 1951 and 1952 studies are reprinted, with new commentary, and Carl Beck and J. Thomas McKechnie, *Political Elites: A Select Computerized Bibliography* (Cambridge, Mass.: M.I.T. Press, 1968).

came up with distinctive types, such as the typical Nazi administrator as a "plebeian on the make," the Nazi propagandist as an
"alienated intellectual," and all of the Nazi elite as "socially marginal" in the sense of being deviant from the averages of the
population.[59] The Chinese Kuomintang and Communist elites,
finally, were found to come predominantly from the upper
classes, to be Western or Russian-educated, and to have gone
into politics without a prior career or from a military background.
Toward the time of the rise of Communist China both elites exhibited an increasing element of lower-class origin, and the
Communists even brought in a strong peasant element.

Elite recruitment in new nations

The study of elite recruitment in new nations can illuminate the
dynamics of change as well as national solidarity—economic
change from *agraria* to an urban industrial way of life, imbal-
ances in the values and distribution of influence among the groups
and associations, and the level of popular participation in politics.
Recruitment patterns reflect a society's values, its judgments regarding personal excellence, and its relation to the highest political roles. They also show the distribution of status and prestige
and the system of social stratification. Values, roles and role
structure, and social stratification all may change over a period
of time, and this will show up in longitudinal recruitment studies. Besides reflecting society, moreover, recruitment patterns
also may change it, especially its public policies and future recruitment patterns. Finally, the stability and continuous development of a new nation depend vitally on the cooperation, quality,
and integrity of its political elites through the disruptive changes
that development inevitably brings.

Integration of elites

The integration of the elite of a "new nation," or of a developed
country for that matter, is crucial to the functioning and devel-

[59] This concept of "marginality" led to some rather absurd conclusions: among those considered marginal were all Catholics, persons with
only an elementary education, and peasants. The original set of studies
also included one by Maxwell Knight, which compared German political
executive elites of the Empire, the Weimar Republic, and the Third
Reich. Its most striking finding was the difference in age between the
Nazi executives and their predecessors.

opment of the political system. In the older democratic nations, a commitment to common values and constitutional structures and to the rules of the political game helps greatly with the integration of oppositional elites, who are often included in some fashion in the making of policy. Most of all, the processes of competition among rival elites and the bargaining and compromises among different group interests are generally accepted among the populace and the elites themselves. Harmony among competing leadership groups is also enhanced by the effective neutrality and instrumentalist attitude of what are increasingly *professional politicians.* To the extent that political elites have come from the same social and cultural background and gone to the same schools, as in England and France, their political socialization is likely to have created strong bonds of underlying harmony. The socialization into political careers among the legislative, administrative, scientific, and propaganda experts of a modern system, furthemore, will create communities of skills with their own ethos and unwritten standards, which can overcome the political cleavages present.

Again the British political elite, and notably members of Parliament, is an excellent example of how institutional setting of venerable tradition can socialize even rebellious new parties and deputies. The French National Assembly or the United States Senate similarly constitute *le salon,* "the club," a socializing environment comparable to a well-integrated modern corps of high civil servants.

Although it is difficult to generalize, the integration among developing political elites, by comparison, seems poor. Independence movements are unified, but postindependence institutional settings are often too new to have integrating power. Competition is often kept hidden, because conflict, bargaining, and compromise may be odious to the public. The political socialization of the elites is heterogeneous and often split by major cleavages. Elite differences of opinion, moreover, in many cases tend to be ideologic and doctrinaire. Oppositions are viewed as subversive rather than as "loyal opposition," and their functioning tends to be conspiratorial. Popular and elite conduct is content with expressing emotions rather than aiming at functional achievement. And the gaining of power by election may be viewed by friend and foe alike as an opportunity for acquiring it permanently, whatever the price. Small wonder that the development of the new states is often bedeviled by dissensions and the breakdown of the brittle elite consensus necessary to advance modernization.

As Lester Seligman has pointed out, the legitimation of the elites of the new states consists largely in the manner in which they embody or evoke the sacred values of the system. The leaders of the old nationalistic movements, in particular, thus acquire legitimacy as leaders of the independent nations. This is particularly true of charismatic leaders, such as Nasser, Nehru, Sukarno, Sekou Touré, or Ho Chi-minh. They are highly functional in the new states, according to Seligman, because they stand above the traditional cleavages, as heroes of the past struggle against colonialism and as symbols of a unified nation yet to come. They also have a major recruitment function in attracting and engaging the services of younger men trained in the political, economic, technical, and planning skills essential to development. For the time being, at least, their undisputed charismatic authority saves the fragile new nation from the almost insurmountable problems of generating political consensus in the unfinished state of its political system. The value of this moratorium of new nationhood becomes at once apparent when we consider the effects of formal democratization amid the dissolving old values and social bases and the conflict between modern and traditional elements.[60]

Recruitment patterns in new nations

The actual recruitment patterns in the new states vary considerably among the different cultures. In general they contrast sharply with those in developed societies, where the political elites can usually claim to embody only a small part of the dominant values of society, leaving the rest to separate religious, economic, and communication elites, including the arts, science, and education. In developing countries, the political elites seem to enjoy a monopoly of social values, except for those represented by tra-

---

[60] Seligman, *Leadership in a New Nation,* pp. 6–11. The literature on elites of developing nations is growing so prodigiously that no attempt can be made here even to list it. As an example of first-rate elite studies see Frederick W. Frey, *The Turkish Political Elite.* Cambridge, Mass.: M.I.T. Press, 1965.

ditional or revolutionary counterelites. In some developing nations, such as Saudi Arabia or, until rather recently, Yemen, the top leadership is still ascriptive, and membership in the socially highest families will determine eligibility for office. From this extreme, the exclusiveness of eligibility varies by degrees all the way to the popular choice of amateurs, the custom in some developed democratic societies at the other extreme. The difference rests in large part on the increasingly legitimizing character of the procedure of election itself. In other words, while Saudi Arabians may require titles or ascriptive family membership to lend the aura of authority to an officeholder, the mere fact of election by a majority will constitute legitimate authority in the United States regardless of an individual's origins or antecedents. It should be noted, however, that in spite of the popular myth the selection of political amateurs in the United States is a very rare occurrence and hardly desirable in itself. Its rareness stems in large part from the need for organized support and very considerable funds for a successful election campaign, but also from the requirement of broad experience in public affairs and skills of a rather specialized nature. Between these extremes, moreover, there lie plenty of gradations and, in particular, mediating structures, which are at work in all countries.

Mediating structures The most important mediating structures are group representation and political parties. Group representation is equally important in highly stratified and in polycommunal societies, in which the elite recruited from a particular subculture derives its legitimacy from its presumed corporate representation of the body of members of that subculture. A representative link of sorts may also be at work in a noncorporate fashion where political elite members are recruited only or chiefly from the social elites of a society, which presumably "represent" the best values of that society. Political parties are sometimes entangled with this process of group representation [61] but

[61] This type of party is called either "sectarian" if it restricts its representative function to single religious, ethnic, or ideological group, or "pluralistic" if it attempts to aggregate several. Seligman, *Leadership in a New Nation,* p. 13 and chap. 5. See also S. M. Lipset and Aldo Solari, *Elites in Latin America.* New York: Oxford, 1968, chap. 4.

can also be "populistic," espousing an overriding national purpose that is said to precede any sectional interest. In either case, they act as recruiting and selecting devices for the holding of public office, narrowing the choice of the electorate down to a mere handful of eligibles.

Breakdowns in recruitment

Finally, let us consider the frequent occurrence of breakdown in recruitment. When a military coup or other revolutionary takeover by a minority occurs in a developing country and it maintains itself by force, suppressing all opposition, doubts arise about the character of the processes mentioned previously. A military dictatorship of the kind that has seized power in many new nations may well claim to represent the highest values of the society and to be bent on its optimal development. But its claims sound hollow if force is used to silence doubters and critics of its policies. And while it may indeed leave an impact on society, such a dictatorship can hardly be said to reflect much about the society except its weakness or perhaps its lack of consensus. Nevertheless, the military in many developing countries is often among the more modern groups and more likely to continue society on a modernizing course than most other elites. Not infrequently, the army of countries like Brazil or the Philippines also performs specific functions of engineering, road building, and teaching the operation of modern motor equipment. The political socialization provided by the professional military career, as Pye suggests, also seems to be more successful than comparable processes in developing nations in inculcating modern civic attitudes without the underlying insecurity and volatility characteristic of the impact of industrialization and urbanization.[62] In Red China, the army has even taken on broad popular socialization functions. But even if we consider these advantages, the effect of military rule in developing nations is a disruption of the normal recruitment and socialization processes; even at its best it supplies no more than a moratorium for a society developing toward political maturity.

[62] See especially Lucian Pye in John J. Johnson, *The Role of the Military in Underdeveloped Countries.* Princeton, N.J.: Princeton University Press, 1962, pp. 80–84.

POLITICAL SOCIALIZATION AND PARTICIPATION

Degrees of participation

In a modern, participation-oriented democracy, where the political elites themselves are more deeply involved, the average citizen is only partially involved. Lester W. Milbrath has suggested a scale of political involvement that gives degrees and kinds of participants as distinguished from "apathetics." [63] The scale begins with *spectator activities* that run from "exposing oneself to political stimuli" to such expressions of commitment as trying to influence someone's vote or exhibiting a campaign button or automobile bumper sticker. Then comes *transitional activities,* such as contacting elective officials or political leaders, contributing funds, and attending political rallies. Finally there are *gladiatorial activities,* such as volunteering of time, active party membership, fund raising, and running for and holding public or party office.[64] Recruitment studies would not consider anything but the last group of activities. This scale does not include demonstrations, political strikes, guerrilla warfare, or violent revolution, all of which are very important outside of the United States and especially in the developing areas of Africa, Latin America, and Asia today. Milbrath's list is evidently a scale of levels of active involvement with a stable, developed system. Massive incidence of the more dramatic kind, and especially of violent activities, is a sign of great instability and imminent breakdown of the political system. Needless to add, such activity was quite common during the great revolutions of Western countries and has recurred in periods of crisis, as in the Weimar Republic of Germany.[65]

In American politics, the percentage of adults participating in any of these ways declines sharply with increasing levels of involvement, apart from fluctuating from one occasion to an-

[63] Nonparticipation is so widespread as to be the norm in many developing societies or developing parts of societies, especially as long as the basic physical needs for food, shelter, and other necessities have not been met. See, for example, James C. Davies, *Human Nature in Politics.* New York: Wiley, 1963, chaps. 1–2.

[64] See Lester W. Milbrath, *Political Participation.* Skokie, Ill.: Rand McNally, 1965, p. 18.

[65] See especially Barrington Moore. *Social Origins of Dictatorship and Democracy.* Boston: Beacon Press, 1966, chaps. 2, 3, 4, 5, and 9.

other. No more than 5 percent are active in a party and get involved in campaigns, although another 5 percent may contribute to a party or candidate. No more than 15 percent are involved enough to display a campaign button or bumper sticker. The voting turnout, on the other hand, may run as high as 70 percent in a presidential election, although state and local elections, and certain areas, remain at a mere fraction of this percentage. Comparable information on the participation levels of other democracies is rather sketchy at best. Some of it will be discussed below.

Almond and Verba's cross-national study

The broadest cross-national study of political participation to date is still Almond and Verba's *The Civic Culture.* The authors carefully explored the patterns of popular knowledge and feeling toward government and political parties in the United States, Great Britain, Germany, Italy, and Mexico. Then they asked their respondents to indicate how active they thought an ordinary man should be in his local community. They obtained a scale of from 51 to 10 percent of their national samples—in a ranking order of the United States, Great Britain, Mexico, Germany, and Italy—who expressed the belief that an ordinary man should participate actively. Another third felt he should participate passively.[66] While this may not reflect what the respondents actually do in the way of participation, it does indicate their notions of what a good citizen ought to do. In all five countries, a high sense of civic duty to participate was positively correlated with high levels of education and occupational status.

The authors of that classic study also tried to ascertain their respondents' sense of political efficacy or competence by asking whether they thought they could influence an unjust local or national regulation and how. The results were quite similar, except for some interesting differences among the nations. Germans and Italians, the posttotalitarian citizens of nation-states unified only a century ago, showed significantly less sense of political efficacy toward their national government than toward local government. As to the strategy of opposition proposed, Americans

[66] The difference between active and passive was defined according to specific activities. Joining community organizations and attending meetings was considered "active," voting and keeping informed "passive." Almond and Verba, *The Civic Culture,* pp. 169–179.

and Englishmen were far more ready to resort to cooperative action such as organizing friends and neighbors; Englishmen also proposed to enlist the help of an elected local official; while Germans, Mexicans, and Italians proposed to complain to administrative as well as elected local officials.[67]

Styles of participation

The patterns of political participation vary also with regard to style. In developing nations, more than in modern democracies, participation is likely to be affective and expressive rather than instrumentally oriented. The grand spectacle of achieving independence, the flamboyance of charismatic men on horseback, and the direct appeals to subconscious personality needs cater to the expressive style. So do the violent eruptions, riots, and demonstrations by means of which protest can express itself far more dramatically than with petitions or ballots.[68]

Revolutionary peasant movements   A particularly interesting example of evolving styles of participation is the contemporary experience with revolutionary peasant movements in Latin America or Asia. According to E. J. Hobsbawm's study of "primitive rebels," prenationalistic peasant mass movements are often the result of foreign invasion or the organization of an underground resistance that mobilizes prepolitical men and women into forms of political and military organization far ahead of any other political development in their countries.[69] Since the 1930s, peasant movements in Latin America have become distinctly politicized, an advance over the earlier types of social banditry or Indian revolt movements. The new forms of agrarian revolt are either reformist-agrarian, like APRA in Peru or Acción Democratica

[67] *The Civic Culture,* pp. 191 and 203. The structure of local government, of course, is another factor that should be considered here.

[68] See p. 139, and Samuel E. Finer, *The Man on Horseback* (New York: Praeger, 1962), chaps. 8 and 9, who speaks of three levels of political culture—developed, low, and minimal—which differ chiefly in the presence or absence of an articulate public opinion. In the last-mentioned, *personalismo,* or *caudillismo,* is a kind of vicarious participation in politics.

[69] E. J. Hobsbawm, *Social Bandits and Primitive Rebels.* New York: Free Press, 1959. See also Johnson, *Peasant Nationalism and Communist Power,* chaps. 1 and 6.

in Venezuela; revolutionary-agrarian, like the "red republics" of Colombia, Peru, and the peasant leagues of Brazil, at least in some of their actions; or finally, political banditry, like the *violencia* in Colombia since 1948. The style and expressions of political activity vary according to the goals, the social setting, and the governmental measures for or against the peasants.[70]

Totalitarian movements   Another special pattern of political participation is displayed in communist or other totalitarian countries. By definition, modern totalitarian movements not only consist of politically hyperactive members,[71] but they also aim at mobilizing and channeling mass participation in the desired direction. Once the totalitarian movement is in power, it ceaselessly "propagandizes and agitates," and frequently cajoles and threatens masses of people into actions of acclaim and support for the regime as well as the innumerable small measures of mass participation demanded of the ordinary citizen. These small measures and gestures in communist China, Russia, and the Eastern European satellite countries, and in Nazi Germany usually command a prima facie righteousness that apathetic or even hostile citizens find hard to face down. Chinese students are asked to wage a war against flies or rats and mice. Russian workers are called upon to work harder to fulfill production quotas vital to the industrial process. Germans under Hitler or under Ulbricht are asked to put the welfare of the community ahead of their private selfishness. Who can refuse such specific exhortations under the watchful eye of his dear neighbors and colleagues, not to mention the government? Perhaps the initial acts of otherwise uncommitted citizens are merely routine performances of what a decent person would or ought to do anyway, though commanded by the new masters. Perhaps the manipulated citizen only goes through the motions because he has been put on the spot. Any such obeying and cooperating, however, already denote subtle commitments and involvements that give

[70] See A. Q. Obregon in Lipset and Solari, *Elites in Latin America,* chap. 9. Also Anderson *et al., Issues of Political Development,* chaps. 5–8 on the functions of political violence in Burma, Colombia, and the Congo.

[71] See Almond, *The Appeals of Communism,* chaps. 1–2 as well as pt. III.

the regime immediate support and, in the long run, become a well-routinized form of implicitly political participation.

After a campaign against rats and mice or selfishness, acts of specifically political support can be evoked with almost the same ease. By the time a new generation has grown up in totalitarian schools and youth organizations, participation has become self-propelled and enthusiastic. The young communists may never ask for a real share in the decision-making process. Nevertheless, their enthusiastic support and participation are genuine and should be so considered. Since totalitarian dictatorships usually begin with societies in a transitional stage and rely heavily on the transitional elements of the population, such as young people, peasants, recent migrants to urban-industrial areas, and other newly politicized social strata,[72] one can compare the manipulated participation in totalitarian countries to the affective-expressive style of developing societies. The applauding masses are just trying to express the sentiments drummed into them by totalitarian propaganda, rather than participating in an instrumentalist way as modern democracies tend to do. This approach explains at least the more visible mass phenomena in totalitarian states. But there remain plenty of actions, such as those inspired by "Soviet patriotism," that are instrumental and meant to accomplish specific political and social purposes.[73]

Participation and suffrage

Although we shall defer the discussion of partisan politics until a later chapter, it is worth our while to reflect here on the link between the gradual extension of suffrage in various countries and the rise of mass participation. The rise of stable mass parties in the nineteenth and twentieth centuries in many European

[72] Another important element are persons alienated from society, such as members of the declining old upper classes or intellectuals in the broadest sense of the word, who cannot find employment appropriate to their training.

[73] See Barghoorn, *Politics in the USSR,* pp. 20–21, 30–33, and C. E. Black, ed., *The Transformation of Russian Society.* Cambridge, Mass.: Harvard University Press, 1961, *passim.* Also Friedrich and Brzezinski, *Totalitarian Dictatorship and Autocracy,* 2d ed., chaps. 11–13, and Chalmers Johnson, "Building a Communist Nation in Asia," in Robert A. Scalapino, ed., *The Communist Revolution in Asia.* Englewood Cliffs, N.J.: Prentice-Hall, 1965, pp. 47–81.

countries, today having a formal membership of from one fourth to one third of the electorate of such countries as Great Britain, Austria, Sweden, and Israel, has been the most visible consequence of this development.[74] These party members constitute an activist core deeply involved in electioneering and other partisan activities. As for the least politicized masses, Norwegian political scientist Stein Rokkan has drawn up ingenious charts showing the comparative timetables of the different steps of enfranchisement for Belgium, Denmark, France, Germany, Great Britain, Norway, and Sweden, comparing (1) the series of decisions regarding the formal conditions for the enfranchisement of hitherto unmobilized masses, (2) the actual rates of their mobilization and the conditions influencing the consequent level of activity, and (3) the conditions for different linkages between participation in parties and in other organizations.[75]

Thresholds of mass participation

In a later work, Rokkan and Lipset present a theory of thresholds in the way of the political mobilization and eventual power of the inarticulate masses, cataloging the "openness" of various European societies to protest and dissent from outside the power structure. The thresholds are (a) the legitimation of protest as such, (b) the permissibility of the incorporation of protest in the choice of parliamentary representatives, (c) protest representation in new parties in the representative assemblies, and (d) the threshold of majority power. These thresholds indicate the phases of democratic participation in most Western democracies so that they can be compared cross-nationally.[76]

[74] See, for example, Maurice Duverger, *Political Parties.* London: Methuen, 1954, chap. 2; or Leon D. Epstein, *Political Parties in Western Democracies.* New York: Praeger, 1967, pp. 111–122.

[75] See Stein Rokkan, "The Comparative Study of Political Participation," in Austin Ranney, ed., *Essays on the Behavioral Study of Politics.* Urbana, Ill.: University of Illinois Press, 1962, pp. 47–91 and the sources cited there; Otto Stammer, ed., *Party Systems, Party Organizations and the Politics of the New Masses.* Berlin: Institute for Political Science, 1968, pp. 26–65.

[76] See Seymour Lipset and Stein Rokkan, eds., *Party Systems and Voter Alignments: Cross-National Perspectives.* New York: Free Press, 1967, pp. 26–33 and the literature cited there. See also Rokkan's contribution to *Party Systems, Party Organizations and the Politics of the New Masses.* Berlin: Institute for Political Science, 1968, pp. 26–65.

For the developing nations, however, the fit is not quite adequate. One reason is the absence or weakness of an institutional framework preceding the modern development of participation patterns, which was present in most Western countries. Another reason is the role of colonial rule, which in some cases may have helped to bring about a gradual growth of participation, but which in every case had the inherently disruptive effect of foreign conquest and occupation. Often it imparted a powerful impetus to mobilization and social change. A third difference is the prevalance of communal participation. Political parties in Nigeria, elsewhere in Africa, and in parts of Asia soon discovered the usefulness of the customary tribal-cultural, religious, and village organizations to supplement their inadequate local structure. Communal participation, of course, strengthens these traditional institutions at the same time that it takes advanage of their emotional ties to their constituents.[77] The fact that the party leaders making the appeal or using the traditional structures are part of a rising new class of associational elites does not seem to interfere too much with this marriage of the old and the new.

Participation and democratic theory

This survey has shown the extraordinary variety of patterns of political socialization, recruitment, and participation and the pivotal significance of understanding their processes in depth in any country if we are to understand its politics. As for participation, which is only one dimension of the process of socialization and recruitment, the findings of area studies suggest a considerable revision of the popular concept of civic participation in democratic theory. From the days of democratic Athens, when slaves carrying ropes painted with vermilion were supposed to drive the laggard citizenry toward the town meeting of the *ekklesia*, we have believed that democracy requires a high measure of political participation in order to function well. A survey of participation patterns around the world and at different periods of history, however, supplies many object lessons to modify

[77] See Richard L. Sklar and C. S. Whitaker, Jr., in James S. Coleman and Carl G. Rosberg, Jr., *Political Parties and National Integration in Tropical Africa*. Berkeley, Calif.: University of California Press, 1966, pp. 619–624.

that idea. On the one hand, many developing societies have hardly any participation, and large parts of all societies seem to experience little inducement to political participation in the process of their political socialization at home or at school. On the other hand, some forms of mass participation, erupting in particular among these otherwise inarticulate people, are so violent and disruptive that they would break up democracies no less than traditional obligarchies.

Such a breakdown of a working democracy occurred, for example, in the Weimar Republic, showing all too clearly the link from violent mass participation to the manipulated mass participation of totalitarian movements and governments. Extremist propaganda, demonstrations, and revolutionary violence by hundreds of thousands of militant revolutionaries of the extreme left and even more thousands of the extreme right led to continual confrontations, which polarized partisan politics around these two camps, each feeding on the threat posed by the other. The democratic politics of ballots and persuasion was soon superseded by the marching and fighting of uniformed, paramilitary organizations—communist, National Socialist, ultramilitaristic, and loyal republican. With the appointment of Adolf Hitler as Chancellor in 1933, the Nazi private armies and their totalitarian million-member movement simply took over, putting an end to German democracy. Similarly, the rise of totalitarian dictatorships in fascist Italy, Spain, or Eastern Europe and of communist rule in Russia was accompanied by violent political participation that crowded out the democratic kind.[78]

It would seem clear, then, that only the nonviolent, democratic kind of political participation can be a functional prerequisite of modern democracy. The low voting turnout in many local elections in Western democracies and civic indifference of the sort shown in France are, of course, serious problems for a democracy. In terms of Milbrath's scale of political involvement, however, it would seem to be a virtue rather than a vice in a democracy if the percentage of citizens engaging in "gladiatorial activities" for antagonistic political camps remains relatively small. The percentage of eligible voters who do turn out, on

---

[78] See F. L. Carsten, *The Rise of Fascism*. Berkeley, Calif.: University of California Press, 1967, pp. 52–65 and *passim*.

the other hand, can hardly be high enough. Only with this optimal combination of many "spectator citizens" and few gladiators can a democracy hope to steer safely between the Scylla of civic indifference and the Charybdis of threatening civil war.[79]

[79] See also Millbrath, *Political Participation,* chap. 6.

3
POLITICAL CULTURES

"Politics is a struggle for power," wrote Samuel H. Beer in his classic work on Great Britain,[1] "but a struggle that is deeply conditioned by fundamental moral concerns." The fundamental differences between the contemporary Tory and Labour models of democratic representation, he went on to point out, lies in the British ambiguity over the social significance of class distinctions —to some, a divisive force, to others, a unifying device for the sake of the social order. And it is no coincidence that the British attitude toward social class has to be stated in this dialectic, "yes-and-no" fashion. Erik H. Erikson also speaks of the identity or character of a nation as derived from the ways in which its history has "counterpointed certain opposite potentialities," from which it developed a unique style of civilization.[2] Fundamental moral concerns, the social significance of class distinctions, national identity or character—these are important themes and elements of *political culture*.

[1] Samuel H. Beer, *British Politics in the Collectivist Age.* New York: Knopf, 1965, pp. xi–xii.

[2] Erik H. Erikson, *Childhood and Society.* New York: Norton, 1950, p. 285. He volunteers such pairs of opposite themes in American identity as "open roads of immigration and jealous islands of tradition, outgoing internationalism and defiant isolationism, boisterous competition and self-effacing cooperation."

TOWARD A DEFINITION OF POLITICAL CULTURE

"Every political system," according to Gabriel Almond, "is embedded in a particular pattern of orientations to political action . . . the political culture." [3] The concept of political culture, still relatively new, must be explained and reconciled with such widely current earlier terms as "ideology," "national character," "legitimacy," and "citizenship." The general cultural system, it will be recalled, embraces the entire social system, including even a society's tools and artifacts. The political culture is a part of the general cultural system, though it may enjoy some degree of autonomy from it.

Like the general culture, political culture is *transmitted* by means of political socialization; thus it is *learned* rather than manifested as some kind of phylogenetic racial heritage. Political socialization, like all socialization processes, is the gradual internalization of politicocultural values and of social and political codes of behavior. It may be true that much of political life involves legal coercion and centralized power. But by far the most important determinant of political behavior consists of the voluntary acceptance of unenforceable values and codes, found in the political culture and forming the content of the political socialization process at all levels.

Political culture can also be *created* by individuals or groups in the process of adapting to new situations or of meeting the challenges of cultural conflict or social change. Such creation may constitute the deliberate or unconscious adoption of ideologies. It may be a living faith that grows from the confrontations of everyday life, the carefully reasoned philosophy of an intellectual ivory tower, or a mixture of both. As a complex symbolic system, moreover, political culture is shared, although not uniformly, by the members of a political system, and is at once a product and a determinant of the system of political interaction among the actors and roles that make it up. Like the general culture, also, political culture produces cultural objects of various degrees of reification, such as expressive symbols, political ideas, and political institutions, which may take on a life of their own. [4]

[3] Gabriel Almond, "Comparative Political Systems," *The Journal of Politics,* 18 (1956), 395.

[4] See Talcott Parsons, *The Social System.* New York: Free Press, 1964, pp. 45–53, 56–58, and chaps. 8 and 9. See also the extensive dis-

Some definitions of political culture

The individual actor in the political system, according to Talcott Parsons, partakes of its political culture in three basic ways: (a) by means of his subjective *interest* in it, or in terms of the gratification or denial of his needs; (b) by means of his *participation,* whether instrumental for achieving a particular purpose, purely expressive, or to commune with his fellow men; and (c) by means of his *value orientation,* or political beliefs.[5] All three of these involve several elements amenable to empirical public-opinion research, such as Almond and Verba carried on in their study of civic attitudes. Since all three reflect the political orientation and motivation of the individual actor, they depend on the first element, his (or her) *cognitive map* of the political system. Some people may have more accurate maps than others, and everybody is likely to project into his map at least a little of what he would like to see. There may even be severe distortions that will interfere with the gratification of one's interests or with one's political participation; these are likely to be rationalized with a convenient political belief system. A second common element is the *affective* (cathectic) *orientation*—a person's affects, feelings of loyalty or alienation, or ego involvement with political objects. A politically alienated person may be at the same time very well informed about politics. A third common element is the *evaluative process* by which the individual assigns "meaning" to political objects and events, and by which he may even have to choose between his interests and his values. Evaluation includes an actor's definition of the situation, his choice of instruments of action, and his style of using them, but not the action or interaction itself.

The civic culture study by Almond and Verba adapted these basic terms to the needs of studying the attitudes underlying patterns of democratic participation in Great Britain, West Germany, Italy, Mexico, and the United States. For this purpose, it focused particular attention on the psychological orientations of individual members of these polities toward (1) the political system in general, (2) the *input* activities of citizens, such as

cussion of human needs and situational determinants in James C. Davies, *Human Nature in Politics.* New York: Wiley, 1963.

[5] Cf. *The Social System,* pp. 57–58.

electoral and other participation, (3) the *output* activities of the government, such as financial aids or regulating activities, and (4) the self as an active participant in the political system. Varying combinations of these major variables would make up such archetypes of political culture as a parochial, subject, or participant orientation. A parochial orientation is very low in knowledge, feelings, and judgment toward all four of these objects and generally is typical of backward societies or of backward elements of modern societies, such as some young people, women, or rural populations. A subject orientation is equally low in its knowledge and involvement with input activities and with the self as a political participant, but well aware of the political system as such and with its output. This archetype is typified by civilizations in which a benevolent bureaucracy plays a major role. It is also represented in modern totalitarian societies, although in conjunction with well-staged rituals of massive participation. The participant orientation, finally, is defined by awareness and positive involvement with all four of these aspects of political culture. Actual "civic cultures," in any case, consist of varying combinations of the three archetypes.[6]

Sidney Verba in a later work defines political culture as "the subjective orientation to politics" or "the system of empirical beliefs, expressive symbols, and values which define the situation in which political action takes place."[7] He carefully seeks to separate what people believe about the interaction between political actors, citizens, parties, and government agencies from the interaction itself, which he excludes from the concept of political culture. The political behavior of the members of a system, in other words, may be affected by the beliefs they hold about the world of politics, but it is only the beliefs that constitute the element of political culture. On the other hand, since basic belief systems involve goals and norms of behavior, political culture is a system of internal controls[8] that determine such

[6] Gabriel Almond and Sidney Verba, *The Civic Culture*. Princeton, N.J.: Princeton University Press, 1963, chap. 1. See also the definitions in Gabriel Almond and Bingham Powell, *Comparative Politics*. Boston: Little, Brown, 1967, pp. 50–52, and Almond's first article on "Comparative Political Systems," *The Journal of Politics*, 18 (1956).

[7] Lucian W. Pye and Sidney Verba, *Political Culture and Political Development*. Princeton, N.J.: Princeton University Press, 1966, p. 513.

[8] See also Parsons, *The Social System*, p. 297, 348–383.

patterns of interaction as who votes for whom or how a given constitution or ideology comes to life once it is adopted by a given political culture. Verba is less concerned with such specific resultants than he is with the basic and fundamental beliefs—"the primitive beliefs," to speak with Milton Rokeach—about the nature and identity of a political system and the character of other political actors.[9] These beliefs and norms of political conduct must be held more or less in common in a political community if it is to deserve the name community and if a system of governmental institutions built upon it is to endure. A rupture of this basic consensus heralds civil unrest, secession, or revolution. Developing societies are very likely to lose their basic consensus in transition and may have to reestablish a new one with painstaking efforts. In a traditional or at least spatially relatively immobile society the local or tribal communities are so self-contained that they can afford to be each of homogeneous basic beliefs. With mobilization and development, however, their consensus is increasingly disrupted as members of one community move to another or as individuals from many different communities find themselves thrown together in an urban or industrial melting pot.

Lucian Pye's trail-blazing study of the political culture of Burma, beginning with the basic attitudes and orientations of various key groups in the society toward the political process, soon discovered the "human dimension" underlying the passage from colonialism to national sovereignty. Underneath the well-known objective difficulties of national development, which are the subject of political microanalysis, lay a microanalytical level of human aspirations, anxieties, and psychological difficulties connected with the process of acculturation to a more modern way of life. Pye's politicians and administrators deeply identified with the collective straining toward a new national identity. The fear of failure of the nation-building enterprise, however, became for them a crippling inhibition, undermining their activities in their appointed roles. The anxieties of the transitional collectivity translated themselves into an individual fear of innovation.

[9] See Milton Rokeach, *The Open and the Closed Mind* (New York: Basic Books, 1960), where the belief in one's own identity and in the nature of the environment constitute a faith so basic it is almost never even put in words, much less questioned.

As Pye's successful bridging of the gap between psychological microanalysis and convention macroanalysis [10] demonstrates, it is not only possible but desirable to link broad conceptual approaches, which have been the tradition of political science since Aristotle, with the study in depth of "the subjective orientation to politics." It is, in fact, the special merit of traditional concepts such as authority, liberty, legitimacy, and consent that they help to pinpoint the areas for inquiry into basic political attitudes. The understandable tendency of students to be fascinated by the discovery of new dimensions of our subject and to belittle what we already know should not prevent us from achieving a balanced view of political culture. The new knowledge is neither useful nor even conceivable without some of the old.

The political culture of a given country, say France, is a tremendously encompassing phenomenon and by no means a new subject of study. In the past it has been explored chiefly from the angle of broad concepts, such as "the idea of liberty" or "the idea of the state in France," and the results of such inquiry have often been incorporated into a macroanalytical frame of historical or anthropological study of France. The political-culture approach *adds* to this many further insights, which may indeed refine or make obsolete parts of earlier findings, as is the nature of all scientific research. To the traditional understanding of French ideas of liberty in the minds of what might turn out to be chiefly well-educated members of the French middle class, for example, may be added the preoccupation with economic security of the lower classes and a quantitative measure of how many Frenchmen have what kind of latent reservations about ideals that always used to be taken with a grain of salt anyway. An understanding of French political culture as a whole

[10] Lucian W. Pye, *Politics, Personality, and Nation-Building*. New Haven, Conn.: Yale University Press, 1962, p. xv, chaps. 1, 15–18, and *passim*. There have been critics of the psychocultural approaches such as Robert T. Holt and John E. Turner, *The Political Basis of Economic Development* (Princeton, N.J.: Van Nostrand, 1966), pp. 24–34, who question whether it can bridge the micro-macro gap or whether it can actually explain or predict collective behavior. It should be noted, however, that the psychocultural approach was never meant to be a substitute for, but rather a complement to, decision-making studies. No serious psychoculturist would propose to "reduce" collective political behavior to individual psychology.

includes both the old and the new knowledge, differentiated by social groups into political subcultures and integrated into a more meaningful picture whose parts are more systematically related to one another than before.

Traditional concepts

Ideologies How then do some of the traditional concepts in this area relate to the political-culture approach? Ideologies and other elaborate systems of political beliefs and values obviously are important, but they have traditionally been studied as political theories and expected to be logically sophisticated and consistent, perhaps even as elegant as a mathematical theorem. To the extent that ideologies have been originated or refined by particular philosophers, their examination has often been simply the study of the "great books." Students of European socialism, for example, would chiefly read and interpret the "great theorists" of the socialist tradition [11] or perhaps also the "great programs" of socialist parties, although the latter already implied a dilution of the the purity of ideological thought with the practical considerations of electoral politics. The political-culture approach takes the results of the traditional study as background for what it really wants to know—namely, what Socialist party leaders, members, and voters actually believe.

Socialists or adherents of other political creeds form communities of faith, so to speak. An empirical investigation of the attitudes and value orientations of such a given political subculture usually yields beliefs that are far from logical consistency and intellectual distinction. It may unearth underlying psychological motives or social compulsions [12] and show up unexpected links between the beliefs and one's perception of one's interest. Many people join parties not so much after a rational decision in favor of an ideology, but rather under the influence of family, friends, or fellow workers. And they may stay with a party more because of the familiar social atmosphere than because of the ideology as such. Investigation may also show the complex in-

---

[11] See, for example, Alexander Gray, *The Socialist Tradition*. London: Longmans, Green & Co., 1946. On ideology, see also the section on "Values and belief systems" later in this chapter.

[12] See especially Robert Lane's superb analysis in *Political Ideology*. New York: Free Press, 1962, secs. 5 and 6.

terplay of contradictory motivations and of political with religious or aesthetic beliefs.

Authority   Where does *authority* fit in, or *liberty,* or, in Thomas Macaulay's words, "the doctrine of divine right, which has now come back to us, like a thief from transportation, under the alias of *legitimacy*" (italics added). Authority and liberty are words and concepts hallowed by centuries of a proud intellectual tradition, and their bearing on the analysis of political cultures is still unquestioned. Legitimacy is about as old as the regimes restored under its banner after the French Revolution. The political-culture approach, again, is not content with a philosophical definition of legitimate authority or of liberty as such, but seeks to ascertain how the members of a given political culture actually conceive of offices and powers of authority or of the procedure by which a person acquires or acts with legitimate authority.

Widely differing sets of attitudes toward authority in its various forms—paternal, social, or governmental—are operative in different countries and settings and with different groups, not to mention different historical periods. The concept of authority held by many ordinary people may be illogical or even incapable of being spelled out. Yet even children and illiterates act unmistakably according to implicit ideas of who should have authority to do what sort of things with respect to whom. Even if they cannot readily describe these ideas, they seem to have clear notions of parental, age or sex-related, social stratification-related, governmental, and police authority to issue commands to them and expect compliance.[13] There is no reason why a research team could not interview a representative sample of any political culture or subculture and try to solicit responses to imaginary police actions or governmental acts. One would have to make

[13] Most of the literature dealing with these aspects was cited in Chap. 2, which covers political socialization. See also Samuel H. Beer and Adam B. Ulam, *Patterns of Government,* 2d ed. (New York: Random House, 1962), pp. 33–36, where the concept is used, albeit with some reservations as to methodological rigor. On the philosophical concept of authority, see Carl J. Friedrich, ed., *Authority.* New York: Atherton Press, 1958. One outstanding early example of empirical exploration of authority patterns is Margaret Mead, *Soviet Attitudes toward Authority.* New York: McGraw-Hill, for the Rand Corporation, 1951.

allowances, however, for possible differences between theoretical and actual responses.

The investigation of attitudes toward liberty, too, is a matter of operationalizing the complex aspects of one or several of the concepts of liberty used by various political theorists. It is not difficult to juxtapose individual self-interest and voluntary conformity so concretely that any adult citizen can communicate his idea of his personal, economic, cultural, or any other freedoms. Here too, there may be a gap between a person's theoretical and actual responses to a challenge.

National character　What, finally, is the place of the controversial notion of national character in the context of political culture? Continental Europeans born before the turn of this century frequently held strong and emotional beliefs about their own and other national identities, viewing national character as something so ingrained and inescapable that their feeling bordered on racialism and resembled current race phobias. Here obviously was a significant clue to their political attitudes and behavior. The interest of American social scientists in national character ran very high in the decade following World War II, evidently in reaction to the American encounter with many nations, both old and new, around the globe. In a way, the search for definitions of national character is as old and as widespread as have been the "nationalisms" of various peoples—as old as their anxious search to define their identities. And although many social scientists since the mid-1950s have become suspicious of the term itself and of its misuse to denote something genetic rather than learned, the materials and literature on national character are as useful today as before.

Individuals, during their process of socialization, take on the national identity as part of their own. Notions of identity, whether personal or collective, are somewhat difficult to ascertain and to compare in a rigorously empirical manner, because a person's sense of identity is so central and basic to his personality that he cannot say much about it except when it is threatened by a major crisis. Nevertheless, the subjective images of oneself and one's nation in politics are crucially important to an understanding of domestic and foreign policies. As we shall see later, there are many dimensions to a collective sense of identity, and all of them deserve careful analysis.[14]

Advantages of the political-culture approach

The advantages of the political-culture approach over the earlier concepts are three. First, political culture is capable of empirical verification and disproof, unlike the Platonic search for the only true ideology or for the "true nature" or "essence" of authority, legitimacy, liberty, or a given national character. Second, political-culture research can clearly demonstrate the changes likely, over a period of time, in popularly held notions of authority, liberty, or identity: there is nothing necessarily permanent about a particular nation's political culture. Such research may also show considerable differences among the groups or subcultures of a society and may enable us to compare cross-nationally and in neutral, quantitative terms what has hitherto been compared chiefly in qualitative terms. Third, political culture allows us to integrate these various, separate, and isolated concepts into our models of the political system—or at least into our conception of a particular political system.

DIMENSIONS OF POLITICAL CULTURE

There are many ways of approaching political culture as a system. One rather obvious method is derived from our discussions in Chapters 1 and 2. Political socialization, especially, involves political culture as the content of the learning process by which a child or immigrant becomes a full-fledged member of a political community. Erikson's eight ages of man, for example, are nearly all of immediate relevance to basic political attitudes.

Social trust

Erikson begins with *social trust,* from which he develops reflections on irrational hostility and breakdowns of trust and faith in the adult world. The sense of trust a person feels toward

---

[14] On the concept of national character in different social sciences, see also *National Character in the Perspective of the Social Sciences,* Annals of the American Academy of Political and Social Science, March 1967.

his social peers and fellow citizens very likely determines whether he is able and willing to cooperate with them for all kinds of social, economic, and political purposes. A total sense of social distrust, in fact, is pathological, and it would make impossible a personal role in social clubs, political parties, or any economic enterprise that involves selling or buying, not to mention credit. Democratic elections and all public administrative, judicial, and police activity are inconceivable without social trust. Any sort of formal education presupposes a large measure of mutual trust.

Patterns of social distrust Although a basic sense of social trust seems optimal for the functioning of society and politics, there are examples galore of patterns of social distrust. The most pervasive is probably the familistic pattern of confining social trust to the members of the family, often regardless of how some family members may misbehave. It is very human, although there may be little rhyme or reason in it, to forgive the abusive father, the negligent mother, or the thieving or scheming relatives what no person in his right mind would forgive a total stranger. The political consequences of hostility and distrust "beyond the foyer" are quite evident in such societies as that of southern France, southern Italy, India, or Burma. Another pervasive pattern, especially among people in modernizing societies who resent the more modern elements, is the particularistic confinement of social trust to members of the local community, including local social elites and political power holders. A phobia of strangers, "outside agitators," or simply "them" as the symbol of the hostile outside world is the logical complement of in-group trust. When such feelings are projected upon one's own nation, a feeling of trust for one's fellow citizens results together with xenophobia, or hostility toward foreigners—familiar hallmarks of nationalism.[15]

Finally, a pattern of social distrust underlies contemporary manifestations of race or other group prejudice. During the anti-

[15] A typical manifestation of this, as Hans Kohn has pointed out in his classic *The Idea of Nationalism*, is the *Fremdheitserlebnis*—the shock of recognition of strange languages or customs one may encounter among foreigners or foreign populations or, for that matter, among socially deviant subcultures of one's own people.

Japanese hysteria that led to the unjust internment of Japanese-Americans during World War II, one agitator verbalized his ethnic prejudice by suggesting: "every time one of their young men looks at a Caucasian girl he thinks of sexual intercourse." Thus he skillfully polarized the sentiments of his audience, evoking images of how members of the distrusted group might act. Life is full of ambiguous situations in which, on the basis of our trust in our fellow man, we simply assume without proof that he will engage in the best rather than the worst of a range of possible behavior. Parallel examples could easily be found in the code of discrimination against Negroes in the United States that Gunnar Myrdal has described [16] or in its current manifestations in real estate transactions, housing, and employment. A lack of trust for ethnic reasons or others, such as religion or sex, reduces one's chances of election to public office. Witness the very considerable, if slowly declining, portions of the American electorate who have told Gallup pollsters they would not vote for an "otherwise qualified presidential candidate" who was a Catholic, Jew, Negro, or woman.

There is, perhaps, no country on earth outside the idylls of a happy childhood in which social trust reigns unrestricted. In Great Britain, according to Richard Rose, "a sense of trust is pervasive in the political culture," [17] and *The Civic Culture* rather bears him out. Yet, even there, patterns of anti-Catholic, anti-Semitic, and anticolored prejudice, not to mention antifeminism, have played a major historical role to this day. The British system exhibits trust especially in the extraordinary way in which government and administration are run in the absence of constitutional restraints—on good faith and collegiality, so to speak. Englishmen show a very considerable amount of trust in their leaders as long as the latter abide by the ethical canons of responsible leadership and frequent collective consultation. Americans have inherited some of this trust, but with a strong and corrosive undercurrent of hostility toward the men they elect to

[16] Gunnar Myrdal, *An American Dilemma,* ed. by Arnold Rose, 2 vols. New York, 1944.

[17] Richard Rose, *Politics in England.* Boston: Little, Brown, 1964, p. 43. Rose also points to the basis in social trust of the old legal principle "the king can do no wrong," a statement probably applicable to all constitutional monarchies.

high office, and worse toward their hapless civil servants. It is worth noting that American hate-your-leaders cults and anti-bureaucratic phobias are often the stock-in-trade of the radical right, along with rank ethnic prejudices—all resulting evidently from a deep-seated lack of social trust. By way of contrast, the conservative right wing of such declining constitutional monarchies as Imperial Germany was possessed of a childlike faith in the integrity of its government, "under which things had always been clean, orderly, and proper," regardless of any evidence to the contrary. It was only after liberals, Catholics, and socialists took over the reins following the fall of the monarchy that the German Right discovered its total lack of trust in their political leadership, although still not in the civil service and judiciary.

Sense of autonomy

Erikson's *sense of autonomy*—an individualistic order with law and justice—is perhaps typical of the political cultures of Western societies. In the great democracies of the Western world, this sense of individual autonomy is basic to the entire edifice of electoral representation and individual rights, which we have enshrined in solemn bills of rights and hedged about with procedural safeguards. Our mechanistic conception of government with its separation of powers, judicial independence, and federal checks and balances, as contrasted to Swiss or British-style "government by committee," also shows a faith in the blessings of individual autonomy in high office. We need to be reminded of the habits of voting with communal unanimity and of arguing to consensus of many developing countries of Africa and Asia to realize the peculiar character of our individual decisions in the polling booth. And it takes the example of communist China, the Soviet Union, and Eastern Europe, not to mention the one-party states of the Third World, to make clear that not everybody in this world prefers a competitive system of politics. Actually, Western Europe also preferred organic, communal theories of society and government at one time in its traditional past. And there are still antiindividualistic vestiges and revivals of this thinking in European conservative thinking, in theories of "the state" and the "public interest," and especially in the British traditions.

Sense of initiative

Erikson's third item, *initiative,* restrained by a sense of guilt, can take on great political significance; for "political initiative" as an attribute of individuals in the mass spells participation, and it may also spell revolt against an evil regime. The Almond-Verba study, for example, asked its respondents what they would do if their local or national government made an unjust decision; the responses obtained were then tabulated. Such a research procedure perhaps too readily equates actual behavior with what people say they would do. Actually, the behavioral question plumbs existential depths that try men's souls. What is it that holds many people back from political action even when they clearly understand there is an evil to be stopped? Is it really only laziness or cowardice, or is it not more likely an individual sense of guilt, a fatalistic knowledge that one is a rather imperfect person in a rather imperfect world, that leaves the initiative to "the hypocrites"? A sense of political initiative, by comparison, would seem to require, if not hypocrisy, a well-rooted self-esteem.

Sense of industry

Item four, a *sense of industry* or technological ethos, appears to have little bearing on political culture. And yet, significant differences in underlying attitude here are linked to item seven, a *sense of generativity,* and can serve to distinguish stagnant or regressive political cultures from those that want to progress. A sense of industry and generativity in this respect would separate a traditional political orientation, or one that wants modern governors to be mere time servers who administer present holdings as cheaply as possible, from the attitude that government involves major tasks of social organization and construction for the benefit of future generations.

Capacity for intimacy; generativity; ego integrity

Erikson's sixth item, the *capacity for intimacy* or for giving of oneself, again together with *generativity* and the eighth item, *ego integrity,* helps to define leadership styles. Not only are a wide variety of styles preferred in different parts of the world, but frequently the leaders reflect merely the weaknesses of the followers.

It takes an unusual degree of political maturity to pick and follow a man of outstanding integrity for a leader. Instances where a people chooses the most qualified person are rare indeed, even though political theory has been preoccupied with the "rule of the best" (aristocracy) since the days of the Greeks, when the question of a rational choice of governors was first examined with care.

The selection or at least confirmation of leaders by some kind of democratic process and the maintenance of loyalty by democratic consent throw a penetrating light upon the limited capacity of men to choose well. Instead of being attracted by a capacity for intimacy they almost invariably prefer a leader who is aloof, a man of lonely and hence probably irresponsible decisions. Not able to maintain their respect in a situation of familiarity, they prefer an air of mystery, although the mystery may hide from their sight things they ought to know. And instead of seeking intimate personal contact with the persons of their choice in order to know them well, they are more than ever content with the artificial images created by public relations men. Instead of preferring leaders of true generativity and concern for future generations, the newly enfranchised nations, and old nations as well, often prefer leaders who only minister to their need for childlike dependency—father images and presumably wise old men. Or, worse yet, they pick men on horseback who appeal to their juvenile romanticism and secret longing for death—maniacal leaders who would ride their nations into a glorious catastrophe with no regard for the fate of future generations.

The sense of identity

The fifth item suggested by Erikson, *the sense of identity,* has been saved until now as a particularly crucial aspect of political culture. It is very hard to define in terms that can be applied from one political culture to the next. Since such topics as modal personality and collective identity are further explored in a section below, the present discussion will consider only the general relevance of the concept to the study of political culture.

Individual identity First, we should note that an individual sense of social and political identity is of particular interest to political scientists where it is lacking or deficient. Human beings appear to have an existential need to identify with an image of themselves that contains the following elements: (1) their place in history, in geography, and in the group world of society; (2) an appropriate role to play in the world—an ethic or a mission; and (3) a definite notion of the origin, nature, and purpose of their existence, such as only religion or an ideological faith can bestow. Young people approaching the threshold of puberty suddenly awaken to the world they live in and reach out to make it their own. If at this point their sense of identity has not already been well established by a gradual childhood socialization within the lap of a stable family and harmonious peer-group environment, they may experience an *identity crisis*. There is, perhaps, no better illustration than the identity problems of the black man in the United States. The current campaign to include recognizable black faces in various roles in the readers for the elementary grades is aimed at the crucial early school years. The drive to reinsert the missing great Negro scientists, pioneers, and civic leaders into American history texts on all levels, and to teach Negro history, aims at the preteens, teen-agers, and young adults. All of these measures are designed to do what black nationalists, Black Muslims, and the more sensible "black power" advocates have been trying to do for decades: to instill a sense of identity of which black people of all ages can be proud in place of the dismal, negative image of darkies, plantation slaves, or menial laborers.

Is it possible to be a person without an identity, a man without a shadow? It is probably inconceivable, this side of sanity, for a human being to be entirely without a sense of who he or she is. But if we restrict the meaning more closely to a sense of social and political identity, admitting the likely presence of gnawing doubts about one's identity at deeper personality levels, we are very close to what the *identity crisis* means in a political context. There is a Grimms fairy tale about a little girl who was so impatient she could never wait for anything. Finally, a good spirit presented her with a button that, whenever she turned it, would make the time go by in a hurry. A flick of her wrist and supper time came. Another twist and it was Christmas or her next birthday. Another turn and she was a teen-ager. One more and she was getting married. And a few turns more and she had become a mother, her children had grown, and she was an old woman whose life had hurried by she knew not how, because life consists of waiting periods of maturation, of moratiums that have to be endured if not enjoyed.

A well-established sense of identity gives a person the strength and the peace of mind to live through the moratoriums of his life with an abiding sense of purpose and self-realization. The teen-ager or young adult desperately groping for an identity may withdraw from political activity into a sense of nonbeing or hide his "nobodiness" behind feverish activity in hobbies or aimless pursuits. But he may also feel driven into a wild political activism, rebellion, or dedication to extremist causes. He may feel an urge to engage in violent action in what he sees as a just war, or in a riot or a "just revolution." Activism and fighting will lend a strong, if temporary, sense of purpose to a mind torn by disorientation.

Collective identity   Also of prime relevance to the study of political culture is a sense of collective identity. When young individuals step by step become full-fledged members of a given pluralistic community, they tend to build large parts of their self-image from the identity elements of the various groups with which they identify. It is these aspects of individual identity, rather than the bottomless pit of individual idiosyncrasies, that we are looking for. It means something to a person when he says "I am an American" or "I am a Frenchman," especially vis-à-vis other countries. Saying so, among other things, connotes a sense of identification with one's land, fellow nationals, and the history of one's nation. Sometimes, for the sake of a sense of national identity, it may be necessary to invent or embellish the national history or to reinterpret it in ideological or religious terms of "a mission." A person may also identify himself with a particular locality, region, or neighborhood. In ethnic America (which is both a state of mind and a period of American history) one expresses a distinct sense of identity in saying "I am a Polish-American and a Catholic" or "I am of Japanese descent." In a society of sharp class divisions and class consciousness, there is meaning in being a worker and trade unionist, proud of what one does and stands for.

Last but not least, there is a strong sense of vocational identity in many European, Middle Eastern, and Asian countries historically steeped in the pride of craftsmanship, and increasingly in the United States. As a man may feel "called to the priesthood," all kinds of trades and professions including the professional military can become "callings"—harbors of worthwhile activity during the biggest moratorium, adulthood—that are preferred to the stormy life of an American jack-of-all trades. There is a kind of salvation at times transcending all other group identities, even nationalism, in being a conscientious doctor, scientist, or carpenter. Even the professional military of advanced countries still lives with the rudiments of an earlier code of military chivalry and the privileges and obligations of the officer ranks that transcend national identities among combatants in war.

Relative importance of identity elements   A third aspect is the composition of the sense of identity of a given population. With respect to the group identities that make up the individual's knowledge of who he is, it is worth knowing how important a role each identity element plays in a given society. Their relative strength may indeed make it a society of prominent ethnic, geographic, social-class, or vocational distinctions. Since we live in a world of nation-states, moreover, it is particularly noteworthy how strongly a sense of national identity is present. The "new nations" of the Third World, in particular, have a difficult time developing a sense of national identity, unless they are among the lucky few, such as Thailand, Ethiopia, or Morocco, that already have a well-established identity of long standing. With the older, established nation-states, it is just as important that countries such as England and France established their identity centuries ago, whereas modern Germany, Belgium, and Italy are still trying to live down their periods of national unification. *Fatta l' Italia, bisogna fare gli Italiani* (with Italy a reality now, we need to create Italians). In polycommunal new states such as India and other colonial creations, the national sense of identity can barely survive the centrifugal pressure of the linguistic subnational identities. The internal turmoil and disorientation of social mobilization, in particular, make a strong sense of national identity crucial to effective and healthy social and political development.

Development of new identities   This brings us to the fourth aspect of a sense of identity, which deals with the development of new identities. Our discussion thus has moved from the lack of an individual or collective sense of identity over the structural question of its varying composition to questions of content. The passing of traditional society requires the development of a new sense of individual and collective identity, a modern sense of who we are and where we are going. As the reader will recall from Chapter 1, this modern sense of identity is very difficult to come by, even after the shell of traditional culture has been shattered by momentous changes in the role of the individual, family life, social stratification, the economy, and the cultural system. There is usually a long transitional period during which old and new ways of life grapple with each other, rival faiths of salvation work at cross-purposes, and intelligent people are suspended in a limbo of indecision, understanding nearly every alternative and believing in none. For a modernizing society, this too is a prolonged crisis of identity, and the greater the resistance to modernity, the deeper the sloughs of despondent cultural pessimism and the more desperate the feeling of disorientation. Sometimes it takes a total breakdown or overwhelming challenge and defeat from abroad to break the deadlock of cultural development and to set free the birth of a new sense of collective identity. For the new identity is possible only upon repudiation and destruction of the old identity. Like Erikson's young man Luther, individuals and nations have to go through painful crisis and symbolic self-destruction before their rebirth in a new, "Protestant" faith becomes possible.

There are many telling examples of these processes in recent European history. The paroxysm of the French Revolution lasted twenty-five years, while riot and insurrection took turns with major reforms, relapses, and the establishment of dictatorship, both Jacobin and Napoleonic. Civil war and military rule were the beginning; the end was an international crusade to spread the blessings of the French Revolution all over the Continent, until a mighty alliance of foreign powers broke the back of the revolutionary Empire and restored the old rulers everywhere. But the immense bloodshed and waste of material and spiritual effort were not all in vain. They gave birth to a new sense of French identity, a thoroughly modern identity, which in spite of decades of further setbacks eventually came to dominate modern France. The important role of revolutionary ideology and violence in this process will be discused later in this chapter.

Another example of the painful modernization of a sense of identity is Germany, where the initial identity problems of national unification and of modernization were temporarily buried under a reinforced pseudotraditional identity of aristocracy, Empire, and military prowess. While it made great concessions to the need for economic, scientific, and administrative modernity, Imperial Germany—in a twist quite characteristic of modernizing nations—fancied that it could modernize "in its own way," especially without Western-style parliamentary democracy. This pseudotraditional identity collapsed in World War I, and there followed three decades of a violent identity crisis, superseded only in the last decades by the new collective identities that developed in East and West Germany.

The development of a new political identity in a nation is closely linked with the degree to which the political socialization of the new generations is reasonably uniform and coordinated. In a country that enjoys long periods of gradual, continuous development, harmonious and convergent patterns of socialization may well make for the growth and stability of the sense of national identity. The earlier the first four stages of political development have been completed—one stage at a time and with long intervals in between—the more settled can be the sense of identity over the centuries. But where there has not been sufficient time, and where unsettling crises and upheavals have intervened, all-out efforts of indoctrination are often necessary to establish a new identity. Overwhelming collective socializing experiences such as major wars and revolutions, too, may create a common sense of identity where there was none before; witness the example of the "revolutionary tradition" in Mexico.[18]

COMPARATIVE POLITICAL-CULTURE RESEARCH

One way of gauging the measurable dimensions of political cultures is to examine the range of questions asked in relevant cross-national research. A number of the recent studies discussed at

[18] See Robert Scott in Pye and Verba, *Political Culture and Political Development*, pp. 330–395.

the end of Chapter 1 are pertinent here. We shall limit ourselve
at this point to some comments on the Almond-Verba study o
democratic political cultures and on further research not men
tioned elsewhere in this book.

What makes *The Civic Culture* so valuable a study is th
ingenious way in which theories link hard data, such as the leve
of education of respondents, with the soft data measuring atti
tudes and orientations. Most earlier cross-national comparison
(such as those of Daniel Lerner or Seymour M. Lipset) are rela
tively crude in that they cannot fully explain why some countrie
may rank higher than others on a scale of hard data of moderni
zation, but lower on a scale of democratic character. Almond
and Verba actually attempted to measure the psychologica
orientations and then, with the help of a knowledge of nationa
histories and sociological and anthropological literature, to relate
them to the hard indices—although they could easily be faulted
for not having gone far enough into the idiosyncratic difference
of each of their five nations. In any case, it is worthwhile to take
a look at some of the specific measurements attempted by the
study.

Measurements attempted by Almond and Verba

In researching the cognitive patterns of their respondents, fo
example, the designers of the *Civic Culture* study skillfully broke
down the political awareness of their respondents into (1) aware
ness of government output at the local and national levels, and
judgment of how much of an effect it has on one's daily life and
on conditions in general; (2) degree of attention to reports in
the various media on political campaigns; (3) attention to ac
counts of public affairs; and (4) ability to name party leader
and governmental ministries. Since it is difficult to give much
depth to standard questions, additional probing with smalle
samples was used to elicit more elaborate explanations, which
fleshed out, for example, the orientations of "parochials," largely
unaware of government and politics, and of "alienates," con
vinced of injustice and corruption in government.

Further questions sought to ascertain the feelings of re
spondents toward government and politics by asking (1) o
what aspects of their nation respondents were proud; (2) wha
treatment they expected from the bureaucracy and police; (3)

how often they talked politics with other people; and (4) how free they felt to discuss political and governmental affairs. Still further questions assessed their sense of civic competence by asking (5) how active the ordinary man should be in his community; (6) whether respondents felt satisfaction about the act of voting; and (7) what respondents would do to influence local or national government in case of an unjust governmental action. Almond and Verba also attempted to measure, among other things, the degree of social trust or distrust toward other people, their respondents' preferred leisure activities,[19] and their membership in voluntary organizations. The *Civic Culture* study obviously provides a lengthy checklist of measurable items that can indicate important dimensions of the political cultures of these five democracies, even though it hardly exhausts the subject.

Selected research examples

Of the many other pieces of recent cross-national political-culture research, a selected few will illustrate the great variety of appropriate studies going on, although rarely under the label of political culture. First of all, the systematic study of within-nation differences should be mentioned, since true comparative study need not confine itself to being "cross-national" in that sense, and also because within-nation differences are an essential part of international comparison. *The Civic Culture* placed very little stress on within-nation differences except in relationship to partisan identification and to differentiation of groups by labels, such as "parochial." There are many different kinds of studies of within-nation differences; we shall discuss a few representative of geographic, age, and partisan groupings and offer some random remarks about other distinctive groupings.

"The eight Spains"   An excellent example of the study of within-nation differences is a comparison of "the eight Spains" by Juan

---

[19] The object was to see whether respondents preferring "outgoing" leisure activities would also be politically more active and interested. See also Verba, "Political Participation and Strategies of Influence: A Comparative Study," *Acta Sociologica*, 6 (1962), 22–42, which relates the subjective sense of political competence of respondents in the five nations to their patterns and strategies of political participation.

J. Linz and Amando de Miguel [20] on the basis of aggregate data. Linz and Miguel specifically emphasize how an international comparison, say of Spain and Italy, can be made far more accurate by breaking down each of the countries into smaller units. The researcher then can hold constant such modernization indices as the degree of industrialization or urbanization and thus tease out of his data the true differences between Spanish and Italian social development or political attitudes, an operation impossible with direct cross-polity comparison. The authors mention as examples of questions for regional comparison varying perceptions of social class by people of similar occupation in regions of differing patterns of social inequality or rate of proletarianization, varying density of voluntary associations among regions of differing economic development or cultural traditions, varying attitudes of businessmen according to whether they reside in developed or underdeveloped regions of Spain, and varying elite-recruitment patterns among regions differing in social structure. The differences among regions in Spain and their past and present desire for maximal autonomy, it should be noted, are extreme and have been the source of some of the crises of recent Spanish history. The article on "the eight Spains" lists about ten categories, including economic development, social structure, language and cultural traditions, religious climate, social participation, media exposure, political traditions, modal personality, values and norms, and family patterns. The combinations vary from secular but traditional Andalusia to religiously devout and highly industrialized Basque country. The "eight Spains" that emerge with distinctive sociocultural character have labels such as "bourgeois Spain," "gentry Spain," "gentry-in-transition Spain," and "proletarian Spain."

Communist leadership in northern and southern Italy   Another fruitful angle of within-nation comparison of political culture [21]

[20] Juan J. Linz and Amando de Miguel, "Within-Nation Differences and Comparisons: The Eight Spains," in Richard Lawrence Merritt and Stein Rokkan, eds., *Comparing Nations*. New Haven, Conn.: Yale University Press, 1966, pp. 267–319. See also Linz's "An Authoritarian Regime: Spain" in Erik Allardt and Yrjö Littunen, eds., *Cleavages, Ideologies and Party Systems* (Helsinki: Academic Bookstore, 1964), pp. 291–341, where the author discusses the significance of unequal socioeconomic development in the political integration of Spain.

[21] See also the many other excellent articles on within-nation dif-

is taken by Sidney Tarrow in comparing the composition of the Communist party (PCI) leadership in southern and northern Italy. Here, along with the regional differences, elite-recruitment patterns are compared within the same radical left party. The differences Tarrow found among the provincial party leaders in the north and south were striking indeed. The majority of the northerners joined the PCI from the World War II Resistance movement, while the strongest element of the southern province leaders came either from the labor or peasant movements or from a college or professional background. In terms of family background, too, nearly two thirds of the northerners were of lower or lower-middle-class origin, while the southerners came in nearly the same proportion from the middle and upper classes and included twice as many professional people as the northerners. The upshot of the comparison was clearly that even the proletarian PCI has to cater to the different political cultures of north and south. In southern Italian society, middle-class intellectuals, lawyers, and doctors still dominate radical political life, while the predominance of functionaries of trade unions, cooperatives, and the Catholic and other mass organizations colors northern Italian politics.[22]

Varieties of comparative studies Many comparative party studies could be named here also, both studies of the attitudes and orientations within different parties of the same country and studies of the differing orientations and ideologies of analogous parties in different countries.[23] Excellent comparative studies are based, for example, on "electoral geography" as pioneered by André Siegfried, attributing different configurations of political culture to the different regions and localities of a country. Many surveys compare the ideologies and attitudes, say, of Conservatives, Liberals, and Labourites in Great Britain or of the mem-

---

ferences in Merritt and Rokkan, *Comparing Nations,* and in Allardt and Littunen, *Cleavages, Ideologies, and Party Systems.*

[22] See Sidney Tarrow, *Peasant Communism in Southern Italy.* New Haven, Conn.: Yale University Press, 1967, chap. 9.

[23] For a detailed discussion see Chap. 5. For surveys of ideologies in a comparative context, see especially Paul Sigmund, ed., *Ideologies of the Developing Nations.* New York: Praeger, 1962, and William H. Friedland and Carl G. Rosberg, eds., *African Socialism.* Stanford, Calif.: Stanford University Press, 1964.

bership and faithful voters of the different parties of India. Outstanding comparative studies of socialist parties and the labor movement in many countries bring out such revealing information as that the dues-paying membership of socialist parties is only about 100,000 in France, but 150,000 in the Netherlands with a population only one-fifth that of France. The comparative study of communist parties in the Soviet Union, China, the communist satellites, and countries of the Free World can hardly help exposing considerable differences in attitudes and ideologies, revealing the impact of national political cultures on what was meant to be a highly disciplined and uniform movement everywhere.[24] Some comparative historical works on fascist and right-wing movements and left-wing intellectuals in the period between the world wars, too, are steeped in the kind of attitudinal and biographical awareness without which comparative study would miss the "human dimension." [25]

There are also penetrating studies of the political orientation and ideologies of other distinctive groups of society. Among the best researched are trade-union movements in many countries of the world.[26] And there is a growing literature on the

[24] See, for example, Robert A. Scalapino, ed., *The Communist Revolution in Asia.* Englewood Cliffs, N.J.: Prentice-Hall, 1965, especially chap. 1, and Alvin Z. Rubinstein, ed., *Communist Political Systems.* Englewood Cliffs, N.J.: Prentice-Hall, 1966. Also R. V. Burks, *The Dynamics of Communism in Eastern Europe.* Princeton, N.J.: Princeton University Press, 1961, and Luis E. Aguilar, ed., *Marxism in Latin America.* New York: Knopf, 1968, as well as Gabriel Almond's *The Appeals of Communism.* Princeton, N.J.: Princeton University Press, 1954.

[25] See, for example, Eugen Weber and Hans Rogger, *The European Right.* Berkeley, Calif.: University of California Press, 1964; Francis L. Carsten, *The Rise of Fascism.* Berkeley, Calif.: University of California Press, 1967; and Ernst Nolte, *The Three Faces of Fascism.* New York: Holt, Rinehart and Winston, Inc., 1966 (first German edition 1963). Also Walter Laqueur and George L. Mosse, eds., *The Left-Wing Intellectuals between the Wars, 1919–1939.* New York: Harper Torchbook, 1966, and, by the same editors, *International Fascism, 1920–1945.* New York: Harper Torchbook, 1966.

[26] See, for example, Adolf Sturmthal, *The Tragedy of European Labor* and *Unity and Diversity in European Labor.* New York: Free Press, 1957; Walter Galenson, *Trade Union Democracy in Western Europe.* Berkeley, Calif.: University of California Press, 1961; and Bruce Millen, *The Political Role of Labor in Developing Countries.* Washington, D.C.: Brookings, 1964.

ideology of youth movements and student rebellion,[27] peasants and peasant movements, white-collar workers and their organizations,[28] public employees or civil servants and their associations,[29] and last but not least the comparative literature on the professional military.[30] Largely lacking is a literature on the political views of priests, scientists, journalists, and many other groups.

Most of these studies, to be sure, are not exclusively or even chiefly devoted to an understanding of the political culture of a given subculture but rather touch upon it along with many other aspects, such as the history, organization, or setting in which a given group finds itself. To pick out the elements of political culture obviously requires a clear idea of what political culture is, both in the individual mind and among masses of people. It is not so much the history of a group, but how the group *interprets* its history; not so much the role it plays, but what role *it thinks* it ought to play; not the situation in which it finds itself or the nature of the system of which it is a part, but its *assessment* of the situation and its *image* of and *preference* in the nature of the political system.

Studies of cultural "rules of the game"   Another kind of comparative study of political cultures concentrates on what John Fisher has called "the rules of the game of politics"—in the American case, the norms underlying pluralistic bargaining. To form a ruling majority in a society of many distinct groups, it is necessary to bring about by compromises and concessions a mighty coalition of groups. A candidate running for election,

[27] See also, for example, Lewis Feuer, *The Conflict of Generations.* New York: Basic Books, 1968.

[28] See, for example, Sturmthal, ed., *White Collar Trade Unions.* Urbana, Ill.: University of Illinois, 1966.

[29] For an example from a vast literature, see Joseph La Palombara, ed., *Bureaucracy and Political Development.* Princeton, N.J.: Princeton University Press, 1963.

[30] See, for example, Samuel E. Finer, *The Man on Horseback.* New York: Praeger, 1962; Morris Janowitz, *The Professional Soldier.* New York: Free Press, 1960, and his *The Military in the Political Development of the New Nations.* Chicago: University of Chicago Press, 1964; John J. Johnson, ed., *The Role of the Military in Underdeveloped Countries.* Princeton, N.J.: Princeton University Press, 1962; and Samuel P. Huntington, *The Soldier and the State.* New York: Random House, 1964.

furthermore, must avoid antagonizing any of a number of powerful "veto groups." Parties often try to play the multiethnic game,
representing each important ethnic group with a candidate on
their ticket.

Many other such "games" are played in various societies,
some so intricate and with so many overlapping patterns that it
is very hazardous to offer any one generalization for a whole
system. One of the oldest games is that of the hierarchy of status
and age, which simply subordinates "lower classes" to their
"superiors" and young people to their elders. Other authoritarian
patterns may resolve disagreements by deference to religious
authority or to an establishment claiming superior intelligence.
The latter kind of oligarchic game is quite typical of most Western European societies. In Great Britain, for example, elements
of traditional authority and the "intelligent establishment" are
mixed but enjoy like deference. The authoritarianism of communist regimes is a subspecies of such an establishment, the
Communist party, which claims the authority of superior intelligence about the social and economic process of development,
backing up this authority with brute force when necessary. All
of these hierarchic or oligarchic systems, as far as they are the
popularly accepted *modus operandi,* are noncompetitive in character.

By way of contrast there is the "competitive game," described by Max Weber and Joseph A. Schumpeter as typical of
contemporary civilizations. Here two or more rival political elites
compete with promises and specific favors for the votes of the
electorate. Perhaps derived from and obviously reinforced by
certain patterns of economic competition, this game may well
figure significantly in the thinking of politicians and parties during election campaigns. Many voters, likewise, may pay tribute
to the images of gamesmanship and fair play, regarding an election as a "horse race." Such notions, however, may coexist in
their minds with hierarchic notions of deference to authority or
limits upon competition. Their actual political behavior may
vacillate or attempt a compromise among the contradictory
notions.

On a more refined and yet broader level, Herbert J. Spiro
suggested comparative "styles of conflict resolution" and decision making. Such styles include bargaining and compromise

among various purposive material interests, violence, reliance on an ideology, and reliance on legal mechanisms for the settlement of social disputes. The latter two, "ideologism" and "legalism," describe very common Western approaches; like all such set procedures they have their pitfalls. Legalism has a way of snagging fundamental political decision-making processes in the coils of rigid legal procedures. Ideologism originates in a historical crisis of participaticn when new groups of society, such as the bourgeois middle class or the working classes, find themselves barred from the legitimate sharing of power.[31]

Styles of opposition   Styles of opposition have also formed the framework for the highly imaginative comparative political-culture research of Robert A. Dahl.[32] Dahl is interested in the "characteristic patterns" of consensus or cleavage within a given political and governmental structure. He characterized political oppositions in the United States as usually "not very distinctive," lacking organizational cohesion, and of varying oppositional strategies. Equally intent on winning elections and on logrolling and pressure-group tactics, they generally prefer to work through one or both major parties, as their goals are limited and, until recently, did not "challenge the major institutions or the prevailing American system of beliefs." The two parties are highly competitive in national elections, yet their members in Congress tend to cooperate as well as compete. For all of these items, counterexamples abroad will readily come to mind, such as the distinctive, well-organized communist counterculture in Italy, which opposes the government chiefly in elections and propaganda, professes goals that fundamentally challenge Italian institutions and prevailing beliefs, and generally refuses to cooperate with the government in parliament.

In reviewing the patterns of opposition of ten Western democracies discussed in his book, Dahl specified as the most important variables (1) the organizational cohesion, (2) competitiveness, (3) distinctiveness, (4) goals and (5) strategies of the opposition, and (6) the site for the encounter between gov-

---

[31] Herbert J. Spiro, *Government by Constitution*. New York: Random House, 1959, chaps. 13–15.

[32] In Robert A. Dahl, *Political Oppositions in Western Democracies*. New Haven, Conn.: Yale University Press, 1966.

ernment and opposition. Upon this basis he developed categories of systems distinguished by (a) the internal cohesion of the parties, rather than two-party and multiparty systems alone; (b) a competitiveness scale running from strictly competitive, cooperative-competitive, and coalescent-competitive, to strictly coalescent; and (c) a scale of goals ranging from pure office-seeking and pressure-group goals over limited structural opposition (reformism) to major structural opposition predicated on complete political or social reform or violent revolution.

Dahl also inquired into such causes for a particular opposition pattern as constitutional structure, electoral systems, widely shared political-cultural premises, particular subcultures, past grievances, socioeconomic differences, patterns of cleavage and consensus, and the extent of polarization of opinion. All of these, of course, are related to political culture as we defined it. On his third point, political-cultural premises, he considered such by-now-familiar variables as the orientations to (1) the political system, such as allegiant or alienated, (2) other people, trustful or distrustful, (3) collective action, cooperative or individualistic-noncooperative, and (4) problem solving, such as empiricopragmatic or rationalistic.[33]

Orientation toward problem solving The last point, orientation toward problem solving, has long been featured in the literature comparing Western democracy with European authoritarian systems.[34] Actually, the distinction is not as easy to draw as it might seem. It is quite true that American democracy, for example, has

[33] Dahl, *Political Oppositions in Western Democracies*, chaps. 2, 11, and 12.

[34] See, for example, William Ebenstein, *Today's Isms*, 5th ed. Englewood Cliffs, N.J.: Prentice-Hall, 1967, or Franz Neumann, *The Democratic and the Authoritarian State*. New York: Free Press, 1957. But compare also, Herbert McCloskey, "Consensus and Ideology in American Politics," *American Political Science Review*, 58 (June 1964), 361–379, and Philip E. Converse and Georges Dupeux, "Politicization of the Electorate in France and the United States," *Public Opinion Quarterly*, 26 (Spring 1962), 1–23, two classic attempts to dispel misconceptions about the nature of American politics. On Great Britain, see especially Stanley Rothman, "Modernity and Tradition in Britain," *Social Research*, Autumn 1961, pp. 297–320. An excellent source on French attitudes toward problem solving is Michel Crozier, *The Bureaucratic Phenomenon*. Chicago, Ill.: University of Chicago Press, 1964.

always tended toward a nonideological, empirical pragmatism in the popular approaches to social and economic problems. Even this statement deserves modification; one should point out the considerable resistance to compromise among the many distinct groups at the grass-roots level as well as the extraordinary willingness to compromise principles in, say, the selection of presidential candidates and national party platforms. The British attitude toward political problem solving may be pragmatic and empirical. It is hardly as nonideological and unencumbered with social-class prejudices as that of American politicians. French problem-solving attitudes tend to be determined by sharp ideological and social-class patterns as well as by the French tradition of rational empiricism. French politicians take a dim view of British-style "muddling through," yet they admit the possibility of doubt and error and have a sharp eye for human frailty. A rationalistic attitude can be skeptical, empirical-experimental, or ideological in the religious or political sense.

Ideological attitudes toward problem solving, again, can be classified along scales running from high commitment to low commitment (ideology mixed with other motives) and also ranging from instrumental over consummatory to expressive. An instrumental attitude is oriented toward achieving the ideological goal by various means judged according to their effectiveness. A consummatory attitude makes a kind of religious cult of activities conforming to the ideology and of acts of homage to its ideals or symbols. An expressive attitude differs from the consummatory primarily in the depth of commitment. Neither is much oriented toward actually solving practical problems, which marks them both off from a modern achievement orientation. If they were typified by two revolutionary movements, the consummatory movement might establish a postrevolutionary religious or ideological state dedicated to the worship of its faith. The expressively oriented movement would simply go back to its everyday pursuits of eating, drinking, and making love after it had blown off steam with the revolutionary symbols borrowed from the ideology in question.

Mass versus elite culture   A final aspect of comparative political-culture research to concern us here is the inquiry into the relationships between a system's mass political culture and its elite political culture, and between political culture and development. Both were the subject of sophisticated comparison under the editorial guidance of Lucian W. Pye and Sidney Verba. A major finding of the study was the marked division of mass and elite political culture in even the most democratic countries. As Pye points out, both deserve detailed attention, although it is not always easy to learn much about the views of the masses of people in developing countries without public opinion polls. The relationship and interaction between mass and elite cultures can help us classify systems. In the more traditional systems, such as Ethiopia, India, and Mexico, elite political cultures tend to be completely separate subcultures; whereas in a country like Great Britain the process of political socialization for the elite includes socialization in the mass culture as well.[35]

Political culture and development   The survey also discovered patterns of fusion and of separation between modern and traditional elements in a modernizing society. In countries such as India and Egypt, mass culture tends to be traditional and elite culture modern, or rather of the type of the "marginal man," who has one foot in the past and one in the future. Nevertheless, the trend seems to be toward a fusion of traditional and modern, either by modernization of a part of mass culture (India) or by what Leonard Binder has called the "integrative revolution" in Egypt—the links established between the urban modernization elite and new rural leadership. Richard Rose's work on Great Britain centers around the theme of fusion of traditional and modern elements, the felicitous habit of always putting the new wine in familiar old bottles or in Rose's phrase the "traditionally modern political culture" of Britain that has sustained development. The development of Japan and Turkey, too, has been relatively fusional in their adaptation of new ways to old. By contrast, the discongruous socialization processes of countries like Italy or Mexico tend to create isolated fragments of rival traditionalisms and modernisms, each locked in its own subculture. Or they may result in a pervasive feeling of alienation and

[35] Lucian W. Pye and Sidney Verba, eds., *Political Culture and Political Development*. Princeton, N.J.: Princeton University Press, 1965, pp. 15–17.

cynicism, because the various cultural "messages" received from different agents of socialization contradict one another.[36]

POLITICAL VIOLENCE AND REVOLUTION

Orientations toward political violence, too, belong among the subjects of the study of political culture. Charges and counter-charges resound in current American politics as to whether American political culture is inclined toward violence and as to who is responsible for the recurrent outbreaks in our time. But the charge can be broadened to include all Western societies and perhaps the entire modern political tradition, whether we like the thought or not. Quite apart from the understandable reluctance of many Americans to acknowledge a violent strain in American culture and society, powerful social taboos also obstruct a clear-eyed view of this issue. All human beings living in social communities would much rather brand the use of violence as deviant behavior than to admit it as a basic feature of social existence. And yet unquestionably the notion of violence lies at the roots of modern individual and collective life and is far from obsolete or archaic, much as we may regret it. Let us take a closer look at some of the theories rationalizing the use of violence in Western political cultures.

The right to revolution

Modern Western political philosophy pays homage to the notion of violence most clearly in the doctrine of the *right to revolution* and in what seems at first blush its very antithesis: the writings of the antirevolutionary political philosopher Thomas Hobbes. Hobbes begins with the intellectual fiction of the individual in the "state of nature," which is a state of total and murderous anarchy, a "war of every man against every man." Man's instinct of self-preservation, or his fear of violent death, induces him to leave the isolated state of nature for organized society and to put himself under its rules (social contract) and under an absolute sovereign. It is one of the chief functions of the sovereign to protect the lives of his subjects against violence, and as long as he

[36] See Myron Weiner, Leonard Binder, Richard Rose, Robert Ward, Dankwart Rustow, Joseph La Palombara, and Robert Scott in Pye and Verba, eds., *Political Culture and Political Development*.

does so the subjects owe him unquestioning allegiance. Only when the sovereign ruler fails to protect them against foreign invasion or when he sends his bailiff to arrest them for trial and possible execution, are subjects free from all bonds of obligation and at liberty to defend their lives as best they can.[37] Society and the state, in other words, are established principally to contain the individual and collective capacity for violence, as one would contain the destructive power of fire within the hearth. Violence by no means disappears in the process, but is put to presumably beneficial use by the agencies of society and government.

Hobbes's formulation was perhaps somewhat extreme and one-sided. Other philosophers (such as John Locke) and statesmen (such as the authors of the American Declaration of Independence) shared his basic assumptions about radical individualism, the hypothetical "state of nature," and the chief rationale for maintaining a society and government. But they were careful not to take away all the residual rights of the individual to defend his interests, violently if necessary. Thus, unlike Hobbes, who preferred to sign these rights over to the sovereign, and unlike earlier writers who had carefully qualified the right to revolution, the Declaration of Independence said in ringing language in 1776: ". . . whenever any Form of Government becomes destructive to these ends, it is the Right of the People to alter or abolish it, and to institute new Government. . . ." It is unlikely that the authors of the Declaration of Independence expected to accomplish such altering or abolition of the existing government without force. The clear implication, spelled out elsewhere in the Declaration and later also in the French and American bills of rights, was that the modern individual (always thought of as a male) had certain rights, and he was not going to be pushed around or deprived of his rights without throwing life and limb into the scales against the organized force of the state, which likewise asserted its sovereign right to enforce obedience.

The state's monopoly of violence

The practice of modern government bears out the evidence from Western philosophy, at home and abroad. The modern state, in

[37] See *Leviathan* and George H. Sabine, *A History of Political Theory,* 3d ed. New York: Holt, Rinehart and Winston, Inc., 1961, chap. 23.

Europe as elsewhere, has indeed acquired what sociologists like to call "a monopoly of violence." Legal scholars used to define the nature of sovereignty and of a duly passed law by pointing to the right of the state to enforce its will. With the exception of the United States, nearly all civilized governments insist on their exclusive control of all military weapons of any consequence and have outlawed private armies of any sort. Individuals, private groups, and corporations are specifically enjoined from any use of violence or from taking the law into their own hands. People who commit acts of violence are subjected to police arrest, court trial, and the penalties of the law. The police and the army are the sole legitimate guardians of the fires of violence, which implies not only their controlling or preventing the violence of others, but also their *deliberate use of violence* in the interest of government and state.

In the growth process of the young, too, violence of sorts is employed in many cultures to enforce discipline, either by threats or by actual physical punishment. But there is also the popular assumption that at a particular point a young man or woman is too big to be disciplined in this fashion, often for the unacknowledged reason that the fully grown young person may be capable of defending himself against the threatened violence. In many cultures, there are specific initiation rites in which the young man has to show his physical prowess. By that time, of course, he may also be quite ready to conform to the mores of society or to listen to the voices of persuasion. But it is worth noting that his adult role began, so to speak, when he was able and willing to use his physical capacity for violence, because later on there may well come a time when that same mature man refuses to accept from his government or police a similar command laced with the threat of violence. The current student rebellions all over the world characteristically began, to quote one of the Berkeley rebel leaders, "when we learned we could stop 'them' with our bodies." On both sides, students and police, explicit or latent assumptions about the legitimate use of force underlie its actual use.

In the international world, the insistence on "sovereign independence," as the United Nations' Charter puts it, is the cornerstone of the state system. Sovereignty today, in spite of the growth of regional and international organizations, is still considered to be most intimately connected with a government's control over its own defense and with the capacity to ward off or deter attack. This, after all, has been the whole point of Charles de Gaulle's nuclear *force de frappe* or *force de dissuasion:* to have a prop to French sovereignty in a world dominated by the nuclear superpowers. Any international or regional control over a country's defense policy is still interpreted as a design upon its sovereignty. And the soldiers themselves, in a curious limbo of roles, are at once both agents of their state, who cannot refuse orders, and the patriotic defenders of their homeland. Ever since the *levée en masse* of the French revolutionary armies against foreign invaders who were trying to put down the popular revolution, conscripted soldiers have been regarded as truculent modern individuals, revolting against the potential tyranny of a foreign power.

In any event, the armed forces, too, are guarding the fires of violence. They control violence on such a gigantic scale today that revolutionaries have little chance against them, unless they organize guerrilla warfare or happen to gain the support of the military. In the latter case the civilian government does not stand a chance. Such a revolutionary role of the military is quite common in many developing countries of Asia, Africa, and Latin America.

Police and military attitudes toward violence

Since the dawn of organized society both the professional military and the police forces have been frequently accused of loving the use of violence for its own sake. Especially since the nineteenth century, generals have been pictured by their detractors as fire-breathing warmongers, thinking of little but how best to apply violence to an enemy that frequently included the opposition at home. The cry of "police brutality" or excessive use of force in the discharge of duty has been directed at police not just in the United States, but from Japan to Western Europe, wherever the control of crime and of street riots has been popularly perceived as oppression of an underdog group by the established authorities. It appears plausible that military or police careers would attract people who were, to say the least, not repelled by the need to use violence. It is also clear that neither the professional military nor the police forces would be served well by anyone who cared more for the fighting than for its objectives, though there have always been some persons in the military and police everywhere who give this impression.

The basic orientation of professional soldiers and police officers toward violence is a prime concern of students of political cultures. Their attitude often is not easily ascertained, because it is bound up with an elaborate system of beliefs about values such as individual and collective honor and self-respect, expressive symbols such as uniforms and flags, codes of hierarchic ranks and obedience to the commands of a superior officer, as well as of solidarity and comradeship among equals, and very specific negative images of the enemy or law violator. Their attitude toward violence is not generally verbalized except during the extremities of actual events. One can also try to elicit expressions of attitudes from reactions to fictitious situations. One can ask a professional military man in the United States, for example, "What should be done if a small communist satellite country suddenly seized an American intelligence ship with some eighty crew members on the high seas and held it captive?" Or one can ask a French police officer, "Supposing a fellow police officer had been hit by a pavement stone thrown by student rioters, what would you do?" There may still be a gap between reaction to a fictitious situation and spontaneous behavior in an actual one, when the physical contagion of witnessed violence, provocation, rage, and fear might escalate the response. But the gap is not as large as many people think, and it could also be in the other direction, response being diminished by ulterior motives of various sorts. Among these may be the specific norms taught in military and police training regarding the distinction between combatants and noncombatants, or between bystanders and active rioters or persons refusing to obey legitimate police commands or resisting arrest. There are also fairly specific norms that attempt to match the violence of the "appropriate reaction" to that of the original action, although these relationships tend to become confused in the rapid succession of reactions. Once violence begins, it tends to escalate precisely because the appropriateness of reactions is a norm easily lost in the heat of battle. Collective violent action also looks very different at varying levels of command over the situation. To the extent that it remains under the control of seasoned leadership, there are generally deliberate decisions made to escalate, deescalate or redirect violent action as the broader objectives of the leadership may suggest. For the leadership, in other words, violence is a tool.

Rebel attitudes toward violence

If the official guardians of violence have well-defined attitudes toward it, what about criminals, revolutionaries, strikers, or demonstrators in domestic encounters with adversaries, the police, or the army? Degrees of explicitness may distinguish novices from seasoned practitioners; but even novices have attitudes toward their own use of violence when under duress. The habitual criminal has a fairly elaborate idea of the real or fancied hostility of society toward him and, on this basis, of how he may have to use violence to overcome resistance or to ward off attack on his person. The spontaneous or first-time striker or demonstrator may not have thought much about how he would respond to provocation or physical coercion; but he surely has a definite concept of who the enemy is, how antagonistic or downright mean he expects him to be, and also of the generally hostile nature of their relations with one another. In the thick of the physical encounter, then, ideas and images of violent interaction quickly merge, as epithets are hurled and the individual demonstrator finds himself not just egged on but often physically pushed from behind into the jaws of the presumably violent adversary. The adversary—police or whoever—by the same token will believe himself under direct mob attack and respond with his own means of violence.

Violence suffered or observed at close hand tends to break down the last crust of civilization holding back the beast inside man. A husband-and-wife team at the University of Tennessee, Bruce and Annemarie Welch, in research with mice found neurochemical changes in the central nervous system as a direct response to witnessing other mice fight. Both men and mice, evidently, are stimulated to join the fray when they see violence, as fans of boxing matches have always known. In mob situations, where fear and direct threat are added to other stimuli, and where the participant already has a strong projective image of his adversary as mean and violent, the patterning effect on the attitudes of both sides is likely to be lasting.

The seasoned veteran or organizer of strikes and demonstrations or the "professional revolutionary," say, of communist or fascist parties, is not only accustomed to dealing out and receiving violence; to his mind it has become an inevitable part of his life as an organizer, agitator, or strong-armed guard. Revolutionary ideologies such as communism or fascism, of course, supply broad rationalizations for the use of violence, although the activist hardly requires any. Twentieth-century revolutionary movements have developed different functional roles for their purposes, most of which involve violence. In the Weimar Republic of Germany, for example, the chief function of members of parliamentary organizations such as the communist Red Front, the republican Reichsbanner, or the Nazi storm troopers was one of hand-to-hand combat with their political adversaries during raids of each other's quarters, meetings, rallies, or demonstrations. Their attitudes toward violence reflected their military training and, for many of them, experience of violence in World War I and the border fights and revolutionary and counterrevolutionary episodes following it. Some also had volunteer military training or police experience, so that military and police pattern of attitudes may explain much of their orientation to the use of violence.

In popular opinion these brown or red guards were all sadistic bullies who enjoyed beating up their adversaries. However, a study of a large collection of autobiographical statements by early members of the Nazi party,[38] including many storm troopers, reveals in the overwhelming majority of cases a pervasive masochism mixed with Messianic hopes for the victory of the movement. The typical storm trooper who reported many violent encounters evidently felt sorry for himself and his buddies and was more preoccupied with the lumps and injuries received than with conquering the enemy. This may well apply to the Italian fascist squads and fascist movements in other countries as well.

Propagandists and strategists of violence   Other revolutionary roles that involve orientations to violence more indirectly include that of propagandistic agitation by the written and spoken word

[38] The collection was made by Theodore Abel, whose book about it was reissued as *The Nazi Movement*. New York: Atherton Press, 1966. This writer is currently engaged in a secondary analysis of the social origins, political behavior, and attitudes of Abel's vitae of early members (pre-1933) of the German Nazi party.

and that of the strategist. Those in the propagandist role range from the sophisticated editorial writer or speech writer to the common agitator in factory, neighborhood, and marketplace. The sophisticated approach involves manipulating the general attitudes of the audience about the enemy and his nature as well as interpreting political events in the light of these concepts. Rather than issuing calls to violence, the propagandist tries to make it acceptable and rational, as in the violence of his own movement and by pointing to the violence the adversary did or might commit toward members of the propagandist's audience.

The strategist has a leadership role. Its connection with violence is indirect, but momentous, because the strategist can create and manipulate situations of violent encounter to suit his purposes of manipulating people. He can use violent clashes in order to shake up and solidify his own people, to mobilize neutral bystanders, or to goad public opinion into compassion for or a backlash against his boys, as the leaders of revolutionary movements have long been well aware. An instructive case in point is Joseph Goebbels' "conquest of Berlin" in the final phase of Hitler's rise to power. The Nazi strategist won majority support in the city by sending his handful of storm troopers again and again into the "reddest" parts of the city, provoking violent clashes and using their bloodied heads to propagandize and mobilize non-Socialist opinion on the Nazi side. In a few years he managed to parlay the position of a tiny, ignored fringe group into the national center of Nazi power and propaganda.

Revolutionary violence

The scholarly literature on revolutions and revolutionary violence is immense and not lacking in glimpses of politicocultural perspectives [39] if we are careful to focus on the orientations rather than the violent interactions among rebels and establishment forces. To begin with, popular attitudes toward the political uses of violence appear to fluctuate considerably with the changing attitudes toward legitimate authority. When the popular regard for established authority wanes (or is low), the expectation of

---

[39] For a recent survey of the literature on revolutionary violence, see Harry Eckstein, "On the Etiology of Internal Wars," Eckstein, ed., *Internal War*. New York: Free Press, 1964, pp. 133–163.

violence rises and so does public toleration of it. Regimes high in legitimacy or institutions supported by an abiding popular faith rarely face the challenge of violence and have little difficulty in meeting it.[40] Ineffective or decaying institutions, on the other hand, seem to attract revolutionary violence as if by a subtle but powerful social mechanism. As state building in Western political philosophy is said to contain violence like fire within the hearth, the disintegration of the state's authority seems to release it again in the public mind. Witness the tottering Russian Empire in the defeats of 1915 and 1917, or the desertion of the old regimes of France or England by their intellectuals, whose role in weaving or undoing the web of political culture is notorious. A failure of the entire political system to socialize the young, or substantial portions of the young, into patterns of political loyalty to the established regime is the most likely explanation of how legitimate authority wanes, although the impact of external humiliation may well have been an added factor in the case of Russia. A failure to maintain the loyalty of the "guardians of violence," furthermore, will clinch the future of a weakening regime.[41]

A very perceptive recent comparative essay on political violence and development by Charles Anderson, Fred von der Mehden, and Crawford Young devoted a lengthy section to cultural, social, and psychological factors worth mentioning here. The authors direct attention, though with considerable skepticism,

[40] In this respect, there are also considerable differences between "tight" and "loose" societies regarding the narrowness or latitude with which social and political deviancy are defined in theory and practice. See also the distinctions drawn by Lucian W. Pye between the lenient attitude toward insurgency of newly independent regimes and the far more repressive one of colonial administrators in Eckstein, ed., *Internal War,* pp. 167–178.

[41] For a review of the concepts of revolution of a variety of current writers, see also Carl Leiden and Karl M. Schmitt, *The Politics of Violence: Revolution in the Modern World.* Englewood Cliffs, N.J.: Prentice-Hall, 1968, pp. 3–9. See also the brilliant survey of revolutions by Barrington Moore, Jr., *The Social Origins of Dictatorship and Democracy.* Boston: Beacon, 1966; Chalmers Johnson, *Revolution and the Social System.* Stanford, Calif.: Hoover Institute, 1964; and Cyril E. Black and Thomas P. Thornton, eds., *Communism and Revolution: The Strategic Uses of Political Violence.* Princeton, N.J.: Princeton University Press, 1964, the latter being a review of revolutionary communism in a dozen areas.

to the large literature attributing a "warrior culture" or a propensity toward violence to certain nations and tribes in order to explain Japanese and German militarism in the past or the endemic violence of Spanish and Latin-American politics. The cult of masculinity (*machismo*) in some Latin countries and the child-rearing practices of Burma, Java, and Indian Latin America are widely held to be responsible for the easy resort to violence. Such analysis of "national character," the authors conclude, is hazardous in the absence of sound research but not to be rejected out of hand. The differences in the degree of morbidity (a "love of death") and between "courage" and "ingenuity" cultures are too great and obvious to be ignored. We shall return to this topic later.

The survey also suggests that protracted violence connected with the struggle for colonial independence may spread arms and clandestine organizations in a developing country and thus condition it to postindependence violence. We have already noted the significance of large numbers of underemployed veterans or vigilantes seasoned in war and violence. The authors then present a catalog of motives for joining violent movements in developing areas, for which there are obvious parallels in the more advanced countries as well. The romantic allure of a guerrilla career as contrasted to the boredom of peasant life or of soldiering for the government, a quest for the heroic and for political activism, and indignation about "injustice, stupidity, and tyranny" are prominent among the motives. The book also notes the disproportionate numbers of members of oppressed ethnic minorities in revolutionary movements and the manner in which guerrilla terror often forces otherwise neutral peasants into massive violence and participation on the side of the guerrillas.[42]

[42] See Charles Anderson, Fred von der Mehden, and Crawford Young, *Issues of Political Development*. Englewood Cliffs, N.J.: Prentice-Hall, 1967, chap. 5. A special case of such recruitment to massive violence is the "cultural revolution" in China, which, according to Robert Jay Lifton, resulted from popular anxiety about the anticipated death of the great leader and the "death of the revolution" itself, which gives it a kinship to the quest for heroic action mentioned above together with the well-known yearning of old revolutionaries to continue to ride the historical wave of the future no matter what. See "Mao Tse-tung and the 'Death of the Revolution,'" *Trans-Action*, September 1968, pp. 6–13.

Ethnic persecution   In this connection the phenomenon of ethnic persecution from pogroms to genocidal massacres should also be mentioned, for it involves, in addition to the employment of violence, ethnic prejudice on a massive scale. The evidence of the nineteenth and twentieth centuries is global and grim. The massacre of the Armenians by the Turks in the 1920s; the current fate of the Kurds in the Middle East, the Balubas of the Congo and Ibos of Nigeria, the Chinese of Indonesia and certain mountain tribes of India and South East Asia; the fate of the Indians of North America and even in racially tolerant Brazil; and, in particular, the massive persecution of the Jews in Eastern and Central Europe add up to a disheartening chronicle of human savagery.

Interpretations of totalitarian violence

The interpretations of totalitarian violence run the gamut from ideological explanations [43] to feeble attempts at finding a utilitarian rationale, but none has been entirely convincing.[44] To blame terror and violence solely on ideological motivation begs the question, since ideologies are highly ambiguous and, if anything, nonviolent on the question of what should be done to "the capitalists" or the Jews, or whomever they designate as "the enemy." The attempts at attributing some utility to mass killing have never shown convincingly that any given objective could not have been achieved better with other means. The most plausible explanation so far has been that the generation of terror and fear by the concentration camps and secret police has the function of keeping much larger audiences than its direct victims in line. Carl J. Friedrich and Zbigniew Brzezinski have argued this case convincingly, even though they have of late deemphasized the central role of terror in the analysis of totalitarianism. Hannah Arendt in her classic *Origins of Totalitarianism* [45] saw in the

[43] For discussions of the role of violence in Marxist ideology, see Robert C. Tucker in Carl J. Friedrich, ed., *Revolution*. New York: Atherton Press, 1966, chap. 10, and Henry B. Mayo, *Introduction to Marxist Theory*. New York: Oxford, 1960, pp. 38–62.

[44] See also Hannah Arendt's thesis of the "banality of evil" in her book *Eichmann in Jerusalem*. New York: Viking, 1964, pp. 276–298.

[45] Hannah Arendt, *Origins of Totalitarianism*. New York: Harcourt, 1967.

secret police rather than in the totalitarian party the center of the system. Friedrich and Brzezinski toned down their emphasis on the significance of systematic violence in totalitarian regimes quite significantly in the revised edition of their authoritative *Totalitarian Dictatorship and Autocracy*.[46] The first edition agreed with Arendt's thesis that it is an inherent characteristic of totalitarianism for the terror to increase as the regime becomes stable. The second edition attributed the increasing terror in Hitler's Germany and Stalin's Soviet Russia more to the leadership and other circumstances, such as the defeat of the original internal enemies and the redirection of terror against the population and one's own movement. Totalitarian terror still serves the function of instantaneous generation of unanimous consensus along the path to Utopia.[47] But such systematic terror can also be found in other autocracies, and even in some democracies in wartime or in "zones of terror," such as may be constituted by a persecuted minority.

Recent comparative studies of political violence

This section concludes by describing a few recent comparative studies of political violence to introduce the reader to a significant current in the discipline. The urban crisis and racial disorders in America have helped to focus attention on the systematic study of violence [48] and will no doubt produce further sophistication in cross-national research as well.

[46] Both editions published in New York: Praeger, 1961 and 1965. See especially chaps. 13 and 14. In a paper delivered at the annual APSA convention in 1967, Friedrich also stressed the role of massive physical terror in Cuba and Red China—far in excess of Stalin's and Hitler's terror, according to the author—and the "decentralization of violence" in contemporary Russia and China, where local vengeance and community pressure take the place of the old centralized terror as a consequence of the internalization of the norms enforced.

[47] In this connection, the idea that totalitarian government is an attempt to make revolution permanent and to retain its momentum is worth reiterating. See, for example, Sigmund Neumann, *Permanent Revolution.* New York: Praeger, 1965 (first issued in 1942 by Harper), and the literature cited there.

[48] See, for example, the contributions to Louis H. Masotti, ed., "Urban Violence and Disorder," *American Behavioral Scientist,* March–April 1968, and Masotti and Don R. Bowen, eds., *Riots and Rebellion.* Beverly Hills, Calif.: Sage Publications, 1968.

Frustration and aggression   One of the pioneering studies in this field is by Ivo K. and R. L. Feierabend, who applied to a large number of countries between 1948 and 1962 the hypothesis that sudden frustration breeds aggression. The hypothesis is based essentially on a measurement of rapid social improvements in terms of expanding educational opportunities and a better diet, and correlation with the increased incidence of political violence. Evidently, the "revolution of rising expectations" of upwardly mobile strata tends to outrun the actual improvements, and the resulting frustration triggers aggression such as revolutionary violence.[49] There have also been laboratory experiments with animals to demonstrate the causal link between frustration and aggression. And James C. Davies based a theory of revolutions on the observation, also made by de Tocqueville, Brinton, and Eric Hoffer, that the great Western revolutions were triggered by a sudden, sharp worsening of improving living standards rather than by prolonged, severe deprivation.[50]

Dimensions of violence   Another pioneering enterprise was the cross-national attempt by R. J. Rummel and later also by Raymond Tanter [51] to explore "basic dimensions" of violence indicated by such events as riots, strikes, demonstrations, assassinations, and major governmental crises. Rummel analyzed 77 nations for the three-year period 1955–1957 in terms of nine domestic-conflict variables and three dimensions: subversion, revolution, and spontaneous riots and assorted civil disorders. Tanter, in replicating Rummel's study for the following three years, collapsed the first two dimensions into one called "internal

[49] Ivo K. and R. L. Feierabend, "Aggressive Behaviors within Polities, 1948–1962: A Cross-National Study," *Journal of Conflict Resolution,* 10 (1966), 249–271. See also Ted Gurr and Charles Ruttenberg, *The Conditions of Civil Violence.* Princeton, N.J.: Center of International Studies Monograph, 1967.

[50] James C. Davies, "Toward a Theory of Revolution," *American Sociological Review,* 27 (1962), 5–19. See also the survey of studies by Huntington, *Political Order in Changing Societies,* pp. 4, 40–47.

[51] R. J. Rummel, "Dimensions of Conflict Behavior within and between Nations," *General Systems Yearbook,* 8 (1963), pp. 1–50 and "Dimensions of Conflict Behavior within Nations, 1946–1959," *Journal of Conflict Resolution,* 10 (March 1966), 65–73; and Raymond Tanter, "Dimensions of Conflict Behavior within and between Nations, 1958–1960," *Journal of Conflict Resolution,* pp. 41–64.

war" (organized internal conflict), and this dichotomy between internal war and "turmoil" was recently taken over and applied to Latin America by Douglas Bwy, who also took into account the relation of internal conflict to "psychosocial dissatisfaction," legitimacy, and the level of violent governmental retribution.[52] Bwy found that organized internal conflict (internal war) such as guerrilla warfare, revolutionary activities, terrorism, and sabotage in his 65 Latin-American provinces correlated quite differently with his other variables than did spontaneous, disorganized internal conflict (turmoil). *Elite instability,* such as cabinet or legislative dissolution, resignations, or dismissals, for example, was more likely to accompany "turmoil" than "internal war," though it often preceded the latter. *Legitimacy* was negatively correlated with both, and especially with organized violent activity. When the popular sense of satisfaction was low,[53] *turmoil* was more likely, while *internal war* occurred more often in times of relative satisfaction.

Other quantitative studies   There are a great many other quantitative studies of political violence, varying in emphasis, which we can only categorize here. Many researchers, in gauging how violent a given nation seems to be in all its domestic and international relations, like to include criminal violence along with the more specifically political kind. It may interest Americans, for example, to know how the United States compares with other Western nations. According to John P. Siegel, director of the Lemberg Center for the Study of Violence at Brandeis University, this country heads the list of 27 Western countries in homicides, has a very high rate of assassination attempts on Presidents and of waves of rioting, though not revolutions, and a moderately high record of involvement in wars. And while there are still insufficient data to prove it, the probability is high that the inten-

---

[52] See also the approach of Robert A. LeVine, "Anti-European Violence in Africa: A Comparative Analysis," *Journal of Conflict Resolution,* 3 (December 1959), 420–429.

[53] That is, when respondents rated themselves low on the Self-Anchoring Striving Scale or when they said they were "worse off than in the past." See "Dimensions of Social Conflict in Latin America," *American Behavioral Scientist,* March–April 1968, pp. 39–50, and the sources cited there.

sive exposure of American children to warlike games and toys as well as to violence on television is causally related to the popular attitudes toward the use of violence, just as bullfight entertainment may be in certain countries. Researchers of international conflict also have long been interested in the relationship between national perceptions and attributes and foreign-conflict behavior, or warlikeness.[54] The attitudes and expressions of hostility toward other nations considered in these research projects find their parallel in the studies of group hostility and prejudice within nations, as among urban rioters in the United States or in the controversy about the significance of looting and other property offenses in American urban riots. It is an interesting question, of course, whether American blacks riot because they find "whitey" hateful or because they crave the affluence they see on television.[55]

Violence and political development   As a last example, cross-polity comparisons have found striking patterns of correlation between a measurement of political violence and political development. On a continuum of political development beginning with Asian and African traditional and conservative oligarchies, and the lowest literacy and per capita GNP scores, the measurement of political violence suddenly jumps from low to very high as the development scale reaches Asian and African modernizing oligarchies and tutelary democracies and Latin-American authoritarian regimes, all with significantly higher literacy and GNPs. From this high point, violence gradually decreases again, as literacy and GNP rise further and political development passes through such phases as Asian and African political democracy,

[54] See, for example, the contributions to J. David Singer, ed., *Quantitative International Politics* (New York: Free Press, 1965), of Rudolph J. Rummel, Dina A. Zinnes, and Ole R. Holsti, Robert C. North, and Richard Brody, as well as Michael Haas, "Social Change and National Aggressiveness, 1900–1960," where economic strains, types of society, and such indices of psychological strain as suicides, homicides, and alcoholic death were ingeniously related to military aggressiveness.

[55] See especially Allen D. Grimshaw, "Three Views of Urban Violence: Civil Disturbance, Racial Revolt, Class Assault," *American Behavioral Scientist,* March–April 1968, and other essay in the same issue. Also Russell Dynks and E. L. Quarantelli, "Looting in American Cities: A New Explanation," *Trans-Action,* May 1968.

Latin-American semicompetitive and competitive systems, and developed and/or European democracies. The political-violence score is as low with the traditional oligarchies having a literacy median score of 2.5 and per capita GNP of $92 as it is with the developed category measuring 98.5 on literacy and $943 in GNP.[56] The clear implication is that it is chiefly in the long transitional phase between the two that strains and frustration generate violence.

VALUE AND BELIEF SYSTEMS IN POLITICS

Much of the conventional study of revolutionary violence has assumed that it can be explained sufficiently by its perpetrators' strong beliefs. By denying that ideological, religious, or other convictions supply a *sufficient motivation,* we do not discount the importance of these elements in all political life, including violence and revolution. Nearly all revolutionary movements are held together by systems of belief, as are their governmental antagonists, and beliefs are often cited to justify violent deeds. Beliefs may include such things as hateful images of the enemy and ideas about the nature of the antagonistic interaction, such as "the class struggle." But they are hardly the sole and generally not even an important cause of political violence, by contrast with such other factors as the presence of what Harold Lasswell and Daniel Lerner called the "specialists of violence," [57] and deliberate strategies of violent confrontation.

Political value and belief systems, in fact, deserve to be studied regardless of whether or not they produce cleavages or lead to revolutionary violence, as a rather autonomous and very important part of political cultures.

Varieties of political belief systems

Political belief systems differ not only in content but also in explicitness. Some modern belief systems are so explicit that they

[56] See Table 10 of the paper "Scalogram Analysis of Political Violence: A Cross-National Analysis," delivered by Betty Nesvold at the 1967 American Political Science Association meeting.

[57] See especially Harold Lasswell and Daniel Lerner, *World Revolutionary Elites.* Cambridge, Mass.: M.I.T. Press, 1965, pp. 252 and *passim*. The essays were first published in 1951.

can be and often are spelled out in considerable detail, upon which controversies and competing interpretations have battened. Others, such as the ethnocentric "idols of the tribe," are implicitly understood or sensed, and are spelled out even in small part only when they face a major challenge. Political belief systems always go considerably beyond specific programs and ideological doctrines, such as the New Deal in America, Marxism, or the gospel of any given religion. They tend to incorporate doctrines into the history and way of life of a people, relate it to political action and goals, and thus make a given ideology at once more specific and more subject to the exigencies of social and political change.[58] Thus the Chinese communism of 1970 as a belief system differed substantially from the Soviet communism of 1970, which in turn differed from its equivalent of 1934, not to mention 1893. Different histories, situations, and ways of life as well as the socioeconomic changes of Chinese and Russian society account for much of the difference. Changing leadership and the changing political situation likewise make for incisive differences. The liberal doctrines of the Glorious Revolution of 1688 meant something very different in England than in the France of Louis XIV and his successors. The political faith producing the French Declaration of the Rights of Man was rather different from the one that inspired our Bill of Rights. By the same token, Czechoslovak communism was something distinctly different to its supporters in 1945, 1953, and 1968;[59] and German National Socialist beliefs before 1933 and after 1939 are rather at variance in spite of the substantially unchanged leadership.

[58] Alex Inkeles, for example, speaks of the "mutual adjustment between (Communist) ideology and social realities" as the determinants of Soviet policy. Alex Inkeles, *Public Opinion in Soviet Russia: A Study in Mass Persuasion*. Cambridge, Mass.: Harvard University Press, 1950. In the "capitalistic" Western countries, official ideology for lack of propaganda effort is even more likely to be adapted beyond recognition and also to be limited to a small well-educated elite. See especially Philip Converse, "The Nature of Belief Systems in Mass Publics," in David Apter, *Ideology and Discontent*. New York: Free Press, 1964, chap. 6.

[59] The sudden reversal of communist liberalization in Czechoslovakia by Soviet intervention particularly dramatizes the contrast between, on the one hand, "Communist normalization" by means of tanks, censorship, and police surveillance, and, on the other, Ludvik Svoboda's "Josephine Communism" of the brief liberalization era, named after the enlightened absolutist Emperor Joseph II of Hapsburg.

Religion and political belief

Too, the nature of contemporary political belief systems can hardly be understood if we ignore their intimate relationship to religion. Modern ideological movements, such as European liberalism and socialism, grew largely out of a kind of moral reaction to traditional or semitraditional societies and political systems heavily infused with orthodox religious beliefs. The *anciens régimes* of continental Europe represented so close a union of throne and altar, aristocracy and priest, that the liberal revolutionaries had to juxtapose to it a new moral faith with standards of personal conduct and ethical values every bit as exalted as those it sought to replace. There is, perhaps, no more persuasive evidence of the analogous nature of the new and old faiths as the launching of a "religion of reason," complete with rites and idols of worship, at the height of the French Revolution. Socialist reform movements of the nineteenth century likewise had to oppose a new quasi-religious faith to the defense of property rights by traditional religion and by the rather moralistic liberal bourgeoisie. In both cases, the new belief systems often received help from organized religion, especially from British nonconformism and some Protestant clerics on the Continent, sometimes even from small left-wing Catholic groups. At the same time, orthodox religion played a major role in all the conservative camps, Episcopal, Catholic, or Protestant, so that in a sense the ideological struggle took place within a framework basically similar to the great heresy struggles of the Middle Ages.

Both European liberalism and socialism in their most expansive days also bore distinct salvational overtones. The coming of an age of economic and personal freedom and of national self-determination—or, in terms of Marxist socialism, the final revolution and the advent of "socialized man" in a classless society—offered as potent a utopia as the coming of the Messiah. And liberalism and socialism became no more scientific, only better rationalized, by virtue of being couched in theories of inexorable social development. The liberal faith in the progress of human freedom and the socialist expectation of an end to the exploitation of man by man are both basically religious notions that can only be believed, not proven. The twentieth century, with its totalitarian utopias of worldwide communist revolution and the racist paradise of fascist visions, on the other hand, has taught us an unholy revulsion against the salvational impulse in this world. And these twentieth-century movements also demonstrate that the dynamic belief of systems of contemporary politics can become more rather than less like religious crusades.[60]

In advanced Western societies, then, religious and religion-like political ideologies are not absent. They may even compete with each other. The secularization of social, economic, and political functions typical of modernity, moreover, tends to rest on another religionlike belief system widely shared among the members of such a society and held particularly by its functional elites. This is the ideology of science and of functional utility in social life, a belief system ultimately as much based on faith and on the actual rule of the established functional elites as any theocracy of the distant past.[61] Secularism evidently is not so much a change in the forms of thinking as in its content. And such seemingly antireligious movements as militant atheism or anticlericalism no less than the great ideological mass movements of our age conform closely to the religious cast of mind of the past, albeit with a negative effect.

Belief in developing nations   The political belief systems of the developing nations of Asia and Africa fit somewhere between those of traditional religion-based societies and governments and the secular functionalism and scientific-managerial faith of developed societies. The African cultural heritage today, according to K. A. Busia, is "intensely and pervasively religious." Common elements of African religion deeply affected the brand of African socialism associated with Leopold Senghor. The African idea of community and tribal solidarity, as in "communitarian socialism," is of religious orgin—especially where it is also symbolized in the chieftaincy, as with the Ashanti tribesmen.[62] Religion also supplied a major element of Burmese (U Nu) so-

[60] See on this point also Raymond Aron, *The Opium of the Intellectuals.* New York: Norton, 1962, pt. 2.

[61] See also David Apter's remarks in *Ideology and Discontent.* New York: Free Press, 1964, pp. 30–39.

[62] See K. A. Busia, *Africa in Search of Democracy.* New York: Praeger, 1967, chaps. on the religious and political heritage; and Anderson *et al., Issues of Political Development,* pp. 191–192.

cialism. The most prevalent link between ideology and the religious and particularistic traditions in Africa, as in the West and in Arab and Asian countries, is found in nationalistic beliefs, since each new nation seeks to find a national identity in common and largely traditional images, in which religion is bound to play a prominent role.[63] Fred von der Mehden has described in detail the wide variety of Indonesian, Philippine, and Burmese attempts to use Islam, Buddhism, Christianity, and even anticlericalism as organizing levers against the colonial overlords. Nationalist movements in the developing countries over a period of time can be anything from religious protest to secularism or Marxism.[64]

Islamic tradition   Manfred Halpern has examined the close link between Islamic traditions in the Middle East and the political community and its traditional government, the sultanate. Among his most pertinent examples are the varieties of Neo-Islamic totalitarianism, such as the Moslem Brotherhood in Egypt, and similar movements in Iran, Pakistan, Syria, and Jordan, which are for the most part millenarian groups of religious fanatics. They are anti-Western, anti-Communist, and anti reform-Islam, and equally against nationalism and secular politics, which they regard as false gods. Their violence and stress on a charismatic leader and on absolute solidarity within the movement give them a superficial similarity to Western fascist movements, with whom they also share a vehement intolerance at home and imperialistic appetites abroad.[65] That a waning faith should mobilize totalitarian energies to prop itself up by enforcing and crusading violence is a well-known phenomenon from the history of Catholicism and Protestantism. It is also true that most Western fascist movements enjoyed considerable support from religious conservatives. It should be noted, however, that such major fascist movements

[63] See, for example, Leonard Binder in *Ideology and Discontent*, pp. 136–139, 143–150; and Eisenstadt, *Modernization: Protest and Change*, p. 119.

[64] Fred von der Mehden, *Religion and Nationalism in South East Asia*. Madison, Wis.: University of Wisconsin Press, 1963.

[65] Manfred Halpern, *The Politics of Social Change in the Middle East and North Africa*. Princeton, N.J.: Princeton University Press, 1963, chaps. 1 and 8.

as those in Italy and Germany and their leadership were not themselves propelled by any kind of orthodox religious zealotry, although they may have had a chiliasm of their own.[66]

Christian democracy   A final category of religion-based political belief systems are the varieties of Christian Democracy in Europe and Latin America. In Europe their origins date back to nineteenth-century groups and thinkers of a left-wing opposition within Catholicism, which was eventually allowed by the pope to compete in the political arena against the often anticlerical liberals and socialist parties and trade unions of the day. Mass parties of this description sprang up in Germany in the 1870s and in Italy with the Partito Popolare of 1919. After World War II, Christian Democratic parties became dominant in these two countries and temporarily important in France, as well as eventually in Chile, Venezuela, and other parts of Latin America. Their ideologies have always varied considerably from socialism to conservatism. At their most expansive, however, the Christian trade unions and often the priestly element, as well as many other Catholic associations, have usually stressed the socialist tenor of the religious message.

Dimensions of political belief systems

Whether we deal with religion-based political belief systems or the "idols of the tribe" of ethnocentric nationalism or with potent and well-established ideologies such as communism in communist countries, there are a number of dimensions we must be aware of.

Prevalence   First, there is the extent to which the particular belief system prevails among the members of a political system. Quite often, a belief system is limited to a given ethnic or other social subculture or to either the elites or the masses of a given society. Furthermore, within a given belief system there is a wide

[66] Roumania's Codreanu was perhaps the most important exception to the rather irreligious nature of European fascist movements. His inspiration seemed to be the same Christian millenarianism that motivated movements in fourteenth and sixteenth-century Western and Central Europe. See, for example, Eugen Weber, *Varieties of Fascism*. New York: Van Nostrand, 1964, chap. 9.

range of attitudes that is crucial for its role in politics. In any political faith there will be zealots of varying intensity as well as mere conventional followers, who may think along the same lines as the zealots but for rather different reasons. There may also be heretics who passionately believe in a different version and unbelievers indifferent to the faith.[67]

Aging   Belief systems also have a kind of "age" that can be stated in terms of the process of political socialization. A "new" faith is born with significant circumstances and events of the outside world. It "ages" with the generation that conceived it, quite possibly deteriorating with changing circumstances or becoming more pragmatic as its holders grow older. And while victorious revolutionary or intensely ideological party movements often try hard to pass on the faith to new generations, such a transmission is unlikely without major modifications in content and underlying attitudes. This is part of the reason why revolutionaries such as Mao's generation of Chinese leaders have been so concerned about the "softening" of the revolutionary spirit, partly the source of the egregious rationalizations why Stalin had to wipe out the Old Bolsheviks of the Russian Revolution and replace them with docile administrators. Some elements, such as a sense of the enemy's identity and of one's own leadership, seem easier to pass on than a sense of purpose, or a vision of utopia, or specific attitudes toward activities beneficial to the movement. For this reason, among other things, the "idols of the tribe" or nation seem to survive better from generation to generation than universalistic political ideologies.

Transfer   In many societies, and especially in developing nations, the prevailing belief system appears to vacillate or change with surprising frequency. As David Apter has shown, the "new nations" still have to sort out primordial sentiments relating to identity and solidarity, such as tribal, ethnic, or language problems that have long been resolved in the older nations. Their

[67] Again the article of Philip Converse on "The Nature of Belief Systems in Mass Publics" should be cited where the declining political awareness of a given issue pattern among the masses is demonstrated. In Apter, ed., *Ideology and Discontent*, pp. 224–240.

"nationalism," therefore, is a constant in their belief systems, even though it often appears less salient than the vague socialism professed by many of their leaders.[68] The latter symbolizes their commitment to national independence and egalitarian development and their repudiation of traditionalism and colonialism, but is curiously silent on such mainstays of the original doctrine as property, class struggles, or religion. From the last push toward independence to the postindependence establishment of the new active governments, developing nations often swing strongly from social revolutionary themes of belief to an assertion of the new national identity. From this point of "national apotheosis," cultural and social contradictions are likely to drive the pendulum back to a sweeping "progressive" evaluation of government and society, at the high point of which some new regimes may become militantly socialist states such as Algeria, Guinea, Mali, the United Arab Republic, Burma, or Indonesia. Others choose moderate socialism, and for them the pendulum may return again to a moderate point of nationalism.[69]

Role of the intellectuals

The strategic role played by the transmission and domestication of such European ideologies as socialism to the developing nations, where they may serve all sorts of important functions, naturally focuses attention also upon the people most directly instrumental in this transmission and adaptation—the indigenous intelligentsia, who are undoubtedly responsible for the management of the political belief systems in the broadest sense. Edward Shils, who credits them with "the gestation, birth, and continuing life of the new states," defines them as all persons with an advanced modern education and, generally, a diploma to prove their exposure to *modern culture.* They are employed in the fields

[68] Anderson and his coauthors, in *Issues of Political Developments,* p. 218, concluded from a survey of 81 developing countries of Asia, Africa, the Middle East, and Latin America that about a third of them have been committed since independence, and about half off and on, to "development socialism," while another 11 countries have a socialist movement as the principal opposition.

[69] Apter, *Ideology and Discontent,* pp. 22–28. See also the contributions of Clifford Geertz, Joseph Elder, and Charles F. Andrain to the Apter volume and Friedland and Rosberg, *African Socialism,* pp. 1–11.

of civil service, journalism, law, teaching, and medicine and are generally intensely involved in the political independence movements. Their composition and politics undergo marked changes as their countries approach independence. A first stage features notables such as lawyers and journalists who favor some kind of liberal constitutionalism under colonialism, a philosophy they absorbed while studying abroad in Western countries. At the same time, intellectuals often seek a moral renewal of the traditional culture, comparable perhaps to the phase of "cultural nationalism" among European literati of the eighteenth and nineteenth centuries. A second stage of highly political nationalism follows, characterized by a broad and increasingly differentiated Westernized intelligentsia, who are quite aware of European socialist movements, including anarchistic and other violent varieties of it, and often join international radical movements. At the third stage, the native intellectuals have taken over the reins of the new states, and they immediately dissociate themselves from the rest of their intellectual class.[70]

John H. Kautsky also sees in the role of the intellectuals a special leaven of development, because as a social class along with labor and capital they are in the "paradoxical position of being a product of modernization before modernization has reached or become widespread in their own country." In Kautsky's view, nationalism and the communist movements in Russia, China, or for that matter India, are so highly convergent that the Soviet Union will support nationalism in developing states as much and even more than native communist groups. Furthermore, Kautsky's native intellectuals are so attached to the use of political power for forced economic development that they are quite likely to impose a "totalitarianism of the intellectuals," which may range from the communist variety to somewhat less violent and also less effective development dictatorships from Egypt to Cuba.[71]

[70] Edward Shils, "The Intellectuals in the Political Development of the New States," *World Politics,* 12 (April 1960), 329–368. See also the article by Harry J. Benda, "Non-western Intelligentsias as Political Elites," reprinted in John H. Kautsky, ed., *Political Change in Underdeveloped Countries.* New York: Wiley, 1962.

[71] See Kautsky, *Political Change in Underdeveloped Countries,* pp. 44, 106 and *passim.*

The end of the ideological age

On a related theme, Raymond Aron wrote about "the opium of the intellectuals" in the narrower, French sense of politically and aesthetically motivated writers, artists, and journalists. Their "opium," to paraphrase Simone Weil, has been Marxism and the "sacred words"—the Left, Revolution, and the Proletariat. Their aims have often been best fulfilled where the working class is least numerous, since the real emancipation of the working class in advanced countries has always been a rather dull affair as compared to the attraction of "ideal emancipation." Aron is quite aware of the different degrees to which intellect and the intellectual love of doctrinaire ideologies are taken seriously—in France and Italy more than in England, and anywhere more than in the United States. But he also posits the "end of the ideological age," owing to a waning of proselytizing conviction, the fragmentation of the intellectual universe, and the dulling of fanaticism among intellectuals, who once desperately longed to commune with the people and to unite an underdog class with an idea and a will.[72]

Class basis of ideology   The thesis of the "end of ideology" was advanced by many writers from another angle, that of *social class*. Karl Marx and many others argued that from the beginning of the great ideological movements of European liberalism, conservatism, and socialism, ideology was "nothing but the total *Weltanschauung* (vision of the world) of a given social class," a "superstructure" determined by the economic technology of the society, the material conditions of life of that class, and the antagonism among the classes. Thus, in opposing the dominant feudal order of the old regimes, the bourgeois middle class of urban property owners and entrepreneurs was said to have developed its own distinctive ideology, classical liberalism, a unifying doctrine and battle-cry against ancient oppression and superstition. The high-minded principles of the liberal faith, however, turned out to be little more than a facade for the self-interest of

[72] Aron, *The Opium of the Intellectuals*, chaps. 1–3, 7–9, and Conclusion. Since the time of his writing, 1955, there has been plenty of evidence of reideologization in some intellectual quarters. The international movement to oppose the war in Vietnam and the universal student revolts of the second half of the 1960s are cases in point.

the bourgeois class when applied to the vital interests of the next lower class, the working class emerging as the result of industrialization. The traditional classes of nobility, landowners, and clergy responded to the liberal challenge by formulating their own class ideology, conservatism, defending other high-minded principles that cloaked their vested interests. And the industrial working class, once it had become conscious of its exploitation by bourgeois and feudal interests, likewise adopted an ideology closely identifying and defending its class interests, Marxist socialism. The struggle among these classes over the concrete and vital interests of each thus intensified the faith in the ideologies and politicized to the point of imminent revolution the "economic and social contradictions" of capitalist society.

Ideology and development   The class-based theory of ideology strongly emphasizes the process of development in terms of evolving social classes and their antagonisms, with or without specifically Marxist interpretation. Hence, John H. Kautsky wrote about how industrialization in a traditional society produces such distinct classes as the business, labor, and intellectual elements, of which only traces are present before industrialization. Business and labor correspond, of course, to bourgeois and proletarian interests, whereas Kautsky's intellectuals are the professional and white-collar strata developed with further modernization in government and private industry. Social and economic development in the advanced countries actually continue to produce further differentiated group interests as well as further differentiated ideologies. Meanwhile, the older classes and their interests and ideologies decline or begin to merge with middle-class views, so that ideological and class antagonism inevitably focuses on the struggle for emancipation of the most numerous class, such as the organized working classes in Western Europe during the first half of the twentieth century. After this period of acute "class struggle," the working classes had largely won their place in society, enjoyed unprecedented standards of living, and became so differentiated themselves as to feel little common cause anymore. In short, the traditional class antagonisms of Western societies were disappearing and so was ideology, except for pockets of stagnation and underdevelopment in Europe.[73]

[73] See on this issue especially Seymour M. Lipset, "The Changing Class Structure and Contemporary European Politics" and Rolf Dahren-

Ideology and social mobilization The rise and decline of ideology in some countries can also be discussed from the vantage point of social mobilization. A good example would be the phenomenon of rural emigration in large parts of southern Europe. Prior to emigration, the rural population may well be living lives of hopelessness, such as Edward Banfield described with reference to Calabria in southern Italy. Their politics may be restricted to supporting, regardless of party or ideology, certain bosses and local potentates who provide favors and services for their clienteles (*clientelismo*). With the ferment of social discontent, however, large parts of these peasant masses grow tired of paternalism and clientelism and turn toward active self-help by means of political organizations. Their social mobilization drives them to reject their miserable status in society and soon motivates them to emigrate to the industrial centers of northern Italy and, at least temporarily, to work opportunities abroad in France or West Germany. During the period of their discontent at home, as well as after emigration or while they return temporarily to vote, they are likely to be under the spell of doctrinaire ideologies that rationalize their bitterness and hostility, such as communism or revolutionary socialism.[74] During their first years in an alien and often unfriendly world at Turin, Valdagno, or Milan, they are still as likely as ever to follow ideological extremes and to engage in violent labor disputes for the sake of the struggle rather than the rewards. However, as they get older and become adjusted to their new life, their interest in political activism increasingly wanes. Like the older native workers of these developed industrial areas, they fall under the sway of what the French call *dépolitisation* and settle down to the satisfactions of higher living standards. There is every reason to believe that social mobilization in the rural developing areas of many countries, together with the difficulties of migration and adjustment, indeed account for much of the ideological extremism of nationalistic or communist movements, although there has been too little evidence so far to confirm the political contentment of those who reach their goal.

---

dorf, "Recent Changes in the Class Structure of European Societies," both in *Daedalus*, Winter 1964, pp. 225–303, as well as Daniel Bell's *End of Ideology*, which reflects on the deideologization of politics in the 1950s in America.

[74] See especially Tarrow, *Peasant Communism in Southern Italy*.

COLLECTIVE IDENTITY AND MODAL PERSONALITY

It is a truism of method, although honored by political scientists chiefly in the breach, that an understanding in depth of any nation's ways of thinking involves a broad familiarity with its literature and popular culture. The reading of its contemporary fiction classics, biographies, memoirs, as well as its pulp magazines, dime-store novels, and comic strips may not directly lend itself to quantitative research, though such research has been done. It can, however, give even the untrained mind a wealth of insight into the all-important setting in which politics takes place.

Low personal salience of politics

The reluctance to cross traditional disciplinary boundaries, moreover, should certainly fall, when we consider that for most persons political interest and activity is neither an obvious nor a natural preoccupation. However salient the subject of politics may seem to its students, the broad public is unlikely to give it priority over other areas of human interest, except in moments of acute political conflict, distress, or exaltation. Who would seriously think, in all honesty, that politics would be more important to any healthy young man than sex or that family ties, other personal relationships, making a living in a world of poverty, or matters of "ultimate concern," such as religion, would not take precedence over the troublesome subject of politics? Whether as students of politics we like it or not, political concerns are intimately dependent on the total matrix of social life in any given country and should not be studied in isolation.

Quantitative versus qualitative study

As we have seen earlier, the extent of interest in politics has been ascertained empirically by the Almond and Verba study as well as other opinion studies in different countries. For example, according to an opinion poll of the DOXA Institute in the middle of the 1968 Italian parliamentary election campaign, 56.4 percent of a representative national sample said they were not at all interested in politics, while another 30.3 percent evinced "little interest"; yet well over 90 percent of the Italian voters have turned out at every election since 1948.[75] The startling figures

---

[75] It should be mentioned here that not voting in Italy does draw a penalty in the form of an entry in a person's legal record, without any other consequences.

hardly explain the unique way in which political participation and interest in Italy fit the culture of the country and the personality of the individual. Only depth interviews, such as Robert Lane conducted in New Haven,[76] or a reading of the writings of such men as Ignazio Silone, Carlo Levi, Luigi Barzini, Giovanni Guareschi, and many others can begin to give us an insight into Italian culture and personality.

Let us pick a book at random for an illustration: Silone's *Adventures of a Poor Christian,* the story of the old pious monk from the Abruzzi who in 1294 was elected Pope Celestine V because of his reputation for saintliness, charity, and purity of heart. Appalled at the life at court, the *raison d'état,* and the political machinations in which he finds himself embroiled, the "poor Christian" abdicates after a few months to seek prayer and solitude. Instead he finds himself hunted and taken prisoner by the competing powers of the Anjous and his successor, while his followers, under police repression, form an underground. The story is a parable on Italian attitudes toward authority in any form: organized power, the institutional oppression by the state and the church, and the internal tyranny of political parties such as the Communist party, from which Silone was a noted defector in the 1930s. Silone calls his novels "antipolitical in the sense that they deal with men who resist political power," absolute moralists striving after a utopia equally derived from socialism and Christian charity toward the poor. Many such interpretive works could be named for nearly every country and culture.

The anthropological and the sociological approach

If we need to study the personality and culture of a country in order to grasp what may be relevant to its political habits and values, the significant spadework done by anthropologists and sociologists in this area deserves credit and attention. We should be aware also of some discrepancies between approaches and of the objection of great anthropologists like Margaret Mead to equating the culture of large contemporary communities with culture and personality in fairly homogeneous tribal societies.

---

[76] See Lane, *Political Ideology* and also his new book *Political Thinking and Consciousness.* Chicago: Markham Publishing Co., 1969. For an illuminating discussion of personality theories in a political context, see also Fred Greenstein, *Personality and Politics.* Chicago: Markham Publishing Co., 1969.

Modern nations, according to the best anthropological knowledge, tend to be rather recent and artificial unions of citizens from many cultures, held together by a political will and common convictions that an anthropologist would be reluctant to analyze in the manner customary to the discipline. Anthropologists generally derive their insights from interviews in depth with rather arbitrarily chosen informants, whose respective positions in an already familiar social structure supply a prismatic and coherent view of a whole society. Sociologists and social psychologists, on the other hand, prefer to use statistically representative samples of the entire population in order to obtain accurate cross sections of the society they are studying.[77] To a student of comparative politics, both methods have virtue. The anthropological approach, using interviews to lay bare the structure and functioning of a society, is superbly designed to reveal precisely the kind of information the sociological approach will not readily reveal, such as the presence and value systems of subcultures, the significance of cleavages, and the presence of organized structures that make a political system a system.

The sociological and sociopsychological approach, on the other hand, is better for an accurate measurement of attitudes in a large, heterogeneous society whose structure and cleavages we already know. A typical example of the anthropological approach in political study is the study of the political ideology of average Americans by Robert E. Lane, *Political Ideology,* or some of the sociopsychological studies of the attitudes of political subcultures. The national election studies of the Survey Research Center of the University of Michigan and similar operations in the United States and in other countries, on the other hand, are good examples of the sociological, or atomistic, approach. This approach is particularly well adapted to the electoral decision-making process in democratic countries, where adult individuals each have the same vote and make their de-

[77] See, for example, the discussion of problems and definitions by Mead, "National Character," in A. L. Kroeber, *Anthropology Today: An Encyclopedic Inventory.* Chicago: University of Chicago Press, 1953, p. 643, and A. Inkeles and D. J. Levinson, "National Character: The Study of Modal Personality and Sociocultural Systems," in G. Linzey, ed., *Handbook of Social Psychology,* 2 vols. Reading, Mass.: Addison-Wesley, 1954.

cisions more as individuals than as members of social groups. Its potential weaknesses can be dramatized easily enough: imagine an eager American Ph.D. candidate going to India, or any other basically different society he does not really understand, to administer a Gallup-type opinion poll to what may be, for the sake of the argument, statistically a perfectly representative sample. The content and aim of his questions would make his undertaking foolish. Since the significance of his questions depends on what are meaningful relationships in a given value system and social structure, he would find it impossible to design a meaningful questionnaire without first knowing the society he is investigating.[78]

The modal personality

We should add here a few remarks about what anthropologists and psychologists call the "modal personality." Investigating the character and habits of small, homogeneous tribal societies, anthropologists can easily construct a basic personality type for a given culture, the archetype of its "character." Allowing a certain leeway for deviant groups and individuals, and perhaps for subcultures within the society, the basic outline of the typical personality structure in a given society can be specifically described. Such a "modal personality" can also be derived from data of psychological analysis in depth, gathered perhaps from psychiatric casework or a study of literature and popular culture. The patients in the mental wards and the comic books read by the masses often reveal the inner conflicts of culture and personality better than the thousands of normal, average citizens, who evidently have developed ways of coping with and covering up the personal problems growing out of their culture.

Modal personality, however, should not be understood as a straitjacket of character development for every individual of a society, precisely because most normal members have learned to cope with society's dilemmas. Nor should it be confused with

[78] For two excellent surveys of anthropological and sociological literature on this subject, see the essays by E. Adamson Hoebel and Don Martindale in *National Character in the Perspective of the Social Sciences* (Annals) and the sources cited there, and Alex Inkeles' article on national character in Francis L. K. Hsu, ed., *Psychological Anthropology: Approaches to Culture and Personality*. Homewood, Ill.: Dorsey Press, 1961.

statistical constructs, such as the "average American" or "typical Italian." Just as the statistically "average Mr. or Mrs. American" is a lifeless abstraction unrecognizable to living Americans and nearly devoid of explanatory power, the "average Signor (or Signora) Italiano" has little life or meaning, except perhaps to compare indices such as standards of living across national boundaries. An American or Italian "modal personality" conceived by an anthropologist, social psychologist, or great novelist, on the other hand, may have extraordinary explanatory power, even though it may lack a sound statistical basis. It can explain past conduct and present attitudes, and in the hands of a skillful researcher, it can even predict future reactions and policies. A brilliant example of what anthropological insight can accomplish, without the benefit of statistically representative samples and even without the researcher's presence in the country, was Ruth Benedict's *The Chrysanthemum and the Sword: Patterns of Japanese Culture* (1946), which in translation impressed the Japanese as much as it had its American audience.

To show how studies of the modal personality may throw light on the political culture of a given country, several such studies will be discussed here.

Mexican machismo In Mexico, our first example, the *mestizo* population of the central region has been under the close scrutiny of Erich Fromm, Michael Maccoby, and others. Drawing heavily upon the writings of Mexican intellectuals about their own national character, Maccoby notes the obsessive concern with the historical trauma of the conquest, the crushing of the indigenous culture, a sense of inferiority, and the tendency to imitate powerful foreigners.[79] The national sense of inadequacy in the encounter with powerful foreign nations, together with a fear of betrayal from within, has an obvious bearing on Mexican nationalism and Mexican foreign policy vis-à-vis the United States or the other Latin-American countries. At the same time, Mexicans, unlike other peasant societies in Southern Europe, Asia, or the Middle East, do possess a strong political faith,

[79] The latter is referred to as *malinchismo,* after Cortes' mistress and interpreter Malinche, and looked upon as a tendency to betray the native population in favor of the conquering Spanish, French, and now Americans.

the heritage of the revolution of 1910 and earlier revolts, which give them a sense of political pride and spur them on to civic participation.[80]

To these explicitly political notions should be added the apparent prevalence of an intense conflict between the sexes, which generates politically significant phenomena. Many male psychiatric cases exhibit a compulsive masculinity *(machismo)* that hides a deep-seated dependence on the mother. Feelings of sexual castration and creative impotence are complemented by encounters with women who cannot love men, according to the case histories. The social evidence lies in the many fatherless families that were either abandoned by, or threw out, fathers who were unable to support them or who were brutally *macho* in asserting their patriarchal authority. Some interpretations are historical derivations, centering upon Spanish conquerors who married Indian women and left Indian men displaced and impotent, or upon ancient conflicts between pre-Columbian matriarchal and patriarchal family systems. Other interpretations center on the masochistic and yet love-hoarding character of Mexican women which provokes male sadism as a "despairing attempt to obtain a response from a body we fear is totally insensitive." [81] Mexican men fight their side of the battle of the sexes by betraying their wives, even setting up supplementary households *(casa chica)*. The wives may retaliate by undermining the relationship between fathers and sons and by raising their daughters to be equally frigid and distrustful of all men.

How does this conflict between the sexes affect Mexican politics? One might expect it to throw up barriers that keep women from political participation [82] and reserve politics to the men. Furthermore, such basic personal conflicts might tend to immerse individuals in their private problems, giving a low priority to elections, civic life, and public issues. At the same time, a

---

[80] This was also established statistically by the Almond and Verba study of five nations, in which Mexicans showed considerable more civic pride than West Germans and Italians.

[81] Quoted by Maccoby in *National Character in the Perspective of the Social Sciences* (Annals), p. 70. Maccoby also cites Mexican popular cartoons to corroborate his interpretation.

[82] See also Robert E. Scott in Pye and Verba, *Political Culture and Political Development,* p. 352, and Almond and Verba, *The Civic Culture,* pp. 209–212, 315–316, and 387–397.

considerable number of men, especially young men, might take out their frustrations and loneliness in violent politics, a phenomenon still rare in the United States.[83] Maccoby's study of a Mexican village of 900 inhabitants found about 11 percent of the men with extreme traits of *machismo* and another 30 percent with a milder version. The *supermachos* were characterized by intense dependence on the mother and by the "authoritarian-exploitative syndrome," which implies contempt for the weak and the worship of power.[84] The *supermachos,* in other words, may be a ready-made supply of aggressive and overbearing leaders and followers of fascist or other totalitarian movements, as well as a constant source of oppression and suffering for others. When the time is ripe for a political movement to recruit itself from these circles, the result may well be comparable to the rise of fascist or communist dictatorships elsewhere in the world.

British self-restraint　Next we consider Great Britain, or, more precisely, the four fifths of the British population who consider themselves middle or working class.[85] By far the more numerous,· the working class in the last 150 years appears to have undergone marked changes in social character, which Geoffrey Gorer has cataloged under the headings of control of aggression, sexuality, and hunger. Until the 1850s, the urban working class in England rather freely expressed its aggression in sports and punishments, the victims being suffering animals or those humans marked off as criminals or the insane. With the rise of the Victorian Age, however, the habitual self-restraint of the English upper and middle classes spread among the working classes, turning callousness into squeamishness and truculence into law-abidance.

　　Symbolizing the new attitude was the ideal of sportsmanship

---

[83] See especially Scott, in Pye and Verba, *Political Culture and Political Development,* pp. 338 and 354.

[84] See Maccoby, *National Character in the Perspective of the Social Sciences* (Annals), pp. 64–73, and the sources and references cited there.

[85] Although insignificant statistically, the remaining one fifth, the upper class, upper and lower middle class, and upper working class, have contributed far more than their share of the political leadership of the nation. There is also a predominantly rural, small, lower working class.

in competitive games, a classic device for channeling physical aggression along acceptable lines by means of rules, a spirit of fairness, and the civil acceptance of the outcome. A good sport restrains himself and is rewarded by the "fairness" of the other players, who refrain from taking advantage of his self-restraint. Sportsmanship and "fair shares for all" have obvious equivalents throughout social life, especially in the politics of the Labour party and of the welfare state. Aggression still figures in causes held to be moral and inherently just, such as crusades and "just wars" against enemies considered morally reprehensible or of superior strength, when the authoritarian conscience releases the brake on aggressive drives and controls.

Gorer finds the origins of the English preoccupation with controlling aggression both in the Calvinistic-Puritan folk psychology, which sees "a limb of Satan" in the natural urges of the child, and in the philosophy and practice of "not spoiling children." Being unspoiled means to English parents an absence of destructiveness or temper tantrums and the ability to accept frustration and discipline without resentment. The habitual control of aggression also used to account for the proverbial shyness and bashfulness in the life between the sexes in England, for shyness involves, among other things, projective fears about the aggressiveness of others.

The satisfaction of hunger, finally, has constituted a major preoccupation of the British working classes until 1945. For generations, the class lines between middle and working classes manifested themselves in the undernourished state and comparative ill health of the majority of the workers.[86] As the public health and conscription records of many industrialized nations demonstrate, the differential of nutrition and health is often so marked that it can be considered a major factor keeping the lower classes in their place. With the British working classes, the centuries-long experience and fear of hunger goes a long way toward explaining their habitual security-mindedness, foresight, and "saving up for a rainy day." Translated into politics, again, the experience and fear of hunger might account for habits of moderation and of taking the long-range view of issues rather

[86] See, for example, John Burnett, *Plenty and Want: A Social History of Diet in England from 1815 to the Present Day*. London: Nelson, 1966.

than insisting on immediate gratifications.[87] Yet it could also make for a shortsighted tendency to maintain the status quo— "I'm all right, Jack"—or for featherbedding in industry and similar stagnating economic practices. Last but not least, it might indicate a low threshold for political panic. Anything vaguely symbolizing a food crisis or impending hunger might knock the props from under the prized political rationality and foresight of the British voter. By the same token, the substantial equalization of working-class nutrition with middle-class standards since World War II signifies a new working-class freedom from anxiety and want, which cannot but modify profoundly the psychological implications of nearly two centuries of hunger. Today's vibrant youth styles in clothing and music from the midst of working-class Britain readily testify to that.

Hindu passivity   Our third example of modal personality is that of Indian or, more precisely, Hindu character, as described by Dhirendra Narain.[88] The Hindu population of India developed a pervasive sense of national inferiority when they were subjugated, first by the Muslims, whose long rule included Hindu persecution and discrimination, and then by the British. The Hindu reaction to the Muslims, in particular, engendered a paralyzing passivity and sense of helplessness, which individual Indians until independence seemed able to shake off only under extraordinary stimuli such as a foreign education. The encounter with British colonialism, on the other hand, had long-range effects that are becoming visible only now. The two Indian leaders Gandhi and Nehru in their day symbolized alternative routes to national development—and, by implication, alternative identities. Gandhi's group of Indian intellectuals sought the salvation of the country in its past traditions. Nehru was the great Westernizer; thanks to him, the majority of the Indian elites are today committed to the Western road of development.[89]

[87] See Geoffrey Gorer, *Exploring English Character*. London: Cresset, 1955.

[88] See Dhirendra Narain, *Hindu Character* (Bombay: University of Bombay, 1957) and his contribution to *National Character in the Perspective of the Social Sciences* (Annals).

[89] On the ambivalence of Indian attitudes in the clash between tradition and Western rationality see also Edward Shils, *The Intellectual between Tradition and Modernity: The Indian Situation*. The Hague: Houton, 1961.

Narain places great emphasis on the lack of sustained feeling and commitment in Indian character, the inability to carry through a task, to fulfill promises completely, or to persevere in the early enthusiasm shown for collective objectives. The lack of commitment may be related to the depersonalizing childhood identification with the many adults of the extended family, the erratic nature of discipline from so many hands, and the absence of praise for children. The caste system, of course, demands commitment, but it is involuntary and inescapable. The identification of young males with the father is particularly weak; there seems to be, in fact, a lack of masculine qualities in the culture, which manifests itself also in the absence of "tough guy" images in literature and movies. Movie heroes often surrender their beloved in the face of difficulties.

Politically, this evident lack of assertiveness and autonomy signifies both extreme dependence and distrust toward authority at home and in the government. Where Englishmen expect and demand fair treatment from their government, Indians expect an unpredictable mixture of blows and indulgence, as from the adults and older brothers of the family, and without any particular performance on their part. The relative absence of aggression and anxiety in the highly formal and seemingly affectless world of Indian social relations does not denote their total absence but, rather, the lack of channeling of aggressive drives. When outraged emotions do erupt, there is an utter collapse of self-control, which can spell senseless violence as well as collective inability to meet crises with purposive action. The recurrent famines and scarcities that have always characterized life experiences in India have not led to controlled anxiety and appropriate attitudes of foresight or problem solving as in England. The lethal problems are "solved" with words only, while individual waste continues and the real crisis closes in.

Uses of the concept of national character

This brief excursion into the realm of national character studies would not be complete without a critical discussion of the traditional uses and abuses of the idea.

Failure to live up to national ideals   As compared to most other nations, Americans are very much aware of the potentially destructive impact of stereotypes of national origin. As a nation made up of immigrants of many nationalities, the United States from the beginning adopted what the Swedish sociologist Gunnar Myrdal has called the American creed: a deeply held conviction that every person is entitled to equal respect and opportunity regardless of his (or her) national origin. Much as we may deplore it, holding a conviction firmly need not imply that it is always honored in practice nor that there may not be large groups of persons whose socialization in the home and among peer groups, perhaps even at school, includes significant mental reservations or even contradictory principles of discrimination.[90] Does a collective sense of identity have to be so sincerely held and lived up to that no compromise is conceivable? Our example directly points to one of the common fallacies in defining national identity.

The pitfall of moralism A conviction held and taught throughout a nation does signify how people think of themselves and how they would like others to think of them, regardless of certain lapses or foibles. As such, then, it is a major aspect of what one may call "national identity" or "national character," even among those people for whom it may serve as little more than a verbal defense before their own deeds. This notion may seem self-contradictory if not shocking at first. The reader should be reminded, however, of the opening statements of this chapter about the dialectic nature of collective identity. Americans raised on the American creed but acting contrary to it, in other words, still pay it the homage of hypocrisy. They will feel conflict and guilt whenever they are made aware of the discrepancy between their principles and actions, which is not to say that they will then adjust their policy to their professed beliefs. They are just as likely to be offended or to think up more elaborate excuses for the discrepancy. Nevertheless, it is not the concern of the study of collective identities to moralize but rather to catalog the *self-images* and *themes of obsessive concern* of a given collectivity, perhaps along with a record of actual performance. But the emphasis should be on the theme itself, or else the analysis becomes a mere servant to a moralistic desire to decry or punish rather than to explain.

[90] See also the comments by C. Vann Woodward in "The Search for Southern Identity," *Virginia Quarterly Review,* Summer 1958, pp. 321–338, on the different sense of identity of the American South.

The pitfall of moralism is an old acquaintance among the wrong ways of studying national character. After more than a century of serious writing on that subject it is as true as ever that a description of any national character often tells more about the observer—and possibly the character of his own nation —than about the nation he describes. Far too often the analysis of another nation's identity has been used chiefly as a club with which to administer a verbal beating. And no less often the description of one's own nation has been either an unabashed apologia or an example of rather myopic, partisan social criticism. In order to salvage what may be worthwhile in the traditional studies of national character, then, everything tainted by these false premises needs to be discarded.

Other pitfalls   There are further pitfalls to which the student of national identity should be alerted. One is the tendency of national-character writings to reify their subject as if it were some kind of natural law, inescapable fate, or collective soul beyond the will of any individual to escape or of a whole people to change. "Mr. X is a nice guy but, of course, he is a you-know-what." Closely related to this mistake is the assumption of unity and uniformity of the "modal personality" throughout large and heterogeneous nations in direct contradiction to even the most modest gathering of empirical evidence. It is no doubt easier on the mental capacity of both writer and reader to assign one descriptive formula to all Spaniards from San Sebastian to Cadiz, especially if one attempts to contrast the Spanish against the Portuguese, Italians, or French. And yet such an exercise in literary logic is demonstrably untrue to the considerable regional variety, the differences among Catalans, Basques, and Andalusians, between town and country, men and women, and among the social classes of Spain, not to mention Portugal, Italy, or France.

Nor does it make sense to picture the national character of a given nation as something unchangeable over the course of time. A nation as noted for stability, respect for law, and moral squeamishness as the English today, for example, in the eighteenth century had a reputation for lawlessness and riotous license. Most modern nations, moreover, have undergone cycles leading from political quiescence and stagnation to generations of revolutionary upheaval and back again. Seventeenth-century England with its civil wars, the execution of a king, and its brilliant abundance of revolutionary political doctrines must have looked just as shocking to the conservative French as did revolutionary France in the 1790s to the conservative Edmund Burke. It is the task of the responsible study of national character to determine the dimensions of its subject differentiated by time, group, and region and not to commit itself to nonfactual notions of an eternal, uniform "essence of a people."

Origin of Israeli collective identity

A excellent example of how collective identity originates, how it is distributed, and how it should be studied is the analysis of Israeli identity by S. N. Eisenstadt.[91] The self-image of the Israeli community and its state, like that of many modern nation-states throughout the world, originated with a revolutionary nationalistic movement with an ideology tied to the dynamics of social modernization, albeit with thematic variations ranging from revolutionary socialism and militant trade unionism to orthodox Judaism. The movement grew up in the 1890s among Jews in the Diaspora in Central and Eastern Europe who wanted their own nation-state in Palestine in order to escape either cultural annihilation by assimilation or the hostility and persecution of the awakening nations among whom they lived.

Revolutionary nationalistic movements vary widely in their balance between universalistic assimilativeness and xenophobic exclusiveness. Few are quite as openly universalistic as was the spirit of the French Revolution, which meant to carry the rights and institutions of free men to all the nations of the world.[92] Other national movements or nations, by contrast, are far more intent on living along their own rationale, with their own religions, folkways, and idiosyncrasies. With some, the balance between universalism and exclusiveness may also reflect their

[91] See his essay in *National Character in the Perspective of the Social Sciences* (Annals), pp. 117–123.

[92] Even French colonial policy, unlike that of the British, was predicated on the theory that the colonial peoples could become cultured Frenchmen with all the rights and privileges attached to that status, at least in theory. Americans, too, by dint of their revolutionary heritage and as a nation of immigrants seeking dignity and freedom, are highly universalistic.

experiences of oppression or conquest by stronger neighbors.[93] The Zionist movement likewise had to find its own balance between universalistic and ethnocentric values. It also had to arrive at working compromises on the language to be used in the new state and the role religion was to play considering the range of religious and secular groups in the new community.

In the diversity of motives and group orientations, a common symbol of the collective identity was found in the image of the egalitarian pioneer, selfless, spartan, and collectivity-oriented, building a new nation of new individuals by manual and agricultural labor. As with the "natural man" of the French Revolution or the "new Soviet man," individual and collective rebirth were logical corollaries of the utopian vision. Their realization took the form of the communal settlements (kibbutzim and moshavim) in which individuals took on the new identity in communal labor, preparation for defense against hostile neighbors, and in inspired cultural creativity.

As Eisenstadt explains, the ideology spread and penetrated to strategic points of the Israeli social system, where it began to determine aspects of the institutional structure. Elites designated as bearers of the ideology, such as the members of certain kibbutzim, began to be recognized by the community, especially by the workers. Political, economic, and cultural elites closely identified themselves with the pioneer symbols and implanted them into the institutional structure, most of all in the workers' education and youth movements and in the common style of life. The spread of the pioneer ideology was greatly facilitated by the absence of significant counterideologies and by the strongly felt need for a unifying faith among the various immigrant groups. Once the ideology had provided a framework for a new set of individual and collective identities, its content also came to dominate the criteria for the allocation of rewards and the recruitment for positions of importance in the community. Mem-

---

[93] As one of the foremost historians of nationalism, Hans Kohn, once suggested, a nation's attitude toward immigration is a telltale indication of its exclusiveness. If an immigrant to the United States fails to become a citizen after an appropriate number of years, Americans tend to ask, "Why doesn't he?" If a foreigner in Switzerland tries to become a Swiss citizen, on the other hand, the people of that venerable democracy would wonder from what he could be running away.

bership and stature in the various pioneering sects or in the General Federation of Labor (Histadrut) was a prized prerequisite for community leadership.

POLITICAL CULTURE AND INSTITUTIONS

Institutionalization of ideology

As is customary during the institutionalization of an ideology, a certain flattening and erosion of the earlier vividness of the pioneer ideology began with the establishment of the state of Israel and the socioeconomic differentiation of modern Israeli society. The ideological charisma became routinized as pioneer leaders became the functionally specialized administrators, military planners, and politicians of the new state or the managers and entrepreneurs of its private sectors. The elites themselves, who derive legitimacy from the common ideology and its symbols, have a vested interest in turning the system into an ideological movement regime—as they have indeed done in some new nations such as Guinea.[94] But the rationale of functional specialization and differentiation decrees otherwise, provided the society is a "free society"—that is, one whose subsystems are functionally autonomous. Such functional autonomy is lacking in such movement regimes as the communist states of our day, perhaps because they did not possess the same degree of social differentiation at the time of the communist takeover. In Israel the attempt to keep the various educational, professional, and occupational groups from becoming autonomous from the integral value system of the major collective organizations, such as the state, Histadrut, and the pioneer groups, was a failure. Yet the ideology remained to provide a sense of collective identity within which pluralism could evolve.[95]

[94] For a discussion of movement regimes, see also Robert C. Tucker, "Toward a Comparative Politics of Movement Regimes," *American Political Science Review,* 55 (June 1961), 281–289.

[95] See also Leonard J. Fein, *Politics in Israel.* Boston: Little, Brown, 1967, chaps. 2–4, and Oscar Kraines, *Government and Politics in Israel.* Boston: Houghton Mifflin, 1961, chaps. 4, 9, and 10, and the sources cited there.

The example of the institutionalization of ideology in Israel [96] leads us back to basic questions of the role of political culture within the political system. Ideological movements, when successful, attempt to translate their political beliefs into specific structures, such as institutions, procedures, and roles. This translation, always difficult, is fraught with the danger that differences of ideological interpretation will give rise to internal discontent and disaffection and eventually destroy, rather than enhance, the unity of the collectivity. On the other hand, as Aristotle remarked in a scathing comment on Plato's utopia, too much unity and conformity in a political community is far worse than pluralistic diversity. Twentieth-century witch hunts and totalitarian forms of government have underscored this dictum with blood. In any case, the relationship between the political culture in all its aspects (cognition, affect, and evaluation) and political structures requires further discussion here.

Origin of institutions

Several theories explain how institutions and other structures come to be, and none of them quite follows the simplistic idea that "the father of our country gave us our constitution," a popular myth of evidently religious inspiration. One theory derives institutions from the exchanges of personal attitudes, sentiments, and activities within small informal groups and face-to-face settings. The satisfactions of these interpersonal exchanges create patterns and norms and serve as crystallization points for broader institutional norms and settings, where tangible rewards will take the place of the personal satisfactions of the small groups.[97] Politically, this could indeed be the process by which new orientations of political culture arise from cooperation in small groups among like-minded individuals. The new orientations in turn create stable, new behavior patterns or institutions, or they maintain the existing structures. The governmental institutions of a given system thus would possess legitimate authority to the extent that their norms and values had not yet been superseded

---

[96] On the general subject of the institutionalization of ideologies oriented toward "the evaluative integration of the collectivity," see especially Parsons, *The Social System*, pp. 348–383.

[97] George C. Homans, *Social Behavior*, pp. 292 and *passim*.

by new norms and values growing from the life of the informal groups of society.[98]

Roles and norms   Another theory, developed in particular by the structural-functional school to link individual behavior and societal functions, stresses the *crystallization of individual roles,* which are said to be the units of the social and political systems. David Riesman, for example, has shown how the same social role may "harness" different types of personalities and not be materially affected by the different subjective meanings people get out of playing it.[99] In politics, of course, roles are the very basis of comparison, whether they have been given legal sanction or not. And they are capable of change by innovation or systemic change stemming from the changes in the system of which they are a rather narrowly defined part. New roles are crystallizing and being differentiated all the time, even in the most stable societies, thus adding to the *role map of its social system.* The standards of expected behavior of each role are its *norms* which can be codified in legal systems or left to custom, as were nearly all norms in the days of premodern society, when people were less inclined to demand "there ought to be a law" about any bagatelle.

Norms are closely related to the values and beliefs shared by the members of a well-integrated system. As long as values and beliefs are widely shared, the enforcement of existing norms and enactment of new norms will seem painless. But when the prevailing values are challenged by dissension and the cry for "law and order" is heard, then the enforcement of the legal norms becomes the harsh and prominent feature of the political system.[100] Roles themselves also can become unstable as a result

[98] Several assumptions underlie this argument, however, such as the similarity of the exchanges at both levels or their interchangeability, although the processes at the institutional level are indirect and more varied and use generalized media of exchange, casting doubt on the analogy. See S. N. Eisenstadt, *Essays on Comparative Institutions.* New York: Wiley, 1965, pp. 24–25.

[99] In Alfred H. Stanton and Stewart E. Percy, eds., *Personality and Political Crisis.* New York: Free Press, 1951, p. 81.

[100] Social status, it should be added here, is the structural dimension of the individual role, assigning to its bearer rights, obligations, and a position in the system of social stratification.

of the role confusion when the same person plays several roles, or because of conflicting or lacking norms, as in the case of *lacunae* in the law. Since political roles often have distinct goals or purposes as well, confusion could also come from conflicting goals or from conflicts among goals, norms, and values, as in the case of an officeholder who fails to follow the norm when its command violates his deeply held beliefs.[101]

Whether institutions are derived from small-group interaction or role crystallization, the relevance of political culture is obvious in many ways. Whether legal norms and institutions are derived from roles and the relations among roles or from the values and beliefs of the members of the political system (including its face-to-face groups), they always reflect the attitudes and the belief system of society. Once roles and structures have become more permanent, they also form objects of the political orientation of the individual member of the system. They become a part of his cognitive map of the system. Whether the role is his own or someone else's, or whether there is a whole structure of roles making up a public institution, he can have positive or negative feelings toward it—pride, distrust, or contempt. He can also draw the role into his evaluative grasp of the political situation and base his own political actions on his judgment of it.

There is a difference, of course, between attitudes toward one's own role and toward the roles of others. Mechanisms of ego involvement make it rather unlikely in most cases that a citizen voter, party member, or elected or appointed public official would view his own role with contempt. Still, there is considerable leeway in an individual's performance (or nonperformance) of various roles and his upholding of the legal and customary norms of his role, depending on his evaluation of how they relate to his own goals or values. Sociopsychology research has suggested that childhood and adolescent socialization may inculcate modes of transacting exchanges or priorities of desires that modify the role substantially. Adult socialization, too, may create new patterns, such as susceptibility to bribe or an inclination toward nonperformance among other likeminded role players.

[101] See also the discussion of other theories of institutionalization and institutional change by Eisenstadt, *Essays on Comparative Institutions,* chap. 1.

The problems are compounded when the individual role is a part of a larger whole. A citizen and voter necessarily thinks of his own role in conjunction with the entire body politic. A party member identifies his role with the activities of the entire party, feeling slighted when his party is slighted. Notions of group and personal identity, self-respect, and perhaps also self-interest are tied up with his involvement in and performance of his role. It is quite possible to identify strongly with one's country and government and to be a poor citizen and a nonvoter. And the attitudes toward one's own party can run the gamut from purely nominal membership for ulterior motives to dedicated activism, or from a kind of personal activism combined with contempt for the party to a passive, but positive, identification—to mention only a few possibilities among many.

Members of large public bodies—civil servants, judges, and legislators—usually have role images that mix professional orientations and concept of their public function. They generally develop in their line of work an expertise of sorts that can be a source of pride in craftsmanship or in specialized knowledge. They also acquire a definite concept of the public duties of "a good civil servant" or public employee, "a responsible judge," or "a man of the people" in the legislature that mirrors the rationale of the governmental system, the *esprit de corps* of their public body, and their own earnest convictions. As for the rationale of the system, for example, there are enormous differences from country to country regarding civil service and judiciary, depending on such variables as recruitment, training, and the prevailing legal system. Legislators differ considerably in the same country in their conception of how to represent their constituents. Some may take a Burkean stance, wanting to make statesmen-like decisions for the good of the country and, if necessary, regardless of the wishes of their own constituents. Others may feel that they are merely carrying out the will of their voters, possibly against special interests. A third type may try to balance, as an honest broker, the competing interests of voters, special interests, and the country. In the French National Assembly it has long been the custom for the individual deputy, believing himself a tribune of the people, to stand up to the presumably oppressive government on the floor of the legislature but to feel out of his depth when called upon to run that government as a cabinet member.

Attitudes toward authority

Some further aspects of attitudes of citizens and voters toward public-officeholders are worth mentioning. As a given system leaves its traditional past on the road toward modernity, popular attitudes toward authority in any form—paternal, social, or political—undergo significant changes. An assessment of such attitudes will very likely have to distinguish between the authoritarian attitude of traditional society (and its remainders in a significant number of families even in such countries as the United States today) and what has been called "authoritarianism" by such social scientists as Theodor W. Adorno, Else Frenkel-Brunswick, and Samuel H. Flowerman.[102] The traditional authoritarianism was a self-reinforcing system in which to be authoritarian was to be normal.[103] The presence of traditional authoritarians in democratic societies raises problems of discongruity that may also lead to personality conflicts, provided such authoritarians do not live among like-minded people. The concept of the "authoritarian personality," however, focused chiefly on people who were not the genuine products of an authoritarian upbringing, but rather of severe social strains and maladjustment that produced striking patterns of ethnic prejudice, intolerance, and a propensity for violence together with a profoundly ambiguous attitude toward authority. The typical "authoritarian" of this definition was capable of worshiping a new leader who created his own role in deliberate confrontation with established role images. The authoritarian then debunks incumbent leadership, thus implying a strongly negative affect toward the established institutions as such.

In a well-conceived symposium on leadership research organized by Lewis Edinger, several contributors each in his own way approached the question of the ambiguity of political leadership authority in industrialized societies. A German psychiatrist argued that the passing of traditional authority amid specialization and routinization of socioeconomic functions has left us

[102] See especially Theodor W. Adorno *et al., The Authoritarian Personality.* New York: Harper & Row, 1950, and Flowerman's essay reprinted in Macridis and Brown, *Comparative Politics.* Homewood, Ill.: Dorsey Press, 1961.

[103] See also the description of authoritarian and innovative personality types in Everett Hagen, *On the Theory of Social Change.* Homewood, Ill.: Dorsey Press, 1962, chap. 5.

psychologically fatherless and at the mercy of rival sibling leaders. A political scientist, Samuel H. Barnes, stressed instead the limitations political leaders face in mobilizing mass support. On the basis of survey research among Italian Socialists, Barnes concluded that leadership style goes with the sense of political competence of the masses of followers. When the latter feel incompetent to influence leaders and decisions, they can be effectively mobilized without a sense of participation. In a word, nondemocratic leadership is acceptable to them, even though democracy may be the end of the movement.[104] If this conclusion applies to industrial societies, of course, one can hardly blame developing nations barely past the traditional stage for preferring undemocratic leadership roles and choosing flamboyant men on horseback such as Nasser, Nkrumah, or Sukarno. Nor is there an unlimited supply of those who can engage loyalty in this manner. Latin America once was the classic country of military *caudillos* ruling with brute force over prostrate populations. But the winds of change have brought about an involuntary and unstable pluralism of old *politicos,* new functional elites, and occasional hangovers from the days of the triumvirate of landowners, the church, and the military.[105] Leadership crises of different kinds are more prevalent in the world today than an excess of all-too-solid despotism.

Communist leadership crises   One typical variety of leadership crisis can be found in early communist regimes, which have to reconcile the odd mixture of Marxist anarchic antiauthoritarianism and the worship of political and industrial authority typical of developmental dictatorship.[106] Robert A. Scalapino supplied a convenient typology of Asian communist leaders, for example, by distinguishing (1) *ideologues,* generally intellectuals burning

[104] See their contributions in Lewis Edinger, ed., *Political Leadership in Industrialized Societies.* New York: Wiley, 1967, and Samuel H. Barnes, *Party Democracy: Politics in an Italian Socialist Federation.* New Haven, Conn.: Yale University Press, 1967.

[105] See, for example, Robert E. Scott in Seymour M. Lipset and Aldo Solari, eds., *Elites in Latin America.* New York: Oxford, 1967, and Irving Louis Horowitz, "Political Legitimacy and the Institutionalization of Crisis," *Comparative Political Studies,* 1 (April 1968), 45–69.

[106] See also Adam Ulam, *The Unfinished Revolution.* New York: Random House, 1960.

with frustration and resentment [107] and yearning to be the philosopher-kings of rapid socioeconomic change; (2) *activists* anxious to satisfy their thirst for dramatic action and to show their leadership skills; and (3) *careerists* from low social origins, to whom advancement in the party promises a rewarding career and who are more typical of communist countries or movements in possession of local power. The first of the three types, like Cassius in Shakespeare's *Julius Caesar,* is probably the most likely "troublemaker" in communist movements or regimes, because "he thinks too much" and harbors in his bosom the essential irreconcilability of anarchism and the totalitarian mystique. Scalapino also surveyed the styles of leadership over the range from dominance of one man or of a small clique, to collective leadership for nearly twenty Asian communist parties; he noted the increasing conformity to the Chinese pattern (also that of the early Soviet Union), which moved from collective leadership to one-man dominance.[108]

Alfred G. Meyer, on the other hand, found in communist systems a series of stages of development of authority that have their parallels in non-Communist industrial societies.[109] At the time of revolution and civil war, the antiauthoritarian, utopian strain in communism comes to the fore, to the point of ignoring major parts of the communist doctrine, such as that on land reform. Once the charisma of successful revolution passes, the new regimes feel a desperate need to acquire legitimate authority by organization, coercion, ideological persuasion, and concessions to potential enemies within and outside the country. During this extended "system building" phase, which was the Stalinist era in the Soviet Union, drastic and wholesale changes of all sorts take place under a facade of ideological unity manifested symbolically in the person and unquestioned authority of the role of the leader himself. Underneath this facade, disorganized authority patterns shift with the restructuring of society, even of

[107] The role of personal resentment and reverted prejudice in the makeup of militants of ideological movements was stressed already by the German social scientists Max Scheler and Werner Sombart in the 1920s.

[108] Scalapino, *The Communist Revolution in Asia,* chap. 1.

[109] In Edinger, *Political Leadership in Industrialized Societies,* pp. 84–107.

concepts of reality, and of all leadership patterns except for the "pseudocharisma" of the top.[110] Following the phase of system building, in now-industrialized Russia and Eastern Europe, a new phase of "system management" has evoked a continuing revolt against overcentralized, authoritarian bureaucracy, often spearheaded by professional elites competing with the party, such as economists, diplomats, writers, or military men.

Western leadership crises　There have also been many attempts to understand the leadership crises occurring in industrialized Western societies from time to time, and the crisis leadership they often produce. Recalling Barnes's thesis of citizen competence and nondemocratic leadership, it is easy to argue that even a democratically competent people—and there are degrees of competence—may feel overwhelmed by foreign or domestic crises and look for a dictator for a time. The ancient Romans used to have such an office, and most Western constitutions provide for emergency powers of "constitutional dictatorship," to use Rossiter's phrase. The British gave such powers to Winston Churchill when the onslaught of the Axis powers appeared overwhelming. The Germans gave a combined majority to National Socialist and Communist totalitarianism in 1932, when economic crisis and governmental ineffectiveness had reached their peak. E. Victor Wolfenstein examined with special reference to Churchill and Hitler the personality type that is attracted to the role of crisis leadership. The psychodynamics of the crisis leaders, whatever their origin, mark them off as deviants from the normal leadership styles of their countries. But when their time comes, their style of performance turns out to be so congruent with the role expectations and emotional needs of the masses that they can mobilize mass support with ease.[111] Similar things have been said about Charles de Gaulle.[112]

[110] See also Mead, "Soviet Attitudes toward Authority," and Jeremiah F. Wolpert, "Toward a Sociology of Authority," in Alvin W. Gouldner, ed., *Studies in Leadership*. New York: Harper & Row, 1950. Further, see the discussion of the role of ideology by Raymond A. Bauer, Alex Inkeles, and Clyde Kluckhohn, *How the Soviet System Works*. Cambridge, Mass.: Harvard University Press, 1956, chap. 3.

[111] See his article in Edinger, *Political Leadership in Industrialized Societies,* chap. 6. See also Edinger, "Political Science and Political Biography," *Journal of Politics,* 26 (May–August 1964), and his "psycho-

Attitudes toward complex governments Popular attitudes toward single governmental roles or complexes of roles are relatively simple by comparison with those required by pluralistic political structures, such as whole party or governmental systems. The whole edifice of western constitutional tradition assumes that the people will understand and appreciate carefully contrived systems of several public bodies with divided authority and prescribed balances among them. As one may recall from the Almond and Verba study, the extent of popular knowledge about the system of government and the incumbents of its roles is a significant variable of political cultures. Furthermore, people must feel positively toward the attempt to secure popular liberty by setting up checks and balances, even though the practice of such constitutional governments may often appear more like a prescription for deadlock and confusion. It would be easier, perhaps, for the confused citizen to love a monistic government, such as that ruled by a king or dictator. Finally, as a politically active citizen, one has to channel one's own actions in the right direction, such as electioneering for elective offices, lobbying with both administrators and legislators, or respectfully petitioning judges or executive chiefs.

The attitudinal problems involved in complex constitutional forms of government may be illustrated by the following examples: One of the difficulties that arose early in the political development of both Japan and pre-Hitler Germany was the considerable difference in popular esteem of government bureaucrats as compared to party politicians and of military officers as compared to businessmen. The military and the administration were still identified with the social status they had enjoyed in traditional society. Consequently, modern parliaments, effective party government, and even a modern market economy with its bargaining way of life were relatively weak and helpless against the challenge of other groups. It was not until after 1945 that parliamentary democracy in Japan and Germany began to enjoy the popular respect it needed in order to work. Another telling

---

biography," *Kurt Schumacher*. Stanford, Calif.: Stanford University Press, 1966.

[112] But see Stanley Hoffmann's contrary interpretation of French leadership styles in Edinger, *Political Leadership in Industrialized Societies*, chap. 5.

example is the notable stability of the constitutional monarchies of Great Britain, Scandinavia, Belgium, and the Netherlands as compared to the turbulent demise of republican regimes in Spain, Portugal, Germany, or Austria. The explanation widely accepted for the greater staying power of those nominal monarchies during extended crises has been that the common man finds monarchy easier to understand and to identify with, a gratifying symbol of unity above the clash of parties and opinions.

Hardly less complex are the attitudinal sets involved in such participatory institutions as political parties, associations, and media such as the press or television. A person may be deeply involved with one party whose victory he desires while at the same time he is expected to tolerate its competitors and find party competition desirable. Worse yet, his predilections are supposed to be limited to a "workable party system," such as a two-party system. Small wonder if he develops a case of role confusion or role strain, provided he does not tire of understanding and cooperating with the system's complexities. Similar considerations apply to interest groups and to the freedom of the press. It is a lot to expect of anyone to tolerate dissenting opinions other than one's own.

Political culture and policy making

This brings us to the end of our somewhat sketchy survey of aspects of political culture and their relationship to the study of political interaction and decision making. The materials available are still somewhat too scattered and unrelated to fall into place with ease. Nevertheless, the need for ordering and comparing psychocultural and sociocultural information about given political systems has emerged clearly and with cogency. Empirical comparative politics can no longer be carried on without accounting for what the people of different systems think and feel. The largest gap in our current understanding of political culture still concerns the process of *evaluation*. Knowledge of a situation and feelings toward political objects lead at best to an awareness of the options for action. How these individuals or groups decide which option to pursue or when to start the action is still an obscure process. Moreover, the student of political cultures should be forewarned of the remaining complexities of linking the micropolitical understanding of individuals with the macropolitical analysis of whole systems and their behavior. Notwithstanding Plato, the state is not—and never can be— "man writ large." The orientations of mass political culture and its various subcultures come to bear on collective behavior and governmental policies only via the complex channels of spatially distributed governmental structures, systems of group interaction, and formal decision-making processes in governmental institutions, such as the following chapters will discuss.

4

THE CENTER AND THE PERIPHERY
Local-national relationships

With rare exceptions, the prevalent form of political organization today is the nation-state, a body politic of extensive size and a population ranging from a few to hundreds of millions. Even such dwarf states as the Maldives far exceed in size and population the ancient preference for a *polis* of no more than 50,000 inhabitants, a face-to-face community capable of gathering in the marketplace within earshot of a speaker.[1]

Man's personal habitat remains relatively small and localized, at least in relation to his entire nation-state. A modern citizen usually grows up in a family of moderate size, even if we add his further relatives. He (or she) lives in a face-to-face community relationship with friends, fellow workers, and neighbors numbering at the most several hundred. Beyond this, his (or her) relationships become increasingly indirect and vague. There is a sense of kinship and of common sentiment, perhaps, with larger groups—ethnic, occupational, socioeconomic, religious, or partisan—but no real contact. There may be an awareness of governmental institutions and of elected representatives, but again only the most tenuous personal contact. There may be moments of intense identification with all of one's conationals in the flush of patriotic sentiment or with a national leader at a

[1] See the discussion of this point in Carl J. Friedrich, *Man and His Government*. New York: McGraw-Hill, 1963, pp. 532–533.

time of trial and confrontation, but again the contact is mostly symbolic and soon recedes behind everyday, parochial concerns.

The drama of modern politics is staged for the most part against a background of vast geographical and human distances separating these communal habitats. The distances impose barriers to communication and to identification. They make it difficult for some people to recognize that they have problems in common with others who live many miles away—difficult also to get together with others and to decide how to cope with their common problems. If there are problems to solve, changes to bring about, and resistance to overcome, furthermore, distances become major obstacles; an all-out effort is required if political action is to be effective. The relations between the center of a modern nation-state and the communal periphery, and also among the peripheral communal habitats, constitute one of the chief dimensions of political analysis.

LOCALISM AND NATIONALISM

Traditional societies for the most part are based on stable local communities, which almost totally confine the whole world of the vast majority of individuals. The only major exceptions are nomadic tribes, whose communal habitat is the mobile tribe and its laws and mores.[2] Modernizing societies, by contrast, strain toward breaking down the exclusiveness of local identification and replacing it with a cross-local, supraregional, more or less national identification. This transition from localism to nationalism is the universal trend in all developing societies, although there is no society as yet, however developed, whose citizens identify exclusively with the nation-state. Nevertheless, one could build a scale of individual orientations shifting from

[2] Daniel Lerner in *The Passing of Traditional Society* (New York: Free Press, 1957) and others as well have shown how, for example, Bedouin tribes may shield themselves against the disturbing realities of urban life with mental walls of prejudice and superstition. Nevertheless, nomadic life appears also to be substantially different from most agricultural societies, manifesting itself, for example, in some egalitarianism and, as among the Somalis, in a kind of pastoral democracy in which all adult males deliberate with the tribal elders.

the local to national concerns—parallel to the progress of modernization—and perhaps also account for the frequent occurrence of a regional, in-between step of cross-local identification short of the eventual national orientation.

Achieving national unity

For the optimal formation and functioning of the modern state and the modern society a good deal of national unity is required. The process of achieving this unity has to start somewhere. It often begins in many places at once, consisting in a kind of will of the people in the communal habitats to grow together into a large integrated community. Or it may start from an advanced center of government and social development, from which the unifying effort penetrates into the periphery. Very often, the *integration* efforts of the periphery and the *penetration* efforts of the center spur each other, speeding up the social and political unification of the nation-state.

In the early evolution of the modern state and society in Europe, the prevalent process was one of penetration from the center. A good case in point is the legal unification of England by the circuit-riding "king's judges," who in the twelfth century spread the English common law over the fragmented feudal jurisdictions. The "reception" of entire Roman law systems and codes by kings and princes on the European continent also amounted to an attempt by the centers to unify countries by penetrating the thicket of local legal conventions. To this day, the highest national courts, especially in federations, see one of their most important tasks in the maintenance, by way of judicial appeal, of unity and uniformity in the interpretation of the law throughout the country. And national parliaments likewise continue to assure penetration and unification through legislation—their primary task from the beginning of the nation-building era.

Administrative penetration Another instrument of effective penetration from the center was administrative. England in the twelfth century and France and Prussia in the seventeenth century show the significance of replacing local, decentralized power structures with a centrally directed administrative service recruited from persons independent of local support.[3] In a feudal society of particularistic patterns of authority, the establishment of a modern, rationalized administration was a revolutionary device in itself. To give the monarch the perfect instrument to make his royal will prevail in the last recesses of his kingdom, after having broken down the resistance of such intermediate structures as the aristocracy and the church, established a direct link between the sovereign center and the subjects at the periphery. In the developing countries of our own age, there are telling analogies whenever central governments strive to reach people in the more remote areas of their nation.

The national governments of most new countries of Asia, Africa, and Latin America are endemically too weak to maintain close relations with the local villages even in the more densely populated areas. The more remote areas inhabited by ethnic minorities or aborigines are hardly penetrated at all. The highlands of Vietnam, for example, home of tribes of prehistoric stock and of Indonesian, Mongolian, and Melanesian migrations of long ago, were hardly ever entered by the Vietnamese or their governments, North or South, until they became staging areas and battleground of the National Liberation Front.[4] India likewise has its mountain tribes and remote areas where the national government is considered a foreign invader. The transport and organizational difficulties alone are so great that the Indian national elections of 1951–1952, for example, were spread out over three months to allow voters to adjust to climatic and travel conditions.[5]

Kalman Silvert has given us a moving glimpse of the collapse of the inward-looking structure of a village society under the impact of nationalism in Guatemala. In his interviews of two

[3] On England and Prussia, see especially Carl J. Friedrich, *Constitutional Government and Democracy,* 4th ed. Waltham, Mass.: Blaisdell, 1968, pp. 39–43.

[4] See Robert Scigliano, *South Vietnam: Nation under Stress.* Boston: Houghton Mifflin, 1963, pp. 2–3. See also the penetrating account of the Indian problem of surmounting the "distance between government and society," the villages, by Reinhard Bendix, *Nation-Building and Citizenship.* New York: Wiley, 1964, pp. 255–259, 266–298.

[5] See Vera Micheles Dean, *New Patterns of Democracy in India.* Cambridge, Mass.: Harvard University Press, 1959, p. 93.

townships of 4000 and 30,000 inhabitants, respectively, an Indian majority of about 80 percent distinguished itself sharply in political ignorance and traditional culture from the more nationally oriented minority of *ladinos* (*mestizos*). The respondents in the smaller *municipio* also differed from those in the larger in that none of them thought "every Guatemalan had a real chance to become President," a question answered in the affirmative by half of the respondents of the larger *municipio*. A similarly large number of the latter, when asked what they would do if they had enough time and money, expressed a desire to "get out of their town," while most of the small-town respondents opted for "going into business and buying a farm." The increasing tendency toward political and spatial mobility among *ladinos* and in the more urban environments is obvious.[6]

Military penetration   The most dramatic and oldest method of penetration of large territories from the center is military. From the dawn of history, conquerors, usurpers, and ordinary rulers have used armed force to extend their command to the farthest corners of a country. When parts of a country rebel or threaten to secede, in particular, even the most benign or democratic regime is likely to resort to military force and occupation to restore the sway of central power, whether secession threatened in the Congo or in the American South. The examples of modern nation building with the help of the military range from the communist civil war in Russia and conquest of China, through the national unification of Germany and Italy in the 1860s, to the independence struggles and civil war of many an ex-colonial new nation in the recent past. In many developing countries of Asia, Africa, and Latin America, moreover, the army frequently performs certain administrative services and construction activities that would normally fall to development administration. For reasons of its superior education and or-

[6] See Kalman H. Silvert, *The Conflict Society,* rev. ed. New York: American Universities Field Staff, 1966, chap. 3. The substance of this process has also been elucidated by Lerner in *The Passing of Traditional Society* and by Karl W. Deutsch in "Social Mobilization and Political Development," *American Political Science Review,* 55 (September 1961), 493–514.

ganization, the army in these countries is often better equipped and has a better public image for these purposes than the feeble administrative service.[7]

Penetration by economic development   Economic development, too, has penetration aspects, either in central planning and regulation or in the activity of private economic enterprise, pushing its markets and the exploitation of resources into peripheral areas. Governmental planning, development aid, and regulation are particularly at home in contemporary societies, both developed and developing. The most dramatic impact of industrial revolution and expanding capitalistic activity today is limited to developing areas and backward parts of advanced societies. Nevertheless, in a more limited sense penetration occurs whenever new technologies or new products are disseminated.

In striking contrast to unity by penetration from the center, modern nation building thrives also on voluntary *integration*, the growing together of peripheral communities into a larger, common whole. This impulse lies at the heart of all nationalistic movements, whether they desire greater unity in an existing body politic, national independence from a foreign overlord, or national unification of previously separate units. On an individual level, the desire for voluntary integration into a larger, cross-local community can even be said to underlie much of the mechanism of internal migration and spatial mobility. Kalman's urbanites in the larger of the two communities he studied wanted to travel or go to Guatemala City primarily to become a part of the larger, national community.

[7] See especially Lucian W. Pye in John J. Johnson, *The Role of the Military in Underdeveloped Countries.* Princeton, N.J.: Princeton University Press, 1962, pp. 82–83, 245–246, and 250. See also Clifford Geertz's description of premodern Indonesia: "The early polities were thus not so much solitary territorial units as loose congeries of villages oriented toward a common urban center, each such center competing with others for ascendancy. Whatever degree of regional or, at moments, interregional hegemony prevailed depended, not on the systematic administrative organization of extensive territory under a single king, but on the varying abilities of kings to mobilize and apply effective striking forces with which to sack rival capitals, abilities that were believed to rest on essentially religious . . . grounds." In David E. Apter, *Ideology and Discontent.* New York: Free Press, 1964, p. 66.

Integration by representative government   Finally, one of the most distinctive instrumentalities of the Western tradition, *representative government,* deserves to be considered in some detail as a major device for integrating large territories. From its medieval beginnings, when legislative activity was insignificant and the British Parliament was considered more as a court and as a check on the taxing powers of the monarchy, the integrative purpose of representation was already abundantly clear. Kings might supply a symbol of unity or a virtual representation of the realm, but there is nothing so representative as an assembly of men elected from all the parts of the country to gather in one spot and decide matters for the whole country. Whether it represents regions, estates, social classes, parties, interest groups, or individuals—whatever may be considered legitimate in a given system—the parliament is a kind of a miniature version of the whole body politic. And even if it should expend its energies laying taxes upon or declaring war for the people, it represents the voluntary element of consent and participation —which has always sweetened the bitter pill. The consensus reached by the representatives in Parliament in theory *represents* the unified consensus in the whole country, even though actual agreement among the populace may be quite impossible.

THE ORGANIZATION OF THE PERIPHERY

The building of the national community in nation-states has also depended vitally on the political organization of the communal periphery and its relation to the center. In all but the most miniature states it is obviously impractical to relate each individual citizen solely and directly to the center. The people of a locality prefer to have a substantial part of their governmental institutions close to home, and the center, too, has a decided interest in decentralizing some of its governmental functions. The prima facie case for democratic government is to be made in a local more than in a national setting. Indeed, there have been strong premodern elements of democracy in many traditional village communities, even in such an unlikely place as autocratic czarist Russia, where the *mir* was praised by famous writers such as Tolstoy and the anarchists Bakunin and Prince Kropotkin as the fountainhead of popular government.

Varieties of local government

The variety of types of local government the world over is stupefying. All units of government below the national level of unitary state, and below the state level of federations, are called local government. It is, of course, possible to distinguish local units by the level at which they operate between the lowest and the state or federal level, such as rural or urban communes, districts, counties, provinces, regions, and the like. There also appear to be several distinctive forms of governmental organization, which can serve as ideal types from which others deviate only in minor ways. One such type, which was probably universal among all societies at one time, is the traditional village community. Another type is that pioneered by the French Revolution and Napoleon and adopted by many nations of Europe and the Third World. A third type is the Anglo-American approach to local government; and a fourth is that of the Soviet Union and some other communist countries.

The traditional village community

The traditional local community is usually held together by the social power of a tribe, a clan, or the extended family. It may be composed of an isolated village or a group of villages. It would take an anthropologist to unravel the roles of custom, communal property, ritual, and religious notions that make up the traditional law of the village. There is usually a chief, headman, or village patriarch, frequently assisted by a council of elders. The mode of their attaining and continuing to hold office varies widely from democratic election to the oligarchy of age, family, or social class. Their way of making decisions likewise varies from public discussion and community consent to sheer autocracy. The communal mores, in any case, are far more powerful and restrictive than even a village autocrat can afford to be, unless his power is based on external support.

Traditional village government in most parts of Europe as well as in Japan, India, and China became amalgamated with a feudal structure throughout the Middle Ages and the modern era. The utter complexity and variety of feudal arrangements defies general description. In theory, at least, it signified a "national" web of personal and quasi-property relationships. As in the crusader's kingdom of Jerusalem, the king "owned" the whole kingdom, and in exchange for loyalty and military and other services he would "loan" parts of it to a group of high lords, who in turn "loaned" it to lesser lords, and so on through many layers. At the communal level, the result was the *manorial system* whose *villeins* and serfs held their land in fief in exchange for services to the *seigneur* of the manor, who in turn owed them protection. Where the manorial system was in effect, the local power structure was largely overshadowed by the feudal presence. The only place where the dead hand of feudalism could no longer interfere with local self-government was in the new cities rising all over Europe, where the growing *bourgeoisie* (from *bourge,* "town") began to explore urban, secular ways of governing peripheral communes.

French local organization

In France, when the modern nation-state fashioned by the absolutist era and the Revolution of 1789 was established, the French type of local organization superseded village and feudal antecedents. The *ancien régime* had already created administrative districts, each under the control of a royal *intendant.* The old communes and municipalities were revived from their long slumber under the prerevolutionary autocracy with some of the first legislation of the revolutionary Constituent Assembly. Each commune could elect its own mayor and council and govern itself as it pleased, except for the occasional appearance of an inspector from Paris. The revolutionary upheaval, however, soon made necessary the reestablishment of more effective state control. Napoleon in 1800 gave French local government its present form. There is a direct administrative link from the central government down through the departments and *arrondissements* to the smallest rural commune. Departments are supervised by a prefect (*arrondissements,* by subprefects), responsible to the Ministry of Interior, which penetrated the structure from above, while mayors and councilmen integrated it from below. The mayor has to follow the directives of his council as well as the ministerial decrees governing all public services. Local jurisdiction is not narrowly defined otherwise, although there is always the threat of administrative intervention on the part of prefects and subprefects.[8]

With minor modifications, this French system has been adopted in nearly all the European countries entered by Napoleon. The Near East and parts of Africa, Central and South America, and parts of Asia likewise adopted it, although in many cases the environment modified its practice considerably.[9] In French Africa, for example, major compromises were made in such areas as the position of the native chiefs in the colonial administration or the granting of more representative self-government. In Middle Eastern villages there are often strong survivals of the traditional village system rather than the French pattern. In Brazil the autonomous powers of municipalities are great, but lack of local finances has forced state and federal authorities to take over many of the services and functions normally performed by the municipal authorities.

The Anglo-American pattern

The Anglo-American pattern, including local government in the old and newer Commonwealth nations, owes much to the evolution of local government in England. The tradition of the municipal corporation with powers defined by charter or central legislation and almost complete independence from the center is an ancient one, being traceable to the times before the Norman Conquest. The boroughs had their own officers, often including a justice of the peace, and had representatives in Parliament. After a period of decline in the seventeenth and eighteenth centuries, the Municipal Corporation Act of 1835 democratized the system by creating elective borough councils. In 1888 there followed elective *county borough* councils with broad powers and rights of supervision over urban and rural areas.[10] Administrative counties for health, police, roads, public assistance, and

[8] See, for example, Brian Chapman, *Introduction to French Local Government*. London: G. Allen, 1953.

[9] See especially Harold Alderfer, *Local Government in Developing Countries*. New York: McGraw-Hill, 1964, pp. 18–90 and chap. 3.

[10] For five centuries before 1888, counties were run by the justices of the peace. On this subject see especially Herman Finer, *English Local Government*. New York: Columbia University Press, 1934, and the literature cited there.

education, as well as noncounty boroughs and urban and rural districts, round out the picture in England. There are also a limited number of parish councils and parish meetings.

All of these units are generally free from control by other local authorities, in contrast to the French hierarchy of levels of government, where the higher levels have financial and administrative control over the lower levels. Unlike the numerous *special districts* used in the United States, the English local units have broad powers to make policies in a variety of areas. The policy-making bodies are unpaid elective councils, which run their administration with the help of council committees rather than with managers as in the United States. National control in Great Britain is accomplished by the regulatory powers of Parliament and such ministries as the Home Secretary (Interior) or the Ministry of Health. The national ministries also can send inspectors and veto certain actions and appointments.[11]

The British pattern made its appearance also in the practices of British colonial government in Africa. The emirs of northern Nigeria were recognized and left "in office," as long as there was no serious complaint against them. The British district officers were supposed to act not as executives, but as sympathetic guides along the path to efficiency and democratic evolution. This practice of *indirect rule* has sometimes been blamed for favoring the traditional forces of African society rather than the educated, urban elites. In any case, the basic pattern of leaving real policy-making authority to the local level is the same as in Great Britain, just as French colonial administration reflected the system in France, preferring direct rule.[12]

The Soviet system

The Soviet system was superimposed on a pattern of local organization seemingly modeled on the French pattern down to the level of the cantons. Czarist government sought to solve the

[11] For further sources on local government, see especially J. A. G. Griffith, *Central Departments and Local Authorities*. London: G. Allen, 1966; William Eric Jackson, *Local Government in England and Wales*, 3d ed. Baltimore, Md.: Pelican, 1963; and William A. Robson, *Local Government in Crisis*. London: G. Allen, 1966.

[12] See also L. Gray Cowan, *Local Government in West Africa* (New York: Columbia University Press), and the large literature on Nigeria.

problem of dealing with the vastness of the country by an extraordinary degree of centralization, leaving even the governors of provinces and regions with little policy-making power. The Municipal Act of 1870 enfranchised all local taxpayers and gave them the right to hold positions on the municipal boards. The village commune, the *mir,* had always been run by an elected headman and an assembly of all householders. The Russian Revolution of 1917 introduced *soviets* at all levels of government, anything below the All-Union, Union Republic, and Autonomous Republic level being considered local government. The highest local level of soviets are the *krais, oblasts, okrugs,* and the larger cities. The next lower soviets are rural and city *raions* and medium-sized cities. Finally, there are the village, small-town, and settlement soviets.

All of these levels are, of course, tightly controlled by the Communist party, from which they have also adopted the principle of "democratic centralism." [13] The practical implication for Soviet local government appears to be that local soviets are not policy-making agencies but merely carry out the policies made at the center. Local soviets elect their executive officers and committees, who are then responsible not only to their constituents but also to the executive committee of the next higher soviet. Both the governmental machinery and the Communist party apparatus are geared to *deconcentration* rather than *decentralization* of political power. The local agencies, each within its geographic range, only carry out the decisions made by the central authorities rather than exercising decentralized policy-making powers.

Many other communist states, such as Poland, East Germany, and Outer Mongolia, have similar patterns of local government. In Yugoslavia, however, the entire governmental system rests on a strong and democratically functioning local level, which has broad powers. The Yugoslav state is, at least in theory, a body composed of communes that control even the bulk of public

---

[13] According to party regulations, democratic centralism signifies the election of all party bodies and periodic reports of the party bodies, but also strict party discipline, subordination of the minority to the majority and of the lower bodies to the decisions of the higher bodies. In practice, both democratic elections and free discussion are made irrelevant to the party's autocratic mode of operation.

economic enterprises. As compared to the Soviet Union, moreover, the Yugoslav Communist party has only moderate influence on the political process at the local level.[14]

ONE CENTER OR SEVERAL?

Contemporary unitarism

Thus far we have taken it for granted that the development of nation-states proceeds along *unitary* lines, or, in other words, that there is only one center to which the periphery is related. Most contemporary states are indeed examples of *unitarism,* such as Great Britain, France, Turkey, China, or Japan. During their period of nation building they usually went through either a process of penetration from one center, as with the prerevolutionary French monarchy, or of integration into one indivisible whole by a revolutionary nationalistic movement such as the French Jacobins, or of both.[15]

Simply as an aid to the voters' understanding its simplicity in governmental organization makes unitarism attractive. The legal theory of indivisible sovereignty favors a single locus of the supreme power of the state—the central government—from which, theoretically, all the lower levels derive their authority. As long as this central government must receive a single mandate from the people in fairly frequent parliamentary elections,[16] it can be kept responsible to the people. The British system, where a strong two-party system and an all-powerful national Parliament control the executive, the judiciary, and all local government, is an ideal type of democratic unitarism.

[14] See Alderfer, *Local Government in Developing Countries,* chap. 4, and the sources cited there.

[15] See the large literature on nationalism. Also Barbara Ward, *Nationalism and Ideology.* New York: Norton, 1966, and the excellent contributions to Karl W. Deutsch and William J. Foltz, *Nation-Building.* New York: Atherton Press, 1963.

[16] As will be seen in Chap. 7 the issue is clear only in unitary, parliamentary regimes, where there is only one national elective organ, the parliament. Federalism and the separation of powers belong to a different tradition of constitutional government, whose stress on checks and balances tends to conflict with the doctrine of political responsibility.

Origin of federal states

In fact, however, many contemporary nation-states are not unitary in structure. Since modern nationalism is a relatively new phenomenon, dating back not much farther than the French Revolution, many national movements started with populations scattered under several well-established states. These existing states and their peoples had to be induced to form a political union—sometimes by contract, sometimes by force, but nearly always in such a way that they would not completely lose their earlier identity and autonomy upon entering the union. Cases in point are the national unification of the United States in the 1780s and Germany in the 1860s. There are also federal unions of formerly independent states, such as the European Common Market, which may yet flower into a political union of what have hitherto been sovereign nation-states.

In some cases a federal union may result by devolution from a more unified empire in disintegration. Thus the British Commonwealth for a while took on a quasi-federal form in transition from the Empire to the separate nationhood of many states.[17] The original thirteen American colonies similarly became separate independent states following the War of Independence, subsequently joining in a confederation and, finally, a federal union. The British colonies of India and Nigeria also devolved from imperial unity into a federal union of fairly autonomous states, of which some, Pakistan and Biafra, even seceded. Strong language and tribal communities, in these cases, made the granting of regional autonomy unavoidable.

Confederations

When a new nation-state is formed by formerly independent units, except perhaps where revolutionary nationalists have overthrown the old rulers of the original states, the logical choice is *confederation* rather than federal union. Until the advent of the American Constitution, confederation was, in fact, the only arrangement known for uniting existing states. In a confederal union, the original and several political centers do not merge,

[17] See also K. C. Wheare, *The Constitutional Structure of the Commonwealth.* New York: Oxford, 1960.

nor do they even part with much of their earlier freedom and identity. Instead, a solemn compact is concluded among the sovereign states in which they pledge to stay together and to abstain from policies inimical to the union.[18] In place of a full-fledged new central government, confederations prefer an "international assembly" or congress of delegates from each state government, which can make decisions only with the unanimous consent of each state delegation. The central authorities often have neither executive nor judicial organs and no practical enforcement powers over member states that fail to meet their obligation. The system denies the central authorities any power, fiscal or legislative, over individual citizens in the several states.[19]

The closest contemporary equivalent to the once widespread confederate form of multicenter government is the functional regional organization, such as the Schuman Plan (ECSC), the Common Market (EEC), Euratom, or the North Atlantic Treaty Organization (NATO). These organizations by definition are concerned only with a limited social function, such as economics, nuclear energy, or common defense. They possess assemblies or councils with advisory powers and high authorities or executive commissions with limited supranational authority. But the real power still lies with the sovereign member governments, who are represented in the Councils of Ministers of the organizations and in bilateral negotiations. As the successful veto of British entry into the EEC demonstrates, it is still possible for the government of one member state to block an action acceptable to all the others.

Federal unions

The fatal weaknesses of a confederate form of government in an age increasingly aware of the vast capabilities of government for human advancement led to its replacement in the United

---

[18] Such forsworn policies include especially hostilities against another member state and treaties with foreign powers that are prejudicial to other member states or to the union.

[19] One result of this institutional weakness, which was crucial in the case of the American Articles of Confederation, was the chronic lack of funds to discharge the duties and obligations of the central authorities. The Continental Congress could not even pay its armies after they had won independence.

States, Switzerland, Germany, and many newer federations with what the *Federalist Papers* called a mixture of national, or unitary, and confederate government, namely *federal union*. Most modern federations originated in response to extraordinary challenges from abroad and at home. They sought the greater security and international power of a larger state, sometimes in the face of an immediate threat of aggression. They also strove to create optimal conditions for large-scale economic development.[20] Both motives suggested governmental centralization and the consolidation of governmental power. At the same time, they wanted to retain the comforts and advantages of the existing political communities, whose governments and political elites would have opposed a complete unitarization in any case. And so they created a hybrid of unitarism and confederation, or of monocentrism and multicenter government, which has proved as durable and practical as it is difficult to define.

Characteristics of federal government   In terms of center and periphery, federal government is characterized by the superimposition of a new center over a multicenter form of government. Each original center still maintains its position vis-à-vis its periphery, and the new center has the whole federation as a periphery. The two layers of centers share governmental functions and services, and the greater new community makes for a general merging and amalgamation of the original constituent communities via the free mobility of goods and persons. The original centers, whether they are called states, provinces, *Länder,* or cantons, enjoy certain inalienable rights and immunities, such as territorial integrity and other guarantees of their continued existence and identity.

Social change and development, and occasional major crises, have brought about such notable shifts in the respective functions of the local, state, and federal governments that it is often difficult to draw a hard and fast distinction between a state of a federal system and strong regional or metropolitan authorities. From an administrative perspective, these are all just different functional levels of governmental activity, justified by their con-

---

[20] See also William Riker, *Federalism: Origin, Operation, Significance.* Boston: Little, Brown, 1964, and Friedrich, *Constitutional Government and Democracy,* pp. 200–201.

venience rather than by elaborate legal theories of states' rights and sovereignty. There are often patterns of administrative cooperation between federal and state governments that belie the theory of checks and balances operative in federalism. Frequently, the federal government also cooperates with local levels over the heads of the state governments. Except for the special constitutional privileges of the states, especially in national representative organs, the practice of federal governments appears to differ chiefly in the special limitations imposed on the central authorities in their dealings with the lower levels. The central government of a unitary state can issue direct legislative or executive commands to the local authorities. It can finance and enforce programs at any local level, whereas a federal government faces many barriers to direct action. Federal programs, therefore, require persuasion and voluntary cooperation for local execution. And while federal grants-in-aid may be very nearly as persuasive to local governments as direct commands, enforcement of the federal specifications of a locally or state-adopted program is quite difficult.

Representation in federal governments The patterns of representation of federal governments vividly show the complexity of the arrangement. The clear and exclusive legislative mandate that the voters of unitary states or of each member state of a confederation give their central legislatures is curiously split in federations. The federal and the state legislatures each receive a full mandate from the sovereign voter, and however carefully the legislative functions are divided between the two, there is always the possibility of conflict. All federal constitutions, therefore, give federal legislation the power to override state action, which suggests that the mandates for the two legislatures are not of the same order. The federal legislatures, moreover, are invariably bicameral, with an upper house representing the states in some fashion.[21] Thus the overriding mandate of the federal legislature is itself amalgamated from several elements, including a popular mandate and one made up of state elements.[22]

[21] The mode of representation, however, varies widely according to how the upper chamber is elected or appointed, what role it plays vis-à-vis the lower house, and whether each state has the same vote.

[22] There may well be a further level of representation along con-

PATTERNS OF FEDERAL ORGANIZATION

With more than half of the inhabited territory (large states are more likely to be federal than small states) of the world living under this "hybrid" of unitary and confederate government, it should cause little surprise that considerable differences exist in the patterns of federalism that evolved all over the world. Leaving aside for the moment the older and looser forms of federation as well as the cases whose federal nature is questioned by most authorities, there appear to be at least three distinctive patterns of federal union. The *Anglo-American pattern* is typical of the United States and of many states of the British Commonwealth,[23] although Great Britain is a unitary state. The *German pattern* is also in use, with some modifications in Austria and Switzerland. The *Soviet pattern,* finally, has been imitated, although with a difference, in Yugoslavia. As will be seen, the differences among these patterns owe a great deal to the circumstances of the origins of particular federal systems. The patterns differ both in the basic relationship between the federal and the regional centers and in the division of governmental functions among them.

The Anglo-American pattern

Kenneth C. Wheare in his classic study of federal institutions[24] proposes as the distinguishing criterion of all truly federal government that both federal and state (province, *Land,* canton) governments be *coordinate* in their spheres of action rather than one dependent upon the other. Although American, Canadian, and Australian federalism differ in some ways, these systems indeed attempt to separate clearly the two levels and to give each a fairly complete set of governmental organs and of legislative, executive, judicial, and fiscal powers. The pattern

---

federal lines, as for example in the form of official councils of state organs that can make policies on the basis of unanimous consent. Such an authority is the Permanent Conference of *Länder* Ministers of Culture and Education in West Germany, which makes common educational policies.

[23] See William Livingston's *Federalism in the Commonwealth.* London: Cassell, 1963, and the sources cited there; also Carl J. Friedrich, *Trends of Federalism in Theory and Practice.* New York: Praeger, 1968.

[24] *Federal Government,* 4th ed. New York: Oxford, 1963, pp. 2–3.

was evidently set by the United States Constitution, whose framers were faced with the well-established power of the state governments under the Articles of Confederation. Fearing that their newly designed federal government might become as dependent on the states as under the confederate system, they went out of their way to give the new federal center all the powers and organs needed for its independence. To be sure, there were still some links of dependence on the states, such as the selection of United States senators in the nineteenth century by the state legislatures. There were also the opposite links of state dependence on the federal government, as in the federal supremacy clause and the federal court power to review state actions and to act as an arbiter among the states and between the union and the states.[25] The Commonwealth federal systems likewise exhibit some remaining links of dependence, and, like the United States, have developed many a link of administrative cooperation.

German federalism

The German pattern of federalism, as evident in the German constitutions of 1871, 1919, and 1949, made no such attempt at separating the levels of government. The Bismarckian Constitution of 1871 set a precedent of deliberate mutual dependence for several reasons. Bismarck had no intention of creating a new central government independent of the states, but rather wished to create a constitutional facade for the dominance of his own state, Prussia, over the rest of Germany. Thus the king of Prussia became the German kaiser, and a member of the Prussian cabinet became the chancellor of the Reich (federal) government.

A second motive lay in the monarchic nature of the federation, most of whose member states were monarchies with little-developed institutions of representative government. Since the national unification required a good deal of unifying legislation, the state monarchies were willing to grant a federal legislature, the Reichstag, sweeping legislative powers. At the same time,

---

[25] This obvious superordination of federal over state governments appears to gainsay the criterion of "coordinate" spheres in a crucial way. It would be more accurate to speak of a striving for mutual independence between the spheres.

they were not prepared to part with their executive prerogatives and their administrative establishments, the pride of continental monarchs. They retained their administrative powers except in fields such as foreign relations and secured executive control, under Prussian leadership, in the Bundesrat (Federal Council). This council resembled the old Congress of the German Confederation (1815-1867) and became simultaneously the nominal executive council of the Reich and the upper house of the federal legislature. Whatever the reasons for its original design, this federal-council type of federalism endeared itself so much to German politicians that it was continued in 1919 and readopted in 1949, long after Prussia had been dissolved and under vastly different circumstances. Swiss and Austrian federalism resemble this type of organization, too.[26]

The German and the Anglo-American types of federalism differ chiefly in the following characteristics. In German federalism the bulk of the legislative authority lies with the federation, leaving only a few functions, such as education, police, and local government, with the *Länder*. The bulk of administrative and judicial power, however, remain with the *Länder,* so that most federal laws are administered and adjudicated by the latter. The federal administration is responsible only for foreign relations, defense, and raising its own revenue; or the latter can be delegated to the *Länder* fiscal administrations. Most federal ministries only draft laws and have no field administration whatsoever. The separation of legislative and administrative or judicial functions by the federal-state dichotomy requires certain additional federal powers to unify the operation of the system. Thus the federal government has certain rights of supervising and investigating the administration of the federal laws by the *Länder*. If it is not satisfied with the state administration, it can bring complaints before the Bundesrat and the Constitutional Court. The federal government also prescribes the administrative and judicial procedures and organization as well as the recruitment and training of the *Land* civil service and judges for the sake of unity. There are also some federal courts whose sole purpose is to keep uniform the interpretation of federal laws by the

[26] The Swiss Council of States is more like the American Senate, but the distribution of legislative and administrative powers between the cantons and the federal government is the same.

Länder courts. An elaborate procedure for equalizing the financial resources of the *Länder* government completes the list of features otherwise associated more with unitary than with federal governments.[27]

The Bundesrat   If these features appear to make the *Länder* rather dependent on the federal government, there is still the Bundesrat to be accounted for among the peculiarities of this pattern of federalism. No American or Australian state can boast the degree of direct participation in all aspects of national politics that the *Länder* governments enjoy. This distinctive institution still has considerable authority over all administrative and financial matters at the same time that it is the upper house of the federal legislature. Bundesrat delegations are not elected; rather they are appointed officials of the *Länder* cabinets, whose instructions they must follow in voting. Judging from the position of the Bundesrat in a federal-council type of federal system, the federal government is dependent on the *Länder* at least as much as the reverse.

Soviet federalism

The Soviet pattern of federalism differs from the other types discussed along somewhat similar lines as did Soviet local government from the other prototypes. It is a system of *deconcentration* rather than *decentralization*. The Union Republic and Autonomous Republic Supreme Soviets have no real policy-making authority, and neither do their party central committees. Their function is, rather, to adapt the policies and plans of the federal authorities to their respective geographical confines. Since, moreover, the Western approach to federalism, far more than that to local government, is suffused with notions of constitutionalism, checks and balances, and the voluntary, pluralistic character of group life, it is important to notice their complete absence in the Soviet Union. The relevant provisions of the Soviet Constitution, including the guaranteed right of seces-

[27] It is worth noting that the present federal system of the Bonn Republic is no longer an example of the integration of preexisting states, but rather of devolution from the totalitarian unity of the Third Reich. Federalism was a deliberate choice rather than, as it so often is, a product of circumstances.

sion, are a complete sham. The strength of Soviet federalism lies in the accommodation of the more than a hundred nationalities and their cultures in its many units. The parallel structure of the well-disciplined Communist party takes care that the solidarity of the "international proletariat" in the national units will not be subordinated to the "bourgeois nationalism" that multinational union might indulge. The same remarks apply to Yugoslav federalism, of which Carl J. Friedrich said that its federal character "depends upon the degree of self-restraint that the Communist party will exercise in the deployment of its concentrated power." [28] In the Soviet Union, the party has shown no such restraint.

POLITICAL INTEGRATION AND SOCIAL COMMUNICATION

Karl W. Deutsch has drawn attention to the common fallacy of accepting as given the political boundaries of states, federations, and whole nation-states. The breakup of larger units and the polycommunal composition of new nations indeed suggest the existence of a more potent social reality beneath the legal and constitutional definitions, namely, *political communities.* Such communities are held together by systems of *political communications,* set in more general systems of social communications of a wide variety of media and functions. "A people," according to Deutsch, is "a community of social communication habits" such that "language, or common cultural memories, permitted them to understand one another's ideas. . . ." He proposed to study these systems of social communication by surveying "the concentrations of population, patterns of settlement, the volumes of traffic and migration, the distribution of radio audiences and newspaper readership, the frequency and range of face-to-face contacts." [29] The patterns of social communication habits and of communication barriers such as different languages, transportation obstacles, illiteracy, and cultural or ethnic prejudice

[28] Carl J. Friedrich, *Trends of Federalism in Theory and Practice,* p. 168.

[29] Karl W. Deutsch, *The Nerves of Government.* New York: Free Press, 1966 (1st ed., 1963), p. 177. See also his earlier *Nationalism and Social Communication.* Cambridge, Mass.: M.I.T. Press, 1953.

in a given country could show the difficulties of social learning that any process of political integration would encounter. The extension of the communications systems to wider and more inclusive audiences is a direct measure of social development and very likely of political development as well.[30]

The study of political communications

The study of political communications, after some fitful advances decades ago, has progressed impressively in recent years. Communication aspects are rather crucial for almost any study of public opinion, propaganda, political culture, political socialization, election campaigns, and decision making on either the domestic or the international plane. The study of political organizations such as parties and interest groups, or of the bureaucracy and its relations with various publics, likewise has important communications aspects.[31] Gabriel Almond even stated that "all of the functions performed in the political system . . . are performed *by means* of communication," [32] which is not to say, however, that they can *all* be reduced to a communications model. But there can be little doubt that communications aspects are ubiquitous in all political phenomena; all kinds of systems can, therefore, serve as the material for comparative methods and models.

Communications models   Richard R. Fagen, for example, proposed different models of the organization of communications and political life for (1) classical democracy, (2) compromise democracy, (3) autocracy, and (4) totalitarianism. The different answers to six questions regarding leadership recruitment and

[30] For a fuller discussion of the theories behind it, see Deutsch, *The Nerves of Government,* chaps. 5, 6, 9–13. The communications process can be conceptualized as the transmission and differentiated reception of information, or as a process of steering by government itself (as in cybernetics), or in many other ways.

[31] There is a survey in depth, with bibliography, of the study of political communication and control for the years 1962 to 1966 in Deutsch, *The Nerves of Government,* pp. vii–xxiii. See also the literature cited in Richard R. Fagen, *Politics and Communication.* Boston: Little, Brown, 1966, chap. 1.

[32] Gabriel Almond, *The Politics of the Developing Areas.* Princeton, N.J.: Princeton University Press, 1961, p. 4.

succession, the definition of political problems and alternatives, policy participation, the scope of legitimate dissent, the dissemination of political information, and the limits of political non-participation add up to models of their communications flow.[33] The importance of communications patterns as a distinguishing characteristic of democratic, oligarchic, and totalitarian systems has, of course, always been known. The crucial importance of a free and competitive press in democracies has long preoccupied students of democratic government. The link between political nonparticipation and lack of political communications among the inert masses of an oligarchy is also familiar, as is the totalitarian governments' absolute monopoly on all political communications and its enormous domestic and international propaganda output.

Mass media   The mass media are probably the most familiar communications channel linking the center, or several centers, with the populations of the periphery. Marshall McLuhan, the author of *Understanding Media,* goes so far as to assert that "the new electronic interdependence" of television and radio is turning the world into a global village with a sort of face-to-face contact. In Japan and Western countries saturated with television, and even during the heyday of the radio anywhere, the immediacy of national communications has been real enough. There is at least the potential of the living room's becoming a "voting booth" with instant participation in war, revolution, and other political events.[34] While nearly everyone may do some television watching in these countries, however, there is considerable doubt about how many actually expose themselves to the rare political communications and how willingly they accept the political messages thus received. The same, of course, applies to the radio and to the press. The facility of reading corresponds only imperfectly to the actual use of communications media, and even the cover-to-cover readers of newspapers may not all be willing to accept

[33] Fagen, *Politics and Communication,* chap. 2. See also Robert A. Dahl, *A Preface to Democratic Theory.* Chicago, Ill.: University of Chicago Press, 1956, and *Who Governs?* New Haven: Yale University Press, 1961.

[34] Marshall McLuhan and Quentin Fiore, *The Medium Is the Massage.* New York: Bantam Books, 1967, pp. 22, 67.

their slant. It takes a certain measure of prior agreement, or at least a propensity, to close the circuit of communications between the center and the periphery.

Partisan press For this reason of agreement, or complementarity, political communication flow is highest within groups and organizations of the like-minded. Political parties, especially in Europe, often have their own daily or weekly press. The mass readership of the Italian Communist daily *L' Unità,* for example, probably is more inclined to agree with much of what the paper says and to take its political counsel and recommendation than is the larger readership of the nonpartisan daily press. In comparing political systems, it is a matter of considerable importance to note how large the independent press is as compared to the partisan press, and whether there is a substantial partisan press. In a deeply divided country, presumably, the different political, social, and ethnic groups may in a very concrete sense not be communicating with one another, each having its own communications system. There are also communities defined by their readership of the trade-union press, farmers' association press, religious or ethnic press, or that of any politically significant group even if its membership seems small. Organizational ties, of course, in themselves create communication channels among the like-minded though rarely with as regular a communication flow or as explicit a content as their journals can transmit.

From the complementary views that facilitate communication it is but a small step to the content of new views and attitudes, of a whole new framework of ideas established in the minds of a willing audience by those who control the media. As Lucian Pye points out, the communications process establishes the basis for a rational discussion of political problems, actions by leaders, and alternative policies by providing a common fund of knowledge and information. On this basis, the people can also assess their future and recognize what causes what or even what is politically relevant on the distant stage of national politics.[35]

[35] Lucian W. Pye, ed., *Communications and Political Development.* Princeton, N.J.: Princeton University Press, 1963, pp. 6–7. Pye edited the volume and added introductions to its several parts, concerning, for example, the distinction between communications in traditional and modern societies and the professions of communication.

For a new or disrupted nation, the communication process is also the obvious way to build a new consensus and a mode of social integration for all parts of society.

Evolution of communications patterns

Pye also describes the basic differences between the communications patterns of traditional, transitional, and modern societies. In traditional societies, in particular, there are no professional communicators such as journalists or public relations men. Instead, communication flows along the lines of the particularistic social hierarchy in each community. The evaluation and response to the communicated messages, consequently, is determined strongly by status considerations, which in the case of low-status persons may mean that they have "no opinion" on most matters.[36] The emergence of professional communicators signifies not only the onset of the great transition, but also the development of a relatively objective "public opinion," which largely supersedes the particularistic maze of individual and group views of traditional society.[37] The professional communicators of transitional society still lack the money, the power, and the professional integrity to survive in a corrupting world. The communication of mass media hardly reaches the villages. The new, objective public opinion is still easily swayed or deceived and may scarcely be able to impress its views upon government. People still tend also to accept communications on the basis of their personal relationship with the source of the message, and the early journalists lack the status of the traditional elites.

[36] Public-opinion polls in relatively developed countries generally show those having "no opinion" to be heavily concentrated among the lower classes, farmers, and women. Dependent youth and domestic servants are other likely categories not accustomed to voicing opinions and hence not participating in the communications circuit.

[37] According to Pye, *Communications and Political Development,* pp. 78–79, the dichotomy is between partisan and politically neutral communications, but this appears to draw a rather narrow conclusion from the American experience alone. Partisanship in European societies was often a universalistic force actively engaged in the nation-building process. There is no logical progression from partisanship to a neutral press, although the latter may be typical of the consensual style of American politics.

Modern communications A modern communications system consists of the highly structured mass media of public opinion as well as a network of informal opinion leaders who communicate face to face. The structure is technologically elaborate and professionally organized and should be independent of government and other social forces. This requirement raises immediate questions regarding influence, "news management," and censorship in the Western countries and the stark fact of totalitarian control over the mass media in advanced fascist or communist countries. The recent developments in Czechoslovakia and the Soviet Union, in particular, suggest that there is a point at which modernization and a controlled press clash head on and that a choice must be made between further modernization and the communist dictatorship. Since control of the mass media and propaganda expansion have served the communists well in developing or rural nations, it is all the more interesting to observe the point at which communist-enforced modernization appears to break down from its "internal contradictions."

In captive and free societies alike, modern communications become extraordinarily differentiated into innumerable specialized channels along with the more general ones. Opinion leaders, too, fall into specialized (expert) and general (moral-political) categories, and their publics tend to listen only to some and not to others. Within established circuits of communication, at least in democratic societies, there is also a good deal of feedback that has a direct adjusting effect upon the content of the messages transmitted. In totalitarian societies, as in early transitional ones, feedback is hindered by the mechanism of social control. But where in early transitional societies free criticism is hindered by status considerations, totalitarian feedback is impeded by ideological and political considerations. Loyal citizens of totalitarian regimes are reluctant to speak up because ideology demands that small complaints be subordinated to the grand goals of the regime. And the political elites of the regime rarely encourage criticism because they regard it as a political challenge to their monopoly of power. Only for short periods, such as the "Let a hundred flowers bloom" campaign in China and short eras of literary thaw in Eastern Europe and the Soviet Union, can criticism raise its head in the overpoliticized atmosphere of totalitarian government, soon to be put down again. The use of self-criticism or mutual criticism in these countries is not an example of feedback, but rather a device to increase individual adjustment and group solidarity, not unlike "sensitivity training" or group therapy in the United States.

Further aspects of political communications

Three more important aspects of communications in political development need to be stressed here: political socialization, ideology, and charismatic leadership. All three are significant vehicles of attitude change from a more traditional to a more modern posture.

Political socialization   Political socialization in traditional polities, it will be remembered, is greatly retarded by the traditional character of the family and social setting, in which even formal education, as far as it is available, can make only a small dent. Once the dependent youth has grown into an independent young adult, the mass media continue, so to speak, his political socialization. They can work at turning a nation of parochials into one of politically well-informed subjects and participants. Much of their effort may lack the depth of earlier socialization, and many parochials may indeed never be converted, yet the effort is surely not lost altogether.

Ideology   Ideology may have a role here in helping the communications process enter into vital interaction with the needs, fears, and aspirations of the audience. An ideology such as Arab nationalism, African socialism, or Burmese Buddhist socialism is at least potentially an extraordinary vehicle for transporting large masses of transitionals from the attitudes typical of a stagnant society into rapid modernization. Consider the effect of European socialism, for example, in picking up the alienated rural-urban migrant, organizing him in parties and trade unions, and giving him a sense of identity rooted in social class consciousness and a vision of the future. A potent political ideology, properly communicated by organization, campaign, and mass media, can inculcate a new set of values, attitudes, and modes of behavior in place of the older ones taught by the environment. On a macropolitical level, it can make a nation out of a collection of villages by giving them a creed or a myth to believe in, or by perpetuating an existential experience of war or revolution, as in Mexico or in many other developing countries.[38] Since membership in nations has precious little to do with physical characteristics and a great deal to do with what Ernest Renan called the *plébiscite des tous les jours,* an act of will, it is up to the communications process to facilitate the identification of every would-be national with the ideology of the nation.[39]

Charismatic leaders   What is true of the role of ideology applies also to that of charismatic leaders in developing and transitional societies. As Ann and Dorothy Willner have argued, charismatic appeal "depends on the leader's ability to draw upon and manipulate the body of myth in a given culture and the actions and values associated with these myths." The breakdown of traditional authority and often of the unity of the new states gives special importance to a leader's skill in legitimizing his authority, associating himself with the sacred historical traditions at the same time that he may be planning to plunge ahead with the modernization of his country.[40] Nor is this phenomenon limited to the early phases of the great transition. Stalin's leadership cult and Hitler's elaborate appeals to Prussian tradition were intimately wedded to the political ideologies of their types of national mobilization. Publicity-wise heads of modern states can still conjure the symbols of the past for a rededication of national effort. And the communications process, skillfully used, mobilizes the many who can more easily identify with an individual father or hero figure than grasp the abstract needs for specific or wholesale social change. The images the communications process transmits from the center to the periphery bring the charismatic leader up

[38] Clifford Geertz points out in his article, "Ideology as a Cultural System," that there are many ways of conceptualizing the role of ideology, one being that of "a patterned reaction to the patterned strains of a social role," the symbolic outlet for social strains and disequilibrium. Apter, *Ideology and Discontent,* chap. 1. See also the articles by Philip E. Converse and Leonard Binder in the same book.

[39] See also Kalman H. Silvert, "Nationalism in Latin America," in *Latin America's Nationalistic Revolutions,* Annals of the American Academy of Political and Social Science, March 1961, pp. 1–9.

[40] "The Rise and Role of Charismatic Leaders," in *New Nations: The Problem of Political Development,* Annals of the American Academy of Political and Social Science, March 1965, pp. 77–88.

close in human terms, however artificial his public-relations image.

Thus all kinds of relationships and interchanges may connect the center with the periphery, including some that may be offensive to discriminating tastes. What, however, are the alternatives? Daniel Lerner has reminded us that center-periphery relations can also consist of the center's ignoring the periphery, as did the Sublime Porte of the Ottoman Empire, or splendid Paris bleeding dry the French provinces, or prerevolutionary Moscow and St. Petersburg. Such neglect and exclusiveness are not necessarily the result of the center's incapacity to penetrate nor of hopeless backwardness at the periphery. Indeed, as history shows, the periphery may in time rise up to destroy the selfish center and the self-sufficient fools who govern it.[41]

[41] "Some Comments on Center-Periphery Relations" in Richard Merritt and Stein Rokkan, *Comparing Nations*. New Haven, Conn.: Yale University Press, 1966, pp. 259–265. See also Merritt's article on Berlin in the same book.

5

THE STUDY OF POLITICAL PARTIES AND PARTY SYSTEMS

Today political parties are a universal and central feature of most political systems. It is almost impossible to describe a macropolitical process or relationship of any significance without including a discussion of the functioning of the party system of a given country. What exactly a party is, or how party systems can be classified and distinguished from one another, is a matter of controversy. Most contemporary parties and party systems, moreover, reflect the growth of mass organizations and their penetration of parties and governmental agencies.[1] The definition of the role of the party system in theories of the political system has been further entangled in empirically precarious theories: Parties in developed countries are supposed to be "autonomous subsystems." But is the British Labour party really autonomous from the Trade Union Congress? How autonomous are other European trade unions from their respective parties? Is the tail sometimes wagging the dog, and, if so, which is the tail and which the dog?

Political parties have always been a rather elusive phenomenon, often acknowledged only in negative terms. The earlier

[1] See also S. M. Lipset's introduction to Robert Michels, *Political Parties*. New York: Free Press, 1966, pp. 15–20.

term "faction," for example, smacked of conspiracy and special interests, which responsible statesmen of the eighteenth century condemned in clear language. George Washington and John Adams took a dim view of party, and in *Federalist Paper* No. 10 James Madison argued the special merits of a federal constitution as a device for controlling the "effects of faction." In autocratic and colonial regimes the very thought of party suggested uncontrollable opposition. Only much later did the public function of parties come to be recognized—often with frequent misgivings— and to be scrutinized by political scientists. Some of the earlier mistrust of parties, and especially of *partisan oppositions,* still plays a considerable role in the popular suspicion of politics. It is still more respectable to attribute a policy to a prime minister and his cabinet than to their party as such, even though the decision may be clearly attributable to the latter. We pretend, in other words, that the "party in office" is less real than the individual officeholders and their authority. In the same vein, people are reluctant to acknowledge the "party in the electorate" and would rather attribute electoral decisions to the voter's spontaneous choice than to his partisanship.

APPROACHES TO THE STUDY OF PARTIES

As the central importance of parties was increasingly recognized in the twentieth century, the comparative study of political parties became an open challenge to some of the century's finest social scientists. From Max Weber's *Politics as a Vocation,* M. Y. Ostrogorski's *Democracy and the Organization of Political Parties,* Robert Michels' *Political Parties,* and Sigmund Neumann's *German Parties* down to Maurice Duverger's *Political Parties* and Otto Kirchheimer's concept of the European "catch-all party," a tradition of classical European party theory has supplied many of the terms of reference.[2] While this heritage has been a source

[2] Weber's essay is reprinted in H. H. Gerth and C. W. Mills, *From Max Weber.* New York: Oxford, 1946, pp. 77–128. Ostrogorski appeared in 1902 with Macmillan of New York, Neumann in 1932 with Junker and Duennhaupt of Berlin, Duverger in 1951 with Armand Colin of Paris, and Kirchheimer is represented in Joseph La Palombara and Myron Weiner, *Political Parties and Political Development.* Princeton, N.J.: Princeton University Press, 1966, chap. 6.

of insights, it has also been, at times, rather confining. For example, it was considered *de rigueur* in most of the scholarly treatises to start out with an abstract definition of the concept of the political party, usually deriving the word from the Latin word *pars* (part) and juxtaposing the "partiality" of its views and interests to the "wholeness" of the public interest, or the state. Such verbal shadowboxing, however, could hardly cover the great variety of structures and processes that deserve the name party in different systems. Parties are highly adaptable phenomena that can fit themselves into vastly different political systems and, in isolation from these systems, defy meaningful generalization.

There are two promising routes for avoiding such pitfalls. One consists in the reduction of the structures and processes of parties to basic political functions and activities, of which some parties may perform all or only a few. Thus party activities could be dissected into an expressive (or representative) and a governing function, or into such functions as leadership recruitment or candidate selection, electioneering, voter organization, political socialization, political communications, program selection, policy making, and the like, and parties could be classified as to what they actually do in a particular system. American political parties for some time have been studied in this fashion. One can also view given political parties as an integral part of the larger political system and study them as a *party system,* or as the macropolitical functions of parties in their specific settings. The latter perspective can be found, for example, in the suggestion that parties are an important part of what David Easton and Gabriel Almond have called the "conversion functions," which transform political demands and supports into specific governmental policies.[3]

Both approaches—the reduction to smaller elements and the relation of parties to the system—tend to be intertwined in practice. Reducing party activity to specific functions inevitably lays bare a structure of major macropolitical, systemic functions that parties seem to serve. Studying parties as systems, rather than by individual parties, directs attention to the broader proc-

[3] See, for example, Gabriel Almond and G. Bingham Powell, Jr., *Comparative Politics: A Developmental Approach.* Boston: Little, Brown, 1966, chap. 5, and David Easton, "An Approach to the Analysis of Political Systems," *World Politics,* April 1957, pp. 387–388.

esses of policy making, recruitment, socialization, and communications of the whole system, sparing us the need to delimit parties from the environment that sustains them and that is generally difficult to separate from them. Both approaches, therefore, tend to draw into consideration large areas beyond the political parties, extending the study of party systems nearly as far as the entire political system. Understanding a party system obviously involves an understanding of the institutional setting, the entire group system and its cleavages, the political culture, and the processes of political socialization and recruitment. Even in areas expressly removed from the sway of parties, such as the civil service, the judiciary, and broad fields of culture and education, the influence of partisanship is almost never completely absent.

THEORIES OF POLITICAL PARTIES

This is not the place for a detailed review of the large literature on political parties.[4] Several basic notions of party, however, deserve to be introduced in order to lay a foundation for later discussion in a systematic context. Parties can be defined on an empirical basis as social groups, vehicles for political conflict, or devices of representation and integration, or as channels of political communications with hardly a reference to the political system.

Parties as social groups

The theory of the party as a social group sheds light on what may well be its most important nonfunctional aspect. From the beginnings of party theory, political parties have been described as gatherings of politically like-minded people (by Edmund Burke and Sir Ernest Barker) or as social units with common goals, a division of roles, communication channels, and a hierarchic authority structure (by Samuel J. Eldersveld). A party is a kind of

[4] For such a review see, for instance, Samuel J. Eldersveld, *Political Parties: A Behavioral Analysis*. Chicago: Rand McNally, 1962, pp. 14–23; Avery Leiserson, *Parties and Politics: An Institutional and Behavioral Approach*. Knopf, 1958, chaps. 2, 8, and 9; or David E. Apter in Harry Eckstein and David E. Apter, *Comparative Politics: A Reader*. New York: Free Press, 1963, pp. 327–332. Also Neil A. McDonald, *The Study of Political Parties*. New York: Random House, Inc., 1955.

polity that recruits and socializes new members, selects leaders through internal processes of representation and elections, resolves internal disputes, and makes decisions regarding its policies toward the outside world.[5] In parties of highly activistic membership, such as European socialist parties of a generation ago or political club movements of all stripes, members may literally live within the party as the social context that gives meaning and direction to their lives. The parties can be thus quite autonomous social as well as political subsystems, having a distinctive political subculture far beyond specific programs or ideologies. Many writers on such European parties liken them to religious communities, "chapels," or sects devoted to a common faith and united by constant close interaction and identification. Sigmund Neumann considered their "integration" of the private citizen via their own community into the larger community one of their chief modern functions.[6] In loosely structured parties of no specific membership or low activism, such as in the United States, the political parties may function as social communities only intermittently. Their networks of interpersonal relationships may shrink and even atrophy between elections.

Parties and their clientele   As Samuel J. Eldersveld has pointed out, political parties differ from other social formations or groups by their "primary structural properties." In particular, a democratic party is a specialized system of action having the goal of occupying governmental offices, a competitive-electoral relationship with similar organizations, and a special pattern of public support and adaptation strategies. Parties are oriented toward a clientele of present and potential voters, although the presence of a substantial floating vote may vary from system to system. The party and its clientele, even its members, in a sense use each other for their mutual advantage; this contributes to the open, multifactional character of most parties.[7] On the other hand,

---

[5] See especially Eldersveld, *Political Parties,* pp. 1–3.

[6] See Sigmund Neumann, *Modern Political Parties.* Chicago: University of Chicago Press, 1954, pp. 396–397.

[7] A typical example of far-reaching factionalism are the Italian Christian Democratic and Socialist (PSU) parties whose factions are so independent that they can frustrate any common decision making. In the case of the former, factional independence even implies the presentation of separate lists of candidates for party offices and, in some cases, factional news organs.

some close-knit parties, such as the totalitarian parties of the left and right, suppress factionalism.[8]

Interest aggregation

Parties also are tied by "subcoalitions" to socioeconomic interests seeking political recognition, if not control. This feature intimately relates parties to the function of *interest articulation* as well as to the *aggregation of interests* (Almond and Coleman).[9] The interests are generally articulated prior to or for the purpose of their linkage with politics via a party. It is to their advantage to seek expression and influence through a party, sometimes through several parties. The party's advantage, on the other hand, lies in forming a large alliance, or aggregation of such subcoalitions, preferably an alliance assuring it a majority in the representative bodies. Less than a majority would fail to give the party political control. An alliance of far more than a majority, on the other hand, might obligate it toward too many partners, all of whom expect a payoff of sorts.[10] Aggregating different subcoalitions in one and the same party requires considerable organizational skill and effort. Their interests are likely to conflict and must be reconciled also with the common goals of the party. The resulting inner tensions have to be carefully managed by a party leadership that knows how to meet group demands in exchange for their commitment to the cause.

Hierarchic organization

Like many writers since Robert Michels, Eldersveld also stresses the hierarchic, oligarchic structure of political parties, which combines patterns of "downward deference" toward the base with centralized command. The leadership itself can be recruited from many different sources or career patterns, or it can become an entrenched, self-serving oligarchic clique such as Michels described. In any case, and regardless of downward deference

---

[8] Eldersveld, *Political Parties,* pp. 3–5.

[9] A good example of parties helping a socioeconomic interest to organize is the founding of trade unions by political parties as in Imperial Germany, both by the Socialists and the Center party. There are also examples of trade unions' establishing a political party, as with the British Labour party, which is still composed largely of the unions.

[10] See also William Riker, *The Theory of Political Coalition.* New Haven, Conn.: Yale University Press, 1962.

patterns, even the most democratic parties are likely to be dominated by leadership perspectives on policy rather than by the
initiative of the rank and file. Party leaders are elected and supported primarily to lead the party to victory and not just to carry
out the instructions of the rank and file. This emphasis on leadership evidently stems from the competitive character of parties
and differs considerably from what is normally expected of governmental leadership. When party leaders become government
leaders, consequently, there *should* be a major change in their
conduct and attitude as they serve their new constituency, the
public.[11]

The logic of collective action   Samuel H. Barnes recently
brought to light a whole new dimension of internal party life in
his study of the Italian Socialist party. His point of departure was
the "logic of collective action," [12] which suggests that in large
groups, such as an interest group or a modern political party,
people are unlikely to engage in the kind of unselfish collective
action familiar from small groups. Instead, they require special
inducements or coercion to make them act in their common interest. Patronage, graft, or regular employment may indeed create
a dynamic political organization. In a lower-class setting the formal organization of a party or union is particularly important,
because these strata lack the multiple memberships and political
competence of the upper classes. But lower-class parties, such
as the predecessors of the Christian Democrats or the Socialists
or the present Communists of Italy, can also rely on a network of
small groups whose emotional incentives for loyalty and collective action enable them to survive decades in the opposition
without the satisfactions of controlling public office. When the
intensive political subculture of the small groups declines, as
with most European socialist and Catholic parties today, Barnes
suggested, then the need to win public office becomes paramount.

[11] While constitutional democracies tend to take this change for
granted, except in cases of impropriety or corruption, extremist parties
often require a formal pledge or presigned letter of resignation of their
legislators or other government leaders, in order to prevent them from
acquiring new loyalties.

[12] See Mancur Olson, Jr., *The Logic of Collective Action*. Cambridge, Mass.: Harvard University Press, 1965.

At this point, perhaps, there emerges what Otto Kirchheimer has called the "catch-all party" [13] of post-1945 Europe, or what German Socialists have described as their transition from a class-based ideological party to a "people's party." As Barnes also points out, the role of ideology in spurring collective action appears to feed upon great status differences and poor communications among the groups in society. It declines when they do. Most Western European communist parties are still far from a decline of the communist subculture and can rely also on a large full-time staff that provides services, organizes action, and disseminates the ideology.[14]

Party structural types

Some scholars, such as Maurice Duverger and Sigmund Neumann, have suggested classifying political parties by their structure or type. Thus Duverger proposed structural distinctions based on the nature of party membership, such as between *cadre parties* and *mass parties* and between *direct* and *indirect* (organizational) membership. Usually, mass parties also have direct membership, whereas cadre parties, such as those of the United States, have no formal membership as such. Indirect parties, as in Great Britain, rest on cadrelike electoral committees chosen by constituent organizations that may really give them a mass-membership base. Duverger also stressed the different local structures of distinctive types of European parties. The *caucus type,* an electoral committee composed of notables, is typical of older European liberal, conservative, or radical parties. In fact, these are also what Neumann called the "parties of individual representation," which are typical of patterns of very limited popular participation beyond voting. Between elections, the electoral organization disappears and the elected representative can enjoy his "absolutely free mandate" to decide only according to his

[13] See La Palombara and Weiner, *Political Parties and Political Development*, p. 184. Also Douglas A. Chalmers, *The Social Democratic Party of Germany*. New Haven, Conn.: Yale University Press, 1964.

[41] *Party Democracy: Politics in an Italian Socialist Federation*. New Haven, Conn.: Yale University Press, 1967, chap. 14, and "Party Democracy and the Logic of Collective Action" in William J. Crotty, ed., *Approaches to the Study of Party Organization*. Boston: Allyn and Bacon, 1968, pp. 107–116.

conscience. The idea of a free mandate, while it may be well rooted indeed in Western theories of representative government, obviously suffered greatly with the rise of lobbies and of party discipline in legislatures.

Duverger's second type of local structure is the *branch,* a fairly large local assembly and discussion club that meets frequently. Typical branch parties were the continental European socialist parties before the development of "catch-all" or "people's" parties among them. These parties were also Neumann's "parties of social integration," mass-membership parties held together by a social fabric of auxiliary associations, including worker's infant care, youth organizations, educational, cultural, and recreational clubs, trade unions, and the like, which literally enveloped the member from all sides throughout the duration of his life. Of course, this political subculture also isolated him largely from nonsocialist society, thereby reinforcing his ideological stereotypes of "the system." [15] Some Catholic and even a few conservative and agrarian parties developed in the same direction. Duverger's third and fourth types of local structure, the small and often clandestine *factory cell* or *area cell* and the *party militia,* have been typical of communist and fascist movements, especially in the 1920s and 1930s. They are usually linked each to the next higher party by *vertical links* only, allowing the practice of *democratic centralism* in communist, and of the *leadership principle* in fascist, structures. The degree of party centralization, discipline, and "strength of articulation" of the whole party also supplies significant distinctions.[16] Neumann characterizes the intensive life of the cells and militias as "total integration," in contrast to "democratic integration," in order to relate the militancy and ideological utopianism of the struggle for power of these parties to the totalitarian dictatorship they are likely to establish, once power is theirs.

Other criteria for classifying political parties have long been accepted in the discipline. One can, of course, classify parties according to their programs or ideologies, or their pragmatism or leadership cults. A distinction is often drawn also among parties defending the status quo (or trying to restore an earlier status quo) and reform and revolutionary parties. The latter distinction

[15] Neumann, *Modern Political Parties,* p. 400.
[16] Duverger, *Political Parties,* pp. 5–40, 63–71.

in constitutional democracies often uses the term "constitutional parties"—parties willing to accept the prevailing constitutional rule including rules for constitutional change—as distinct from parties hostile to the constitution or unwilling to accept its legitimate authority.[17]

One-party systems

A particular problem of definition is posed by the parties of one-party systems. The traditional party literature has tended to exclude such parties automatically from the definition as soon as competition ceased. Sigmund Neumann, for example, declared: "A one-party system is a contradiction in itself." He built the presence of competition into the very definition of political party as the "articulate organization of society's active political agents, those who are concerned with the control of governmental power and who compete for popular support with another group or groups holding divergent views." [18] Neumann and others were understandably concerned about the phenomenon of the one-party dictatorships of the period between the two world wars. Whenever a totalitarian communist or fascist party seized power and suppressed all other parties of a given system, an argument could indeed be made that the basic character of the organization had undergone a drastic change. In many cases, in fact, its taking on of entirely new functions hitherto reserved to the police, army, or the administration suggested strongly that its basic *raison d'être* had changed with the acquisition of a monopoly on power.

The extension of the interest of political scientists to the developing nations, and also to the earliest phases of nation building in the older nations, once more focused attention on the *parti unique,* since most developing systems indeed seem to have started out with only one party, generally a kind of nation building or independence movement. These developing one-party systems may not be competitive, but they are not necessarily dic-

[17] For further classificatory schemes, see Fred W. Riggs, "Comparative Politics and the Study of Political Parties: A Structural Approach" in Crotty, *Approaches to the Study of Party Organization,* pp. 58–69; or Kenneth Janda's approach to creating a computerized bibliography on comparative political parties described in the same work, p. 159, and in his ICPP Reports on the International Comparative Political Parties Project.

[18] Neumann, *Modern Political Parties,* p. 395.

tatorial and may be divided into factions. In time, the nationalistic movement may split in two, and political competition makes its entrance long *after* the first partylike organization appeared. Hence, students of African political parties, for example, carefully avoid tying their definition of parties to the presence of competition; James S. Coleman and Carl Rosberg, for example, define them as "associations formally organized with the explicit and declared purpose of acquiring and/or maintaining legal control, either singly or in coalition or electoral competition with other similar associations, over the personnel and the policy of the government of an actual or prospective sovereign state." [19] Even single parties, in other words, are accepted as parties, if they perform certain societal functions normally ascribed to political parties.

THE FUNCTIONS OF POLITICAL PARTIES

Almost any mention of functions that parties perform will relate them to the political system or at least to an important part of it, such as a subculture or major political institution. Not all parties of different systems, or even within the same system, perform quite the same functions. Major national parties very likely serve broader functions than minor or geographically limited ones. In a well-articulated setting, some functions ordinarily associated with political parties may be performed by interest groups, the bureaucracy, or other leadership cadres. Thus the varying array of functions actually performed by a party may well serve as a basis for classifying both individual parties and whole systems.

Basic party functions

For the initial orientation of the student, the many different political functions attributed to political parties can be divided into a few basic categories:

1.   The recruitment and selection of leadership personnel for the various governmental offices.

2.   The generation of programs and policies for government.

[19] James S. Coleman and Carl Rosberg, *Political Parties and National Integration in Tropical Africa.* Berkeley, Calif.: University of California Press, 1966, p. 2.

3. The coordination and control of governmental organs.
4. Societal integration by the satisfaction and reconciliation of group demands or by generating a common belief system or ideology.
5. The social integration of individuals by the mobilization of support and by political socialization.
6. Oppositional counterorganization or subversion

Such pervasive functions as representation and communications, as well as interest articulation and aggregation, are implicit throughout several of these broad functional areas.

Selection of candidates

As James Bryce declared in describing American political parties before World War I, "The chief thing is the selection of candidates" for public office. Taken broadly, this statement has validity even in such totalitarian one-party dictatorships as those of the communist orbit. Only in military dictatorships and in traditional partyless systems such as Ethiopia are political leaders selected exclusively by agencies other than parties. In modern democracies, moreover, the selection process is ostensibly designed to give the masses of the voters *a real choice,* albeit a choice limited by prior selection on the part of the parties. As E. E. Schattschneider pointed out a generation ago, the voters would be quite incapable of making a meaningful choice if it were not for this prior narrowing of their choice from theoretically everybody to a handful of candidates.

Importance of voters' role   The necessity of prior selection, however, need not obscure the basic issue—that of the very considerable variation in the relative influence of the voters or even the rank and file of party members in choosing a candidate. The United States is still the only country having primary elections that take an important part of the selection process (for all but the presidential candidates) away from party conventions and give it to the registered voters under the "closed" or "open" primary systems, opening up candidate selection to the widest competition within a party and to influence by nonparty members or nonactivists. Even primaries, of course, will not stamp out considerable preprimary selection and promotion efforts by party agencies. In all the other democratic systems, the selection of candidates is carried on as a private affair by party agencies with varying degrees of participation by the rank and file. The selection of a slate of candidates also helps to orient the party's voters. The voters at large, of course, still get to choose among the parties' candidates. But this choice may not amount to much, considering that as much as 60 to 75 percent of the voters of most modern democracies are so attached to their own parties that they are unlikely to vote for anyone else's candidates. In countries with electoral party lists and proportional representation, the party agencies often have sweeping power over the electoral success of a candidate by their authority to determine his place on the ballot. Monopolistic systems, as under communism, generally skip the democratic ritual of public elections. But they too allow the *parti unique* to select by its own process the candidates for leadership positions, and an officeholder can be maintained or dropped in the face of public displeasure.[20]

Candidate recruitment   Like all recruitment processes for important positions, the selection by political parties carries strong qualitative implications. It is necessary to inquire into the principles of selection and to contrast, perhaps, the selection for public office with rival recruitment processes for private industry, the professions, or the civil service in order to know whether recruitment by party aims at the cream of the crop or at the unsalable goods of other recruitment processes. In the American system, for example, with rare exceptions the cream goes to other callings. It is very significant also to note whether party recruitment of political leadership is limited to a particular social class or to a particular geographic, ethnic, or religious clientele. Since the basic distribution of strength among the parties of most systems is fairly constant, it is also worth knowing which recruitment processes actually lead to the top governmental positions and which merely recruit spokesmen for a more or less permanent opposition.

Party role in elections   A related aspect of the selection of candidates in competitive systems is also the organized effort to get

[20] See especially Leon D. Epstein, *Political Parties in Western Democracies*. New York: Praeger, 1967, chap. VIII, and the sources cited there; also Austin Ranney, *Pathways to Parliament*. Madison, Wis.: University of Wisconsin Press, 1965, chaps. 2, 3, 5, and 6.

them elected and reelected. There is a good deal of evidence, in fact, that modern parties, as we know them, largely owe their existence to the need of elected parliamentary representatives to create electoral committees or a grass-roots organization to assure their reelection. At least, this was the origin of permanent party organizations in England and elsewhere upon the widening of the suffrage.

Generation of programs and policies

The second basic function generally attributed to parties is the generation of programs and policies. Given parties may vary widely in their degree of ideological commitment or pragmatism. Whether a given party is regarded as highly ideological or highly pragmatic, in fact, rather depends on the views of the observer. If a party is close to our own views on given policies, it will look more pragmatic as it grapples with concrete issues. If it is rather far from our own viewpoint, it will seem more narrowly ideological in its thought patterns. Nevertheless, some highly ideological parties are distinguished by their own emphasis on cohesive, complex, verbal formulas for the full range of policies. Ideology to them is a means of organization and discipline as well as a matter of conviction. To the individual party member, for example, of a communist or fascist party, ideology often constitutes the real world of meaning, a spiritual home away from his alienated home in the society that surrounds him. A pragmatic party, by contrast, lives in an environment characterized by a basic consensus no matter how pluralistic.

Patterns of pragmatism and ideology   An important example of the differences between pragmatic and highly ideological parties was supplied by the study of one-party systems of tropical Africa. James S. Coleman and Carl G. Rosberg, Jr., speak of two basic patterns: (1) the pragmatic-pluralistic (PP) pattern and (2) the revolutionary-centralizing (RC) trend. Contrasting these two types on various aspects of ideology, popular participation, and organization, the two political scientists arrived at the following characterization. In the degree of ideological preoccupation, declamation, and rationalization, PP was limited while RC was heavy, constant, and compulsive. PP's approach to modernization was adaptive or aggregative of pluralistic group interests, RC's revolutionary and antitraditional. Analogous differences were observed in their attitudes toward neutralism, Pan-Africanism, decolonization, and "Africanization." With PP the patterns of political mobilization and participation were partial and intermittent as well as both direct and indirect in such states as Ivory Coast, Senegal, and Cameroon. With RC political mobilization and participation was high and direct in such party-states as Guinea, Ghana, and Mali. In organization, finally, the pragmatic-pluralistic patterns were hierarchical and variable and comparatively loose in their relationship to other associations and to the government, while the revolutionary-centralizing states were monolithic, punitive toward dissent, and gave the party total monopoly control over associations and the state.

These patterns have their analogies in the European, North American, and Commonwealth settings. The pragmatic-pluralistic pattern there corresponds especially to cadre parties and perhaps also to Kirchheimer's "catch-all" party, which is willing to aggregate nearly every group it can find. Revolutionary movements from the Jacobins of the French Revolution to the early socialists, communists, and fascists, on the other hand, are centralizing parties heavily relying on political mobilization and ideological drive. Wherever they have come to power, as in the revolutionary regime of pre-Napoleonic France or in the so-called totalitarian dictatorships of the twentieth century, they have exhibited the same characteristic attitudes and behavior. They established highly centralized regimes in which the party completely controlled all other associations, the state, and all real or fancied opposition. Popular participation and enthusiastic acclaim were skillfully organized to form a continuous and intense link between the individual and the party-state. The declamation of ideology, and official preoccupation with its images and visions, became indeed heavy, reiterative, and compulsive like a fixed idea in a monomaniacal mind.[21]

Party programs and policies   In any case, even the most pragmatic party has to develop a more or less cohesive response to the constant challenge of policy making. If it is in the opposition, it exhibits a point of view of its own by criticizing those in power. In electoral competition, it generally has to put forth a program

[21] See also Epstein, *Political Parties in Western Democracies,* chaps. 10 and 11.

of policy alternatives in order to make itself attractive to the voters. To be sure, there are many oligarchic systems of policy making where the policies are decided only at the top or where policy making involves chiefly governmental agencies and pressure groups rather than the voters or the rank-and-file membership. But even one-party systems generally feature some internal competition between interests or factions organized informally around alternative policy proposals.

When a party of distinct program is in office, the program generally serves to orient its many officeholders in legislative, executive, and regional or local governments toward common objectives. Since political ideologies and electoral programs of parties beyond glib verbal formulas are rather vague, the program of the party in office is often modified considerably in the execution of day-to-day policies. The followers see what "their party" is doing and identify themselves with it regardless of program details. The unifying program image in the minds of friends of the regime, in other words, has become their perception of what their party in power actually does. The perception of supporters and opponents is, of course, colored by their respective ideologies. But the point is that they do not stick as much to their ideology as to their leaders in office. They tend to identify the actual government or party record, as far as they know it, with their own allegiance or opposition to the party in power.

Elections and party profiles During the electoral competition, likewise, parties present their respective pragmatic profiles, including memories of past performance and promises for the future. The several party profiles interact to define the issues of the campaign and to orient the voters into camps defined by these issues. Of course, issues are not the only determinant of the campaign alignments, which owe a great deal to preexisting party loyalties and to the personalities and larger exigencies of the moment. The magic of charismatic leadership or of profound disaffection with a leader, as well as great political crises such as the threat of war, revolution, or famine, have a way of burying the political discourse over specific issues under waves of primary emotion. Still, most election campaigns take place within a pattern of issue alignments that serve to mold the profile of the parties and help to define a party voter's and member's political identity in a way that he can talk about. These profiles and identities are then disseminated through the network of political communications. As important elements of the political culture, they also serve the purposes of political socialization for those identifying with them as well as for those building their political identity in reaction to them.

Control and coordination of government

The third major function of political parties is the control and coordination of government. It may well be their most important function for the system of which they are a part. One can define parties as a systemic response to the need for organization and coordination of a body politic for the purpose of making decisions and governing itself.[22] The voters by themselves, popular sovereignty notwithstanding, are unable to control and direct government without the benefit of parties. Governing elites likewise need parties to mobilize popular support. Many constitutional democracies possess so many built-in checks and divisions of governmental authority that they would be constantly deadlocking if it were not for the role of the parties in bridging over the artificial chasms opened up by bicameralism, the separation of powers, and federalism. Large, heterogeneous, and new nations would be incapable of maintaining, not to mention increasing, their internal cohesion and political consensus without the help of political parties.

Challenges to party power   To be sure, the basic purpose of parties to help the people govern is frequently challenged and disputed by rival organizations and elites. In Imperial Germany and Japan, for example, the military and the civil service refused to acknowledge the parties' claims to governmental leadership. Traditional elites, whether nobility, landowners, or the churches, have always taken a dim view of parties, although they cannot long hold out against their rise.[23] In countries of pronounced

[22] See Epstein, *Political Parties in Western Democracies,* chap. 12. That parties do not cease being parties as a result of never holding office hardly detracts from the importance of the "governing function" for nearly all political systems except traditional autocracies, personalistic systems, and military dictatorships.

[23] See, for example, the account of the transformation of historical oligarchies in Liberia and Zanzibar by James S. Coleman and Carl G. Rosberg, Jr., *Political Parties and National Integration in Tropical Africa.* Berkeley, Calif.: University of California Press, 1964, chaps. 12 and 13.

pluralistic structure and strong antipolitical biases, such as the United States, national parties may also be so incohesive as to be incapable of exercising power. Instead, it may be left to interest groups, business and social oligarchies, regional and local governments, or to the officeholders as individual leaders.[24] Reliance on personal leadership rather than the mediating structures of political parties is consequently a widespread phenomenon in many transitional and even modern societies. Public opinion polls in most Western countries show clearly that the individual political leader is far better known and more likely to be trusted than his political party, even where the decision-making power is obviously in the hands of the party rather than the man. The popular perception of modern political systems, in other words, is personalistic and rather distorted.

Party government in Great Britain   The contrast between the exercise of this function in Great Britain and in the United States has long preoccupied American political scientsts. But the United States is not the only modern example, or even an extreme example, of parties weak in the governing function. Great Britain affords a rather outstanding example of party government that to a considerable degree is a result of the well-disciplined and cohesive two parties there. The two-party system in Great Britain has helped to create a system of political responsibility, from the prime minister and the cabinet system down to the electorate, that makes the electoral choice more meaningful than just about anywhere. The older countries of the British Commonwealth have tried to adopt the same rationale with varying success, and American political scientists have praised it. But the greatest contrast, perhaps, is between British party government and European continental notions of state authority, reinforced by the problems of multiparty systems.

Nongoverning parties   When Sigmund Neumann coined the term "parties of individual representation," he was referring to an older theory of representation that is still well rooted in most countries of the French, or Rousseauan, tradition of representa-

---

[24] See also E. E. Schattschneider, "U.S.: The Functional Approach to Party Government," in Neumann, *Modern Political Parties*, pp. 194–218.

tive institutions.[25] In France under the Third and Fourth Republics, and in Imperial and Weimar Germany, there was the notion of the neutral, administrative state as the guardian of the public interest but also as a potential oppressor of the people. The representatives of the people and their parties in the National Assembly, and in the Reichstag, saw their function primarily in checking and opposing the state rather than in governing it. The formation of parliamentary governments required coalitions among the many parties. Parties and party leaders felt considerable reluctance to take on the full responsibility of government. And so, continental parliamentary government came to diverge considerably from the British cabinet system from which it had evolved. The tradition of nongoverning parties is still strong in France under the Fifth Republic and in Italy outside of the Christian Democratic party. In West Germany it has been abandoned in favor of the British approach.

Integration of society

The fourth major function of political parties is the integration of society by the satisfaction and reconciliation of group demands. All societies are made up of many different groupings and interests, whose needs and claims frequently conflict with one another. The conflicting demands have a centrifugal effect upon the body politic unless they are countered by periodic unifying efforts, such as those made by major political parties in the process of electoral competition. Parties successful in winning office may actually be able to satisfy some of the group demands. But even in hopeless opposition, a nationwide party may be able to reconcile the groups in its coalition by giving them a voice and lending its nationwide solidarity to what would otherwise be only an isolated group. The unifying or unity-maintaining capacity of political parties can be illustrated with such examples as the major parties of Belgium, which keep the country from being torn apart by the two language communities. Canada until recently and the pre-Civil War Democratic party of the United States are cases in point. Of course, even party ties may eventually be sundered, but while they last they offer divided nations, and es-

---

[25] See also the British analogy, the radical and liberal traditions, as discussed by Beer, *Britain in the Collectivist Age,* chap. 2.

pecially new nations, a concrete hope of survival. Where would India be today without the Congress party?

The process of integrating groups and interests into the greater society is part of the conversion process touched upon earlier, as demands are transformed into policies. But it can also take the form of nonconversion or nonsatisfaction of demands, or rather the substitution of future satisfactions for the unattainable present ones. At the moment of the struggle for national independence, for example, the nationalist movements of the new nations about to be born have very little to deliver in the way of immediate satisfactions for whatever group interests make up their coalition—geographic, socioeconomic, religious, tribal or ethnic, or political. They can only dispense the symbolic satisfactions of national independence, ideology, and identity, and otherwise promise a pie in the sky. The nationalistic faith in the future and the common goals may create as strong a bond of unity as any population in the springtime of social-communications development may be capable of feeling. This integrating faith of nationalism, in fact, is stronger than any distribution of scarce favors can ever hope to be, because it can remain above considerations of scarcity and conflicting demands.

A good example of such an integrating faith generated for a purpose was the Soviet Communist party at the time of Stalin's first Five Year Plan (1928–1933). The decision to industrialize rapidly involved considerable economic sacrifice among individuals and groups who had barely recovered from the hard times of the civil war. The party therefore had to organize a tremendous propaganda effort to generate popular enthusiasm and collaboration for the big push of the country into the twentieth century. Apart from coercion and fast talk, all it had to offer were promises of a better future for all Russians, rich or poor, as much as a generation or more away, bought at the price of present sacrifices.

Social integration of individuals

The fifth major function of political parties is the social integration of individuals into society and the body politic, a vital part of political socialization. All parties perform this function to some degree by involving people in electoral competition, mobilizing their support for the government or opposition, and serving

as channels of political communications. Parties of "social integration" (Neumann), such as the early socialist or Catholic
parties, and even communist and fascist parties, however, do a
good deal more. Their recruits typically consist of masses of
individuals uprooted from the farm, the small town, the urban
ghetto, and other human bonds, and they are greatly in need of
reintegration into human communities. The European socialists
supplied this need literally from the cradle to the grave, with
youth groups, women's clubs, sports and recreational associations, trade unions and professional organizations, workers'
educational leagues, and, to make the cycle complete, funeral
societies. In the 1890s, a generation after the socialists began,
and in competition with them, the German Catholic Center party
also began to build up a similar web of Catholic youth groups,
women's associations, farm and professional associations, and
trade unions. Other Catholic countries likewise developed highly
organized, cohesive organizations enveloping the individuals and
maintaining their loyalty in spite of other processes of social
mobilization. After World War I, vast numbers of people mobilized by the war and by the postwar dislocations were socially
integrated also by the communist and fascist parties. Auxiliary
organizations as well as the intensive social interaction in these
extremist parties generally offered the uprooted, the discontented,
and the alienated "totalitarian integration" into their communities of combat and faith.

Again, an ideology or statement of common beliefs may
perform wonders in helping individuals to merge with the
group. The French political scientist and writer Raymond Aron
demonstrated in his brilliant essays on the "opium of the intellectuals" of Europe the nature of the myths of Marxism and
proletarian revolution, and their attraction. The intellectuals he
describes are deeply alienated from the society around them,
a situation which is their equivalent of rural-urban migration or
uprooting as a result of war or catastrophe. Hence they are
"searching for a religion," for a faith in collective causes that
can integrate them into their societies.[26]

[26] Raymond Aron, *The Opium of the Intellectuals.* New York:
Norton, 1957, pp. 203–304.

Opposition and subversion

The sixth function of parties is the obverse of controlling and coordinating the government, namely counterorganization for opposition or subversion. Calling this a major function is sure to raise questions about its implied threat to legitimate authority and, indeed, its potentially dysfunctional nature. Yet there can be no doubt about its crucial significance to the system and its citizens. Not only is some opposition necessary for political competition, but its institutionalization and recognition as "Her Majesty's loyal opposition" has long become a vital safety valve against the threat of popular revolution. As long as the discontented can vote the incumbents out of office and a new set of leaders in—so the argument goes—things are unlikely to deteriorate to the point of a popular uprising.

Joining the opposition, rebelling against established authority, or engaging in the cloak-and-dagger work of outright subversion, furthermore, seem to appeal romantically to deeply felt needs in many people. The very process of policy making at all levels generates an army of dissent and disappointment. Every time a policy decision or an appointment has to be made, enemies are made as well. Every effort at rallying popular support or a political consensus, and every massive propaganda effort, antagonizes large numbers of people while attracting or persuading other large numbers. If the dissenters are to be politically united and effective, parties are the most useful device and an attractive alternative to isolated protests.

Perhaps the most menacing forms of partisan counterorganization are the revolutionary underground, and the totalitarian party in a democratic party system. Patterning its tactics closely upon the treatment it receives from the government it is plotting to overthrow and vice versa, the counterorganization may be a terroristic underground in a repressive police state, a backwoods guerrilla movement in a predominantly rural society, or an empire of front organizations combined with an electioneering apparatus in a free, developed society. Communist and fascist movements out of power have been the prototypes of this kind of counterorganization, but they have no monopoly on it. In accordance with the situation in which they try to seize power, they recruit large numbers of dissidents and forge them into what Philip Selznick has called the "organizational weapon" against the established order. They seek out its weaknesses, capitalize on its political and economic crises, strive to divide and confuse its supporters, and prepare to seize power when the time is ripe. As with moderate oppositions, their leaders aim at replacing the incumbent government leaders, but with a vital difference: as antisystem parties, they intend to change the entire political system as well.

THE VARIETY OF PARTY SYSTEMS

One common way of comparing and classifying whole party systems is by examining how and by what agencies the party functions are performed. How are government leaders recruited, policies designed, and governments run? How are the various group interests reconciled, individuals politically socialized, and political oppositions organized? The exhaustive answers to these questions add up in every case to a distinctive party-system profile. But several other approaches to defining party systems have long been in use or invite systematic application.

By far the most important aspect of any party system is and has always been the numerical relationship among the parties. This remains as true as ever at the crude level of distinguishing one-party (noncompetitive), two-party, and multiparty systems. It is also true of the more sophisticated numerical classifications and of the numerical relationships unearthed by election studies or political sociology. The number of players and their relative size largely define the nature of the game of electoral and parliamentary competition and coalition. The constant or fluctuating relationship between existing social groupings and voting patterns over a period of time gives the electoral and parliamentary game a time dimension and social perspective.

One-party systems

A catalog of numerical variations would begin with one-party systems, whose most prominent feature is monopoly, or the absence of competition. Nevertheless, there are differences among such systems, such as those categorized by Gabriel Almond as authoritarian, totalitarian, and dominant nonauthoritarian. The two former differ chiefly in their degree of penetration of the social and associational structure of society. Dominant nonauthoritarian one-party systems are said to be typical of recently emancipated nations whose nationalistic movements, such as the Congress party in India, have a practical monopoly without suppressing any opposition parties. Thus there may actually be numerous small opposition parties in competition with the giant, but generally no unified opposition. The openness and broadness of the dominant party, moreover, usually imply great socioeconomic and ideological heterogeneity among its constituent groups and the channeling of most conversion functions through its loose framework.[27] These three types are not too different from Coleman and Rosberg's two types of African party systems.[28]

Two-party systems

From the absence of real competition we move to the two-party systems—by comparison, highly competitive. A two-party system, by definition, need not be free from third or fourth parties as long as the latter are too small to interfere constantly and substantially in the bipolar pattern of competition. The label, however, should be denied to party systems where the competition is not chiefly between the two major parties, either because one party is overwhelmingly preponderant or because the two major parties have formed a rather long-lasting coalition. This restriction immediately raises the question of borderline cases, such as West Germany from 1966 to 1969 or Austria prior to 1966. It is a question of judgment in the individual case whether the hidden competition between the two parties in a "grand coalition" in fact overshadows the competitive patterns outside, or whether indeed any political competition remains

[27] In Gabriel Almond and James S. Coleman, *The Politics of the Developing Areas.* Princeton, N.J.: Princeton University Press, 1961, pp. 40–42. See also Robert E. Scott, *Mexican Government in Transition.* Urbana, Ill.: University of Illinois Press, 1964, pp. 106–109.

[28] The one-party type suggested there can be extended freely to include such totalitarian systems as the Soviet Union, which shares with them even the occasional tendency toward a "no-party state." *Political Parties and National Integration in Tropical Africa,* pp. 676–678.

that is worthy of the name.[29] Leon D. Epstein, in his survey of Western democracies, comments on the relative rarity of two-party systems, naming only Great Britain, Australia, Canada, Austria, the United States, and New Zealand, and perhaps also West Germany.[30] To this might be added some Latin-American systems still dominated by the competition between Blancos and Colorados, or their equivalent, the conservatives and liberals,[31] such as Uruguay, Colombia, Nicaragua, and Honduras. There used to be many more Latin-American countries of this description, but the rise of new parties and the decline or eclipse of the traditional two have reduced their number.

Restraints on two-party competition   Ideally, a two-party system would feature fairly frequent alternation between the two parties and a meaningful choice for the voters at every election. To the small extent that these two criteria are actually met, a two-party system could be an excellent problem-solving mechanism of popular government. On any major problem, the two parties could prepare alternative solutions for the voters to choose between at the next elections. However, actual two-party systems hardly ever function in this fashion. As many as 60 to 75 percent of the voters in Western democracies feel strong loyalties to a particular party and are not, for that reason, independent or purely "rational" voters who consider each issue on its merits.[32] Neither is it easy to reduce the multiplicity of issues

[29] The question of regional one-party dominance has been of great interest to specialists on American parties. See, for example, Paul T. David, "The Changing Political Parties," in Marian D. Irish, ed., *Continuing Crisis in American Politics* (Englewood Cliffs N.J.: Prentice-Hall, 1963), pp. 47–65, or the earlier writings of V. O. Key, Austin Ranney, and Willmoore Kendall.

[30] Epstein, *Political Parties in Western Democracies,* pp. 59–69. See also Leslie Lipson, "Party Systems in the United Kingdom and the Older Commonwealth: Causes, Resemblances and Variations," *Political Studies* (February 1959), 12–31.

[31] See especially Robert J. Alexander, "The Emergence of Modern Political Parties in Latin America," in Joseph Maier and Richard W. Weatherhead, eds., *The Politics of Change in Latin America.* New York: Praeger, 1964, pp. 101–125.

[32] For a discussion of different methodological aspects of this question, see also Anthony Downs, *An Economic Theory of Democracy.* New York: Harper & Row, 1959, and Herbert J. Spiro, *Government by Constitution.* New York: Random House, Inc., 1959.

of an electoral contest to a simple dichotomy between parties *A* and *B*. A voter may well like *A*'s foreign policy but prefer *B*'s domestic policies, or his preferences might be split in even more complex ways. Democratic elections rarely provide unequivocal mandates on any given issue. They are more likely to decide the question of personnel, as the "ins" may be confirmed in power or ousted. And even there, complications arise when the electoral system fails to permit the voter to choose leaders exactly as he would like to. Many electoral laws frustrate or discourage ticket splitting, thus forcing the voter to choose a package of candidates, just as he always has to choose a package of issues.

Actual two-party systems are further limited in their capacity to live up to the ideal. As comparative studies in state politics in the United States have shown, political competition between the two major parties is not as frequent a phenomenon as commonly believed. Outside of urban areas, in particular, one-party dominance is widespread, and the bane of noncompetitive oligarchy is relieved only by internal competition in the primary elections of the dominant party.[33] Nationally, two-party competition in the United States has also been the exception rather than the rule; witness the long periods of nearly uninterrupted Republican and Democratic preponderance in the last one hundred years. Another such example is West Germany, where the presumable development of a two-party system until 1969 always shrank from actual alternation in power. Given the solid block of party loyalty in modern competitive systems, the only hope for real competition lies in a sizable "floating vote" between the parties, which might represent what little "rational" choice there is.

Finally, the institutional framework and its significance for two-party competition should not be overlooked. A unitary and unicameral parliamentary government in a homogeneous nation appears to be most suitably associated with a highly competitive two-party system, in that it would maximize a system of political responsibility between governmental leadership and the voters. Such a system of "responsible party government," of course, is closely approximated only in Great Britain, if there.[34] An upper

[33] See Epstein, *Political Parties in Western Democracies*, pp. 48–55, and the sources cited there.

[34] See also the comments on David E. Butler, "American Myths

house divided along partisan lines already confuses the pattern of competition and muddles the issues, if indeed they were ever very clear. The separation of powers introduces further confusion and can even bring deadlock between executive and legislative branches, as Americans are well aware. Instead of giving the voters a clear-cut choice, in other words, political competition just turns into obscurity of political responsibility and friction between different organs of government.[35]

In federal systems the bipolar pattern can become so complicated as to be nearly unrecognizable. Major federal parties often take on a rather decentralized federal structure themselves and vary considerably in ideology and organization from state to state. In Canada, for example, some provinces have their own distinctive party systems, and in West Germany most *Länder* had multiparty systems, while federal politics in both countries tended toward a two-party system. More confusing still, the patterns of partisan competition can easily become lodged in disputes between the federal government and some of the states, when one party controls the former while the other rules the latter. In all of these cases, responsible party government can hardly be said to operate to its full extent.

Transitions to multiparty systems

Is there a transitional area between two-party and multiparty systems? In a number of instances such a claim appears reasonable on quantitative grounds alone: two-party systems at a point when third-party movements deny either one of the major parties a clear majority; doubtful cases, such as West Germany or Austria; or cases in which the competitive pattern appears to be predominantly bipolar although the number of parties exceeds two. The last-mentioned category is, perhaps, the most interesting in that it includes, for instance, the party system of the Fifth Republic of France, which is half multiparty, half the

---

about British Parties," *Virginia Quarterly Review,* 31 (Winter 1955), 46–56.

[35] These comments are not necessarily an indictment of the American party system, whose other virtues have been argued cogently, for example, by Epstein, *Political Parties in Western Democracies,* and by Julius Turner in his dissent, *American Political Science Review,* 45 (March 1951), 143–152.

dominant (since 1962) Union for the New Republic (UNR), a system rather neatly divided into anti- and pro-Gaullist forces. Another example is the Italian system—whose largest party, the Christian Democrats (DC), is in a similar if momentarily weaker position than the UNR, which won a landslide in 1968. On the other side, in permanent opposition, is the Italian Communist party with 26.9 percent of the vote.[36]

This bipolar multiparty pattern is also typical of the systems of Norway and Sweden, where the socialists are opposed by a nonsocialist coalition of several parties. In spite of the number of parties and the absence of any desire to merge, the patterns of competition appear to be bipolar both in the electoral confrontation and in the governmental coalitions.[37] Of course, at the level of government and opposition, all parliamentary systems will tend to be somewhat bipolar, since it takes a parliamentary majority to control the government and to pass legislation. Nevertheless, in deeply divided systems such as that of Italy today, France under the Fourth Republic, and the Weimar Republic of Germany, partisan conflict raged unabated among the opposition parties and even within the government coalition as well as between government and opposition.

Classification of opposition patterns

Robert A. Dahl in his *Political Oppositions in Western Democracies* has furnished a sophisticated scheme for classifying the Western patterns of opposition and thereby also the patterns of party systems in these countries. We have already discussed the chief features of his work from the point of view of comparative political-culture research.[38] As for the numerical features of a "game of competition," these patterns indicate not only the

[36] See, for example, Giorgio Galli, *Il Bipartitismo Imperfetto*. Bologna: Il Mulino, 1966.

[37] See Harry Eckstein, *Division and Cohesion in Democracy: A Study of Norway*. Princeton, N.J.: Princeton University Press, 1966; Nils Stjernquist, "Sweden: Stability or Deadlock," in Robert A. Dahl, *Political Oppositions in Western Democracies,* pp. 116–146, as well as accounts of Dutch and Belgian politics, as by Val Lorwin in *Political Oppositions in Western Democracies,* pp. 147 ff., or Arend Lijphart, *The Politics of Accommodation*. Berkeley, Calif: University of California Press, 1967.

[38] See Chap. 3, pp. 169–171.

organizational cohesion or division of both the government coalition and the opposition coalition, but also the nature of opposition strategies that may forge coalitions or lead to intra-opposition feuding. An "opposition of principle," as Otto Kirchheimer called it, such as the communist or fascist parties of European democracies in the early 1930s, was as likely to attack fellow opposition parties as the government. In fact, the communists concentrated their venom on the democratic socialists, whom they called "Social Fascists." And the real fascists delighted in attacking conservatives of all stripes. In a similar vein, the McCarthyist opposition in the 1968 elections in the United States was so intent on defeating the Democratic candidate for President, Hubert H. Humphrey, that they enabled the Republican candidate, Richard M. Nixon, to win, although he had shown far less sympathy for any of their causes than Humphrey. This goes to show that political alignments and de facto coalitions *can* form across obvious ideological as well as government-opposition divisions.

Competitiveness and distinctiveness   In addition to distinguishing oppositions by their organizational cohesion, goals, and strategies and by the site of their encounter with the government—in parliament, in the streets, or in the mountains and forests—Dahl also suggested competitiveness and distinctiveness as important variables. Competitiveness, indeed, runs from "strictly competitive" oppositions to those that are "strictly coalescent," such as the Austrian "grand coalition" until 1966. Studies of coalition behavior in democratic assemblies tend to show both of these extremes in clear quantitative terms. A "strictly competitive" system takes action either with a majority composed of only one party or with a bare-majority coalition. A "strictly coalescent" system is characterized by coalitions of all or nearly all parties. Examples of strict competition are generally limited to developed, pluralistic societies in normal times. Strictly coalescent systems include not only many developing countries, but also developed, pluralistic systems under the strains of wars or various emergencies. In the immediate postwar era of West Germany, for example, all-party coalitions at the state level were in vogue because the country was under foreign occupation and no party would have wanted to shoulder responsibility by itself.

West Berlin still prefers a coalition government of nearly all parties because of its state of siege by the communist powers around it.[39]

Class voting   High competitiveness often coincides with high distinctiveness of the opposition.[40] Robert R. Alford, for example, demonstrates that one can measure the degree of "class-voting" by correlating aggregate data and polls with voting statistics. The Labour, or socialist, parties of Great Britain, Australia, New Zealand, and West Germany thus turn out to have a distinctive "class character" that attracts the blue-collar vote. They are also based on powerful trade union movements that give them this distinctive character, whereas there are no such "distinctive class-parties" in the United States or Canada.[41] Such a class-distinctive opposition, or one of religious or ethnic distinctiveness, may well fall short of the size of the floating vote, or capability to alternate, of the less class-conscious two-party systems.

However, a certain fluctuation always occurs at the fringes of the self-defined social class in question, or among the potential "working-class Tories," and may indeed make for alternation, provided the two blocs are almost evenly matched, as in Great Britain. Even in the case of religious and ethnically distinct oppositions, the margin of fluctuation is much larger than is popularly held possible, as plebiscites and elections in Eastern Europe after World War I vividly demonstrated. Being of proletarian status, Polish-Byelorussian origin, or of a Catholic family may be objective givens that influence voting. But to be a militant proletarian, a proud and intransigeant Byelorussian in Poland, or a political Catholic anywhere is a matter of subjective evaluation and choice. A distinctive opposition of this description with any chance of success, in other words, is not so much a measure-

[39] See this writer's article on West German coalition behavior in Sven Groennings, Michael Leiserson, and E. W. Kelley, *The Study of Coalition Behavior.* New York: Holt, Rinehart and Winston, Inc., 1970.

[40] This depends somewhat on the definition of competition. According to writers such as Joseph Schumpeter, a maximum of competition is characterized by a floating vote and hence inhibited by class, religious, or ethnic bloc voting.

[41] See especially Alford and also Alan D. Robinson and Juan Linz in Lipset and Rokkan, *Party Systems and Voter Alignments.*

ment of how many persons of a given "category" exist in a country as of the willingness of this many people to unite behind a certain symbolic image.

Between "strictly competitive" and "strictly coalescent" party systems, there are also "cooperative-competitive" and "coalescent-competitive" stages.[42] Dahl shows how a given system may be highly competitive in the elections while exhibiting a mixture of competition and cooperation in parliament, as in the United States. Other systems manifest the mixture of competition and cooperation also in the elections, for example in the form of electoral alliances, or they go from highly competitive elections into the clinch of an Australian-style grand coalition. Strictly speaking, except in civil war, no party system is so exclusively competitive in its day-to-day operation (if not on substantive aspects of policy) as to forgo the broad patterns of consensus and cooperation implicit in adherence to the rules of competition.

Multipolar systems

From multiparty systems of a more or less bipolar pattern of competition, we move to what Giovanni Sartori has called the "extreme pluralism" of a multipolar system. Sartori's theory presents the Italian party system as a model of "extreme pluralism," defining the latter with the following criteria: (1) the number of poles, or distinctive parties, is five or more; (2) the "distances" between the poles, measured in ideological and socioeconomic terms, and the noncoinciding nature of the cleavages [43] frustrate the formation of a political consensus on the governmental level; (3) there is a large, strategically located "center party" that preempts the center of the spectrum and imparts a centrifugal drive to all oppositions, leaving them to an "irresponsible" strategy of outbidding each other. Italy with its eight or nine distinctive parties and the "central" Christian Democrats is said to exemplify this type of system, which typically includes parties opposed to the system of government itself, as well as some that may accept it only in part. France under

---

[42] See Dahl, *Political Oppositions in Western Democracies,* pp. 336–338, emphasizing the difference between systems where the elections directly determine the new government and those where they do so only after coalition negotiations.

[43] On this point, see also Duverger, *Political Parties,* pp. 234–239.

the Third and Fourth Republics, the Spanish Republic of the 1930s, the Weimar Republic of Germany, and perhaps also Finland and Israel are other examples of extreme pluralism.[44]

By way of a footnote to Sartori's theory, Arend Lijphart in a paper at the 1967 Congress of the International Political Science Association in Brussels presented a comparative table of cumulative percentages of party strengths in descending order of party size for Italy, Switzerland, the Netherlands, Denmark, and Norway. Comparing the strengths of the largest, the two largest, three largest, and so on, parties of each system, he found no marked difference between "stable" and "extreme-pluralistic" multiparty systems that would allow a clear typological separation on the basis of numbers and party sizes alone.[45]

FACTORS AND CAUSES OF PARTY SYSTEMS

Political parties are a highly adaptable phenomenon, the result of the institutionalization of important political functions at several levels. This process of adaptation to the special conditions and felt needs of a particular system at a particular time in history shapes parties and party systems in characteristic ways. Students of comparative politics have traditionally looked upon this process as one of social causation in which certain identifiable "causes" or factors produced certain characteristic forms and procedures. This approach is not in itself wrong as long as we distinguish the many different kinds of such causes,

[44] See Giovanni Sartori, "European Political Parties: The Case of Polarized Pluralism," in La Palombara and Weiner, *Political Parties and Political Development*, pp. 137–176.

[45] See Arend Lijphart, "Typologies of Democratic Systems," *Comparative Political Studies*, 1 (April 1968). In the same article, the author also adds to Dahl's coalescent-competitive dichotomy one distinguishing homogeneous from fragmented political cultures. Thus he produces a stability scale ranging from homogeneous-coalescent "depoliticized democracy" over fragmented-coalescent "consociational democracy" and homogeneous-competitive "centripetal democracy" to fragmented-competitive "centrifugal democracy," the latter being characterized by the inability or unwillingness of the political elites to bridge the gaps between the fragments of society. See also Lijphart, "Consociational Democracy," *World Politics*, 21 (January 1969), 207–225.

or factors, and as long as there is no simplistic reduction of the complexity of social causation to a single cause.[46] We shall survey briefly three kinds of theories relating party systems to different sets of factors. The first hinges on the influence of institutional settings on party origins and survival. The second relates parties to divisions among social groups and their development. The third examines them as a response to historical crises and situations.

Institutional settings

Parliaments   The importance of institutional settings on the formation of parties is the most universally present of the three sets of factors. Many of the earliest Western party systems, especially those of Great Britain and France, originated as it were in the lap of parliaments at a time of widening suffrage. Parliaments, as gatherings of delegates bent on concerted action, soon learn to appreciate the concerted power of factions. Although the factions of early parliaments may themselves originate from aristocratic cliques or notables from a particular region or interest, their presence encourages the other delegates to organize likewise for collective action or in self-defense. The requirement of majority rule in representative assemblies is a strong spur toward the formation of a progovernment faction and an opposition willing to and able to succeed it.

The next step in party development is suggested by the need to assure the reelection of individual delegates and of whole legislative blocs. The best means of securing the permanence of representative tenure is the creation of a permanent electoral committee in the constituency of the individual representative. The best means of perpetuating a faction in an assembly is the creation of a network of electoral committees that select the candidates and help them get elected—in short, a party organization. British parties were impelled along this road by the great electoral reforms of 1832, 1867, and 1885, as the existing legislative factions rose to the challenge of wooing the newly enfranchised masses by creating electoral committees and

[46] On the question of causal interpretations, see also the contributions of Lerner, Parsons, Dahl, and Lewis S. Feuer in Daniel Lerner, ed., *Cause and Effect.* New York: Free Press, 1965.

linking them into a national organization.[47] Maurice Duverger, in his book *Political Parties,* strongly emphasized the "internal creation" of parties—that is, by the parliamentary faction—in contrast to external creation of parties, as by protest movements originating outside of parliaments.

The early parliamentary setting may well help to shape the entire party system to the extent that externally created parties, as in Great Britain, can be absorbed into the internally-created system. Countries in which the national parliament and its cabinet are the dominant political institutions thus may indeed have their party systems patterned by the confrontation of government and opposition. These two camps, of course, could be made up each of more than one party, as long as they tend to form stable coalitions to govern and to oppose. In this fashion parliamentary government, as distinguished from presidential-congressional government, tends to create a bipolar party system. Exceptions to this rule, such as Canada or the Third and Fourth Republics of France, can largely be explained by the presence of competing institutional focuses of political power and by special features of political culture.

Dispersion of institutionalized power   A dispersion of institutionalized power, as in federalism or a system of separation of powers, whether between a president and congress or between the administrative state and the representative process (as in France), is a major factor in dispersing the party system as well. In federal systems, the regional differences often keep the national parties heterogeneous and decentralized, as in the United States, or irreconcilably fragmented, as in Canada. The separation of powers, on the other hand, supplies a unified policy-making focus in the head of the executive branch that is independent of partisan consolidation in the legislature. Thus it takes away the incentive to form a cohesive government majority and a cohesive opposition, leaving the political scene to the

[47] See Robert T. McKenzie, *British Political Parties,* rev. ed. New York: Praeger, 1963, pp. 1–8, and the sources cited there. See also Ostrogorski, *Democracy and the Organization of Political Parties,* vol. 1, for a detailed discussion of the development from the registration societies for the registration of the new voters to the creation of national party organizations by Peel and Disraeli.

ever-present centrifugal forces of interest and cleavage. In the case of the Weimar Republic or of pre-Gaullist France, the result appears to be a highly fragmented party system whose leaders gladly leave actual decisions to the administrative state or to a strong president. In the United States the party system is similarly fragmented in practice, although there is a bipolar element stemming from the electoral competition for the presidency and the clash of partisan establishments in the Congress. The electoral competition for the presidency alone appears sufficient to perpetuate the nominal bipolarity of competition between what are really rather heterogeneous ad hoc coalitions of state parties and other groups, or two "congressional" and two "presidential" parties rather than two major parties.

Electoral systems   One of the most widely discussed "causes" of party systems is the electoral system. Elaborate theories have been developed to prove, on the basis of comparative evidence, that systems electing a candidate by a mere plurality vote in a single-member district "cause" and perpetuate two-party systems, and further, that the requirement of an absolute majority, at least on the second balloting, in such an electoral district of a multiparty system provides some incentive for a consolidation of parties but will not force the small parties to give up their independence. Finally, it is asserted that proportional representation "causes" and perpetuates multipartism.[48] Closer examination reveals a complex set of interacting factors, not the least of which is the choice of voters and the attitudes of party leaders toward other parties. The simple causal relationship suggested by some politicians and political scientists is evidently not present, although it would be equally wrong to deny altogether that electoral laws have strong effects on the outcome of an election.

A careful assessment of the evidence and of the theories advanced to explain the causal links leads to a more modest formulation of the relationships. We must, however, bear in mind the crucial role of the historical settings and political prefer-

---

[48] See especially Ferdinand A. Hermens, *Democracy or Anarchy?* Notre Dame, Ind.: University of Notre Dame Press, 1941, and now also Andrew J. Milnor, *Elections and Political Stability*. Boston: Little, Brown, 1969.

ences for one or the other of these electoral laws (there are many variations of these three systems).

Plurality systems   Generally speaking, variants of plurality or absolute majority (second ballot) in single-member districts were the rule in all democracies prior to World War I. Plurality was particularly favored in the Anglo-American countries, where a two-party tradition gave it enough legitimacy to survive the occasional onslaught of third- and fourth-party movements. It is generally correct to say that a plurality system in a traditional two-party area is heavily biased against the successful rise of extra parties, although the rise of the British Labour party demonstrates that a third party can break through and become one of the two major parties.

Apart from the factor of political tradition, the bipolarizing effect of plurality systems is clear only in each electoral district. Only the two largest parties, party *A* and party *B,* stand a concrete chance of capturing a plurality, especially if they make a "catch-all" appeal to all the important groups in their district. Parties *C, D, E,* and so on have no hope of winning the one seat to be filled. In a regionally diverse country, however, the bipolarizing effect of the plurality system may assure the survival of *A* and *B* in one region, while *C* and *D* survive in another region, *A* and *E,* in a third region and so forth, resulting in a multiparty system in the national parliament. Single-member plurality districts by themselves, consequently, cannot "produce" or maintain a two-party system. They may, however, reinforce other bipolar factors by discouraging new third parties or splinter groups. They also tend to overrepresent narrow majorities at the national level, so that the winner of a two-party contest may get a solid majority of the legislative seats.

Absolute-majority systems   The absolute-majority system with runoff elections was popular among multiparty countries such as France and Germany before World War I, because it allowed a first test of party strength in any one district and then gave the parties a chance to combine their voting strength behind coalition candidates with a chance to win a majority. Thus there was an incentive for groups to merge into permanent major parties, which received a special advantage for getting majorities on the first ballot. At the same time, small parties could survive if no party received a majority on the first ballot by concluding electoral alliances for the runoff. The premium on willingness and ability to form such alliances, furthermore, tended to discriminate against extremist movements and to reward politicians for cooperation across the social and political cleavages of the system. The absolute-majority system was so satisfactory to the French that they returned to it repeatedly after experimenting with other electoral laws and have used it again since 1958. In Germany, on the other hand, during half a century of rapid urbanization without reapportionment, the same system led to such gross disparities in the population size of the electoral districts that the tide of electoral discontent swept it out once and for all in 1919. The Germans, and other polities with similar complaints on the European continent, replaced it with proportional representation. It was under various proportional-representation laws, then, that Weimar Germany and other new continental democracies had to weather the political storms of the 1920s and 1930s, when powerful extremist waves challenged their unstable governments from the left and the right. The collapse or near collapse of many a democratic government in this period is sometimes blamed on proportional representation, although many countries returned to it after 1945.

Proportional-representation systems   Generally speaking, the most popular versions of proportional representation [49] have given minorities and small parties an excellent chance of separate representation in the national parliament. They have accomplished this either by large multimember districts in which even a mere 10 percent of the voters can get a candidate elected or by compensating for the "lost votes" of each district in the national distribution of parliamentary seats or by a combination of both. Proportional representation derives its legitimacy from the arguments that the national parliament should be a mirror of the political forces and opinions in the country, and that the

[49] A reduction of the electoral district to four or three legislative seats with no provision to compensate small parties for their "lost votes" in each district, as debated in recent years in West Germany, would probably tend to rule out small parties and might even lead by attrition to a two-party system.

other two systems cheat voters out of their share of representation if their candidates lose. The experience with proportional representation during the turbulent 1920s and 1930s, however, was not exactly encouraging. Given the fragmented nature of European societies at the time and the extraordinary changes and adjustments they went through, the permissiveness of proportional representation toward minorities of every description, splinter groups, and extremist movements indeed encouraged a proliferation of parties and contributed to the increasing fragmentation and instability of parliamentary governments. The electoral system obviously did not "cause" the growth of new groups but it made it possible for them to succeed. It also failed to discourage the splintering of the existing parties, which the other two systems do by rewarding cooperation and party unity and by punishing secession.[50]

In a system dominated by large, stable groups, proportional representation can have considerable attraction to the second, third, fourth, and further parties, and even to the largest party. The second party may prefer it because proportional representation spares it the substantial underrepresentation of the loser in a plurality system. To the smaller parties it guarantees survival. And the largest party may count on this last effect to keep its closest competitor from taking its place. France, Italy, and Germany returned to versions of proportional representation after 1945, although with mixed emotions. In the 1950s the French attempted a modification of proportional representation by ceding every district in which a party or electoral alliance captured an absolute majority to the candidates of the winners. The result was a considerable, though temporary, setback for the French Communist party. The effect of the innovation was short-lived, because in later elections the parties evidently failed to conclude advance alliances.

The West German electoral law modified proportional representation, setting a minimum hurdle of 5 percent of the popular vote, without which a small party or splinter group will not be represented in the national parliament. This provision

---

[50] Admittedly, the evidence on this latter point is not without ambiguity in an absolute-majority system. Plurality voting, however, is ruthless in its punishment of party splits and dissenters, as the 1968 presidential and congressional elections in the United States again demonstrated.

can be credited with having worn down by attrition all but three of about a dozen parties over a period of twenty years, although it cannot, of course, stop sizable movements of any sort, including neofascists. The West German electoral law also added elements of plurality voting in order to avoid the sterility of party lists typical of the Weimar Republic, where the party bureaucracies were the sole determinants of who was selected as a candidate.[51] At least half of the parliamentary candidates have to be persons of genuine popularity and rapport with their constituencies.[52]

Social groupings

The importance of studying what Seymour M. Lipset and Juan Linz, among others, have called the "social basis" of politics lies in the significance of social groups for the patterns of political competition. When the entire party system of a country recruits itself from a single class or from a fairly homogeneous public, as did the Conservatives and Liberals of nineteenth-century England and the contemporary American Republicans and Democrats, a lively two-party pattern of competition with a considerable floating vote and real alternation in power is feasible. Where parties represent antagonistic social classes or ethnic or religious communities, the pattern is likely to be one of rigid immobilism, ideological dogmatism, and a failure to communicate across the "columns" of politically organized social groups. The mere accident that one antagonistic group forms a numerical majority while the other group is forever in the minority makes for oppression, rebellion, and ultimately violent conflict. Breakdowns occurred in European party systems in the 1920s and 1930s, and some of the polycommunal new nations seem rather close to such explosions today. Group-related party systems will, of course, change over a period of time along with their group basis. In

---

[51] Half of the Bundestag deputies are elected by winning a plurality in a single-member district. The rest are elected from party lists, according to the distribution of the second ballot among the parties.

[52] On the effect of electoral laws, see especially Duverger, *Political Parties,* pp. 216, 239–255; Enid Lakeman and James D. Lambert, *Voting in Democracies.* London: Faber, 1955, especially pp. 149–199; and Milnor, *Elections and Political Stability,* chaps. 2, 3, and 4.

any case, the criterion distinguishing highly group-related from homogeneously based party systems is intimately related to the function of the aggregation of group interests.

Response to historical crises

The theories relating party systems to historical crises and challenges are too numerous to be discussed exhaustively here. One might say that the entire literature on political parties and their development is one continuous essay on this subject. Political parties arise at a particular point in history to fulfill major new functions, such as those previously discussed. What greater crises and challenges can be imagined than those giving rise to national unification or independence movements?—or to organized popular effects to replace traditional elites with new leaders from among the people?—or to party movements in defense of a beleaguered social group? Among the more recent theories of this nature, the most prominent have been advanced by Joseph La Palombara and Myron Weiner and by Seymour Lipset and Stein Rokkan.

Three kinds of crises La Palombara and Weiner suggest three kinds of major historical crises that affect the form and functioning of party systems. The first is the crisis of *legitimacy* that occurs when hitherto accepted governmental authority wanes and requires popular reaffirmation, as for example at times of popular revolution or at the time of the great early suffrage reform. In colonial regimes or declining empires, anticolonial or antiimperial movements spring up to reestablish the spell of legitimacy. If existing and substituted structures of authority are so shaken as to require regeneration on the broadest possible scale, a second kind of crisis may ensue, the crisis of *participation*. Although a legitimacy crisis can be cured by substituting new and more accepted leadership, participation crises require an all-out effort to penetrate the local periphery for organized support for the government. In terms of the history of the widening of the suffrage, only the broadest mass suffrage will do, or else the masses may participate in their own way—by revolution. A third kind of crisis is that of *territorial integration,* calling forth unification and antiunification movements, the latter aiming at the independence and unity of a smaller unit than the nation about to be born.[53]

These three kinds of crises follow no prescribed order and can even come one on top of the other. In the latter case, the crises may so overload the political system that it cannot resolve any of them. The overburdened citizenry and leadership fall into acute political disorganization, or anarchy, and the system collapses. In a variation on the integration-plus-participation crisis, Hans Daalder has stressed the importance of how early political unification occurred and against how much resistance in the various European countries, singling out those latest in attaining unity against considerable resistance, Italy and Germany. He also places considerable weight, along with the relative congruence of political and economic development, on the "reach or permeation" of parties as against other power holders.[54]

Critical junctures in European history   Lipset and Rokkan have supported their theories of the genesis of contemporary European party systems by anchoring them in the great historical crises and challenges that conditioned the political response of rising elites on the eve or at the beginnings of mass suffrage. The first such crisis was the Reformation and Counterreformation of the sixteenth and seventeenth centuries, which made for substantially differing patterns in the Protestant northwest, the Catholic south, and the mixed belt in between.

The second "critical juncture" is the "national revolution" of the nineteenth century, which, in addition to issues of integration and independence, featured the rise of mass education and the struggle for secular or religious control over it. What earlier constituted the forceful emergence of national centers from the dominance of an international center, now becomes the process of internal consolidation, against the resistance of churches and movements of territorial defense, of the national community.

A third crisis is that brought on by the Industrial Revolution, which pits the primary, landed economy of agriculture

---

[53] La Palombara and Weiner, *Political Parties and Political Development,* pp. 14–19, 399–418.

[54] La Palombara and Weiner, *Political Parties and Political Development,* pp. 44–48, 58–67. On the question of the "load" see the same work, pp. 427–433.

against the secondary one of industry. The extended struggles over the Corn Laws and other tariffs protective of agriculture are typical of this confrontation, as are the struggles for state control ₲ver, or freedom of, industrial enterprise of the nineteenth century. This was the basic definition of the conservative and liberal positions in mid-nineteenth-century England, and there have been many shades of it since then in agrarian movements and in contemporary developing countries, such as those of Latin America. The fourth critical juncture, finally, is that of the clash between the employers and the workers, which at the beginning of this century posed anew a conflict between national loyalties and commitment to an international revolutionary movement. The anarchist-syndicalist, socialist, and communist movements owe their existence to this crisis.[55]

Lipset and Rokkan also discuss the genesis of the radical right, in the form of German national socialism, Italian fascism, French Poujadism, or the American right today, as "cleavages in fully mobilized polities." These movements are all said to be integral-nationalistic, authoritarian, and examples of lower-middle-class revolt against the rising elites, organizations, and corporations of modern society. While this generalization may be rather debatable and deficient on several counts, other "critical junctures" of the history of fully mobilized polities could be added to the Lipset-Rokkan framework to account for the more recent partisan forces and alignments of European systems. Such a critical juncture was the "age of imperialism" with its race for colonies and the intense rivalry and eventual war among the great powers. A separate case could be made for the crisis of 1917–1918, which saw four mighty empires tumble and ignite with the flames of social and ethnic revolution. World War I was a landmark in the development of party systems everywhere, signifying in particular the fateful communist secession from socialist movements and the rise of fascist counterrevolutions in response to the "red scare."

Another major crisis was the assault of totalitarian movements and dictatorships on the democratic systems of Europe between the wars. This onslaught deeply transformed all the systems and public opinion and, in the form of the response to

[55] Lipset and Rokkan, *Party Systems and Voter Alignments,* pp. 33–50.

communism, has continued even after the defeat of fascist totalitarianism on the battlefields of World War II. The postwar crisis of decolonization, finally, has also been a major source of partisan dislocation and realignment in a number of countries. And if this crisis seems insufficiently general among European countries, there is the "crisis of ideology" that restructured partisan politics in the last decade. Presumably spurred by the waning of class consciousness, it tended to transform many an ideologically militant class party into a highly aggregative "catchall" party, with corresponding changes in the patterns of party competition.[56] Broadly speaking, of course, every national election is a major crisis and challenge to all the parties, which invariably respond by conjuring up among their supporters visions of the great catastrophe awaiting the country if the party fails to win. Nearly all political action lives on crisis and challenge.

[56] See especially Otto Kirchheimer, "The Transformation of the Western European Party Systems," in La Palombara and Weiner, *Political Parties and Political Development,* chap. 6.

6
GROUPS, INTERESTS, AND CLEAVAGES

Political parties, according to the proponents of *group theory,* are only one variety of the far more inclusive social species of "groups." Policy making and political life can be reduced almost entirely to the role of the different groups of a political system. As Arthur F. Bentley defined the process of government in 1908, "When the groups are adequately stated, everything is stated."

The structure and interaction of social groups indeed constitute the skeleton of society, in which most of its life, including political action, takes place. Politics and government grow out of the internal life of the groups in response to the needs and functions of more inclusive communities, and they continue to depend heavily on their demands and supports. The study of the relation of group processes to politics is a huge and highly controversial field, about which a number of conflicting theories have been advanced. As yet no simple formula can explain the perplexities and conceptual difficulties of the subject to the satisfaction of all political scientists. Instead of a consensus on broad definitions, however, there has evolved a considerable literature on particular groups and their role in their respective political systems.

INTERESTS AND INTEREST GROUPS

Bentley and Truman's group theory

The "group theory" approach of Bentley and of David B. Truman [1] sees the entire polity as composed of hypothetical collectivities called groups, including "potential groups" or "latent (so far inarticulate) interests," the "official groups" of public officeholders, and even such large collectivities as social classes and ethnic or religious communities. According to Charles B. Hagen, a group is a "mass of human activity" directed in favor of or against a proposal of policy.[2] Public policy, in particular, is the result of the interplay of the group forces. As economics deals with the "allocation of scarce goods," political science deals with "authoritative allocation of values" (Easton) by means of the "group process" or "governmental process." Thus the group theorists have created a theoretical fabric to encompass all of politics and also to focus attention on the role in politics of private associations and groups rather than the official, corporate structures. Governmental institutions and policy-making individuals dissolve into groups in action. Ideas and ideologies are real only as thought or not thought by groups. Certain common motivations of group activities are the "interests." And social and political changes really consist of the processes of the protean world of ever-changing groups and of individuals' multiple membership in them.

Bourgeoisie versus proletariat

A drastically contrasting approach is that of Karl Marx and Friedrich Engels, who in the *Communist Manifesto* of 1847 reduced the significance of all group memberships to that of two antagonistic classes. Bourgeoisie and proletariat, defined

---

[1] See David B. Truman, *The Governmental Process.* New York: Knopf, 1951; also his article "Political Group Analysis," *International Encyclopedia of the Social Sciences,* vol. 12. New York: Free Press, 1968. Bentley's book, *Process of Government,* was reissued by Harvard University Press in 1967, edited by Peter H. Odegard, one of the pioneers of American interest group research.

[2] In Roland Young, ed., *Approaches to the Study of Politics.* Evanston, Ill.: Northwestern University Press, 1958, pp. 42, 44–45. See also the writings on American interest groups by Harmon Zeigler, John C. Wahlke, Lester Milbrath, and many others.

and distinguished chiefly by their respective relationships to the productive process of the machine age, are the supergroups of modern society, outside which in the long run there is no existence. Their respective members willy-nilly partake of an ideology, a class consciousness arising from their basic relationship to industrial production—an awareness of their diametrically opposed "class interests," which are inherent in the "internal contradictions" of industrial society. Their awareness of their irreconcilable class interests is the cement that can bind bourgeoisie and proletarians, respectively, into militant, class-based organizations such as political class parties. "The most complete, strongest, and clearest expression of political class struggle is the struggle among the [class] parties," according to Lenin.[3] The bourgeoisie, morover, controls the modern state and its coercive apparatus, while the proletariat may have to rely on trade unions and revolutionary organizations. In any case, both for bourgeoisie and proletariat, ideology, interest, and the class group are intimately connected. The deeper the cleavage between bourgeoisie and proletariat, the more intensely their ideologies are felt.

Elitist theories

A third school comprises the various theories of elitism, which likewise juxtapose two groups—the masses and an elite however constituted. Plato drew the line between his spirited and cerebral "guardians" and the *hoi polloi,* who are slaves to their senses. Other philosophers from Aristotle to Edmund Burke and Ortega y Gasset have been partial to nobility or aristocracy of one sort or another. Contemporary writers have tended to define elite status in terms of wealth, ethnic origin, or membership in a "political class" (Gaetano Mosca), "power elite" (C. Wright Mills), or "functional elite." [4] No matter how the elite group

[3] See the discussion in Henry B. Mayo, *Introduction to Marxist Theory.* New York: Oxford, 1960, chap. 5, and pertinent selections in chaps. 1 and 2 of Robert V. Daniels, *A Documentary History of Communism: From Lenin to Mao.* New York: Random House, Inc., 1960.

[4] The "functional elite" are those well qualified by skill and training to participate in the workings of modern industrial society, in contrast to the poor, the undereducated, the unemployable, and "welfare cases." See also Peter Bachrach, *The Theory of Democratic Elitism: A Critique.* Boston: Little, Brown, 1967.

is defined, the gist of the theory is invariably that the elite does in fact, and perhaps ought to, or ought not to, control governmental power and policy.

Like Marxism, elitist theories at first glance appear to have a great deal of explanatory power that lends itself especially to political polemics and agitation. How strikingly simple it would be, indeed, if all politics could be reduced to class struggle or all power to an identifiable "elite" group! Any attempt at applying either theory in empirical research, however, tends to encounter problems of a curious circularity of thinking, if not paranoid tautologies. Neither type of theory, it would appear, offers a concrete, testable basis on which to "prove" or "disprove" its assertions. Group theory likewise has little empirical relevance. However satisfying it may be to the analyst to reduce everything political to groups, it is precisely this homogenization of diverse political realities that makes group theory an unsatisfactory instrument of political science.[5] If all factors of politics are made out to be "groups," assuming for the sake of argument that all factors in a concrete situation ever *are* groups, then the term "group" has lost its analytical value.

The actual role of groups in politics

Promising research on the actual role of groups in politics will have to avoid the semantic traps of group theory and instead concentrate on the hardnosed pursuit of empirical reality. Instead of seeing groups everywhere, we need to perceive the rise and function of specific groups in a historical, developmental context. Instead of calling all kinds of groups from the family to mass organizations and social classes "groups," we need to explore the vital distinctions among them. And instead of following the tautological circle of group-activity-interest-ideology, we will have to separate these concepts analytically, if indeed they can survive such surgery. In this context, "activity" belongs under the heading of participation, policy making, and perhaps also socialization and recruitment. "Interest" is an awareness of more or less material benefit or damage—in other words, part of the cognitive and evaluative process of political culture.[6]

[5] See especially the critique by Harry Eckstein in Eckstein and Apter, *Comparative Politics: A Reader,* pp. 389–394.

[6] See, however, Mancur Olson, *The Logic of Collective Action.* Cambridge, Mass.: Harvard University Press, 1965, chap. 1.

Ideology also falls in this category, although some communications aspects may suitably be discussed here.

Almond's classification of interest groups   A good start on a classificatory scheme of the politically most relevant kinds of groups other than parties was made by Gabriel A. Almond, who suggested the following types of structures for *interest articulation.* The most conspicuous are today's *associational interest groups,* which are functionally specialized in making explicit the interests of labor and management, agriculture, industry, and the like before each other, the public, and public bodies. They also include ethnic organizations, associations of civil servants, denominational groups, refugee and veterans associations, and all kinds of civic groups. Formally organized, these groups can often document their representative character with open recruitment procedures and membership figures. Since their role in formulating or criticizing public policies is very much in the limelight, their internal processes of making decisons are almost as likely to arouse the curiosity of the public and of political scientists as are those of political parties.

Almond also lists *nonassociational interest groups* such as "kinship and lineage groups, ethnic, regional, religious, status and class groups which articulate interests informally, and intermittently, through individuals, cliques, family and religious heads and the like." [7] He mentions as one of his examples a complaint of an informal delegation regarding language instruction in the public schools on behalf of an unorganized linguistic group, such as, say, the Mexican-Americans of Los Angeles. Implicit in this kind of interest articulation is the relationship between the unorganized, or latent, interest group and its more or less self-appointed spokesmen. It is not easy to distinguish the leadership claims of such a spokesman from the demands of the group.

Structures of a third kind are *institutional interest groups* within legislatures, bureaucracies, armed forces, churches, and other corporations. These groups are part of a highly organized structure, but one constructed for purposes other than what

[7] In Gabriel A. Almond and James S. Coleman, eds. *The Politics of The Developing Areas.*   Princeton, N.J.: Princeton University Press, 1961, pp. 33–34.

concerns us here. Without any need for further organization, groups within these structures can articulate their own interests or that of the corporate entity within or toward the outside world. An ideological clique within the faculty of an educational institution, for example, may represent their own views and those of an outside group toward their fellow faculty members and students and, furthermore, try to promulgate them to the community as the "voice" of the institution. In many such cases the claims of representativeness exceed the truth.

Fourth on Almond's list are *anomic interest groups,* such as rioting mobs and ad hoc demonstrations. Although they may sometimes be carefully organized and harnessed, they derive their label from their disorderly and potentially self-destructive character. They often come into being chiefly where effective channels for voicing complaints are lacking, as in the many peasant revolutions of history throughout the world. By nature their activity is sporadic, but their immediate effect may be powerful enough to overthrow governments or to make them totter, as did the French student uprising in May 1968.

The emphasis in Almond's approach to interest groups, though not the categories, has changed somewhat in his more recent work with G. Bingham Powell, Jr. His earlier stress on the maintenance of the boundary between the society and the polity, from which, in particular, definitions of modernity and of totalitarianism were derived, has given way to increased emphasis on the differentiation and autonomy of the interest-articulating groups. "The subordination of interest groups to political parties may limit the mobility of the political process, create monopolies in the 'political marketplace,' and even stale-mate the system." [8] Denyng an interest independent representation may lead to riots or demonstrations or, in totalitarian countries, require a high price in social control.

The more recent work also concerns itself more with the problems of gaining *access* to decision-making structures, pos-

[8] Gabriel A. Almond and G. Bingham Powell, Jr., *Comparative Politics: A Developmental Approach.* Boston: Little, Brown, 1966, pp. 74–79. On the other hand, there are also situations in which a particular group or interest dominates a party or whole government, as with military predominance, church control over government, or the rule of an elite however defined, including a "master race."

sibly by means of violence and demonstrations. It also deals with such channels of interest representation as *personal connections,* and with different styles of interest articulation. The style of interest articulation, in particular, can either make for effective "aggregation of interests" or, as with riots, for a loss of the message in the din of the noise. Rigid ideologism or particularism can fragment the group process, frustrate aggregation, and prevent a politics of bargaining.[9] Questions of style, including the basic matrix of cleavages or particularism, are highly dependent on attitudes—in other words, on the political culture and the political socialization processes of a given system. To characterize the politics of Great Britain and the United States as a "politics of bargaining" reflects Anglo-American political cultures. By the same token, the various kinds of relatively nonbargaining political cultures—the patterns of ideological absolutism in France and Italy, those of communal particularism in many developing systems—reflect basic ways of life that pattern the formal group structure. The "moral basis of backward societies" is a matter of political culture, of which the presence and activity of groups is only a reflection.

MODERNIZATION AND THE POLITICS OF INTEREST

Early nonassociational groups

The historical and developmental dimensions of the role of certain kinds of groups in politics remain to be exhaustively explored. As cultural evolutionists and political anthropologists suggest, the earliest or "primitive" politics of the stateless societies of Africa, Asia, or Indian America before the arrival of Europeans were generally (with some notable exceptions) of such small scale or weak cross-local links that family ties (kinship, lineage) constituted the predominant grouping. In the absence of political structures and major nonkinship organization, kinship is the chief key to the rudimentary and ephemeral political life that may be called forth by crises or external threat. At this point, also, personal leadership and social stratification may make for political groupings.

As societies grew in scale, for example by conquest or by

[9] Almond and Powell, *Comparative Politics,* pp. 80–91.

banding together against external enemies,[10] they automatically added further nonassociational groups (ethnic, religious, regional) to the prevailing kinship ties. The ancient empires, as well as more recent traditional and semitraditional systems, were familiar with nonassociational interest groups and the intermittent demands they made through leaders or cliques. They also knew anomic groups as well as institutional interest groups, such as might grow out of the priesthood or the military establishment or palace guard.

Transitional mobilization

In the transitional phase of most developing countries today, the patterns of earlier, mostly large-scale societies tend to come into violent motion. Kinship ties, religious and particularistic status groups are challenged by the effects of urbanization and industrialization. Ethnic groups undergo social and political mobilization that predisposes them to break down the existing system of ethnic stratification, which may oppose their rise. Personal leadership of varying derivation looms large. New cross-local social classes arise and tend to supersede earlier social strata. In European societies, for example, the classical bourgeoisie was the first such challenger, soon to be followed by the working classes and the new middle classes.[11] Anomic interest articulation and the intermittent representations of the old and new nonassociational groups continue on a rapidly increasing scale, foreshadowing their need for regular and permanent channels. Institutional interest groups, such as the military and increasingly the public service, loom rather large and influential, because they already possess permanent organization and access to the decision-making process.

As Lucian Pye has pointed out, transitional politics falls considerably short of the ideal of representative politics—an open process by which conflicting interests can be brought out

---

[10] A good illustration would be the growth of settlements in favored locations such as the Yellow River basin, and later the joining in of outlying agricultural areas for protection against outside nomadic raiders.

[11] The old middle classes are distinguished by ownership of income property and commercial or industrial enterprise, whereas the new middle classes are essentially the white-collar groups and the equally dependent professions.

into the open and resolved by bargaining. The most common groups represent "a way of life and a diffuse and unlimited set of interests," and concrete demands appear either as "highly personal demands" of group leaders or as the "unnegotiable" claims of ethnic or religious groups. Government leaders couch their political appeals in broad, diffuse, and emotional language, anxiously avoiding specifics for fear of alienating large parts of their undifferentiated public. Considerable political maturity is required for a new polity to come down to specifics or for its politicians to abandon their early nationalistic perorations and come to grips with specific policy proposals.[12] Increasing modernity, at this point, means functional specialization both among politicians and in group methods for articulating interests. It also means better communication channels and better means of access for group demands. All these indeed must take a decided upswing to bring on modernity.

Early mass organizations

Among the earliest mass organizations in developing countries, other than the nationalist movement itself, are trade unions and farmers' leagues. These associational groups differ from their equivalents in developed countries such as the United States. Bruce H. Millen has characterized both kinds of trade unionism in language that fits the agrarian leagues. He juxtaposes the "economic unionism" of developed countries, which generally leaves politics to the politicians and parties, to the "political unionism" of the transitional phase.[13] The latter is distinguished by the heavy political involvement of the union leadership, the primacy of broad political over narrow economic goals, the frequent use of direct mass action for nonindustrial objectives, and a stress on ideological conformity and on "movementism" to capture power and to carry out political, economic, and social reforms—all of which may make the trade union

[12] See Lucian W. Pye, *Aspects of Political Development*. Boston: Little, Brown, 1966, pp. 81–85. Pye stresses in particular the dilemma of the politicians of the new states, who must modernize without offending their audience, amidst an extraordinary confusion of standards of performance.

[13] Bruce H. Millen, *The Political Role of Labor in Developing Countries*. Washington, D.C.: Brookings, 1963, pp. 8–10.

resemble a political party. Similar statements could be made about the early agrarian and, incidentally, also about early labor and farmers' movements in Western countries, such as the early Grange or the Knights of Labor in nineteenth-century America.

Contemporary trade unions   Contemporary American trade unions have evolved their style of interest articulation since the turn of the century, if not earlier, in reaction to ideological politics. A typical manifestation of this style of unionism was Samuel Gompers' "trade unionism pure and simple," which was concerned chiefly with such bread-and-butter issues as more wages, shorter hours, and better working conditions. Distinguishing itself carefully from its persecuted socialist and other radical offspring, the American labor movement found it more profitable to establish regular channels of collective bargaining over the respective shares of the common enterprise of management and labor. The trade union movements of northwestern Europe combine a similar emphasis on collective bargaining, collective control, and economic unionism with close ties to Social Democratic parties. Before World War II, however, these labor movements were more fragmented along ideological and religious lines, as Italian and French unions still are among several socialist, communist, and Catholic party groups. With increasing fragmentation, also, there comes more of the political unionism described by Millen. At the time of his writing, in fact, trade unionism in India, Ceylon, Indonesia, Lebanon, Nigeria, and many developing countries of Africa and Latin America was highly fragmented and rather amorphous in structure, and collective contracts were rare.[14]

Farmers' organizations   Farmers' organizations have undergone a somewhat similar evolution, although their clientele, except perhaps in Latin America, has been considerably less inclined toward revolution and violence. Current farmers' or-

---

[14] Millen, *The Political Role of Labor in Developing Countries,* pp. 11–34, and the literature cited there. Unionization, moreover, often begins with white-collar workers in industry and government, such as the railway unions of India or transport workers and government employees in Africa. See also Walter Galenson, ed., *Labor and Economic Development.* New York: Wiley, 1959.

ganizations in Italy and France are split into powerful communist, socialist, and Catholic wings that fight and excommunicate each other. Even worse fragmentation along ideological, religious, regional, and socioeconomic lines prevailed among the farm organizations of Weimar and Imperial Germany, although the posttotalitarian farm interests in the Bonn Republic are as well consolidated into a single organization as is organized labor. The overcoming of ideological splits in both cases reflects a notable meeting of minds on the grounds of economic interest and pragmatism. Thus a modern politics can arise from a transitional phase by means of structural changes that immeasurably increase a group's real bargaining position. The ability to speak for all of German labor or all of German agriculture greatly facilitates the establishment of regular channels of access to the parties, the legislature, the bureaucracy, other groups, and the public at large.

ORGANIZED INTERESTS IN THE MODERN POLITY

Once the process of modernization has become clear, our curiosity naturally falls upon the presumable end product, the politics of interest in a fully developed polity. To begin with, there are likely to be many hundreds, even thousands, of associational interest groups that dominate form and style of modern interest articulation. In comparison to earlier phases, nonassociational interests rarely are expressed now, and anomic interest articulation is even rarer, except when a new or left-out group demonstrates or strikes to gain access to the decision-making process. The associational groups are strong also because their members have increasingly assigned their interest-specific concerns to the paid lobbyists and staff of the organization. A closer look at a study of the British Medical Association (BMA) will illustrate the advanced stage of the politics of interest.

Focus of modern pressure-group politics

Great Britain According to Harry Eckstein's examination of the British Medical Association, modern "pressure-group politics" is determined by three variables: the structure of decision making, the pattern of policy, and the political culture. First, interest groups obviously must aim their activities at the particular agencies or levels of government where the decisions they wish to influence are made. Thus the exact structure of administrative functions and of effective power in governmental institutions determines the *channels* through which interest groups approach government. By way of feedback, governmental decisions and policies can modify these channels or restructure the group itself. A successful one-issue movement, such as the Anti-Saloon League in the United States, may disintegrate once it has achieved its original purpose. Political culture also restricts the channels by specifying what a pressure group can legitimately do without being "too obvious" about it, by producing a backlash, or by raising fears of a corruption of the policy process. British political structure, for instance, discourages interest groups (except for the largest of them) from exerting influence upon the political parties or individual members of parliament. Party discipline and solidarity shield the individual M.P. from all such groups except, in the case of the Labour party, the Trade Union Congress. Instead, the average interest group concentrates its efforts on the executive, from the cabinet level on down to local government.

At the cabinet level, large interest groups are consulted as a matter of routine on all legislation concerning their interests. Since major questions of policy are often controversial among the groups and government, consultation often turns into negotiations and hard bargaining. In other words, the major associational groups, such as the trade unions, the Federation of British Industry, or the National Farmers Union may even be accorded a veto. Only on rare occasions, and only after negotiations to win the consent of a group have failed, will the government impose its policy over the veto of a major group. Negotiations, of course, also require of the group representatives a certain flexibility and skill of advocacy. Smaller groups and nonassociational interests have less leverage and are more likely to be overruled, although the governmental need to consult them and the desire to obtain their consent are strong. Government administrators also feel it necessary to consider and utilize the technical expertise and experience that interest groups can supply for their own regulation. It is not always easy to separate purely technical advice from the bias a group is likely to have regarding its own regulation.[15] A group's advice and consent are sought further at all levels of policy implementation and execution.

Germany and France   These stable links between government and associational groups can also be found in other advanced countries. Gerald Braunthal and Herbert J. Spiro described the relation between the West German manufacturers (BDI) and employers associations (BDA), as well as the trade unions (DGB) and the Bonn government and parties.[16] The West German federal cabinet and the cabinets of the states include concerned interest groups as a matter of routine in "ministerial advisory councils" or in consultations on any pending bill of legislation.[17] In the Fourth Republic of France, according to George E. Lavau, particular interest groups could often count on a "friendly" high official or even a minister, who frequently became identified as a friend when he was still a member of the appropriate interest-specific "parliamentary study group." The groups evidently found it easier to "colonize" the National Assembly and invariably used their leverage there when the executive turned out to be "hostile" to their demands.[18] Under

[15] Harry Eckstein, *Pressure Group Politics.* Stanford, Calif.: Stanford University Press, 1960, chaps. 1 and 7. On British groups, see also Samuel E. Finer, *Anonymous Empire.* London: Pall Mall, 1958, and Samuel H. Beer, *Britain in the Collectivist Age.* New York: Knopf, 1965, pp. 71–88, and chaps. 4 and 12.

[16] See Braunthal in James B. Christopher, ed., *Cases in Comparative Politics.* Boston: Little, Brown, 1965, pp. 241–258, and his *The Federation of German Industry in Politics.* Ithaca N.Y.: Cornell University Press, 1965; also Herbert J. Spiro, *The Politics of German Co-determination.* Cambridge, Mass.: Harvard University Press, 1958.

[17] See, for example, Lewis J. Edinger, *Politics in Germany.* Boston: Little, Brown, 1968, pp. 209–212. See also Heinz Burneleit, *Feindschaft oder Vertrauen zwischen Staat und Wirtschaft?* Frankfurt: Knapp, 1961, pp. 41–48, and Walter Krumholz, *Wie ein Gesetz entsteht.* Berlin-Munich: Humboldt paperback, 1961, pp. 55–59. Krumholz lists the communal associations, the nation chamber of commerce (DIHT), the BDI, BDA, DGB, the Farmers Association (DBV), and the White-Collar Union (DAG) as groups that according to Rules of Order II of the federal ministries are routinely invited to comment on pending bills (para 29). The ministries also solicit independent expert opinions.

[18] In Henry W. Ehrmann, ed., *Interest Groups on Four Continents.* Pittsburgh, Pa.: University of Pittsburgh Press, 1958, pp. 63, 67–74. See

the Fifth Republic, the channels of group influence have shifted noticeably from the legislative arena to the executive and the bureaucracy, where advisory councils composed of group representatives are now attached to all major administrative agencies. Ehrmann speaks of some 500 "councils," 1200 "committees," and 3000 "commissions" at the national level in France, all serving to bring together governmental and group representatives.[19]

The comparison of Great Britain, West Germany, and France, in this order, also shows a significant progression in attitudes toward interest-group activity and regular contacts between lobbyists and government personnel. British political culture is characterized by the least objection to this form of lobbying, while the French are still haunted by a strong fear of special interests, "intermediary bodies" (de Gaulle), and the danger of corruption of the state. Germany during the Weimar years witnessed close interaction between rather narrow political parties and even narrower, energetic interest associations, which both combined to fragment the system, while many conservatively inclined citizens and civil servants mourned the eclipse of "the state" under the onslaught of the pluralistic marketplace. Since 1945, however, organizational consolidation among the groups, the trend toward a bipolar system, and the "end of ideology" have facilitated the rise of a stable, highly integrated system of interest articulation in league with the West German government.[20]

Development of interest-group activity

The bulk of the associational interest groups in a modern polity sprang up more or less simultaneously with the expanding functions of modern government around and since the turn of the century. This, in Chapter 1, constituted our fourth stage of

---

also Ehrmann's *Organized Business in France.* Princeton, N.J.: Princeton University Press, 1957, and *Politics in France.* Boston: Little, Brown, 1968; Jean Meynaud, *Nouvelles Études sur le Groupes des Pression en France.* Paris: Colin, 1962, and Bernard E. Brown, "Pressure Politics in the Fifth Republic," *Journal of Politics,* 25 (August 1963), 509–525.

[19] *Politics in France,* p. 184.

[20] See, for example, Charles E. Frye, "Parties and Pressure Groups in Weimar and Bonn," *World Politics,* 17 (July 1965), 635–655. On great Britain, see also Richard Rose, ed., *Studies in British Politics.* New York: St. Martin's, 1966, chap. 4.

political development. In some cases the groups were organized to defend interests against governmental regulation or against the encroachment of other newly organized associations. In other instances, as with the American Farm Bureau Federation, government activity literally created the interest group. In many cases, however, the group activity comes first and prevails upon government to add new agencies and functions. Ministries of trade or commerce, labor, welfare, transport, and agriculture, as well as various promotional agencies in modern governments, are often the result of organized demands for governmental action in a new field. And once organized business or agriculture, say, gets the government to add a ministry or agency in its field of interest, it makes sure the new minister and/or staff are "friendly" to it. When a new secretary of labor is selected, for example, the trade unions are usually consulted and may well have an opportunity to propose a man of their choice. Thus close and stable relations between large interest groups and the corresponding executive agencies are encouraged and facilitated from the beginning.

Interest groups have similarly "started" many standing or ad hoc legislative committees. If such groups are large and powerful, they can see to it that the committees are composed largely of "friendly" legislators from constituencies where the group is particularly influential. A group's interest in having enough friendly legislators in the legislative assembly or in the relevant committees also drives it to attempt to influence legislators by financial support or propaganda, or at least by mobilizing group members in the constituencies concerned. But just as a group's interest in the executive depends on the decision-making power there, groups will concentrate on legislative committees only where such committees wield considerable power, as in the case of the topical standing committees of the United States Congress, the French National Assembly prior to 1958, the Italian Parliament, or to a lesser degree the Bonn Republic.[21] The "parliamentary study groups" of pre-Gaullist France were interest-specific ad hoc committees, so to speak. In the British

[21] In West Germany and in the Weimar Republic, certain interest groups at times succeeded in persuading political parties to nominate some of their functionaries, who, when elected, immediately strived to get on the "right" committee of the national parliament.

House of Commons, the nontopical committees *A, B, C,* and so on are too weak and unspecialized to be of much service to an interest group.

In a more decentralized governmental system, such as constituted by federalism and the separation of powers in the United States, interest groups naturally attempt to get a foot inside all the doors, executive, regulatory, and legislative, and they often try to exploit the antagonism of the separate agencies and levels of government by playing one against the other. If the executive agency or regulatory commission balks, they turn to Congress. What the Senate will not give, they try to get from the House of Representatives. If the state and local levels will not respond to their demands, they ask for federal action on their behalf. And since elective offices are involved at all levels, they take an intensive interest in elections in order to defeat the "wrong" and advance the "right" candidates. Their power to deny election to a candidate can be formidable. Between elections, likewise, they undertake to influence the public to view their interests favorably and to resist encroachment upon them. Thus the larger organized interests in this country, and in comparable situations elsewhere, tend to be the most cohesive political force amid the many associational and institutional group forces that influence the formation of public policy in certain fields. As "veto groups," to use David Riesman's phrase, if not always as a constructive force, they often overpower the intent of governmental agencies or political parties.[22]

Governmental solidarity as a defense

Even though interest groups may be the most cohesive forces in a pluralistic system, their large number and egocentric single-mindedness prevent real cohesion for the process of public policy making. In order to carry on a consistent course of policy, the executive must avoid becoming dependent on the interest groups, relying instead on devices that make for solidarity and centralization of authority within the entire administration. A centralized, solidary executive branch can consult with interest groups from a position of strength. A decentralized adminis-

---

[22] See also the survey by Samuel J. Eldersveld in Ehrmann, *Interest Groups on Four Continents,* pp. 173–196, and the discussions in the same work, pp. 246–289.

tration, just like a legislature whose actual power is decentralized in standing committees, is wide open to "colonization" by powerful interests. Groups can acquire control over certain personnel positions, a veto over the policies affecting them, and even a voice over significant portions of the budget. In short, they can jointly take over the whole government, whose policies may then indeed become the direct product of the group forces, as group theorists have often hinted.

In legislatures, likewise, the best defense against the organized interests lies in solidarity and centralization of authority, as with a presiding officer, presidium, or steering committee. But solidarity can also come from the presence of cohesive party government. Interest groups naturally wish to impress their demands on parties in and outside of the legislature, and all the more where the parties are the dominant element in policy making. Again, decentralization in the parties opens them up to excessive interest influence, while solidarity and centralization allow them to deal with the organized interests from a position of strength. Political parties usually need financial support [23] from interest groups and, in democracies, are in any case rather inclined to take into consideration the wishes of organized interests in policy making in order to build up support. But they become dependent upon them only at their peril.

Interest-group access to political parties

The relations of associational interest groups to political parties in some ways resemble those between the groups and the government. Groups will try to gain access wherever it seems possible and worthwhile—in other words, wherever important decisions are made.

A decentralized party leaves its candidates the prey of demanding interest groups at the time of nomination and again at election time, so that each of its deputies in the legislature has obligations to interest groups he has to pay off eventually. Such mortgages naturally reduce party cohesion and discipline in a legislature.

---

[23] Some systems, as in West Germany, provide party campaign funds from the treasury in order to lessen the power of interests at this point of the democratic process. See also Rose and Heidenheimer, eds. *Comparative Studies in Political Finance,* special issue of *Journal of Politics,* November 1963, for other systems of party finance.

A strong and centralized party, on the other hand, such as the major parties of Great Britain and Western Germany, is likely to have stable relations with interest groups only at the center of the state or national party organization. The policy demands of the interest groups may be fed into the party's program and policies by more or less formal, topical "advisory committees" attached to the central party organization or at least to the party conventions. And the financial support from organized interests likewise is channeled exclusively through the central organization rather than given directly or denied to each candidate as in the United States.

Decentralized party finance or a mixture of centralized and decentralized campaign financing, however, need not imply an absence of stable relationships and channels between parties and interest groups. Where parties fail to provide for centralized handling of demands and funds, the major interest groups invariably will coordinate their efforts by drawing up uniform lists of policy demands, which each local candidate must accept to gain their campaign support.[24]

SOCIAL AND POLITICAL CLEAVAGES AND LEGITIMACY

"A stable democracy," according to S. M. Lipset,[25] "requires the manifestation of conflict or cleavage [because they] . . . contribute to the integration of societies and organizations. Trade unions, for example, help to integrate their members into the larger body politic and give them a basis for their loyalty to the system." The presence of an important political cleavage can indeed become the focus of integration into a meaningful political group life for masses of individuals who are uprooted and lost in the wake of economic and political change.[26] Conflict in itself brings the combatants together in a

[24] See especially the literature on American party finance and the contributions to Rose and Heidenheimer's theories, *Comparative Studies in Political Finance*, p. 791.

[25] S. M. Lipset, *Political Man*. New York: Anchor Books, 1963, p. 1. See also his recent *Revolution and Counterrevolution* (New York: Basic Books, 1968), where some of his scattered essays have been reproduced and integrated.

[26] Georg Simmel calls it a *sociation,* which is caused by and seeks to resolve such dissociative phenomena as hate, envy, or greed. *Conflict*

kind of interactive society. But a major political cleavage can also escalate the struggle between antagonistic groups to the point of civil war or complete breakdown of the polity. The difference between the integrative and the disintegrative effects of political cleavages, it would appear, lies in the cleavage structure and in the legitimacy of the political institutions and processes of a system.

Social cleavages, which are not necessarily identical with political cleavages, are as numerous throughout societies as are the groups that they separate from one another. Minor social cleavages, for example, separate families, age groups, and neighborhood. Major social cleavages divide communities of religious faith, distinctive social strata or classes, ethnic or territorial communities, occupational groups, and ways of life. All of these social groups have communication systems that help to socialize and integrate their members. Small groups can do with word of mouth, while larger groups have to rely on symbols and on more formal communication processes. In a highly literate, modern society, such communication may well take the form of newspapers, periodicals, or radio or television programs, each having its group clientele. Modern societies, indeed, have thousands of printed group-communications media whose distribution patterns and content characterize specific groups. The social cleavages are relative discontinuities in communication among the groups.[27] This fact is particularly noteworthy when a major social cleavage happens to become a political cleavage, because the group-specific content, say, of trade union journals then also becomes an important part of the political ideology of one of the sides in the political struggle.

Origin of political cleavages

How do political cleavages originate? There is no easy general answer except that political cleavages are invariably responses

---

and the Web of Group Affiliations. New York: Free Press, 1955, p. 13 and *passim.* See also the theoretical discussion by Lewis A. Coser, *The Functions of Social Conflict.* New York: Free Press, 1956, chap. 7.

[27] The presence of multiple group affiliations, of course, makes the discontinuities relative rather than absolute. An independent press and public communications, moreover, add a common communications system to the separate ones of the groups.

to major economic or political change. Political cleavages could not possibly be identical with all or even the major social cleavages without reducing a society to a civil war of all persons and groups against all others. Nevertheless, they often arise from a major social cleavage in reaction to a drastic change in relations between the groups. The French Revolution of 1789, for example, created a political cleavage between the awakening bourgeoisie and the nobility and other mainstays of the old regime, because the latter had oppressed and exploited the former without granting them access to power. Once victorious, the bourgeoisie took such cruel revenge as to perpetuate this cleavage for more than a century as the major divide of the French political system. During this long period of incisive social and economic changes, the prorevolutionary and antirevolutionary cleavage in French politics naturally lost much of its identification with the original social cleavage, becoming instead a meaningful symbol of political affect and orientation, vaguely associated with progress and revolutionary sentiment.

Some later political cleavages remained more closely linked to the social cleavages that gave rise to them. For example, the political cleavages separating the rising working classes from the bourgeoisie, the farmers from the nonfarmers, and loyal Catholics from secular or Protestant elements preserved better their link to the social groups concerned. An important reason for this staying power lay in the formal organization of labor in trade unions and socialist parties, of agriculture in farmers' associations or agrarian parties, and of loyal Catholics in Catholic associations and parties.[28]

Changes in the political structure may also create political cleavages. At the time of unification or foundation of new nation-states, for example, antagonistic forces may dispute the issue of unification or governmental centralization, as did the Federalists and Anti-Federalists of the earliest years of the American republic. The clash of economic interests vying for control of the government, too, may give rise to a major political cleavage. The issues of free trade versus tariff protection pitted

[28] Conflict with "out-groups," according to Lewis Coser, increases internal cohesion, defines the relations among the groups, and creates enemies and friendly coalitions. *The Functions of Social Conflict*, chaps. 5 and 8.

nineteenth-century agriculture against industrial enterprise, and different branches of the latter against one another. Often, also, several issues may add up to a heterogeneous cleavage composed perhaps of historical memories, questions of economic interest, and social cleavages of "turf," class, ethnicity, or religion, as well as issues of structural political change.

Analytical approach to cleavage structure

Any attempt to analyze the present cleavage structure of a political system and to relate it to the operation of the party system will have to begin by drawing some vital analytical distinctions about the levels and nature of political cleavages. Pitting two major parties against one another as an indicator of political cleavage, we need to explain relationships far more complex than a set of coinciding dichotomies.

Social-structural level At the social-structural level, for example, ethnic, geographic, or religious cleavages are *capable* of developing into political cleavages, provided they are salient and reinforced by social mobilization processes that internally solidify the groups and make for friction among them. The same processes of social mobilization could just as easily dissolve these groupings in an industrial or urban melting pot. In most populations the economic, occupational, and educational differences at this level are distributed along a normal curve, which makes it most arbitrary to draw a "class line" at any one point without additional confirmation. Only subjective self-identification with a class and hostile perception of another class, ascertained in interviews and not from aggregate data, can confirm the presence and indicate the precise location of a class cleavage.

A good example of the complex nature of the cleavage structure are the working-class Tories of Great Britain, the goodly portion of the British working classes who for reasons of personality and deferential attitude vote Conservative and not Labour.[29] Similar divisions can be found on the Continent—especially in Catholic populations, where the social-structural

---

[29] See especially Eric Nordlinger, *Working-Class Tories in Great Britain*. Berkeley, Calif.: University of California Press, 1967, and Robert T. McKenzie and Allan Silver in S. M. Lipset and S. Rokkan, *Party Systems and Voter Alignments*. New York: Free Press, 1967, chap. 3.

cleavages alone can never explain why some Catholic workers vote for anticlerical socialist parties while other Catholic proletarians prefer Catholic or Christian Democratic parties.

Nonpolitical organization level　At the next higher level of cleavage are nonpolitical organizations such as churches, ethnic associations, and organized labor or agriculture. These solidary, cohesive groups could indeed account for political antagonism and cleavage, except that their mutual hostility does not follow automatically from the in-group versus out-group mechanism. Quite frequently, in fact, their leadership may be anxious to reduce whatever intergroup tension arises from the members' prejudices. Even more often such groups are allied against a common enemy, and for the sake of the alliance they refrain from hostility among themselves. Only where there is evidence of consistent hostility between two groups can one begin to speak of them as sources of political cleavage.

Electorate level　At the level of the electorate the party voters constitute a reliable indication of political cleavage. Voting studies and political sociology, consequently, have tried to analyze the "social bases" and the organizational memberships [30] of the loyal voters of given parties. From the resulting social profiles of the party electorates, such labels as "class-based" or "ethnic-minority party" have been derived, although rarely with anything like perfect correlation between, say, proletarian status and socialist vote. Political sociologists and the public are quite satisfied when as much as a majority of party voters fit a given label, or when a given group is 50 or 100 percent more frequent among party voters than in the general electorate.[31]

Party member level　Party members can be similarly analyzed. They also vary in their degree of loyalty and solidarity, even though they are "gladiators" (to use Milbrath's term) engaged in competition with other parties. Not every member is an ac-

[30] See, for example, Juan Linz in Lipset and Rokkan, *Party Systems and Voter Alignments,* chap. 6, on West German politics in the 1950s.

[31] See also Mattei Dogan in Lipset and Rokkan, *Party Systems and Voter Alignments,* chap. 4, on French and Italian politics.

tivist of the party.[32] At this point one should take into account a definite desire on the part of party leaders and members to have their group rally around controversial issues and to maintain internal solidarity. This political motivaton, however, may at times inject divisions into the party membership and electorate, just as it may sometimes lead to a coalition with certain other parties for common objectives.

Nonstructural cleavages   Nonstructural cleavages also abound in political life. Political cleavages can easily originate from temporary, major issues of personnel or policy with no relation to social cleavages. Issues, say, such as the personality of Charles de Gaulle or issues of foreign policy, defense, or welfare can polarize a political system into antagonistic camps for decades. The juxtaposition of government and opposition, and other built-in checks and balances of the governmental structure, can likewise produce long-standing major political cleavages. Indeed, we must account for a great many dimensions and levels of cleavage at any one time in order to sketch out the actual cleavage structure of a polity.

Cross-cutting cleavages

Seldom if ever has a simple dichotomy split a whole society neatly into two camps. Even in settings of extreme political polarization, as in the coming of civil wars, not *all* significant cleavages coincide. A Marxist class society of two antagonistic classes presumes the merging of all or most cleavage lines into one.[33] It is far more likely, however, that the various cleavages will run across one another. Parliaments and electorates tend to divide along several noncoinciding lines, such as left-right, rural-urban, and communist-noncommunist. Often workers will read the bourgeois press and farmers the city press. The Flemings and the Walloons of Belgium, in spite of their ethnic strife, tend to belong to the same major parties, such as the Socialists

[32] See especially the recent study of party activists, *L'attivista di partito,* by Francesco Alberoni, Vittorio Capecchi, and others. Bologna: Il Mulino, 1968.

[33] See also Rolf Dahrendorf, *Class and Class Conflict in Industrial Society*. Stanford, Calif.: Stanford University Press, 1959, pp. 213–238.

or Christian Socialists. Both Catholics and Protestants have joined and voted for the West German Christian Democratic Union, and so do both workers and employers. Instead of deep coinciding and irreconcilable cleavages, in other words, most political systems feature cross-cutting cleavages that tie people together even as others divide them.

Effect on stability and legitimacy   The presence of cross-cutting cleavages, according to Simmel and Lipset, is a major factor of stability and legitimacy in a political system. This applies *a contrario* to countries undergoing a crisis of legitimacy, caused by the breakdown of major conservative institutions or the exclusion of major groups from access to the political system. Moderate conflict in a competitive, democratic system will increase or reestablish the legitimacy of the system as long as the contending groups separated by political cleavages have as much in common as divides them. When systems exclude major groups, as they did with the workers of Germany and France, they isolate them from cross-cutting affiliations with participants in the system. Parties or movements that themselves seek to isolate their followers from all cross-cutting influences and loyalties are creating a potentially fatal threat to the legitimacy of the system.[34] With the socialist and Catholic parties of "democratic integration" (Neumann), this was largely a defensive response to political exclusion, although they took many decades to get over their original reactions. With the totalitarian parties of the right and left, however, the objective was the deliberate launching upon the established order of a phalanx of alienated individuals guided by a utopian ideology.

The argument of the beneficial effect of cross-cutting cleavages upon stable democratic processes can also be extended to a preference for two-party over multiparty systems, federalism over unitarism, and territorial representation, such as with plurality in single-member districts, over proportional representation. All of the preferred systems tend to force political decisions into coming to terms with the cross-pressures of multiple group membership and the pluralism of society, while their opposites are

[34] See Lipset, *Political Man*, pp. 65–79, where the tendency toward political extremism is ascribed to all "isolated" occupations and trades. Also Simmel, *Conflict and the Web of Group Affiliations*, pp. 127–130.

more conducive to social single-mindedness and isolation.[35] Large-scale societies also would be preferable to small, communal settings, although it is no secret that the larger nation-states have had substantially more difficulty in developing stable modern systems than the smaller European democracies. The very process of nation building, as Stein Rokkan has demonstrated in the case of Norway, follows a course from struggles between the center and resisting peripheral territories to functional, economic-interest cleavages among groups distributed nationwide.[36] The older cleavages of "turf," in other words, are intersected by cross-cutting cleavages of primary versus secondary economy and labor versus management.

[35] See also Lipset, *Political Man,* pp. 80–82.

[36] In Lipset and Rokkan, *Party Systems and Voter Alignments,* chap. 8; see also his typology of cleavage structures of the smaller European democracies in Otto Stammer, ed., *Party Systems, Party Organizations and the Politics of the New Masses.* Berlin: Free University of Berlin, 1968, pp. 26–65.

7
POLICY-MAKING STRUCTURES AND INSTITUTIONS

Modern currents in comparative politics are clearly distingushed from their immediate predecessors by their treatment—or, more frequently, nontreatment—of the institutional fabric of modern governments. Once the epitome of comparative subjects, the study of political institutions now has been downgraded, if not altogether eliminated from the discipline. Unfortunately, this change often misleads students into thinking they can neglect Western institutional lore and proceed directly to what they consider the livelier aspects of political reality. For this and other reasons the decline of institutional studies merits detailed discussion.

THE LEGAL-INSTITUTIONAL APPROACH

The era of the legal-institutional approach represented a highly effective scholarly response to a historic challenge—the constitution-making and institution-building phase of nineteenth- and twentieth-century Europe and America. Earlier intellectual reflections on politics had been theological and philosophical, as would befit an age still under the waning spell of sacred monarchy and traditional institutions. Not until the traditional fabric broke down, or until major upheavals had questioned or destroyed the legitimacy of the traditional institutions, did the nature and function of governmental institutions become a focus of popular debate.[1] When monarchy itself, for instance, has to give reasons for its existence, or when learned men ask what its usefulness or function might be, the best days of monarchy are over.

The urge to replace tottering older institutions with rationally designed new institutions called forth expert designers of entire constitutions as well as specialists on the optimal, detailed design of particular institutions such as bureaucracies or legislatures. By contrast with the earlier political thinkers, these men may well be called political pragmatists, even nut-and-bolt specialists.

The constitution-making and institution-building age is not over. Besides the many European countries that fashioned new constitutions after World War II, numerous new nations have now designed and adopted constitutions as a kind of birth certificate of nationhood. Partial institutional changes going on constantly in all countries also require constitutional and institutional expertise. Since constitutions are legal documents and modern governments fashion their primary activities—administration and lawmaking—according to legal definitions, the predominance of legalistic approaches to constitutional and institutional change is quite unavoidable. It would appear, then, that regardless of the current preferences of some political scientists, the legal-institutional approach is still strongly represented in legions of practicing politicians and administrators and likely to remain with us for a long time. A student of comparative politics who ignores the legal-institutional approach, in other words, is out of touch with the chief frame of reference of the practitioners of politics, out of touch with the reality they perceive.

To be sure, the legal-institutional approach can well afford

[1] There are some early antecedents in antiquity, such as Aristotle and Polybius, Roman lawyers and thinkers, and, in the Middle Ages, famous churchmen and reformers such as Marsilius of Padua. Nearly all of these became interested in institutions in reactions to major challenges to the legitimacy of prevailing institutional patterns.

to be improved upon with current social-science innovations, such as those discussed in this book. In view of certain exaggerations and blind spots in the study of political institutions, in particular, there appears to be a balance here that needs to be restored. For instance, past writings have often tended to present the "behavior" of a political institution as an abstraction for the whole political process, attributing to it a collective "life" and "consciousness" such as only individuals possess. Earlier writers also have been too easily satisfied with mere description or with normative legal definitions, when they should have inquired into the actual functioning of a given institution. In case of failure or breakdown, too, legal-institutional analysts have rarely gone beyond cryptic formulations, such as mutterings about the "problems" posed by certain institutional designs—their problems actually being mostly matters of legal logic rather than of actual functioning.[2]

The blind spots of legalism generally follow from its exaggerations. Insufficient attention has been paid to the dynamics and details of actual functioning of an institution. The crucial importance of the recruitment and training of the institutional personnel tended to be ignored or underestimated. Problems of the personnel as a group, such as socialization, solidarity, and hierarchy, were rarely recognized, nor were the social relations and interaction with the clientele of a given institution. And the legal-institutional approach also shied away from dealings with the content of policies.[3] When scholars assume a kind of essential immanence in the legal description of institutions, naturally all other aspects seem to fade into insignificance.

To restore the balance, then, a close look at political institutions and processes appears to be in order, with regard to both basic definitions and particular designs, although the available material still limits us mostly to Western examples. The policy-making processes, as distinguished from the structures, will be discussed in the next chapter.

[2] See also Roy Macridis, *The Study of Comparative Government.* New York: Doubleday, 1955.
[3] See, for example, the remarks of Austin Ranney, "The Study of Policy Content," *Social Science Research Council Items,* Vol. 22, No. 3 (September 1968).

A DEVELOPMENTAL VIEW OF INSTITUTIONS

Looking at political institutions from the point of view of development is easier than looking at the complex world of social and economic relationships from the same angle. For with institutions, the time of birth, the transformations undergone, and the onset of decay or breakdown can be dated precisely. They can even be causally related to their environment, or rather more concretely than most social phenomena.

Rise of institutional functions

Structural-functional theory, in particular, can be used to explain the rise of political functions, their differentiation from non-political functions, and the institutionalization of the roles and activities that crystallized in response to the functional needs of a primitive society. Thus "stateless" societies may acquire personal leadership at a time of crisis and may keep it as a result of circumstances or because of the incumbent's skill in maintaining himself. From the accident of lasting personal leadership there may crystallize the role of a chief, definable in terms of powers, rights, and duties, to use the language of the legal-institutional approach. The role becomes an office to which appropriate procedures of succession or recruitment can appoint or elect future incumbents. More complex functions or a larger workload make for more-complex role structures, in which the work is divided among several roles or offices.

The further development and decay of actual institutions pose considerable difficulties for a legal-institutional and perhaps even for the functionalist approach. Once they are established, whether by dint of the charismatic authority of a leader or founder or by the rational authority of a clearly conceived purpose, political institutions show a staying power far beyond charisma and rational purpose. Their claim on popular obedience can become generalized as they acquire legitimacy over the years. Their activities may become multifunctional and may provide fully for institutional self-renewal and self-preservation against other group forces. Having made themselves independent of their original functions, they can acquire new ones right and left. As C. Northcote Parkinson has asserted, they may even grow without increasing their workload or with a diminishing load. It is rather difficult to see, then, how an institution could begin to decay, though decay it may in time.

Institutional decay

Institutional decay may begin, however, with breakdowns in the recruitment and indoctrination of an institutional staff. When markedly different or inferior personnel are recruited, and the new incumbents fall short of public expectations in exercising the customary functions, decay may well set in. Or if the socialization of new recruits is no longer able to overcome competing socializing influences, solidarity and morale suffer. Extreme examples of such rival influences are subversive ideologies and corruption. The norms that are a part of each role fail to bind, the goals become expendable, and the entire role structure breaks up in disarray, as a demobilized army might break ranks and flee before the enemy. Institutions may also fall victim to the competition of more effective institutions. Or they may be destroyed for reasons of economy, when they represent overhead capital that a society feels it can do without.

Constitutional aging

Apart from the more palpable examples of institutional development and decay, there are aging processes that whole constitutional systems and major institutions undergo. A brand-new constitution shows its age, so to speak, by a pervasive sense of uncertainty in a world of power-hungry, if not hostile, group forces. The individual political roles and role structures set forth in the document are not born into a vacuum. Very often they were designed and introduced by a strong nationalist or reform movement, which immediately claims all or most of the important offices for itself. And then the struggle begins, as the movement splits into factions, which together with other organized interest groups may attempt to use their respective roles to advance their interests.[4] Individual roles and role structures are found

---

[4] Whether the original nationalist movement can later split into factions pluralizing the institutional structure depends, of course, also on its character. Totalitarian movements, such as communist or fascist parties, and even the "mobilization regimes" generally permit no such growth of factions or of institutional pluralism.

to limit or conflict with what their incumbents would like to make of them, and the whole system may fail to achieve a working equilibrium. At this point, it is quite common for a new constitution to be disregarded or discarded by the regime, especially if the constitution sought to introduce political competition into a noncompetitive political system. In this latter case, the strain and conflict may occur also between the noncompetitive role structure of a one-party or a no-party system and the imported competitive role structure of a Western constitution.

Consider for contrast an "old constitution," not necessarily as old as those of Great Britain or the United States, but one that has been a going concern for a generation or more. Here the process of crystallization of formal roles is fairly complete.[5] Individuals have been socialized into these roles, which relate their activities and attitudes to other roles. Public expectations and the performance of public agencies have achieved an equilibrium of exchanges. Political groups from within and interest groups from without have congregated around the points of the system where policy decisions are made. Differentiated recruitment processes have become established channels, and political communications within the government and between its agencies and their respective publics provide a routine flow of rules and information. In a system as old as that of Great Britain, there are virtually layers upon layers of different aspects of institutionalization, from ancient rituals and broad community norms to the cutting edge of majority rule on any one current political decision.

Aspects of institutionalization

One can define the major aspects and levels of institutionalization, following S. N. Eisenstadt, as norms and frameworks regulating processes of social exchange. The first such aspect comprises the basic nonexchangeable goals of human existence in a given society. The second aspect defines the initial bargaining positions of individuals and groups of the society. The third establishes generalized media of exchange, such as money or

---

[5] Role crystallization and change, of course, go on continuously in all societies and governmental systems, including the most stable. See especially S. N. Eisenstadt, *Essays on Comparative Institutions.* New York: Wiley, 1965, p. 30.

political support, in each of the different institutional spheres. Fourth, various frameworks, rules, and organizations are set up as regulated channels of exchange, as in legal institutions, economic or political markets, administrative organizations, or communication systems. And finally there comes the legitimation of the norms, of the channels, and of the rates of the exchanges. Institutional change, moreover, may also come about as a result of the different norms held by some groups in the society.[6]

EXECUTIVE ROLE IMAGES

If African tribal chiefs, feudal European monarchs, totalitarian dictators, and the chief executive of a modern state have anything in common, it would seem to be an archetypal image of paternal authority. As political socialization research has shown, even the untutored and the very young have a basic understanding of what executive leadership is—an understanding that does not extend to the other organs of government. Nevertheless, the actual images of modern executive roles differ in significant details, depending on national traditions and on additional functions that certain systems assign to the executive. Let us take a look at some of the more typical role images.

The executive institutions of most countries bear a striking surface resemblance to one another, which is due both to a common heritage and to a certain amount of mutual observation and imitation. The common heritage of all Western governments, including that of the United States, is the replacement—in fact or in effect—of a monarchic executive by a democratic executive. Aspects of the monarchic executive that were considered tried and proven were often retained. In this sense, there are close parallels, for example, between the constitutional position of King George III, the sovereign by divine grace, and that of the American president, whose authority was derived, at least indirectly, from the new sovereign, the people.[7] The relations of

[6] Eisenstadt, *Essays on Comparative Institutions,* pp. 32–34, 40–44. Eisenstadt also discusses the effects of institutionalization on a system as a possible source of contradictions or of internal "antisystems."

[7] A closer parallel, perhaps, can be found in the presidency established by the Weimar Constitution of Germany (1919), which was modeled after the position of the Kaiser before his abdication, again substituting popular election for divine right.

the President with the Senate, especially with regard to foreign relations, were similarly modeled on the king's relations to the House of Lords, down to the formula of "advise and consent." There are similar parallels between the development of the dual executive in Great Britain, king and prime minister, and the presidency and premiership of the Fourth Republic.

Manifestations of national political culture

Manifestations of national psychology also have made for some diversity in the concept of the executive in different Western countries. One can relate, for example, the solitary, powerful figure of the American chief executive and his lonesome decisions to the American fascination with man alone against the elements, a situation richly explored in American literature. The British cabinet government has often been connected with the British habit of "government by committee" or of always entrusting great decisions to a small group and never to an individual. Then there is the peculiarly French ambiguity of attitude toward authority, which has led French government since 1789 to waver constantly between the extreme of a quasi-dictatorial executive, such as the two Napoleons and de Gaulle, and the exact opposite, "government by assembly." There are also the Germans, who from Bismarck to Hitler, and perhaps to Adenauer as well, appear to have set entirely too much trust in executive leadership.

The unique form of the Swiss Federal Council owes much to the deeply ingrained Swiss distaste for the show-off, or the man who "wants" to be chief. The Federal Council was modeled after cantonal executive councils and is composed of seven members of the Nationalrat (federal diet) elected for a four-year term by this body. The federal councillors are normally re-elected for as long as they care to serve, and they act as one body. The Federal Assembly (both houses) annually selects a new president and a vice president of the Confederation from among the councillors, thus taking care not to indulge overly anyone's love of self. Needless to add, the Swiss share this wariness of ambition or personal preeminence with a number of other Western nations, from the ancient Greeks to the British.

That a chief executive can be a great deal more to his people than his office would indicate, is hardly news. Societies in crisis, or even just in the permanent crisis of transition, awaken a need for dependency stemming from the earliest layers of childhood socialization. A modern people threatened by war or economic depression often wants to be taken care of by its leader. Transitional societies nurture charismatic leaders, caudillos, military men on horseback, and founding fathers with an abandon stemming from deep personal needs, whose fulfillment becomes personified in the great man. Totalitarian movements such as communism and fascism have capitalized on these propensities with striking results. The cult of personality, assiduously promoted by propaganda, could manufacture a *Duce* or *Führer* as well as a Stalin or Mao Tse-tung. The lineage of leadership cults can be traced back to Julius Caesar and Bonapartism, and further. Nor can we simply condemn this impulse. What contemporary society, in fact, can claim to be so enlightened that it can do without the charisma of a John F. Kennedy or Charles de Gaulle to unify and mobilize the people in pursuit of peaceful goals?

Development of the dual executive

The development of the dual executive is of particular relevance to executive role images, since it attempts to divide the normal functions of the executive branch into specifically policy-making and more symbolic or ceremonial headship functions. Thus the day-to-day policy of the government, the "governing," is done by the British prime minister, or the German chancellor, while the British queen or the federal president of the West German Republic only "reigns" as a symbol of continuity of the state. The Fourth Republic of France supplies a typical example of the division of functions between the two executive figures: The president presided over the French Union, chaired cabinet meetings and the Constitutional Committee, granted pardons, appointed civil servants and ambassadors, received foreign envoys, signed laws and treaties, and, most important, designated the new premier and appointed his cabinet ministers. In the phrase of one incumbent, Vincent Auriol, his office was the "moral magistracy" of the nation. In spite of this inside role, with a presiding seat on the Council of National Defense and with access to all the diplomatic and other classified documents, the president's political powers were decisively limited by the provision that his official acts had to be countersigned by a cabinet minister. The cabinet, on the other hand, had the authority over the day-to-day policy of the government and was responsible for it to the National Assembly, which could and did topple many a premier during a presidential seven-year term of office.

The powers and position of the West German federal president vis-à-vis the chancellor are almost identical with those of the Fourth Republic, with the possible exception of the appointment of a premier and cabinet. Here the French president frequently exercised a real choice among various possible coalitions, while his West German equivalent has stood in the shadow of a strong chancellor.

In Great Britain, too, the division of authority is very similar, although the venerable traditions and the magic of the monarchy created a curious game of ritual and symbolism in place of the cold language of republican constitutional law. Essentially, the monarch has "the right to be informed, to encourage, to warn," and his (or her) great popularity and long experience in government can make the king or queen an important force behind the scenes. But the few political prerogatives still retained by the crown have in reality long been wielded by the cabinet, which even writes the royal messages to Parliament and decides all official appointments and acts ostensibly discharged by the monarch.

Functional role differentiation

A second important structural aspect of executive roles is their specialization along functional lines. The American Constitution, for example, makes no mention of a cabinet. Yet within the first year of the Union's new government, 1789, departments of State, Treasury, and War were established. By now, there are eleven departments, State, Treasury, Defense, Interior, Agriculture, Justice, Post Office, Commerce, Labor, Housing and Urban Development, Health, Education, and Welfare. Each department, of course, has within it a number of further specialized agencies, not to mention the many independent agencies. The British Ministry is composed of some seventy agencies, of which about seventeen or eighteen make up a typical cabinet today. Within this cabinet, moreover, there is an inner cabinet of about half that size. Among the regular cabinet members are usually the prime minister, the chancellor of the exchequer (Treasury), the home secretary (Interior), the foreign secretary, the secretaries for commonwealth relations, Colonies, and Scotland, the president of the Board of Trade (Commerce), and the ministers of defense, labor, and agriculture and fisheries. The French Council of Ministers has been composed of some twenty ministers since 1946, Key ministries were always Foreign Affairs, Defense, Finance, Justice, and Interior, which on occasion have constituted, together with the premier and whatever other ministers they cared to invite, a kind of inner circle for the making of general policy.

It should be clear from this comparison that executive policy making requires the same functional division of labor that has produced topical committees—with the notable exception of Great Britain—in legislatures. It is in these individual ministries or agencies that most policy proposals originate or are worked out in detail. It is here also that ministers or the cabinet as a body find the expert knowledge required to transform their plans and wishes into reality. In governmental systems where most bills come from the executive branch, the individual ministry can also do the actual legislative drafting, thanks to the legal training and administrative experience of its career personnel. It will also be remembered how a particular interest group can, with the appropriate legislative committee and executive agency, form a triangle of consultation and cooperation for the purpose of developing a new policy within its particular field of interest.

Coordination and development of policy

Executive role structures must also provide for coordination and the development of a unified general policy. Such coordination generally occurs in several ways. One is political coordination by the chief executive leader—the American President, the German chancellor, or the British or French premier—who has to present an image of coherent policies to his own party, to the public, and to the opposition. In the United States the chief executive even runs for office on the basis of such a policy image. In Great Britain and West Germany the image of the prime minister or chancellor dominates the partisan contest in the elections, even though these officials are not directly elected to their posts. The French president of the Fifth Republic is likewise the chief projector of general policy images toward the French public. Coordination is also facilitated by cabinet secretariats or, in the United States, by the Executive Office of the President.

Role of chief executive   The specific manner in which the chief executive coordinates the policies of the different departments or ministries depends also on his relationship to them. President Lincoln could say, when his entire war cabinet voted "nay" on one of his proposals, "the ayes have it." The British prime minister, on the other hand, is only a *primus inter pares,* who must consult with and defer to the majority decisions of his cabinet even though his preeminence has long been generally accepted. The relationship between President de Gaulle and the individual ministers was rather anomalous, in that he left some departments completely to themselves, while others, especially Defense, Foreign Affairs, the French Community, and Algeria, were exposed to such frequent interference as to bring about a near-eclipse of the premier and appropriate ministers. The president himself is not even responsible to the French Parliament. The premier of the Fourth Republic was perhaps in the weakest position, owing to the coalition character of his cabinet, the impatience of the National Assembly with the executive, and his equality with the other members of the cabinet. Individual ministers often served under several premiers in succession, clearly showing their greater staying power.

The constitutional position of the West German chancellor places him somewhere between the British and the American chief executive. With a strong personality and a legislative majority, Adenauer could dominate and, on occasion, ignore or overrule his cabinet. Lacking both, his successors have been no more dominant than the British prime minister, and often less.

Executive solidarity   The relative independence of a ministry or executive agency can be gauged not only as against control by the chief executive, but also as against the cohesion of the cabinet or executive branch as a body. In the American case, individual secretaries often disagree publicly with each other and on occasion with the President without violating any accepted customs of executive solidarity. There are, moreover, a considerable number of independent agencies, such as the Federal Reserve System or the powerful regulatory commissions, whose autonomy has been carefully secured. On the state level, this lack of executive unity is even more pronounced: A typical example is the state of California where, next to the governor and lieutenant governor, the attorney general, state controller, secretary of state, state treasurer, superintendent of public instruction, and the members of the State Board of Equalization are all directly elected by the people. Under this system, only the gubernatorial control over budget and personnel and what legislative leadership a governor can muster against considerable odds can produce any coordination of policy among these separately elected heads of departments.

A look across the Atlantic Ocean shows an extreme contrast in Great Britain, where the cabinet operates in a spirit of extraordinary unity and solidarity, as well as secrecy. Since responsibility is collective, and decisions rest on a firmly implanted consensus that the members of the government are all sitting in the same boat, nobody is allowed to voice his dissent from the majority decision in public. France and Germany are less cohesive than Great Britain—the French cabinet owing to its coalition character and the German cabinet, if not for the same reason, owing to its habits of executive compartmentalization and of valuing autonomous expertise more than political compromise.

Cabinet committees A second device for the coordination of departmental policies comprises the more or less permanent cabinet committees or councils. Even in the United States, where the tendency is great to set up a new executive agency for every new task, there is, for example, the National Security Council, which makes general foreign and defense policy for the Cold War. It is composed of the President, the Vice-President, the Secretaries of State and Defense, the directors of Central Intelligence, of the Office of Defense Mobilization, and often of the U.S. Information Agency, the chairman of the Joint Chiefs of Staff, the Secretary of the Treasury, the director of the Bureau of the Budget, and members of the President's staff. An Operations Coordinating Board and the staff of the council help to implement the policy decisions and supervise and report on the implementation by the various departments involved. The Council of Economic Advisers is another example.

The British especially have gone in for cabinet committees. Since 1945 at least five standing cabinet committees have coordinated government policy for specific purposes. The Legislation Committee, for instance, reviews all bills issuing from individual ministries and, with the help of the whips and leaders of both houses, proposes timing and strategy for submitting the legislative program of the government to Parliament. The Defense Committee resembles the American National Security Council. There are also many interdepartmental ad hoc committees, established to develop a single project or legislative enactment, such as the introduction of the national health service, and dissolved after they have accomplished their goal. The French have their Committee of National Defense, a council on economic policy, and ad hoc interministerial conferences.

In the Bonn Republic the most important ministerial conferences are those among the topical ministers of the federal and state levels or of the states alone, as in the field of education, which are fairly permanent and serve to develop agreed policies in each field. At the federal level there are also frequent interdepartmental meetings below the ministerial level. There are also several ministries, such as those of Economic Cooperation, Justice (for checking the form and constitutionality of bills), and Bundesrat Affairs, whose liaison functions help to coordinate the activity of various ministries. Finally, and this applies also to France, frequent ministerial and subministerial conferences tie together the executive policies of the different members of the Common Market of the Council of Europe.

Centralization of budgetary powers   The third and perhaps the most significant device for the coordination of the executive departments is the centralization of budgetary powers. In the United States Congress, budgetary proposals used to be introduced by as many as nine different House committees and altered by fifteen Senate committees with no reference to Treasury estimates of revenues, until the Budget and Accounting Act of 1921 created the Bureau of the Budget. Today, this bureau is a part of the Executive Office of the President, which bears the primary responsibility for coordinating departmental requests and squaring expenditures with revenues. Departmental budget officers on all levels prepare detailed requests, which must conform to the overall program of the President and anticipate the likely reactions of the Congress. The Bureau of the Budget collects and, as directed by the President, molds the departmental requests into a total spending budget based on Treasury estimates of revenues. The final product of the Bureau's labors is presented in a presidential message to the Congress and is submitted to the House Appropriations and Ways and Means committees. Congress has to authorize the expenditures and thus can still increase or decrease items as its own preferences or pressure from constituencies, interest groups, and executive agencies may suggest. Nevertheless, the centralization of budget making powers gives a considerable measure of control to the chief executive, who can thereby spell out the priorities of a coordinated executive program in dollars and cents. Similar executive budgets are also in use in most American state governments.

In Great Britain, the departmental estimates go to the financial divisions of the Treasury, which has assistants, or undersecretaries, specializing in the needs and ways of each spending department. Each secretary confers with departmental representatives until the budget proposal is whipped into the shape the cabinet desires. The Treasury also controls taxation and the home civil service. Its proverbial skinflint atitude weighs heavily upon the spenders, forcing them to justify their requests in great detail. The fact that the vital money aspects of all government operations go through his hands makes the chancellor of the exchequer, next to the prime minister, the second most powerful figure in the cabinet. Since the House of Commons is given very little authority over the budget and the House of Lords none, cabinet approval for the budget drawn up by the Treasury gives it practically a final character.

The French budgetary process also begins with the collection of departmental requests by the Ministry of Finance, which, however, has less authority than the British Treasury or the American Bureau of the Budget to pare down departmental demands. Only the cabinet as a body has this authority, and the coalition nature of French governments is unlikely to allow rigorous budgetary control anywhere. There is, moreover, the powerful Finance Commission of the National Assembly, the "queen of commissions," which under the Fourth Republic firmly took control of the "executive budget" and turned it into a "legislative budget" at the price of toppling many a cabinet over financial issues. Under the Fifth Republic the "queen of commissions" has been hamstrung with various limitations but on several occasions has succeeded in kicking over the traces.

The German budgetary system fulfills the purpose of executive coordination through the powerful Ministry of Finance in a manner similar to that of the British Treasury, without the legislative eclipse customary in Great Britain. There is the same control of the minister of finance over departmental requests and also a cabinet veto over any increases in spending that the Bundestag may be inclined to vote. On the other hand, the Bundestag and, in particular, its budget committee, as well as the finance committee of the Bundesrat, are given ample opportunity to examine, discuss, and slash items in the budget if they so desire.

LEGISLATIVE ROLE IMAGES AND LEGISLATURES

While in essence the executive leadership roles may be considered a timeless feature of government, traditional or modern, legislatures as the center of the governmental process are distinctively modern. To be sure, the idea of representative government, together with the first representative institutions, can be found in traditional societies such as medieval England.[8] But they were hardly central to government, and not until Elizabethan times did they become serious rivals to the monarchic executive, when the transitional phase was well under way in England. The seventeenth-century struggle for supremacy between king and Parliament as well as the emergence of the Restoration Parliament mark the movement of the representative process into the vital center of British and, eventually, most Western governments. The United States followed older lines of development with its separation of powers. In all the other coun-

[8] See, for example, Gerald P. Bodet, *Early English Parliaments: High Courts, Royal Councils or Representative Assemblies?* Boston: Heath, 1968.

tries following the British or the French patterns, and theoretically even in today's communist dictatorships, the powers emanating from the sovereign people are entrusted chiefly to a representative assembly, which ought to delegate them no farther.

Political responsibility

Executive branches, according to this doctrine of parliamentary government, are responsible to the elected representatives of the people for all important political actions they take. Such *political responsibility* can take several forms; it can even be eclipsed by the actual relationship that evolves between a cabinet and its legislature. The relationship between the representative and those he represents is rife with ambiguities in theory and in fact. Is an elective representative merely the agent of his constituency and of the organized interests that are vocal in it? Does he, by becoming a member of a parliament, acquire a primary obligation toward the whole nation? What does he owe to his party, which in most modern parliaments plays a major role in his nomination, his election, and his legislative activities? And, crucially, how does he view his own role among these potentially conflicting obligations—as an honest broker or mediator, a crusader for an ideological cause, a nation builder, or what? [9] Will he consider himself a critic or supporter of the executive, a policy maker or a critic of policy?

The answers obviously hinge on aspects of political socialization and culture, especially on leadership styles and on a legislator's conception of the whole political system and his place in it. There is a world of difference, for example, between the oppositional cast of mind of most French legislators and the willingness of British members of Parliament to take on governmental responsibility.[10] A great deal also depends on details of

[9] There is by now a growing literature on legislators' self-images, associated with scholars such as Heinz Eulau, David B. Truman, Norman Meller, Marvin Weinbaum, and others.

[10] See also this writer's essay on party government in Germany in Elke Frank, ed., *Lawmakers in a Changing World*. Englewood Cliffs, N.J.: Prentice-Hall, 1966, pp. 65–82, where the oppositional cast of mind of Weimar legislators is contrasted with attitudes in the Bundestag. Samuel H. Beer, *British Politics in the Collectivist Age* (New York: Knopf, 1965), is still a classical source on various theories of representation.

the complex role structure of different legislatures or parts thereof.

Unicameralism versus bicameralism

The first question of the structural design of legislatures is the choice between unicameralism and bicameralism. The constitutional tradition of political responsibility clearly suggests a single legislative assembly in which the popularly elected representatives of the people carry out the will of their constituents, to whom, at the next election, they will have to answer. However, only two Western countries (Denmark since 1954 and New Zealand since 1950) and some state legislatures of federal systems (such as Nebraska in the United States, Queensland in Australia, and most of the *Länder* diets of the West German Republic) are unicameral. Sweden is moving toward unicameralism. There are also a number of approximations of unicameralism, such as the Norwegian Storting, which is elected as one body although it splits subsequently into two parts for purposes of legislation, the Odelsting and the smaller Lagting, a kind of permanent senior committee of the whole parliament. The British House of Commons has won such preponderance over the House of Lords, especially since 1911, that the British system likewise comes close to being unicameral in practice.

Bicameral legislatures   To the constitutional tradition of checks and balances, however, bicameralism appears more desirable. Not only can an additional legislative assembly, an upper house,[11] provide review of the legislative activity or a check on the "popular passions" and "the spirit of faction" of the lower house; it can also bring to bear on the representative process elements of social organization other than individualism and mass parties. While, for example, the United States House of Representatives, the Canadian House of Commons, the West German Bundestag, and the Swiss Nationalrat all represent the individual citizens of their respective countries, the United States Senate, the Canadian Senate, the West German Bundesrat, and the Swiss Council of

[11] Using the terms "first chamber" for the popularly elected and "second chamber" for the upper house can give rise to misunderstanding in comparative study, since Sweden and the Netherlands, for example, assign these names in the opposite manner.

States were meant to represent their states, provinces, *Länder,* or cantons. Similarly, the upper houses of most American state legislatures used to represent counties as if they were the states of federal systems. But whereas these American state senators were directly elected, a more common usage among Western upper houses is indirect election. The upper chamber of the Swedish Riksdag and the upper chambers of the Dutch and Belgian parliaments, for example, are elected by the county and city councils for staggered terms. The Senate (or Council of the Republic) of the Third (1871–1940), Fourth (1946–1958), and Fifth (1958–   ) Republics of France also have been elected indirectly by electoral bodies based on local government units. In all of these cases, the intent of the constitutional design appears to be to juxtapose a "peripheral" elite of local or provincial notables to the influential men and organizations that control national politics at the center of the system.

Two further ways of composing an upper chamber exemplify a different approach to the basic problem. One is that of the British House of Lords, which at first glance appears to be a gathering of men selected according to aristocratic principles of another age. On closer examination, however, more than half the peers, not to mention the high judicial and church officials in it, turn out to be of twentieth-century vintage. The titles often represent high individual merit of former prime ministers, ambassadors, governors-general, writers, or scientists. The members of the Canadian Senate, appointed for a lifetime, also are supposed to represent an elite "quality" by contrast with the reign of sheer numbers in the lower house. Another view of "quality" has tried to represent the great vocational and functional groups of society in so-called economic or social councils. A good example of such an upper house can be found in Ireland, where it is composed of eleven appointees of the prime minister, six elected by the universities, and equal numbers from five panels representing culture and education, agriculture and fisheries, labor, industry and commerce, and public service. The Weimar Republic of Germany (1919–1933) and the Fourth and Fifth Republics of France had economic councils as third chambers, which, unlike the Irish Senate, were limited to an advisory capacity and little used in the legislative process.

Powers of the two houses

Once bicameralism is adopted, another important issue is whether the two houses are to be equal in their legislative powers. It would be a cardinal violation of the principles of democracy if the popularly elected lower house were in the weaker position. If there is to be a check on the majorities of the lower house, or if nonquantitative elements of social organization are to balance the reign of numbers, it is solely a matter of the discretion of the constitution makers how strong this check shall be. Hence, the British House of Lords is given only a delaying period of one month in the case of a budget bill or twelve months with ordinary legislation, after which the bill becomes law in the form in which the House of Commons passed it. The German Bundesrat, in spite of the emphasis on federalism in the West German Basic Law, has on many legislative subjects merely a suspensive veto, which can be overridden by larger majorities in the lower house. The Dutch upper house, to mention a third method of weakening the check on the popularly elected chamber, is not allowed to amend bills, but only to accept or reject them as they stand.

The United States Congress and the Australian parliament, with their equality between the two houses, are rather conspicuous exceptions to what appears to be the rule. If anything, the United States Senate would seem to be in practice the stronger branch. Then there is the example of the Italian, the Swiss, and the Swedish systems, in which the two houses have shared even the control of the executive. More often, however, the presence of executive-legislative relations of a parliamentary type makes for the strengthening of one chamber, the lower house, at the expense of the other.

This trend toward focusing responsibility more clearly need not detract from the usefulness of even a weak chamber of review. In fact, being less involved with the partisan alignment for or against the government often allows an upper house to develop better its peculiar nature to the benefit of the entire system of government. At least, this has been cited as a chief virtue of the British House of Lords, a seemingly anachronistic institution in a modern society. The House of Lords has withstood many attempts at reform in the last half century, largely because almost any modernization would make it a stronger check on the real center of power.

Internal groups in legislatures

The second major question of the design of legislatures concerns their internal organization into groups capable of effective deliberation and of concerted legislative action, such as standing committees or partisan groups. Since a great many different subjects come before a parliament, a division into several smaller, more specialized "little legislatures" seems quite logical. However, there is a great deal more to it.

The United States Congress   The standing committees of the two houses of the United States Congress on such subjects as foreign relations, agriculture, the armed services, and so on are the main legislative agents of these houses, who can make or break almost any piece of legislation before them. Each house tends to accept what its committees lay before it. The committee chairmen, who owe their tenure to seniority only, are among the most powerful men in the Congress. Each house of Congress, therefore, presents a picture of very considerable decentralization and fragmentation of that legislative power which under the constitutional tradition of responsibility is meant to be exercised in a unified manner. In the House of Representatives, at least, the rules committee provides a focus of centralized control that can hold back or advance bills, open them up to crippling amendments, or protect them against changes. The United States Senate lacks a rules committee, has only a weak presiding officer, the vice-president, and allows such excesses of minority power as the filibuster to frustrate the majority will that may be present on crucial issues. Senators have generally felt that the small size and continuity of their "most exclusive club on earth" required no institutional devices for cohesion.

Congressional parties, another grouping capable of producing concerted action, have not been absent in the two houses of Congress, since the members of both houses are generally elected under a partisan label. The majority party receives all the committee chairmanships and proportionate representation on all the committees and elects the speaker of the House of Representatives. Both parties of each house meet frequently in caucus and have floor leaders, whips, and steering committees. Yet the prevalence of smaller factions, the paucity of means by which the party leaders could persuade their followers, and the prominence of other groupings and power centers in both houses decisively weaken partisan control.

In summary, the internal organization of both houses of the United States Congress frustrates the coordination of legislative policy by an unusual degree of decentralization and fragmentation of power, which in practice has led to presidential legislative leadership in spite of the separation of powers. American state legislatures are generally better coordinated and more likely to vote along party lines.

The House of Commons   The organization of the British House of Commons provides an extreme contrast to that of the United States Congress. Following the establishment of parliamentary sovereignty in the seventeenth century, the British House of Commons for a while had fairly strong standing committees on such topics as privileges and elections, religion, grievances, the courts, and trade. With the rise of cabinet leadership from among the membership of Parliament, the cabinet became the sole center of power and the topical committees declined, except for a few of more technical function. Today, in place of the American standing committees, the House of Commons has nontopical committees called by the letters of the alphabet, *A, B, C,* and so on. The speaker of the House of Commons, a neutral figure in the partisan sense, routinely assigns bills to them for their consideration and appoints their chairmen, who are likewise supposed to be neutral guardians of parliamentary practice. Since these standing committees are not topical, they never become the gatherings of materially interested politicians and experts that congressional committees invariably are.

Strong partisan control in the House of Commons further contributes to the centralization of legislative authority in the leadership of the well-disciplined majority party, the cabinet, and the shadow cabinet of the equally well-disciplined opposition. The centralization of partisan control rests not only on tradition and on the relative smallness and social unity of the British Isles, but even more on the control of the party leadership over the nominations on the party ticket—which, unlike the American counterpart, are not encumbered with primary elections and residence rules. The powerful, extra-parliamentary party hierarchies and the British habit of voting for the party rather than for the candidate round out the picture of unified "party government" in Britain. Against this background, the average back-bencher in the House of Commons has little choice but to follow faithfully the party line. He can, of course, communicate his dissent to the leadership via the party whips and make his vote felt in the caucus meetings. Once a decision has been made, however, he is under threat of severe penalties not to bolt the party on a formal vote.

French parliaments   The internal organization of other Western legislatures can be classified somewhere between the American and British extremes. The French Chamber of Deputies of the Third Republic and the National Assembly of the Fourth Republic rather resembled the American model in having powerful topical committees and weak partisan control. The latter was due in part to the French multiparty system, in part to the unstable cohesion of most parties, excepting Communists and Socialists. Thus the parliamentary executive, the center of power in Great Britain, in France always had to be based on a frail coalition of several parties and could hardly assert itself against the other power centers. The constitution of the Fifth Repubic considerably curtailed the general powers of the National Assembly, weakened its committees, and separated a greatly strengthened Council of Ministers (cabinet) from it. These changes have centralized control over the legislative process, but also have centered it outside the National Assembly. The presence of a strong Gaullist faction in the National Assembly facilitates the legislative activities of the cabinet. The peculiar character of de Gaulle's leadership and the two-headed nature of the executive do not permit a comparison between this arrangement and the British party government. It is still too early to predict the development of this relationship under de Gaulle's successors. The Senate of the Fifth Republic, incidentally, has managed to retain some of the oppositional spirit of pre-Gaullist days because it is not under the thumb of the cabinet.

Both houses of the French parliament under the Third, Fourth, and Fifth Republics had a *bureau,* each consisting of a president and a number of vice-presidents and other officers. This institution is typical of the French pattern adopted by continental European legislatures. The presiding officers, representing the duly constituted and officially registered partisan groups, have the function of scheduling and expediting the business before the house. Needless to say, their importance as a center of legislative authority depends largely on the number and importance of the partisan groups in an assembly. The more groups, the less authority.

The Bundestag   The organization of the West German Bundestag approaches more the British rather than the French or American model. There is a strong tradition of party unity and discipline, which relies on active participation and frequent caucus meetings. From this one might expect the British type of perfect fusion of executive and legislative branches by party government. Under the first three chancellors, however, the majority parties in the Bundestag on occasion exhibited considerable independence and even opposition to their own cabinet, especially when the deputies felt that they were not consulted on questions of policy. The equivalent of the French assembly *bureau* is here called the Council of Elders. There are also topical committees, in which Bundestag experts vie with those of the corresponding ministries. But party ties are so strong, even in the committee meetings, that the committees are still far from becoming the centers of legislative power they have always been in the United States.

The Italian Chamber of Deputies   The Italian Chamber of Deputies resembles in some respects the organization of the French parliament before 1940. While party cohesion has grown from weak and vacillating antecedents to considerable strength, committees also are powerful and are frequently even given the authority, *in sede deliberante,* to legislate. The president of the Chamber is in a fairly strong position. The individual legislators enjoy a degree of independence found, perhaps, only in the United States Congress. In no other Western legislature can the members still introduce so many private member bills, and nowhere else are they allowed to vote in secret ballots.[12]

Non-Western legislatures The comparative study of non-Western legislatures is still in the process of gathering and evaluating information from what appears to be a considerable variety of institutional patterns, ranging from traditional representative assemblies to the pseudoplebiscitarian national assemblies or soviets of communist countries and "mobilization regimes." Some of the more developed assemblies in Latin America, Japan, and the Philippines rival any Western legislature in legalistic institutionalization and decentralization of legislative power. Others, such as the Supreme Soviet and other regimes run by an all-powerful party movement, are declaratory sounding boards of party and leadership rather than lawmaking bodies; hence they are lacking in the internal organization and deliberative mechanics previously discussed. Nearly all of them are rather subordinate to the preponderant executive, regardless of whether the executive's strength is a matter of personal charisma, of one-party dominance, or of the support of any other group, such as the landowning oligarchy or the military.

EXECUTIVE-LEGISLATIVE RELATIONS

The most conspicuous diversity in the design of legislative and executive role structures is found in the patterns of executive-legislative relations. The American preference for the separation of powers on the one hand and the evolution of parliamentary government in many countries of Western Europe on the other circumscribe a fundamental disagreement about how public policy making should be organized.[13] The American version of executive-legislative relations is perhaps merely a matter of

[12] While the Italian legislative process still awaits authoritative analysis, excellent spadework has already been undertaken by political scientists such as Joseph La Palombara, Giovanni Sartori, and A. Spreafico, as well as by scholars at the Carlo Cattaneo Institute in Bologna.

[13] A long list of sources is precluded by lack of space. By way of proxy, nevertheless, such distinguished names as Carl J. Friedrich, Herman Finer, Karl Loewenstein, and Herbert J. Spiro should be mentioned as stand-ins for the many who labored with distinction in the vineyards of institutional studies.

historical accident and circumstance, in part perhaps the result of a mechanistic theory of government, and in part, most significantly for other new nations, a reflection of the uses of a single executive figure to hold together a very large and heterogeneous country.

Historical models

The historical models for the fashioning of the American presidency at the Philadelphia Convention of 1787 were the British monarchy in its traditional form and the governorship in many colonies of the British Empire in the eighteenth century, with both of which the American colonists had had ample experience. It would be an exaggeration and simplification to describe the relations between the king and Parliament, or the colonial governor and his legislature, as a system of separation of coordinate powers in the sense of the United States Constitution—although separate they were. The king, in particular, was in a rather anomalous position, exercising traditional royal powers and prerogatives that gave him a preponderant position, although the Act of Settlement of 1701 had once and for all allocated sovereignty to Parliament. His personally appointed representatives in the colonies, the governors, likewise still occupied a very strong position vis-à-vis the elected representatives of the colonists, although development elsewhere in the British Empire later saw the decline of the governor-general and the rise of a parliamentary executive. Thus, the desire of the British colonists outside the original thirteen American colonies for more self-government served in the long run to whittle away the quasi-monarchic authority of the former chief executive and to transfer most of his authority to parliamentary leaders; the American colonists, however, won complete independence from the British crown when it was still strong, and they went on to elect their own strong governors.

Mechanistic theories

At the same time, the mechanistic theories of government of the late eighteenth century, together with a liberal preference for as little government as possible, led Baron de Montesquieu (1869–1755) to write in his *Spirit of the Laws* (1748): "When the legislative and executive powers are united in the same person, or in the same body of magistrates, there can be no liberty . . . lest the same monarch or senate enact tyrannical laws to execute them tyrannically." Writing this under the absolutist regime of the king of France, who had indeed united both functions in his hand, Montesquieu seemed sensible enough in wanting to separate them. His belief that the greater liberty of Englishmen was due to the "separation of powers" between king and Parliament (and the judiciary) should be seen against the background of French absolutism, although historians deny that his description of British government was accurate.

The separation between the executive and legislative branches written into the United States Constitution was, of course, never intended to prohibit cooperation on fundamental governmental tasks. The President still participated in legislation through his message and veto power. The Congress had budgetary control over the executive and could issue legislative commands to it and establish or abolish executive agencies. The Senate, in particular, participated in executive appointments and in the making of foreign policy. Nor was the desired antagonism between the two branches meant to produce a complete deadlock. During the first three or four decades of the young republic, in fact, the social and later the party ties uniting President and congressional leaders were close enough to keep the separation-of-powers system operating smoothly. For a while, the nomination of candidates for President was even in the hands of the congressional parties, a cohesive national political elite who tended to pick a man from their midst.

Needs of a heterogeneous country

But the expansion of the country, the widening of the suffrage, and the incisive social and economic changes through war and peace soon began to transform the presidency into a chief focus of national unity for the most disparate and heterogeneous groups, while the Congress yielded more and more to functional and sectional fragmentation. The special procedures of nomination of a presidential candidate by a party convention were designed to bring about a nearly impossible consensus. Except for Lyndon B. Johnson, indeed, the typical American President of the last one hundred years has been an outsider to the ranks of national party leaders in the Congress, generally a governor of a large state or a popular general of a past war. And the cabinet officers of his choice are not usually selected from among the senior politicians of his party in Congress, who have to accept him as their nominal leader upon whose success the fortunes of the party depend. He may have a following throughout the country and in both houses of Congress, a "presidential party," to which he owes his selection on the floor of the nominating convention. But his presidential party is not identical with the congressional party of the same label. Friction and rivalry develop, and soon, after a brief honeymoon of executive-legislative harmony, deadlock threatens even the most popular President. Despite his awesome concentration of powers and his mandate from at least a plurality of the voters, the single executive is very much alone with his responsibility to the electorate and to the Constitution that he swears to uphold.

The single executive outside America

Although the single executive of the American system appears to have served the country well, there have been few attempts at imitation among the older constitutional democracies and none that lasted. The French adopted it in 1848 only to find their first president, Louis Napoleon, using the office to become Emperor Napoleon III. Most Latin-American nations adopted a presidential regime after their emancipation from colonial rule, but generally with doubtful results. More often than not, their presidents have been *caudillos* and their legislatures little more than rubber stamps. At the very least, the presidents have tended to legislate, leaving their congresses little more than a veto power over legislation and none at all over the liberally used decree and emergency powers of the single executive. The more recent trend toward closer adherence to the standards of constitutional democracy in Latin America often meant replacing the single executive with a plural executive of the cabinet or council type.

In a sense the charismatic leaders of many a new nation of Asia or Africa today would seem to function much more like a single executive than like a prime minister of a cabinet, the title many of them hold. Such a comparison depends chiefly on the plebiscitary nature of the authority of a Sekou Touré, Jomo Kenyatta, Sukarno, or Bourgiba—on the popular stewardship of their role rather than on their juxtaposition to a congress, or, analogously, to their single, dominant party, which they generally control far better than an American President can ever hope to control Congress.

Origin of parliamentarism

It is one of the ironies of constitutional history in the West that the same British tradition that originated the separation of powers also gave birth to parliamentary government—and began to do so, in fact, long before the United States Constitution was written. The causes of the development of the "fusion of powers" in the cabinet can be found both in the rise of parliamentary supremacy and in historical circumstances. The supremacy of Parliament derived from the civil wars of the seventeenth century and the Glorious Revolution of 1688, which put an end to divine-right monarchy. It received further support from the nineteenth-century theories of parliamentary sovereignty, which refused to tolerate even the appearance of a sharing of sovereign power between monarch and Parliament, even though formulas such as "the King in Parliament" preface all laws.

The concatenation of historical accidents began with the weakness of eighteenth-century British monarchs; increasingly they found it necessary to select their advisory cabinet from among parliamentary leaders who could marshal broad support in both houses, such as Sir Robert Walpole (1676–1745), who became not only the first prime minister but also the first head of a cabinet to be overthrown by Parliament. Still, the executive-legislative relations of British government were not clearly recognized to constitute an entirely new and most desirable pattern until the middle of the nineteenth century.

This was the origin of *parliamentary government,* or *parliamentarism,* the generic name reflecting the derivation of the highest governmental authority from Parliament.

British parliamentarism

In its British version, parliamentary government has meant an extraordinary degree of power concentrated in the cabinet, which sits at once at the apex of the national administrative machinery, in full control of the House of Commons, and at the head of the major party of the land that received a popular mandate at the last general election. The centralized and well-disciplined nature of British political parties makes this a system of "responsible party government," because the electorate can make a choice between two competing programs and sets of leaders, thereby enforcing governmental responsibility in the long run. The emergence of a cabinet of sixteen to nineteen members within a ministry of some seventy, of an "inner cabinet" of eight or nine, and of the prime minister as the prominent head of what is otherwise a collegial body further indicates the degree of centralization in policy making. The prominence of the prime minister as government leader, party leader, and steward of the people has become so great that the parliamentary elections, though formally elections to the seats of the House of Commons, are fought largely as a personal duel between the incumbent and the opposition leader and between their "teams," the incumbent cabinet and the "shadow cabinet" of the opposition party.

Selection for high office   The contrast to the American system of separation of powers lies not only in the concentration of powers in one small group rather than in three coordinate branches; [14] it is found also in the nature of the selection process that brings men to the highest executive offices. The prime minister and his cabinet all have acquired a seat in the House of Commons or the House of Lords before they become members of the cabinet. Thus they are never complete outsiders, but can generally look back upon many years of a successful parliamentary career in which they acquired both plenty of experience and the cooperation of their fellow legislators. The prime minister, in particular, must win a seat in the House of Commons; this recent custom has induced many a hopeful contender to divest himself of his aristocratic title and become, say, Sir Alec Douglas-Home (Lord Home) or Quintin Hogg (Lord Hailsham).

The closest way to approach the British practice in the United States would be to select as presidential candidates the floor leaders of both majority and minority parties in the House of Representatives and to recruit their cabinets from among other

---

[14] The British judiciary is independent, but it has no power to rule acts of Parliament unconstitutional.

legislative leaders of either party in House and Senate. Even then it would still take the sharpness of party lines and the cohesion of British parliamentary parties to provide an analogous setting. And the prime minister and cabinet so selected would have to retain their leading positions in the Congress. The next chapter will set forth the dominant role accorded the cabinet in the legislative organization in the House of Commons. The cabinet makes most of the laws and the budget, guides them through the House, has the commissioners of the monarch give the royal assent, and implements the execution of the laws.

Cabinet accountability   The House of Commons, on the other hand, and especially the opposition party in it, has both the duty and ample opportunity to subject the cabinet to public debate on all matters of policy and administration. More specifically, the parliamentary question hour puts the prime minister and his cabinet ministers four times a week through a purgatory of written and oral questions on matters large and small. This process inevitably uncovers mistakes or abuses and injects them into the editorial columns of the press and, potentially, into the campaign arguments of the opposition at the next general elections. Unlike American cabinet officers, who can hide behind the executive prerogative, the British cabinet members have to be present in person and to account for their policies and the actions or omissions of their departments whenever a member of Parliament demands it of them.

Cabinet solidarity   This account would not be complete without a mention of the important role of solidarity in British cabinet government throughout the rise and fall of cabinets. The cabinet is a collective body sharing the responsibility as one man. It is not possible for a cabinet member to carry his dissent from a cabinet meeting in speeches to the outside, as American cabinet members have been known to do. Neither can the House of Commons vote only one cabinet minister out of office. Cabinet solidarity requires that the cabinet sink or swim together, though it can also require that one member play the scapegoat for some common disaster and quietly resign. It is also rather unlikely that a part of the party in power would break ranks and vote with the opposition to bring down the government, however much they may be in disagreement. Since the opposition party is in the minority, then, a government is more likely to fall because of repudiation by public opinion or covert dissension within the party than by a formal vote of no confidence or of censure. Of course, it may also be forced to call elections because by-elections have whittled down its narrow majority or because the five-year term of the House of Commons nears its end.

In any case it is the privilege of the prime minister to choose the time to "go to the people" in such a manner as to favor his reelection. The dissolution of the House by the crown (only at the request of the cabinet) is the decisive step in the quest of the prime minister for a new popular mandate. Often the mere threat of dissolution can help to keep the majority party in line behind him. If the prime minister's party loses its majority in the elections, the implication is a mandate for the opposition, even if, owing to the presence of a third party, the opposition did not receive a majority either. The monarch must honor the popular will as customarily interpreted.

French parliamentarism

In the other great Western European democracy, parliamentary government began in the 1870s after nearly a century of experiments with various forms of government. Several basic differences between Great Britain and France tended to create a rather different setting for French parliamentarism. To begin with, French political parties lacked the discipline and cohesion of their British counterpart. They were often little more than unstable legislative factions with little or no grass-roots organization. There were no two major parties, such as have characterized British politics for centuries, and at first there was little consensus on the form and procedures of government among the monarchistic and republican groups of various coloration. Furthermore, there was the tradition of the strong state, whose civil service and executive prerogatives dated back to before the great revolution of 1789. Faced with such an unyielding monolith, French legislators and parliamentary parties rarely came to feel that they controlled the government and were responsible for its actions. Instead they seem to have conceived their role more as popular tribunes, oppositional representatives of the people against the state.

Ministerial instability   Throughout the nearly seventy years of the Third Republic, the Chamber of Deputies grew in influence at the expense of the Senate and of the president of the Republic. One of its first presidents, Marshal MacMahon, through his high-handed actions, was responsible for much of the decline of the presidency and the rise of assembly supremacy; his unfortunate precedent also discredited for eight decades the use of the executive power of dissolution to discipline the Chamber of Deputies. Without this counterweight against the parliamentary weapon of overthrowing the government, however, a forever unruly assembly toppled one coalition cabinet after the other with awesome regularity. A French social scientist, Auguste Soulier,[15] counted the causes for the fall of over one hundred cabinets of the Third Republic. Most frequently cabinets were toppled by shifts in party strength after an election. Of twenty-eight cabinets receiving an expression of no confidence, seventeen found themselves in the minority at the end of a debate following an *interpellation,* one was not allowed the establishment of normal relations with the Chamber, four resigned after their legislative proposals had been changed substantially, and six left office in a huff and in spite of express endorsement by the Chamber. Another fifteen quit because the Chamber thwarted their plans by denying them the financial means to carry on, and other cabinets resigned after clashes with the powerful committees of both houses, with organized pressure blocs in the Chamber, or with the president himself. Thus surrounded by hostile agents, the typical French cabinet tended to see ministerial responsibility involved in every conceivable detail of its short life. Its average tenure of seven to eight months became shorter toward the latter years of the Third Republic, too short at any rate for a minister to establish firm control over the seasoned high civil servants running his ministry, even though some ministers outlived several cabinets. And the premiers generally seemed to be relieved to lay down their high executive office and to return to their seats in the Chamber, where many other former premiers awaited them.

After the defeat of the Axis powers in 1940 a Constituent Assembly drew up a new constitution for a Fourth Republic.

[15] Auguste Soulier, *L'instabilité ministerielle sous la troisième République.* Paris: Armand Colin, 1939.

The abortive first draft of the constitution would have established a unicameral legislature with tight control over the executive. The second draft modified this extreme design and added a weak upper house, now called the Council of the Republic. Care was taken to provide for the power of dissolution under carefully circumscribed conditions.[16] The three parties in control during the first years were far more cohesive and better organized than those of the Third Republic, but soon the ministerial instability returned. Governments now fell after an average five months in office. Unpopular measures and grave decisions, such as those demanded by the Algerian question, were postponed from cabinet to cabinet, until in 1958 the Fourth Republic collapsed before the threat of military revolt and civil war.

The procedure for setting up a new cabinet in the Fourth Republic was the same as before 1940, although it generally took longer: the president of the Republic chose a likely combination of middle-of-the-road parties and designated a prime minister, who would then try to strike a bargain with the four or five groups needed to form a legislative majority. The ministers were mostly members of the Assembly, to which the cabinet owed responsibility.[17] The life of the cabinet inevitably depended on the uncertain agreement of the coalition partners on a few issues and was threatened as soon as unforeseen, divisive questions came up. Cabinets frequently felt they had to ask for a vote of confidence on important projects and sometimes also on minor matters. The Assembly could also take the initiative and prepare a vote of censure, which if supported by a majority would bring down the cabinet.

The commissions of the National Assembly always took firm control of all pieces of legislation, including cabinet bills, and even of the budget. Under these circumstances, it was easy for cabinets to feel thwarted in their plans and to resign in disgust. The commissions further took on the job of supervising the executive, and often they yielded to the temptation to initiate governmental action themselves. At the same time, the use of

[16] The power of dissolution remained in disuse except in 1956, when Premier Edgar Faure invoked it, only to find himself universally condemned and expelled from his own party.

[17] In the Third Republic many had been senators, and in de Gaulle's Fifth Republic many were experts from outside parliament.

written and oral questions was not as pronounced in French parliamentarism as in Great Britain. Instead, the French deputies either called ministers before one of the commissions to answer questions, or they used the dreaded *interpellation* to bring the cabinet to heel. An interpellation is a question directed at the premier or a particular minister, who has to reply in full. The government's reply is followed by a debate ending with a vote to proceed to the "order of the day." An adverse vote or one requiring the government to take remedial action is quite likely to lead to its resignation.

Thus parliamentary government under the Third and Fourth Republics of France produced a rather different system than in Great Britain. The names "cabinet government" and "assembly government" indicate the chief differences, and they hint at the difficulties of transplanting governmental institutions from one Western country to another, not to mention to a new nation.

The de Gaulle constitution   During the dozen years of the Fourth Republic there was no lack of critics of ministerial instability, one of the most outspoken being General de Gaulle. Several attempts were made to strengthen and stabilize the executive. In 1958, when the parliamentary system broke down in the face of threatening civil war, de Gaulle and his friends were given full powers not only to deal with the crisis but also to rewrite the constitution. The result of their constructive criticisms and of further developments brought about by de Gaulle is the present constitution of the Fifth Republic, the executive-legislative relations of which are a mixture of presidentialism and parliamentarism.

The constitution of the Fifth Republic weakened the powerful commissions of the National Assembly and transferred budgetary authority and the control over the legislative agenda to the cabinet, so that the resulting procedures showed a certain similarity to those in England. But the framers of the new constitution took further steps to make up for the lack in France of a strong two-party system, such as the one that makes cabinet government possible in Great Britain. Instead of resting the strengthened cabinet on a coalition of the "old parties" or even on the large Gaullist Union for the New Republic (UNR), they decided to separate it in various ways from the Assembly: ministers now have to resign their Assembly seats upon appointment and cannot return to them after their cabinet steps down. Many ministers are experts called in from the outside anyway. The cabinet is still responsible to the National Assembly, but the ways in which the Assembly can control, supervise, and censure the cabinet have been curtailed so substantially as to make the parliamentary character of the relationship doubtful. Not only is there far less opportunity for the Assembly to upset a cabinet by frustrating its legislative and budgetary plans, but the cabinet can be overthrown only by a motion of censure supported by an absolute majority of the deputies. The motion of censure also requires a waiting period of 48 hours and can be used only once in a session. The premier can stake the fortunes of his government on any bill, which then becomes law unless the Assembly can mount a successful motion of censure within 24 hours. The question period, finally, was increased and the practice of interpellations ending with a vote was discouraged. While it is still possible for an angry Assembly to bring down a government, the present system hardly looks like one of parliamentary supremacy.

Direct presidential election   Most unorthodox for a parliamentary system, however, was the establishment of a strong presidency, replacing what is ordinarily a figurehead with largely symbolic and ceremonial functions. The presidents of the Third and Fourth Republics were elected by Parliament, clearly the source of their authority. The 1958 constitution instead set up an electoral college of some 80,000 electors, composed of more than three fourths of the municipal councillors and mayors. In 1962, moreover, President de Gaulle changed the election modus to direct popular election, giving French presidents a powerful popular mandate not unlike that derived by Napoleon I and Napoleon III from plebiscites. This method of electing the president, de Gaulle hoped, would remold the French party system into two strong groups.

Even before this plebiscitary turn, the new presidency had enough power to constitute the chief focus of authority in the 1958 constitution. The constitution conferred upon the President the guardianship over the functioning of the governmental organs, together with sweeping emergency powers under article 16. Added to his traditional headship over the entire administration, the armed forces, and the French Community, and his personal prestige as the embodiment of French greatness during the bitter days of defeat in World War II, this grant of powers gave de Gaulle invincible strength in French politics. Vis-à-vis the once proud National Assembly, the constitution put solely in the hands of the president a power of dissolution that, while sending the deputies home for reelection or defeat, affects neither the cabinet nor the president, who has a seven-year term. The cabinet no longer falls with every election. It is selected and appointed by the president and requires no "investiture" by the Assembly, though it can be repudiated by it.

The French president has always presided over cabinet meetings. Since 1958, however, his weighty presence gave him a policy-making role of major importance tending toward the eclipse of the premier and other key ministers. Under President de Gaulle, at least, no premier or foreign minister could be anything but his spokesman and helpmate. Whether de Gaulle's successors will be able to maintain this system or whether they will modify its authoritarian features in the direction of more parliamentarism, only the future can tell.

German parliamentarism

France has not been the only country to experiment with modifications of parliamentary government. Another significant example of such experimentation is provided by the German Republics of Weimar (1919–1933) and Bonn (1949–   ), although they seem to have followed the opposite course from the French.

The Weimar Republic   Executive-legislative relations under the Weimar Republic of 1919 were patterned largely after the preceding imperial regime, which had just allowed its ministers to become responsible to the Reichstag under the impact of impending military defeat. Thus the chancellor and his cabinet were now to be drawn from a majority coalition of the many parties in the lower house, while the Reich president would be directly elected by the new sovereign, the people. Having been denied control over the executive for such a long time, the

Reichstag now introduced French-style questions and interpellations with a vengeance. With a multiparty system incapable of rallying majority parties or even stable coalitions, cabinets fell as frequently as in the Third and Fourth Republics of France. Rising economic crisis and political turmoil in the early 1930s finally made the establishment of cabinets with a parliamentary majority impossible, as the Communists and National Socialists together attained a majority of seats in the Reichstag, not counting the other parties hostile to the republican constitution. During the last two years before the appointment of Hitler, the parliamentary government of the Weimar Republic was forced to depend upon the extraconstitutional emergency powers of the Reich president, who appointed and dismissed cabinets at will.

The strong presidency was thought of by many as the "emergency brake" on the still somewhat unfamiliar processes of party government and parliamentary democracy. This tentative attitude toward parliamentary government also marked other aspects of the "improvised democracy" of Weimar. Cabinet ministers, for example, were often selected from among nonpartisan, outside figures or experts rather than from among the party leaders, in the hope of thereby escaping the violent factionalism that rent the political community. The second Reich president, von Hindenburg (1925–1934), was himself an unpolitical figure, who represented the military glory of the past but was quite unable to penetrate the political crises before him. The tentative attitude toward parliamentary democracy eventually induced many Germans to toy with the idea of replacing it with a more authoritarian regime, such as presidentialism, making even the "constitutional dictatorship" of the emergency powers of the Reich president seem like a normal form of government. The untimely end of parliamentary government in the Weimar Republic was partly due also to the diffidence of the party politicians, who were all too ready to leave authority to the strong president.

The Bonn Republic   The Bonn Republic represents in many ways a strong reaction to the weaknesses of the Weimar Republic. Its executive-legislative relations, in particular, show a determination to establish a system of cabinet government somewhat like that of Great Britain. The framers of the Basic Law of 1949 completely eliminated the strong, popularly elected Reich president of the Weimar model, creating instead in their federal president a figurehead weaker than the president of the Fourth Republic of France. They decided also to stabilize the parliamentary executive, the chancellor, with a novel device, the *constructive no-confidence* vote: the Bundestag can overthrow a chancellor only by electing a successor. The theory behind this clause is that an irresponsible opposition, such as the combination of Communists and National Socialists in the early 1930s, could never agree on a candidate and would thus be unable to topple governments.

In the two decades that the West German Basic Law has been in effect, something approaching a two-party system has brought the earlier propensity toward multipartism under control, so that a government coalition and a fairly unified opposition party now lend stability to the parliamentary system. Nevertheless, the constructive no-confidence vote still weights the scales in favor of not only the executive but also the incumbent leadership within the majority coalition, thus producing some undesirable side effects.

Separation of powers and parliamentarism compared

The question of which is better, the separation of powers or parliamentary government, hinges on the philosophical encounter of theories of constitutional checks and balances with those emphasizing governmental responsibility to the people. A conclusive answer also involves a detailed analysis of a country's political parties, sectional or other divisions, and legal procedures. What has worked well in Great Britain and the United States may not do so elsewhere. However, some basic relationships should be clear. A homogeneous, unified society with a two-party system of centralized, well-disciplined parties (unlike the United States) seems to be well served by parliamentarism. Countries with many parties, or with great sectional and other diversities, on the other hand, are better off entrusting their executive authority to a strong president. Attempts to combine the two systems seem to tend toward a confusion of responsibility and to undermine the role of the prime minister.

Executive and legislative roles and role structures are not

just a matter of institutional blueprint or constitutional design. Although the norms and goals of the constitutional design enter importantly into these roles, other role norms and goals for an executive or legislator derive from the broader political culture and from important subcultures within it. The process of recruitment of political executives and legislators usually involves subtle ways of ascertaining whether the candidate has in fact internalized these latter norms and goals before he is given a formal role. The literature on leadership recruitment contains a good deal of evidence on such underlying criteria for selection in various countries. Occasionally, however, under the impact of crisis or by failure of human judgment, the safeguards on the selection process break down and someone like Adolf Hitler is chosen. Considering the frequency of political crisis and the continual desire for radically new departures and daring new leadership, it is difficult to conceive of selection processes so carefully guarded that they will never make a major mistake. The British prefer to season their future prime ministers in decades of parliamentary experience, for screening as well as training, before they are even considered for office. Yet even such a prolonged apprenticeship is not a surefire guarantee, because its success or failure depends on the accidents of individual personality and of personality change.

ADMINISTRATIVE ROLES, TRAINING, AND RECRUITMENT

If careful selection and training are utopian desiderata in the case of British prime ministers or Platonic philosopher kings, they are routine procedures with administrative personnel.[18] Earlier ages of highly developed public administration and finance had their own selection criteria and training procedures, which were vital to the territorial unification of the modern nation-states in Europe. But as middle-class revolutions in England and France brought absolute monarchy under control, and commerce and industry began to flower in the eighteenth and nineteenth centuries as never before, liberal ideology came to view public administration as authoritarian and meddlesome.

[18] On training, see also Fred Riggs, *Administration in Developing Countries*. Boston: Houghton Mifflin, 1964, chap. 10.

The laissez-faire ideal only had room for representative assemblies and, at most, for judicial enforcement of the laws, but no room for a bureaucracy. With the waning of the interest in administration, the recruitment practices declined, and the public service in such countries as England and the new American republic became a sinecure for persons tired of competition in the marketplace as well as for incompetent relatives and sons of influential families. In the days of the *spoils system* in the United States, administrative offices were used as reward for partisan loyalty and help during election campaigns. It was evidently assumed that administrative activity required neither much formal training nor professional standards of conduct.

Civil service reforms

After long neglect the interest in rational public administration was revived in the latter half of the nineteenth century. A new concern in business and industry for efficient management rather than just efficient machinery, by the application of scientific method to human relationships and society rather than only to nature, soon spread from the private realm to the public. Civil service reforms in England and the United States tackled the most obvious abuses. A Civil Service Commission was established in England in 1855; by 1870, entrance into the Home Civil Service had been restricted to persons who passed *open examinations.* The principles of a career service also spread to the Commonwealth nations. In the United States, the Civil Service Act of 1883 brought the first 10 percent of federal employees under a *merit system,* and today almost everyone in the federal service and increasing numbers of state and local employees are recruited and promoted according to merit systems.

On the European continent, the heritage of absolutism had preserved bureaucracy, although there was also a need to streamline and democratize lingering authoritarian practices. In nineteenth-century France, for example, the executive "departments" set down their own standards and rules of appointment, discipline, and promotion. Despite sporadic attempts to pass uniform civil service legislation, in fact, it was not until 1946 that an Office of Public Service *(Fonction Publique)* was created in Paris to fulfill functions similar to those of the U.S. Civil Service Commission. The establishment of a federal civil service of Germany in the nineteenth century also had to await the creation of the empire of 1871. The dominant influence of the Prussian bureaucratic-authoritarian tradition, however, served to carry over the patterns of the absolutist bureaucracy to the modern German civil service. This is not to say that the resulting practices were not a model of efficiency and integrity, but they were also authoritarian in their relationship to the public.

Characteristics of bureaucratic organization

Given the ubiquity of governmental bureaucracy, some curiosity focuses naturally on social life before its appearance, on its origins, and on its essential nature. As one of the important formal political structures, public administration has attracted the attention of scholars from many disciplines, and some of the best descriptive accounts have come from outsiders. One such definition linking origin and nature and setting forth clearly the salient organizational characteristics is by Max Weber, a German sociologist writing in the first decades of this century. He describes fully developed bureaucratic organization with the following criteria:

1. Fixed and official jurisdictions of each agency, regulated by specific rules or laws
2. Hierarchic organization on several levels in superordination or subordination
3. Extensive, careful, and usually secret record keeping
4. Professional or at least thorough training for staff members
5. Separation of domicile from office and full-time devotion to functions of office
6. Operation according to rather stable and exhaustive rules

It is easy to imagine social life prior to the attainment of all of these criteria.

The crucial importance of the quality of administrative personnel has created characteristic patterns in the civil service systems of modern states. A well-established civil service today constitutes an elaborate system with differentiated recruiting and advancement on several levels and for specialized tasks. The typical civil service has at least three levels: administrative leadership, middle management, and the rank and file. The top executives often include political appointees, such as ministers or department secretaries and undersecretaries, who are not part of the civil service proper, which is not to say that they lack the experience and discipline of a long public career. The rank and file may include a vast pool of secretarial and other man-power outside the career service. Civilian government employees, including local and regional levels of government, number in the millions in today's larger nation-states. In the United States, for example, federal civilian employment alone amounts to almost 2.5 million persons of every description. West Germany, with more than twenty-five million gainfully employed persons, has one tenth of that number on the payrolls of federal, *Land,* and local governments. In France the number in the public employ approaches 2.8 million.

British civil service

The civil service in Great Britain is composed of three major classes, a small Administrative Class of no more than 2500, an Executive Class of about 70,000, and a Clerical Class of perhaps 120,000.[19] It does not include the large staff of the public corporations, which are made up of the industries nationalized after 1945 as well as a number of older public bodies, such as the BOAC or the Central Electricity Board.

The *Administrative Class* is recruited in part from members of the Executive Class who have passed special examinations. Its bulk is recruited directly from the cream of university graduates in their twenties. Graduates with first- or second-class honors need only pass an interview, other graduates a written examination as well. All examinations are geared to test general knowledge in the arts and sciences and well-rounded ability rather than technical qualifications.[20] The Administrative Class in a very real sense runs each department and, by means of continual interdepartmental contacts and conferences, the entire administration. Its members, as top civil servants in each department, are both advisers and troubleshooters for their minister,

[19] These figures stem from official sources of the British Information Service dated 1966; they are somewhat at variance with other descriptions, owing evidently to differences in classification schemes.

[20] The written examinations give the applicant an opportunity to show his knowledge of obscure technical subjects as well as his general knowledge.

whose difficulties with his cabinet, with Parliament, and with the public they must seek to head off or at least to straighten out. They are also entrusted with the preparation of plans or legislative drafts for the use of the policy makers.

The *Executive Class* is concerned with the management of most day-to-day government operations, supplying office directors and supervisors for the most diverse functions. While the members of the Administrative Class have *staff functions,* the Executive Class chiefly directs the *line functions.* It is drawn from eighteen- or nineteen-year-old graduates of academic secondary schools, who have to pass an examination and an interview, again along lines suggested by the educational curriculum. Nevertheless, members of the Executive Class often acquire a great deal of expertise in technical or semiprofessional fields such as taxation, accounting, or the like.

The *Clerical Class,* finally, consists of clerical and sub-clerical workers who are recruited with some secondary education at the age of sixteen or seventeen. The most numerous of the service classes, its members usually work under supervision and according to the instructions of members of the Executive Class. They can also become members of the latter, if they can demonstrate proficiency by passing an appropriate examination.

In addition to these three service classes, the British government has also engaged the services of specialized professional, scientific, and technical personnel. Here, besides an applicant's certified formal training and practical experience, an interview is used to ascertain the subtler requirements of a public career.[21]

American civil service

The American federal service has no equivalent of the British Administrative Class, the highest positions being generally filled with political appointees by successive administrations. This procedure is motivated less by considerations of party patronage than by the belief that the "reform character" of the program of each new President requires a new set of dedicated top-level administrators. Holdovers are rare, although they do occur. The federal career service has a *General Schedule* of eighteen classifi-

[21] Regarding the top civil servants and their relations to the partisan leadership of the cabinet in office, see especially Anthony Sampson, *Anatomy of Britain Today.* New York: Harper & Row, 1965, chap. 14.

cations, which range from clerical jobs to professional and scientific positions at the top. Subclerical positions are covered by a separate *Crafts, Protective, and Custodial Schedule* with another ten grades.

Recruitment to the federal service is by competitive examinations. At the higher levels, an evaluation of academic background and professional experience takes the place of examinations. A college graduate is usually classified at grade GS-5, or lower middle management, but can be promoted in time to the top. By and large, it can be said that the lower positions of the American federal service have been comparatively attractive and have competed well with private industry. The higher levels, however, have rarely held their own against the professions and executive positions outside the government; this situation, along with the lack of tradition and prestige, has often discouraged able men and women from making the government their lifetime career.

French civil service

The French civil service before World War II was characterized by the differing practices and uneven personnel quality of the different executive departments. The Foreign Service, the Conseil d'État, and the Ministries of Finance and the Interior always attracted exceptionally able men, while other ministries had to adjust their examination and promotion standards to the meager crop of applicants. Promotions were generally kept within each department. The reforms of 1945 created two uniform classes of civil servants: the *administrateur civil,* modeled after the British Administrative Class, and the *secrétaire d'administration,* corresponding broadly to the British Executive Class. Two lower classifications include the administrative clerks and the typists and subclerical workers.

French civil administrators have the function of preparing legislative drafts and ministerial directives as well as coordinating the many moving parts of the administrative machinery. They are recruited from among the graduates of the École Nationale d'Administration, which handpicks its students from among large numbers of applicants under thirty, who either have a diploma from a college-level institute of political science or are already officials in the service. Entrance is by a single examination that tests general knowledge and intelligence. The course of studies mixes academic instruction with practical experience in administration, social services, and private industry. The school also offers refresher and advanced courses of experienced officials.

German civil service

The West German civil service has inherited many of the virtues and some of the vices of the Prussian tradition—efficiency, austerity, and authoritarianism. It is divided into four classes. The Higher Service *(Höherer Beamtendienst),* somewhat more numerous than the British Administrative Class, supplies planning and advisory services and administrative coordination, and on the highest level it may represent ministers in parliament or to the press. This Higher Service is recruited almost exclusively from law-school graduates, who must complete an additional three and a half years of in-service training, ending with a second state examination in law. The near-monopoly of legal training, and in Roman law at that, must be contrasted with the breadth of background preferred by the British civil service and with the French efforts, in the civil service reforms of 1945, to give future civil servants a broad training in political and social science. Historically, the German preference for legal training is associated with the nineteenth-century notion of the *Rechtsstaat,* the "administrative state under law" rather than under an arbitrary monarch—a notion more plausible to German Liberals at the time than any thought of democracy. In practice, this excess of legalism has tended to make the German civil service unnecessarily rigid and unresponsive to social needs and pressures.

The other classifications of the German civil service are the Elevated Service *(Gehobener Dienst),* comparable perhaps to the Executive Class in Great Britain, and the Middle and Simple Services, which include minor executive and custodial or messenger services, respectively. There is also a vast army of white-collar employees, typists, and so on, who are not part of the civil service. The Elevated Service requires applicants to have the equivalent of a secondary education and a period of in-service training. The Middle Service expects six years of secondary school and an apprenticeship of one year. The Simple

Service demands that applicants have completed their eight years of elementary school and that they have learned a trade. The numerical proportions are clearest when the civil service of both federation and *Länder* are considered, since their service regulations are uniform and the *Land* administrations constitute by far the bulk of the administrative state in West Germany. For every two members of the Higher Service, there are seven of the Elevated, five of the Middle, and one of the Simple Service, and about ten white-collar employees without civil service tenure. This breakdown does not include the personnel of the federal mails and the railroads, which makes up about half of the public employees of federation and *Länder*.

Almost from the very beginnings of German state bureaucracies, the German civil servant made a bargain with "the state." The civil servant would devote his best efforts to executing his job faithfully if his monarch promised to protect him and to take care of him and his family in sickness and old age. Complete protection in the discharge of his duties, sickness and disability benefits, and pension rights with generous annuities for his widow and orphans were the eventual goal. This bargain, not always kept faithfully by the state in the age of monarchy, became the cornerstone of the "well-acquired rights" of civil servants in the republican period. Obligated to the old order by reason of its composition, the German civil service clung to its privileges rather than become a British-style service class responsive to the wishes of the emerging democratic society. To this day, and despite the efforts of the Allied occupation at reforming the German civil service after 1945, the administrators are too defensive to adapt themselves and their training to the changing society around them. While they have been efficient and relatively free from corruption, they remain exclusive, aloof, and unresponsive.[22]

Civil service horizons

This survey has shown some of the administrative services in operation and compared their varying interpretation of the con-

[22] See also the surveys by Paul Meyer (*Administrative Organization: A Comparative Study of the Organization of Public Administration* [London: Stevens, 1957]) and by Brian Chapman (*The Profession of Government* [London: G. Allen, 1959]).

cept of a lifetime career service under a merit system. The remainders of class barriers in European countries, which have fashioned their highly stratified educational systems, also show up in the classifications of their civil service systems, unlike those of the General Schedule of the American federal government. Yet such countries as Great Britain and France have moved with all deliberate speed to democratize in spirit and training their top civil service, once so aristocratic. With the help of scholarships they have encouraged persons from all social backgrounds to compete on an equal footing for admission to their highest administrative classes, and they have made transfer by examination to the next higher class easier. At the same time, American administrators and social scientists have long been moving toward ever-greater professionalization of the federal and some state civil services. More recently, they have given serious consideration to proposals for the creation of a senior civil service analogous to the British and French models.[23]

FORMAL ROLE STRUCTURES
IN DEVELOPING COUNTRIES

The political institutions of the developing countries have been largely neglected in this chapter. One reason is the scarcity of authoritative accounts of what in many cases amounts to an unstable mixture of changing traditional role structures, vigorous but unstable parties and mass organizations, and a deceptive facade of Western constitutionalism. When the ruler of an African one-party state puts on his native robes to address his people, all three of these elements are happily combined. But neither an understanding of the cultural underpinnings, of the party structure, or of the legalistic trimmings each by itself, nor a recognized formula for combining all three will give a reliable and comprehensive key to understanding the wide variations of executive leadership in developing countries.[24]

[23] The proposals are discussed in P. T. David and Ross Pollock, *Executives in Government.* Washington, D.C.: Brookings, 1958, and M. H. Bernstein, *The Job of the Federal Executive.* Washington, D.C.: Brookings, 1958.

[24] See, for example, Leonard Binder's critique of Gabriel Almond's functional model in *Iran: Political Development in a Changing Society.* Berkeley, Calif.: University of California Press, 1962, pp. 7–10.

Roles of legislatures

Barring new evidence from comparative legislative research currently in progress, legislatures in developing countries seem to offer little more hope of uniform analysis. Their respective roles within their political systems vary considerably to begin with, although they tend to be at least relatively weak vis-à-vis the executive, if not mere rubber stamps of the *parti unique* and its leader. The adopted constitution, in any case, gives us little clue to the real functioning of these institutions, which ought to be at the focus of our interest.[25] Preliminary studies have also shown that whatever the formal rules of order, the proceedings of legislative assemblies everywhere are governed by a fundamental procedural consensus that has its roots in the political culture.

In some Western systems, for example, there is nearly always competitive majority rule on the floor of the legislature, barring major crises or unanimous declaratory actions. In others, and in most developing countries, the stronger tendency is to argue to consensus.[26] In the Japanese Parliament, for example, it would be considered an outrage for the majority simply to vote down the objections of the minority on an important issue. Instead, a compromise solution has to be found that constitutes at least a token of respect for the minority point of view. Further research, it is hoped, will describe the many varieties of basic procedural consensus and eventually supply a more inclusive scheme of classification than is available today. When the comparative study of legislatures has reached this point, we may also be able to compare executive-legislative relations in a more meaningful fashion.

Public administration

The most developed part of institutional comparison beyond the conventional Western powers is the comparative study of

[25] See also the general remarks on this subject by Bernard E. Brown, *New Directions in Comparative Politics.* Calcutta: Asia Publishing House, 1962, pp. 3–4.

[26] See, for example, the account of Indonesian practices in George McT. Kahin, *Major Governments of Asia,* 2d ed. Ithaca, N.Y.: Cornell University Press, 1963, pp. 588–589.

public administration.[27] As Ferrel Heady has pointed out, the part of Almond's functional framework relating to political institutions, namely rule making, rule application, and rule adjudication, has not persuaded students of public administration to abandon their focus on bureaucracy as an institution, however multifunctional.[28] Instead, and in addition to structural concepts, some have tended to go into behavioral definitions; others have studied the "ecology of administration," just as biologists have studied the environment of living organisms.

Riggs's "prismatic society" The most striking "ecological" theory is that of the "prismatic society" by Fred W. Riggs. The prismatic society is a mixed transitional society of functionally diffuse ("fused") and functionally specific (diffracted") structures. Its patterns of power, and especially its administrative subsystem *(sala),* are affected deeply by manifestations of society's prismatic character in the economic sector (bazaar-canteen types) and in the "kaleidoscopic" elite groupings, social structures, and symbolic systems. The administrative subsystem, the *sala,* halfway between the modern "office" and the traditional "chamber," holds an extraordinary amount of power vis-à-vis the other political institutions, even though the scope of bureaucratic power may still be limited and its efficiency low. Administrative functions in the prismatic society are performed not only by regular administrative structures, but also by other structures not primarily oriented toward this function. Bureaucrats, on the other hand, frequently can and do interfere in the political process. The *sala* is often associated also with institutionalized

[27] See especially Dwight Waldo, *Comparative Public Administration: Prologue, Problems and Promise.* Chicago: ASPA, 1964, and Ferrel Heady and Sybil L. Stokes, eds., *Papers in Comparative Public Administration.* Ann Arbor, Mich.: University of Michigan Press, 1962. Also John D. Montgomery and William J. Siffin, eds., *Approaches to Development: Politics, Administration and Change.* New York: McGraw-Hill, 1966, and the Fritz Morstein Marx classic, *The Administrative State.* Chicago: Chicago University Press, 1957.

[28] See Ferrel Heady, *Public Administration: A Comparative Perspective,* Englewood Cliffs, N.J.: Prentice-Hall, 1966, pp. 14–20, and the sources cited there, as well as the discussion of the behavioral dimensions of bureaucracy.

corruption, bureaucratic enclaves of self-protecting management, unequal distribution of services to the public, nepotism, and, quite generally, a wide gap between actual behavior and the norms and standards of administrative conduct.[29]

Heady's categories Ferrel Heady has supplied a classificatory scheme of types of developing administration, ranging from the "classic bureaucracies," such as Germany and France, over the "civic-culture" countries—Great Britain and the United States —and successfully modernizing Japan, to the communist countries and the Third World. The classical bureaucracies are characterized by a tenured, lifetime career service drawing largely from civil-servant and upper-class families, "a semiclosed caste." [30] The civic-culture countries lagged behind considerably in the professionalization of their civil service, especially the United States, where the role of the top administrators is far more in the public limelight and is more an object of political competition than in Great Britain. In both countries, the participant style of the public makes administration subservient to political decision making at all levels.

The modernizing administrators of Japan, by contrast, according to Heady and other observers,[31] play a dominant role in the whole political system. Their top echelons and even their retired civil servants are deeply involved in the representative process and elective politics, owing perhaps to the historic importance of the administrative modernizing role in an authoritarian society. Soviet administration, on the other hand, is "one-party administration," politicized and utilized for the party's purposes of political communications and direction, although party and administration have been kept separate except for interlocking directorates. The Communist party has used the huge administrative apparatus along with the other party-con-

[29] See Riggs, *Administration in Developing Countries,* pp. 23–24 and chaps. 8–10.

[30] On France see also Michel Crozier, *The Bureaucratic Phenomenon.* Chicago: University of Chicago Press, 1964.

[31] See also Reinhard Bendix, *Nation-Building and Citizenship,* chap. 6, and the relevant parts of Robert E. Ward and Dankwart A. Rustow, *Political Modernization in Japan and Turkey.* Princeton, N.J.: Princeton University Press, 1964.

trolled mass organizations for the rapid advancement of modernization.[32] Instead of Marx and Engels' "withering away of the state," there has been unlimited growth of the state machinery and with it coercion and control over individuals and groups.

In the developing countries, administration is largely directed by a consensus on such goals of development as nation building and socioeconomic progress, although in the general population there also tends to be a pervasive oppositional attitude toward government. Next to a political elite committed to development, social scientists are agreed, an effective bureaucracy is essential for progress along the road of modernization. For many reasons, beginning with the extremely limited resources of trained manpower, the bureaucracy often is lacking in effectiveness. The most successful developing administrations appear to be those of former British or French colonies, which learned administrative skills and styles from their former masters.[33]

Heady, finally, distinguishes six types of developing administration:

1. Traditional autocratic systems, where bureaucracy and army serve the ruling families and where administration is fragmented among agencies and nonadministrative structures. As Leonard Binder has shown in his study of Iran, such an administration tends to be conservative in orientation and rather reluctant to modernize society.

2. Bureaucratic elite systems, civil or military, or both, whose officialdom fills the void of one or several mass parties. The bureaucratic or military tutelage over a presumably immature society may be quite devoted to modernization, but can hardly help being mindful of its own perpetuation as well. Pakistan, Thailand, and, perhaps, Japan are named as examples.

3. Polyarchal competitive systems, such as those of the

[32] See also Merle Fainsod, *How Russia Is Ruled,* rev. ed. Cambridge, Mass.: Harvard University Press, 1964, and the same author's contribution to Joseph La Palombara, ed., *Bureaucracy and Political Development.* Princeton, N.J.: Princeton University Press, 1963.

[33] Ferrel Heady rates the British administrative tutelage higher than the French. But this appraisal fails to consider the significance of "indirect rule" in British colonies, as compared to the deep penetration of French colonial administration into the ecological environment of postindependence administration.

Philippines, several Latin-American countries, Turkey, and Israel, which most closely resemble the Western European and American prototypes. Here power is dispersed, and public administration needs the support of major groups to be effective.

4. Dominant-party semicompetitive systems, which correspond to David Apter's mobilization systems or to Robert C. Tucker's "revolutionary mass-movement regimes," although they are not identical with the communist model. Examples are India and Mexico, both of which are developing from rather diffuse antecedents a more effective administrative service, particularly in Mexico, tied indirectly to executive leadership.

5. Dominant-party mobilization systems, such as those of Algeria, Egypt, Guinea, or Bolivia, in which the civil service is strong but subordinate to the party and to the executive leadership.

6. Communist developing countries, such as North Korea or Cuba, where huge and complex administrations are completely dominated and controlled by the Communist party.[34]

INSTITUTIONAL GROWTH AND DECAY

Our discussion would not be complete without a few parting comments on institutional growth and decay. Looking at institutions as formal structures obscures by excessive simplification some of their vital aspects, including the mechanisms of their change and adaptation to changing circumstances. As was pointed out earlier, an analysis of formal structure is quite incapable of telling us how or why political role structures are born and maintained, and how and why they break down. For that, we must have a thorough understanding of the processes by which *institutionalization* occurs and by which it may be reversed. A legislature or administrative agency, for example, is not created by legislative fiat or organizational chart alone. Besides being organized by a previously existing organization or institutional group, it has to take on an *autonomous life* of its

---

[34] Heady, *Public Administration,* chaps. 5 and 6. See also the topics and countries discussed in La Palombara, ed., *Bureaucracy and Political Development,* especially chaps. 1–4.

own, to become *legitimized* with sets of values in the political culture of the general public and in the subculture of its own staff and clientele. Its more significant roles, too, must be taken on in earnest, as a result of the role socialization of newly appointed or elected officials.

By the same token, a well-established institution needs to maintain itself by means of appropriate interaction with its total environment. If the environment changes or the institution's original functions change, it can adapt itself to the new conditions. If its legitimacy in the eyes of outsiders begins to wane, it can even try to reinforce its image in the general political culture. If it weakens in its recruitment and socialization of new leadership, it can try to broaden its sources of recruitment and intensify the indoctrination of its members. Even direct competition from a rival structure need not signify the end of an adaptively flexible institution, as long as its life is not authoritatively terminated, say, by legislative fiat.

But an institution can surely decline and disintegrate if its leadership neglects the devices that can maintain it. In the long run, any of three prime causes—an unmet crisis of legitimacy, dysfunctional recruitment, or insufficient socialization—can ruin a political institution. Very likely, however, one will lead to the deterioration of the other two. Next to sudden crises, of course, political modernization itself poses some of the greatest threats to institution maintenance.[35]

[35] On this general topic see especially the remarks of Samuel P. Huntington, "Some Notes on Political Institutionalization," at the Salzburg Round Table Conference of the International Political Science Association, 1968.

THE POLICY-MAKING PROCESS

"Case studies never 'prove' anything," Harry Eckstein wrote in his classic study of pressure-group politics in Great Britain. "Their purpose is to illustrate generalizations which are established otherwise, or to direct attention to such generalizations." [1] This comment offers perspective on the well-known fact that the experience of an actual case leaves a deeper impression than dozens of organizational charts or constitutional paragraphs. Nobody ever "experiences" a governmental institution or a formal role structure in the way that an elected representative may experience the wrath of the electorate over a particular issue, the heat of a legislative floor fight, or the astute maneuvers of lobbyists or administrators in concrete cases. Some of this experiential sense of politics can be gained, perhaps, by a study of the process of policy making as such—the dynamic aspect of the structures and relationships discussed in Chapter 7.

There are many ways of approaching the policy-making process, and a considerable literature of case studies is available. One school of policy studies, for instance, stresses the content of actual public policies in such fields as foreign affairs and defense,

[1] Harry Eckstein, *Pressure Group Politics*. Stanford, Calif.: Stanford University Press, 1960, p. 15. See also the remarks on case studies of Bernard E. Brown and Martin Landau in James B. Christoph and Bernard E. Brown, eds., *Cases in Comparative Politics*, 2d ed. Boston: Little, Brown, 1966, pp. 3–32.

agriculture, labor, business, social welfare, and so on.[2] Another approach has sought chiefly to identify the various inputs into policy making, either to demonstrate the pluralistic character of the policy process in a democracy or to pinpoint which groups or agencies appeared to be the most powerful.[3] A third approach, favored in this chapter, stresses the procedures and pragmatic steps of policy making. Other observers, especially Karl W. Deutsch, have emphasized the communications aspects of "decision systems." For more than a decade, indeed, decision-making models have been used with varying results by political scientists, economists, and workers in other disciplines.[4] The different approaches vary nearly as widely as the conceptions of politics itself.

For our present purposes, the process of policy making will be examined with constant reference to the role structures considered in the previous chapter. Structures and dynamic action together, it is hoped, will constitute a functioning whole of sufficient detail to allow meaningful comparisons. Policy making in this context is to denote the making of *public* decisions by *public* officials or agencies, although it is surely possible to speak of policies of private groups or individuals. And we shall assume that policy making is a goal-oriented, rational process that requires careful design and strategy to meet such general criteria as effectiveness, efficiency, and integrity. In a democracy, moreover, it also must be tied into the representative process and allow for consultation with any party affected by its decisions.

[2] See also the discussion of policy goals by Harold Lasswell in Lasswell and Lerner, *The Policy Sciences.* Stanford, Calif.: Stanford University Press, 1951, chap. 1.

[3] See also James A. Robinson and R. Roger Majak, "The Theory of Decision-Making" in James C. Charlesworth, ed., *Contemporary Political Analysis.* New York: Free Press, 1967, chap. 10, and the sources cited there as well as by James Rosenau in chap. 11.

[4] See especially Richard Snyder in Roland Young, ed., *Approach to the Study of Politics.* Evanston, Ill.: Northwestern University Press, 1958, and his survey in Austin Ranney, ed., *Essays on the Behavioral Study of Politics.* Urbana, Ill.: University of Illinois Press, 1962. Also the description of the Leviathan simulation program by Sidney C. and Beatrice K. Rome in Harold Borko, ed., *Computer Applications in the Behavioral Sciences.* Englewood Cliffs, N.J.: Prentice-Hall, 1962, chap. 22.

THE NATURE OF THE POLICY PROCESS

To clarify the policy-making process further, it is desirable to arrive at a definition of its chief aspects. Policy in the broadest sense is the deliberate conduct of one entity, such as a person, group, or agency, toward another entity over a period of time. A person with a policy may not be very conscious of how he is acting and why. An organized group is more likely to be conscious of the procedures by which it makes decisions, especially if internal disagreements occur frequently. A public agency amid the pressures of organized interests and modern democratic government can hardly help knowing how its policy arises out of a long series of decisions in which it may often be little more than a broker among the different groups and interests.

The unspoken assumption behind any study of policy making is fhat even large groups and complex governmental agencies can make policy with as much or more rational control and unambiguous intent than an individual person can—that they are capable, as it were, of thinking and acting with one mind. Every day, newspapers will speak of such things as the policy of the United States government toward Laos, or the policy of Congress toward the steel industry, even when the actual policies may be more like a football punted to and fro between the executive branch and Congress, between the two houses of the Congress, or among the committees and prominent members of either house.

The general definition of the making of public policy delineates further areas of inquiry. A public policy, first of all, is ascribed to a specific agency or officeholder, such as the Atomic Energy Commission or the British prime minister. In practice, it is often very difficult to find out to whom a specific policy should be attributed. When British Prime Minister Anthony Eden, during the Hungarian revolution of 1956, gave the orders for the Suez invasion, it was not readily apparent to outsiders whether this decision was his alone, that of the British cabinet, or that of a small group of Tory leaders. The Labour opposition blamed the "diehard reactionaries" or the entire Conservative party, which at the time held a majority in the House of Commons. To the Egyptians, the responsibility seemed to lie with the entire British people, or with all the "colonialist-imperial-istic" powers. The communists attributed the Suez invasion to a conspiracy of "the capitalists" and "imperalist warmongers." People with a lively fantasy, indeed, could think up any number of sinister conspiracies behind the invasion. This example shows the difficulty not only of allocating responsibility for governmental action but also of learning the identity of the origin or maker of specific policies.

As a second aspect, a particular public policy has a definite addressee—a person, group, agency, subject, or foreign state toward whom it is directed. This holds true even if the policy should be one of ignoring a problem or of denying recognition to a foreign government. The addressee usually gives the policy its generic name, such as "labor policy," "foreign policy," or "policy toward the Soviet Union."

A third aspect is the dynamic character of the policy-making process. Not only is a specific policy usually composed of a series of decisions over a period of time, but each decision is the result of interaction among individuals, organized groups, and various public agencies, involving consultations, conferences, smaller decisions, communications, and various pressures and maneuvers by interested parties. This process is quite normal in a free society and likely to take place even without the slightest governmental encouragement, as long as a reasonable amount of publicity attends governmental actions in the making. The rights of petitioning government for grievances, of holding public hearings, and of an inquisitive free press usually give the interested parties sufficient opportunity and early warning so that they can get in on the framing of the governmental action, if the action did not, indeed, originate with them.

Phases of policy making

However, if the making of public policy is not to be left to those special interests that can bring pressure to bear where and when it matters, and if the resulting policy is to be a public policy—that is, the policy of a government elected by a majority to govern on behalf of all the people—then the flow of policy making has to be made to include certain basic phases. There is general agreement about what these phases or steps should be, although the different suggested flow charts vary in some details.

Taking official notice

Policy making begins when government takes official notice of a matter, a situation, or a problem. Such a matter might be brought to its attention by one of the policy makers in executive or legislature, by an administrative agency, by an interest group, by the press, or by the public at large. It could involve the revision of existing laws or policies or the regulation of an entirely new field not hitherto touched upon by governmental action.

Taking official notice of a matter may be limited to a statement as vague as, say, "Air pollution is getting to be a problem." The commitment to action may go no farther than the observation, "Something ought to be done about it." But even at this step, and more so in the later phases of policy making, the prime considerations stem from the rules inherent in the constitutional order: What level of government—local, regional, or national—should concern itself with the problem? What particular agency has jurisdiction over it? What basic limitations, such as those found in the bills of rights of all Western democracies, will inhibit governmental action with respect to the problem at hand?

Fact-finding and consultation

The second step in the flow of policy making involves both fact-finding and consultation with the interested parties. It is difficult in practice to separate these two, for two reasons. (1) In a democracy the opinions and attitudes of interested parties are among the most important kinds of information required for the making of public policy. Although government may have the power to enforce almost any policy it decides upon, there is very little point in ignoring or offending the sentiments of the public the policy affects. For reasons of economy in government, if for no other reason, it is better to rely on the voluntary cooperation of a public satisfied with a new policy, or at least satisfied that it has been heard, than to rely on enforcement alone. (2) The expert knowledge needed for intelligent governmental action is most likely to be found among the interested parties anxious to offer their assistance. To return to the example of air pollution, who would be more qualified to venture an opinion on, say, its legislative regulation, than health authorities, the medical profession, conservation organizations, and automobile engineers? Naturally, the quality of information sources is crucial to policy making, and there can hardly ever be enough effort made to secure independent expertise and to balance antagonistic sources of information against one another.

This second step may involve the holding of public hearings, consultation with organized interests and other agencies, efforts by legislative investigating committees, executive investigators, or commissions of inquiry, and invitations to independent experts or specialists to contribute their knowledge. This is the province also of legislative reference services and of the staff of legislative committees.

Formulating alternative policies

The third phase is the formulation of alternative policies by the public agencies and often also by the interested parties. At this point, we may say, the input of information is tentatively infused with a will, or rather with various desires, to control or refashion the subject under consideration. Even if a policy proposal intends only to make a rule of practices that are already customary, there is still that element of a governmental will that can be authoritatively enforced. At this stage there is also a tendency for camps pro and con to cystallize, for issues to be stated, and for lines to be drawn for the coming battle. Often the formulation of policies is also guided by administrators, who are not only familiar with the subject but also aware of the limited choice of practical measures to achieve various objectives.

Public deliberation

The fourth step involves public deliberation over the alternative policies proposed. This phase takes place largely within the governmental institutions and according to the procedures laid down in the constitution and the customs and usages that have grown up around it. The interests and persons promoting a measure and those opposing it battle each other every step of the way. In a political system such as that of the United States, with its many checks and balances in government, hostile interests can use every single check from powerful legislative committees to the presidential veto and judicial review to oppose an action. In a more streamlined system, such as that of Great Britain, the majority will is so well organized that it possesses what amounts to a practical monopoly on the policy-making process. Nevertheless, the British system allows the major opposing interests their day in court, on the floor of the House of Commons and in the press, without permitting them to obstruct the governmental business.

Owing to the complexities of deliberation under most Western constitutions, the entire process takes place on many levels and in a number of settings—perhaps in several committees and on the floors of both legislative houses, in the executive branch, in party and interest-group conferences outside of the government, among readers' letters and on the editorial pages of newspapers and magazines, at public meetings, and possibly even in the current election campaigns.

Authoritative decision

The fifth part of the flow of policy making brings an authoritative decision. A typical example is the final passage of a law by both houses of a legislature and its signing by the chief executive. At this point the choice between the alternative proposals has been made, and one policy has been designated as "the public policy." Since a law is a kind of command backed by the power of enforcement, this may appear to be the final product—the final output of the policy-making machinery. As will be seen, it is not the end of the flow of policy making.

Many legislative acts are accompanied or supplemented by high-level administrative rule making, which may supply a very substantial part of the content of the policy. If the supplementary rules involve broad policy decisions made at the top of the administrative hierarchy, as distinct from routine decisions at the lowest levels, then they should be regarded as part and parcel of the deliberative process along with the making of laws. Likewise, some executive functions, such as the conduct of foreign relations, may involve very little lawmaking or none at all. Yet they go through the same phases of policy making as the legislative process, except that the deliberative stage is likely to take place among executive agencies, officials, parties, and interest groups, or even representatives of several international powers. The signing of a treaty or a declaration of war marks the authoritative decision at the end of the deliberations.

Implementation

After the authoritative decision come two further steps in the flow. Although their significance may pale by comparison with the decision itself, it would be a gross mistake to ignore them.

First, there is the implementation of the policy decided on, a phase requiring both adequate means and a willingness to abide by the decision. The implementation of a policy may well fall short of success because the policy makers neglected to supply enough funds or an adequate array of rewards and punishments for enforcement. It may fail also because the administrators, police officers, judges, or military men entrusted with the implementation take a dim view of the policy and have ways of getting around it, either by nonenforcement or by deliberate reinterpretation. A system of autonomous government organs and checks and balances particularly invites such abuses. It is not inconceivable, on the other hand, that the implementation of a policy may on occasion be more effective if it substitutes its own proven techniques for those laid down by the framers of the policy, as long as the intent of the policy is maintained.

Feedback

The final phase in the flow of policy making is the feedback. A public policy designed to effect certain results may find its goal elusive or discover unforeseen obstacles. Hence, there should be a feedback process to apprise the policy makers of the shortcomings of their original policy, its failures, loopholes, or unintended by-products. This feedback is frequently supplied by the implementors, who report their experiences in administering or executing a policy, or their dilemmas arising from the adjudication of cases under the policy. Interested parties may also petition or otherwise approach the policy makers for a reconsideration of the decisions made.

In a sense, then, feedback is very likely to reopen the flow of policy making from the beginning by getting the government (1) to take notice of the defects of the existing policy, (2) to have new consultations and to accept the new information along with the earlier results of fact-finding, (3) to formulate new alternative policies amending or repealing the existing policy, (4) to go once more through the stages of the deliberative process, (5) to decide on a new policy, (6) to implement this new policy, and (7) to find out how well it works.

THE LEGISLATIVE PROCESS

Given the legalistic nature of most Western societies and the all-encompassing fabric of customary and civil law, the law-making and law-changing powers of government provide an obvious, central focus for popular self-government. To a much higher degree than in nonlegalistic societies, this legal fabric gives the legislature and executive leadership a ready-made lever to change society.

To be sure, some countries in the throes of modernization will use the massive violence of war or revolution to overcome barriers to social and economic change. Others, such as the mobilization regimes and communist dictatorships, use massive ideological propaganda to change attitudes and goals of the people.[5] But it is no secret how limited and crude violence is in what it can achieve. Revolutionary ideology likewise is a clumsy tool that works only as long as it is believed in fervently. And yet, ideological fervor is itself dysfunctional to rational planning and flexible adaptation, as well as being difficult to maintain. By comparison, the accomplishing of social and economic changes by changing the law, whether by legislative or executive action, can be a superbly sophisticated method, capable of bringing about veritable revolutions without disorder or confusion. In a democratic system, moreover, it is easy to make legislative change follow popular preference by means of the representative process, a feat quite beyond ideological or violent modernization regimes.

It should be noted that the legislative process, although important, is only a part of the entire process of policy making.

[5] For a succinct discussion of legalism, "ideologism," and violence as political styles, see Herbert J. Spiro, *Government by Constitution*. New York: Random House, Inc., 1959, chaps. 13–15. The meaning of the words is not completely identical with the usage here.

We can best see its place by relating legislative activity to each of the steps of policy making discussed earlier.

The initiation and origin of laws

Usually the first step by which policy makers take notice of a problem is related only informally to legislation. Many new subjects of policy making are introduced in connection with the election of lawmakers. Often the competing political parties raise issues, as do organized interests, the public-opinion media, and the public at large, that sometimes lead lawmakers to commit themselves to specific programs if elected. More new subjects of legislative interest are brought to the elected legislators' attention by lobbyists for organized interests and through the channels of public opinion and party organizations outside the legislature.

A third source is the executive branch of government, which in both parliamentary and presidential systems is vitally involved in elections and the issues springing therefrom. It is worth noting that in Great Britain, in the member countries of the British Commonwealth of Nations, and in most continental European legislatures the vast majority of bills proposed come from the executive branch. Seven out of every eight bills before the British House of Commons, for example, are government bills. Three out of every four bills passed by the West German Bundestag are cabinet bills. In the United States Congress, by comparison, most legislative proposals are initiated by individual members or by the party leadership in either house of Congress. This difference in the mode of operation is due largely to the separation of powers in the United States Constitution, which, by barring the President from exercising more than indirect legislative leadership, encourages the initiative of party leaders in House and Senate.

Some Western constitutions also give the right to initiate legislative action to advisory bodies such as economic councils or, by means of the initiative, to the people at large. The latter device was developed to some perfection in Switzerland and on the West Coast of the United States, although it can also be found in many other constitutions, such as Italy's. In the state of California, for example, an "indirect initiative petition" signed by a number of registered voters exceeding 5 percent of the last gubernatorial vote will introduce a measure in the legislature.

If the legislature fails to act within forty days, the measure must be placed directly on the ballot, where it will become constitutional law if approved by a majority of the voters. The initiative in Switzerland, dating back to the 1830s, crystallized in 1891 as follows: A petition signed by 50,000 citizens eligible to vote can introduce a specific matter or a constitutional amendment into the legislature, which within three years must submit a draft corresponding to the intent of the petitioners to a vote of the people at large and in the cantons. At the cantonal level the initiative is also used for ordinary legislation.

Consultation and fact-finding

Consultation and fact-finding are distributed throughout the legislative process and frequently take place informally or during elections. However, there are formal procedures and institutions to ensure the effectiveness of both the consultations with interested groups and the gathering of information. The topical committees of the two houses of the United States Congress, of the West German Bundestag, or of the French or Italian lower house, for example, facilitate the concentration of experts and interest-group-oriented legislators at key points in the legislative process, thus going a long way toward accomplishing the consultation of organized interests. Informal contacts between legislators and lobbyists have become one of the most pervasive aspects of representative government everywhere. The organized interests often seek to create a public climate favorable to their cause by advertising and other forms of publicity, of which the legislator and his constituents sooner or later become aware.

The political parties also provide privileged access to the legislative process to representatives of organized interests who, by campaign contributions, by consistent support, or by personal friendship, have gained an inside track. British political parties, for example, have topical committees that, in consultation with certain interest groups, operate not much differently from legislative committees. Most political parties employ such committees for the drafting of specific planks in campaign platforms.

The topical ministries of the executive branch likewise contribute information and consultation on measures that fall into their fields of specialization. When a bill originates in the executive branch and requires guidance by the cabinet for its passage, as in Great Britain, the topical ministries' expert knowledge as well as their frequent contacts with the appropriate interest groups come to bear on the content of the bill.

Finally, there are routine legislative procedures and institutions for consultation and fact-finding. Most legislatures use investigating committees to gather information relevant to their legislative activity. These investigating committees concentrate sometimes on the conduct of the executive branch, sometimes on any and all goings on in society that may be of legislative interest. The British House of Commons, for example, undertakes none of the investigating made familiar by American congressional and state legislative committees. But it does have two standing committees, Public Accounts and Estimates, which are concerned with the financial conduct of the executive and have the power to send for persons and papers. There are also inquiries by the royal commissions appointed by the crown, which are comparable to some of the presidential commissions in the United States, such as commissions on civil disorders or on violence. Legislative committees and executive agencies in the United States also hold frequent hearings, to which interested groups and executive officials may be invited to supply opinions and information relevant to the policies contemplated. French standing committees can even summon government ministers before them.

Finally, individual legislators, legislative committees, and political parties often have a research staff and the services of a legislative reference service or its equivalent at their disposal to help with the gathering of information. Such legislative services and staff are particularly well developed in the United States. If all else fails in any country, the individual legislator can always gather some of his own facts by means of his contacts with his constituents.

Formulation of alternative policies

The formulation of alternative policies is difficult to isolate as a specific step in the policy-making process, because in one form or another it goes on from its very beginning to the end. Fact-finding and consultation do not necessarily precede the formulation of policy. Normally, the latter occurs in the minds of administrators, legislators, or other public figures after a considerable amount of experience with the problem in question. But frequently the seminal concept of the new policy may be derived a priori from the logic of other extant policies, from a partisan philosophy, or from something called "the best American tradition" or "the best French manner," as the case may be. In either instance, there is likely to be a need for the further gathering of information and for extensive consultation with interested groups regarding the policy's acceptability.

When a policy is formulated by an interest group, moreover, the process of policy making resembles in microcosm that of government itself. When, for example, the Federation of British Industry formulates a policy on foreign trade, it has to take into account an astounding variety of diverging economic-group interests within its own organization, and often it must consult with such other organizations as chambers of commerce, farm interests, and organized labor, not to mention governmental agencies and key personnel. The "inventor" of a specific policy or the officers of an interest group that wishes to adopt the policy often have to spend as much time and effort first on selling their own membership on the policy and then on rallying broad support for it from other interested groups as they spend lobbying. In a typical Western pluralistic society, every organized interest is a little pluralistic group system in itself; each operates much like the whole pluralistic system of organized groups, among which government is only one of many agencies, albeit one with special powers to make its decisions stick. In this world of group balances and compromises, the inventor or formulator of policies, however brilliant, is likely to be like a bull in a china shop unless he uses the only force that can organize enough agents of policy making for action: a concerted effort at persuasion.

By contrast, the policy process in most developing countries is relatively simple. The government party or power holders are too preponderant and the interest groups too few and too weak to be an even match.

Legislative deliberation

Deliberation is the part of the legislative process for which formal constitutional law, standing orders, and other rules of parliamentary procedure have provided in the greatest detail. There are at least two ways of looking at the process of legislative deliberation: one can either consider it as the careful staging of the grand drama of conflicting interests, groups, and personalities on the floor of the legislature and its organs, or one can follow the process of deliberation by means of a flow chart of steps through which a specific measure must pass to become a law. The first approach has been anticipated so broadly in the preceding paragraphs that we can concentrate here on the second manner of analysis, the course of a bill or resolution through a legislature. For the purposes of this discussion, it should be assumed that at the outset there exists at least one complete draft of the bill, which may, of course, be changed substantially before the final decision.

American procedure Legislative procedure in the United States Congress distinguishes chiefly between financial bills, which may originate only in the House, public bills, and special bills. All that is necessary for the introduction of a bill or resolution is that it bear the name of a legislator and be laid on the table of the clerk (House) or secretary (Senate). All bills so introduced receive a number and are referred to one or more of the standing committees. Their titles are printed in the *Congressional Record,* and this is considered the "first reading" of a bill.

The standing committee can, after going through its own process of deliberation, with debates, hearings, establishment of a subcommittee, and so on, take various types of action on the bill. It can amend it, strike out parts, offer an alternative version, or report it unchanged. In the majority of cases, committees decide to "pigeonhole" bills—that is, not to report them to their house at all. To dislodge such an unreported bill from a standing committee requires a "discharge petition" supported by an *absolute majority* of the members of the House. When a bill is reported out by a House committee, it is placed on one of three calendars: tax or appropriation measures on the "Union calendar," other public bills on the "House calendar," and private or special bills on the "Private calendar." These calendars are a device for sorting out the vast number of bills and resolutions coming before the House, and in particular for giving the financial bills the important position they deserve.

The placing of a bill on one of the calendars does not automatically bring it to the floor of the House for debate. Most public bills require a special rule or order from the Rules Committee, which also can amend a bill or pigeonhole it indefinitely as well as determine whether or not the bill is to be open to amendments during the debate. When a bill receives the green light and reaches the floor for its "second reading," the House often transforms itself into the Committee of the Whole in order to relax the rules and quorum requirements of its formal sessions. In this state, the House requires only a quorum of 100, and it can allow every member who desires to speak five minutes to make his point or to offer amendments. During the debate it is customary to give precedence to the spokesmen of the different points of view in the committee reporting the bill before other members of the House are recognized. The opposition to a measure naturally attempts various dilatory maneuvers, such as demanding time-consuming roll calls. But the role of the Speaker as the instrument of the will of the majority party generally enables the will of a majority to prevail. "Closure" can be obtained by a simple majority vote on the "previous question," which is: "Shall the bill be engrossed [reprinted as amended] and read a third time [for final passage]?"

In the American Senate, whose smaller size and greater continuity have rendered unnecessary many of the arrangements of the House for expediting business, even the Committee of the Whole is no longer used except for treaties. But each bill must undergo the three readings and the committee stage. Debate is unlimited except by certain general rules; for example, a senator may not speak more than twice a day on the same subject, and under "unanimous consent" procedures the end of debate is set beforehand. Hence there have been "filibusters," and a number of abortive attempts have been made to impose better controls than the mild and rarely used provisions for closure.

Since the versions of a bill passed by House and Senate must be identical, often a conference committee must be called to arrive at an identical version acceptable to both. This committee usually includes the chairmen and the ranking majority and minority members of the standing committees in charge of the bill in both houses. The agreed final version is accepted or rejected on the floor of both houses without further attempts at amendment. Nevertheless, the conference procedure does allow for a kind of renewal of the preceding legislative battles, again giving the leadership of the standing committee a particular advantage.

Finally, the presidential veto or the "pocket veto" represents another point at which hostile interest can strike down a bill. Since the President is the only federal officer who represents all Americans, his veto power along with his message power and other tools of legislative leadership come closest to being an instrument of pure majority will in the American system. Nevertheless, forcing the reintroduction of a bill or the rallying of two-thirds majorities to override a veto also renews the preceding legislative battles in both houses, allowing the opposition to reenact their defensive skirmishes with the benefit of broader experience.

British procedure   How does the legislative process in Great Britain compare with that in the United States Congress and with similar proceedings in the American state legislatures? The venerable "Mother of Parliaments," as might be expected, in many procedural matters has actually been the originator of our formulas and customs. Even the expression first or second "reading" goes back to the practices of the British Parliament before printing was invented. But there are also some significant variations. Parliament today has very little to do with the actual origination and fashioning of laws. To be sure, congressmen and senators rarely think up and write the laws they introduce, but there can be little doubt about the firm control congressional committees exercise over the form and content of the measures before Congress. The British Parliament, by comparison, has been said to be engaged merely in consenting to laws thought up by parties and organized interests, drawn up by civil servants, and guided through the House of Commons by the government. One should bear in mind, however, that the cabinet and the majority party in the House owe their decisive role to their leadership in the House of Commons and not to an outside source of authority. Parliament may have organized its lawmaking function in a peculiar fashion, but it is still sovereign in Great Britain, though in practice only through its leadership, the cabinet.

Furthermore, there is the same distinction between financial and other public bills, although with rare exceptions bills of both categories now come from the cabinet. Private members' bills and motions have to take their chance by lot on the rare opportunities provided for them. Finally, there are the "private bills," comparable perhaps to our special bills or to the customary petitions for a redress of grievances addressed to Parliament since the earliest days. For these private bills, there are special quasi-judicial proceedings before the Committee on Unopposed Bills or the Committee on Private Bills, the latter holding hearings to allow the opposition to be heard. Money bills in the British system have to originate in the House of Commons, and since the 1911 reform the House of Lords can no longer even amend or reject such a bill. But the Standing Orders of the House of Commons bar it from considering any proposal for the expenditure of funds that is not recommended by the crown. In practice, this means that budgets are made by the chancellor of the exchequer, who collects departmental estimates and, with the help of treasury officials, proposes the revenue measures to match the projected expenditures of the next fiscal year.

When the budget is submitted by the cabinet to the House of Commons, the House sits as Committee of the Whole, either of Ways and Means (revenue) or of Supply (appropriations), to consider it. The unwieldy size and unselected character of this body, by contrast with the expertise and efficiency of the far smaller finance committees of the French and American legislatures, tells much about the preponderance of the British executive in the making of the budget—an activity once considered the bulwark of popular government against the executive. This impression is further confirmed by the reluctance of the cabinet to lift the veil of secrecy from the details of the budget in advance. Its custom of regarding any reduction of items in the budget as an implied vote of no confidence, finally, reduces the role of the House to that of a rubber stamp. Only the loyal opposition, which lacks the vetoes to do any harm, has much opportunity to assert itself during the debate on the budget and to utilize it for attacks on government policy. On the other hand, this centralization of financial power in the hands of the cabinet recommends itself for economy in government, in contrast to the diffusion of spending power among, say, the committees of the American Congress in earlier days.

In the House of Commons, nonfinancial public bills and motions nearly always come from the cabinet, which preempts most of the time available for debate, even though the number of public bills rarely exceeds about seventy-five a year. According to standard procedure, a public bill or motion is introduced when a minister (who is always a member of Parliament) hands a dummy of the bill to the clerk, who reads its title. Upon the "first reading" the bill is printed and distributed. The second reading involves the presentation by the sponsoring minister of the chief purposes and devices of the bill, giving the opposition an opportunity to move for a postponement or to propose alternative solutions to the problems with which the bill deals. The minister is allowed a final rejoinder to the arguments of the opposition. The second reading ends with a vote, upon which the tenure of office of the cabinet depends if the bill is a cabinet bill. A negative vote leads to its resignation and, possibly, the dissolution of the House. An affirmative vote indicates the support of a majority in the House for the basic purposes of the bill, whereupon it is sent to the Committee of the Whole or to one of the standing committees for consideration in detail. Unlike American committees, the British committee in question is not at liberty to change the basic purposes of a bill or to pigeonhole it. It must report the bill as soon as possible, depending on the agenda agreed on by the whips of both parties. When it is reported out, the entire House can consider, and vote on, the bill's details.

At this point, it becomes necessary for the House of Commons to limit debate and to regulate the vast flow of amendments and motions proposed. The Speaker has the power to silence members who stray from the subject and, by his use of the "kangaroo," to select amendments for debate. There is also the "guillotine," a timetable for the discussion of the various stages of a bill, which sets a specific time for a vote on each stage. Closure can be moved at any time, both on the whole bill or any part thereof, but it must be accepted by the Speaker, who will want to be sure the opposition has had its day in court. These powers and the urgency of the governing majority to get its business done give the Speaker an awesome task of maintaining a fair balance between majority and opposition, and between the front and back benchers on both sides of the aisle. If it were not for his scrupulous impartiality, the proceedings might easily become a mere show of democratic encounter and compromise for the benefit of the galleries.

The final adoption of a bill is preceded by the third reading, and at this time only verbal changes to add polish are in order. The bill or resolution must then be accepted or rejected as it stands. Upon passage in the House of Commons, the bill still has to go to the House of Lords, unless it has already been passed there, and to the monarch for approval. Since the reform of 1911, and even more since the Parliament Act of 1949, the House of Lords has lost its equality in legislative power with the House of Commons, which can now override the Lords by passing the bill in question twice (1911–1949: three times) in consecutive sessions, during no less than one year (1911–1949: two years). This still gives the upper house a full veto during a government's last year in office. Custom has it that the House of Lords ought not to defeat a measure for which the government has received a specific mandate at the preceding election.

In the House of Lords, the three readings and the use of a standing committee for the revision of public bills are also the standard procedure. The Lords make much use of the Committee of the Whole and enjoy a reputation for well-considered revision, owing to the absence of pressure of time and constituency groups as well as to their ample supply of well-qualified former prime ministers, high judges, and other experts in the fine art of law-making. The granting of the Royal Assent to legislation, the final, authoritative decision, also takes place in the Lords' Chamber, to which the Gentleman Usher of the Black Rod summons the Commons. The Royal Assent is given in Norman French, the usual formula being *La reine le veult*. Since 1854 the assent has been read not by the monarch himself but by three commissioners. There has not been an executive veto *(la reine s'avisera)* since 1707.

French procedure   In the French parliaments of the Third and Fourth Republics, the procedure differed in many ways from the British approach. The French distinguish chiefly between *projets de loi* (government bills) and *propositions de loi* (private member bills), although the strong *commissions* (committees) of the lower house always took control of both kinds as if they were their own. Bills were introduced by being given to the Assembly president, who read their title, had them printed, and assigned them to the appropriate commission. It should be noted that in France, as in the United States but not in Great Britain, the crucial second reading occurs only after the committee stage. The various topical commissions of foreign affairs or of the interior, or the powerful finance committee, can revise bills any way they want to, and sometimes they come up with draft bills of their own. Each committee appoints from among its members a *rapporteur* to study and prepare a report on each particular bill, a role in which ambitious young deputies invest much effort.

The staging of the floor debate tells much about the distribution of power. The debate is opened by a speech of the rapporteur (or rapporteurs if several committees were involved), setting forth the major objectives of the bill for general discussion. Significantly, the minister or other author of the bill gets a chance to speak only after the rapporteur. The recognized party groups of the chamber may designate spokesmen, who receive a privileged place on the agenda for the presentation of the view of each party. Individual members take their turn in the order in which they have signed in on the president's list of speakers. The general discussion is closed by a vote on the question of "passing to the articles"—that is, to a discussion of details—or, if the Assembly disagrees with the committee report, on returning the bill to the committee. Despite its occasional unruliness and the weak regulatory powers of the Assembly president, the French lower house is comparatively efficient in getting its business done. Closure can be voted by a majority vote as soon as spokesmen for and against a bill have been heard. There is also a special procedure of "urgent discussion," which can be invoked by a minister, a standing commission, and formerly also by private members. Under this rule committees must report within three days, and the debate must follow immediately and continuously until the final vote is taken.

From the lower house of the Third and Fourth Republics of France, a bill still had to go to the indirectly elected upper house, the Senate (Third Republic) or Council of the Republic (Fourth Republic). The Senate had legislative equality with, and acted much like, the Chamber of Deputies. But the Council of the Republic could only initiate laws in the lower house and was allowed two months for the examination of bills passed by the National Assembly. Under "urgent discussion" it could take twice the time taken by the lower house. On financial measures it could neither initiate new expenditures nor reduce revenues, but it was allowed to take just as long with the budget as did the Assembly. Before 1954 the Council of the Republic could, by a negative vote of an absolute majority of its members, force the Assembly to override its veto of a bill with a like majority, an undertaking rarely possible in view of the shaky majorities of governments under the Fourth Republic. In 1954, however, this veto power was taken away and replaced with the Third Republic practice of the *navette,* the shuttling back and forth between the houses, for as long as one hundred days, of bills on which there was no agreement.

As soon as the de Gaulle (Fifth) Republic took over from the Fourth Republic in 1958, the wings of the powerful National Assembly were clipped. Its control over the cabinet was whittled down decisively, its range of legislative activity curtailed, and the other great national institutions—the presidency, the Senate, and the Constitutional Council—strengthened at its expense. These changes are reflected in the processes of legislative deliberation, where the cabinet now exercises a degree of control over its own bills it never possessed before. Government bills have priority in either house and can, at the discretion of the cabinet, be sent either to a standing committee or to a special committee created by the cabinet, evidently for the purpose of circumventing entrenched committee power. This special committee must bring the bill to the floor within three months. The Assembly's power of discussing and amending a bill or any part thereof is hamstrung further by the government's right to object to discussion of any amendment that has not been considered by the committee. Even more incisive is the right of the government to request that the Assembly or Senate accept or reject with a single vote the entire bill or any part thereof in the form determined by the government. This rule can limit the legislative power of the French Parliament to a mere veto, such as the American President has.

Special safeguards also assure executive control over the passage of financial legislation. The finance minister introduces the budget, whereupon it is sent to the finance commission. The report to the floor has to be in very general terms, and there may be no amendments that increase or decrease expenditure.

If the budget for a fiscal year should be delayed beyond its beginning, the government may also request authority to reissue by decree a budget identical with that approved for the preceding year.

German procedure   In the West German Bundestag, the procedure resembles in many ways the deliberations of the French Assembly before 1958. As under the Fourth Republic, for example, the agenda of the Bundestag is made up by the Assembly president sitting together with other party leaders of all recognized groups in the Council of Elders. In the Fourth Republic, the committee chairmen were a part of this council that determined the agenda. In the Fifth Republic, the agenda is determined by the cabinet. The three readings also follow the French model. The committees are small, but there are many more of them than in France, owing perhaps to the German preference for specialization and compartmentalization, which also marks the highly technical character of the proceedings in committee. Committee deliberations are generally carried on in closed session, although the organized interests are allowed ample contact with committee members.

In the plenary debates on a bill the rapporteur and chairman of the reporting committee enjoy some prominence, but not as much as once in France. Speakers have to enter their names on the president's list. Ministers, rapporteurs, and the members of the upper house, the Bundesrat (who are usually ministers or high civil servants in the state governments), may speak whenever they desire. The Bundestag president presides and can silence, and even exclude for the day, speakers who stray from the subject or become disorderly. In sharp contrast to the tone of technical, expert objectivity of the committee meetings, the speeches from the rostrum to the fully assembled Bundestag tend to be aimed at the galleries and, sometimes, at the microphones of radio stations, which have broadcast some of the more important debates. In financial legislation, the Bundestag accords its cabinet almost as much authority as does the British House of Commons. Only the government may introduce or increase proposals for expenditures or taxes. On the other hand, there is a strong finance committee, which can pare down estimates and appropriations, a body far more effective owing to its smallness and concentrated expertise than the British Committee of the Whole.

The West German upper house, the Bundesrat, is unlike any other legislative body in the West in that it has no terms or sessions and its members, the appointees (and often cabinet members) of the state governments, have to vote strictly according to instructions from their governments, somewhat as the members of the United Nations General Assembly. Consequently, there are state delegations but no political parties in the Bundesrat. Topical committees, corresponding to the topical ministries of the *Länder* (states) and the federal government, coordinate the legislative activities of the executive branches on both levels. Each state government has a representative on every committee. Legislative proceedings before the infrequent plenary meetings of the Bundesrat consist chiefly of voting on bills that have already been circulated among the appropriate ministries of both levels and thoroughly discussed in committee. Each *Land*, in rough proportion to its population, has three to five votes, which must be cast *en bloc*. The character of the proceedings only rarely develops into a debate, but permits the Bundesrat to dispose of ten to twenty bills in a single afternoon. In some subjects the participation of the Bundesrat in federal lawmaking is not equal to that of the Bundestag, although in the more important kinds of laws it is. In case of disagreement between the houses, a mediation committee is created, with a representative from each state delegation and a like number of Bundestag members, to produce a compromise acceptable to both houses.

Authoritative decision

The final decisions on each bill occur at several levels and points in the process. Some decisions fall even before a fully drafted version is introduced in the legislature. Some occur in the form of votes in committee and on the floor, both on articles or amendments and on the whole bill. The final decision, for which the procedure is usually laid down in the constitution, occurs when a bill becomes law after having been duly passed by one or two houses of the legislature and signed by the chief executive. Some of these aspects have already been touched upon, especially the stages before submission of a bill to the legislature. The rest require some explanation.

Legislative voting   In the American Congress the most common manner of voting is by sound of voice *(viva voce)* or, in case of doubt, by a *rising vote,* which enables the ayes and noes to be counted. Also, on request of one fifth of a quorum, tellers designated by both sides place themselves in front of the desk of the presiding officer to count first the ayes, then the noes, filing through between them. Finally, there is the roll-call vote, in which the clerk calls off the names and permanently records the votes cast by each member of the house. Owing to the pressures of constituency and organized interests, congressmen and senators are understandably reluctant to go on record in this permanent fashion except on the most uncontroversial subjects. Roll calls are also time-consuming, which makes them a favorite delaying tactic for groups opposing a measure.

In other Western legislatures, the voting procedures differ little from those in the Congress. On the European continent, voting by show of hands is popular both in committee and in the fully assembled house. In the British House of Commons and its Commonwealth equivalents there are also the divisional lobbies, into which the members of Parliament file through "yes" and "no" doors to facilitate counting. This method of voting is also used on the Continent. In German usage it is called *Hammelsprung,* which refers to the leaping of sheep over a low barrier to facilitate counting. However, there are three doors, *yes, no,* and *abstention,* since continental practice allows formal abstention; in Anglo-American usage the unwilling legislator simply does not answer the roll or is absent when the vote is taken.

Executive approval or veto   A duly passed bill does not become a law until it has also been signed and proclaimed by the chief executive, an action which is supposed to follow upon passage through the legislature. In some Western systems of government, the executive has an opportunity at this point to prevent the bill from becoming law by withholding his signature. It will be recalled that the Royal Assent in Great Britain has become a mere formality during the past two and a half centuries. In the United States, however, the presidential veto has become an important instrument of legislative leadership. An outright veto involves returning a bill with the President's objections to the house where it originated, whereupon Congress can attempt either to satisfy the objections or to muster two thirds of the vote in both chambers to override the veto. An unsigned bill in the President's hands will become law without his signature after ten days, provided Congress is still in session by the end of this period. Since there is usually a very considerable volume of legislation passing through the presidential office at the end of a session, this provision gives the President a "pocket veto" that requires no explanation and cannot be overriden.

Still, a presidential veto or pocket veto only empowers the chief executive to accept or reject a bill in its entirety. Presidents have often had to swallow their dissatisfaction with a "rider" tacked onto a bill in order to sign into law the bill itself, of which they approved. The governor of the state of California, by contrast, and the governors of three fourths of the other states of the Union also have an "item veto" that enables them to strike out or reduce (but not to increase) any item of appropriation or expenditure in the budget. A few American state constitutions even allow such an item veto to be exercised toward all legislation. Needless to add, the "item veto" increases executive influence on the final stages of lawmaking to the point of active participation.

In the Fourth Republic, the president also had the function of promulgating the laws within ten days of their passage by Parliament. Within this period he could return the bill for consideration to the two houses of legislature. It was generally understood, however, that these veto powers were a means for remedying technical defects in legislation rather than a tool for presidential policy making. The constitution of the Fifth Republic of France continued the presidential power of returning a bill for reconsideration, lengthening the period for executive scrutiny from ten to fifteen days. The stature of the presidency gives the exercise of this power political overtones. The federal president of the West German Republic also has not only the right but the duty to refuse his signature to a bill containing aspects of questionable constitutionality. The president of the Republic of Italy, by contrast, has a real veto power, to be exercised by returning bills for reconsideration with suggestions for change. Although sparingly used, none of the presidential vetoes has so far been overridden by the Italian parliament.[6]

The British tradition of executive vetoes deserves an additional comment. Although long in disuse in Great Britain itself, the veto is still very much in use in the British colonies, where governors use it along with very considerable decree-making powers on behalf of the crown. Even in the self-governing dominions of the Commonwealth until the early twentieth century, governors-general appointed by the crown exercised the power of "reservation"—reserving bills of dominion legislatures for the signification of the sovereign's pleasure. On some subjects of legislation, such reservation was obligatory. Before 1900, furthermore, the monarch and his cabinet in London could "disallow" (annul) dominion laws duly passed by a dominion legislature and assented to by the dominion governor or governor-general. This, too, is a power now in disuse.

Western legalism

This survey of legislative policy making in developed countries should be understood in the context of the central position of lawmaking. This is the result of two important characteristics of Western government. One is the strong legalistic undercurrent of society, government, and politics, an element quite alien to most of the new nations. The legalistic approach naturally brings out the importance of lawmaking as the mechanism for changing the legal rules of the game. Second, there is general presumption that other governmental functions, such as administration and adjudication, should be subordinated to the laws made by the legislative process. While there is some talk of judicial supremacy in the United States and in West Germany, the bulk of judicial activity in both countries still consists of applying the laws made by the legislatures to specific cases. Despite the specter of executive predominance in America and in France, or of a self-contained administrative state in France, Italy, and West Germany, the legislative power is still a most

[6] It should be noted, however, that the inability of the Italian Chamber of Deputies to rally overriding majorities may be the result of the rigid multiparty system rather than of the authority of the presidency.

potent directive and, at times, corrective force that can exercise a good deal of control over executive and administrative policy.

EXECUTIVE POLICY MAKING

Many of the legislative programs originate and are drafted within the executive branch. The executive generally is also given powers and the responsibility of guiding these programs through the legislature. In addition it controls the execution and administration of these laws, which often require the development of more specific administrative policies within the broad principles laid down by the law. Beyond these lie still further areas of executive policy making, including some that may appear purely technical or "purely administrative." As an example, the executive power over personnel policy in army and civil service and over antidiscrimination clauses in federal contracts and federally insured loans turned out to be major devices to assure to all Americans regardless of color or creed the constitutional rights hitherto denied to some.

Given the size of the modern executive apparatus and its vast involvement in the activities of society, legally, economically, and otherwise, anything government does or fails to do immediately influences, hurts, persuades, or pressures millions of people, often without any clear intent on the part of the executive leaders. Obviously, it is desirable that such extraordinary power be used with skill and for deliberate purposes, for which the executive leadership can be held responsible through the democratic process. Such considerations have motivated the vast efforts of persuasion, the press conferences, fireside chats, radio broadcasts, and television appearances of modern chief executives and their representatives.

There are also large fields of executive activity that normally involve little or no reliance on legislative authorization. In foreign affairs and defense, for example, some of the most crucial decisions for a country's survival or internal development are made exclusively by executive officials, who may even be in civil service tenure positions from which they can be fired only for cause. Less well known are the extensive promotional and regulatory activities that modern executive branches carry on in economy and society, and in Europe even in culture and in the fine arts. There are also the vast management responsibilities of modern governments today, which extend from the management of a nation's resources, the purity of its air and water, the wildlife and health of its forests, or its energy sources, to the management of such public enterprises as the post office, European railroads, or the vast nationalized or public industries and utilities of Great Britain, France, Italy, West Germany, Switzerland, or Scandinavia, not to mention many developing countries.

Nonlegislative rule making

A good deal of executive policy is customarily laid down in legal enactments that for all intents and purposes look like and have the same effect as the laws legislatures make. Essentially three kinds of such legal directives can be found in most Western systems of government: (1) general powers of issuing lawlike decrees or ordinances, sometimes contingent upon a state of emergency or legislative authorization; (2) powers of filling in the details of duly passed legislation, either generally recognized or specifically authorized by the laws in question; and (3) administrative rules relating to the management of the administration. These three categories are not always easy to keep apart. The practices of executive rule making in the major Western countries will, therefore, be discused country by country rather than by categories.

American practice   The American presidential power to issue orders and directives is regarded as inherent in his duty to "take care that the laws be faithfully executed," his pledge to "preserve, protect, and defend the Constitution," and the ordinance-making powers necessary to direct the varied activities of the executive branch. The use of these powers is particularly prevalent in activities that go beyond the mere execution of laws, such as military affairs or the personnel policy of the administration. In the conduct of foreign relations, the practice of concluding "executive agreements" rather than treaties, which would require Senate approval, has long been accepted as an outgrowth of the inherent power of issuing directives in the international field, in which the initiative clearly rests in the hands of the President. In wartime or grave emergency, the power to issue executive decrees becomes practically a general legislative power. President Lincoln upon inauguration proceeded to raise and spend money and to build up the armed forces of the Union for four months before he even called Congress into session. Later wartime Presidents followed not far behind his example in their use of the war power for enactments normally left to the Congress.

The practice of filling in details in duly passed legislation developed naturally with the rising complexity of the regulatory tasks Congress tackled. In the eighteenth and early nineteenth centuries, lawmakers could state their intent in simple, broad principles that required little additional clarification. The regulation of the complex aspects of a modern economy and society has raised a multitude of technical difficulties, so that administrators need considerable discretion in applying a law to widely varying circumstances. Congress has resorted to tacit or express delegations, to the President or to particular departments or agencies, of the power to fill in details. The Trade Agreement Act of 1934, for example, empowered the President at his discretion to lower tariff rates with some countries by as much as 50 percent.

In comparison to the other two categories, administrative rule making may appear a less lofty function, but it is vital to the functioning of any administrative organization. Much administrative rule making pertains to the internal practices of administrative agencies, and it may concern almost any subject from sick-leave provisions to accounting practices. Other administrative rules affect the public, especially those rules made by the regulatory commissions and agencies. Altogether more than a hundred federal agencies have the power to issue rules and regulations. Congress has attempted to safeguard the public with the Administrative Procedures Act of 1946, which directs the regulatory agencies to publicize their organization and procedures and to give interested parties advance notice of proposed rules, a fair hearing, and the right to counsel.

British practice   In Great Britain, the use of genuine executive decrees has waned along with the real power of the monarchy and with the functions of the Privy Council, a large, unwieldy body that once was the monarch's chief instrument of government. It is composed of some three hundred persons, including all present and past cabinet members, Commonwealth prime ministers, and high judicial and church officials. Excepting certain of its committees, such as its judicial committee, the council's functions today are largely ceremonial. The proclamations or "orders in council" issued by the queen are usually made only upon the advice of the cabinet ministers, who are responsible for them to the House of Commons. Typical subjects for an order in council are the granting of town charters or, under the Emergency Powers Act of 1920, the proclamation of a state of emergency for one week, after which period Parliament must confirm the executive emergency powers or allow them to lapse.

The filling in of details in legislation as well as rule-making powers are usually provided for by delegation of power from Parliament to the cabinet, the Privy Council, individual departments and agencies, public corporations such as run the nationalized industries, or private companies. As a result of this delegation of legislative power, so-called statutory instruments have been issued by departments and agencies at a rate of ten and fifteen times the number of laws passed by Parliament. Interested parties are carefully consulted before they are drawn up and the majority of statutory instruments must go before Parliament for validation, or at least a possible veto, according to the legislation on which they are based. The House of Commons, in fact, has established a Select Committee on Statutory Instruments, which scrutinizes these ordinances and, in case of doubt, brings them to the attention of the House. The making of administrative rules falls within the same category, except that these rules rarely have to undergo scrutiny by Parliament. This lapse of popular control led to severe criticisms, most notably by the Lord Chief Justice Hewart, who in his book *The New Despotism* (1929) warned against the creation of a bureaucratic power complex with the unrestrained right to make its own administrative rules and decisions in its dealings with the public. Since that time, recourse by injured parties to the courts has been reinstituted.

French practice   The French have a tradition of using executive decrees to a much greater extent than Anglo-American practice would consider compatible with popular government. In spite of the dominance of the Chamber of Deputies under the Third and of the National Assembly under the Fourth Republic, the number of *decrèt-lois* issued by the executive was quite considerable. Under the Fourth Republic, in particular, the French Parliament twice voted "full powers," first to Premier Paul Reynaud in 1948 and then again to Mendès-France in 1955, to issue decrees covering vast fields of economic regulation, but limited in their duration and effect on the budget. Parliament still had to ratify the decrees.

In 1958, after the leaders of the collapsing Fourth Republic had called on General de Gaulle to take power, the Assembly granted him full powers to deal with the emergency and to draw up a new constitution. The emergency powers applied for six months and covered everything save interferences with fundamental rights and liberties. The constitution of the Fifth Republic, by specifically limiting the jurisdiction of Parliament to a list of enumerated subjects of legislation, has legalized the stream of *decrèt-lois* of the executive. The Conseil d'État, a unique administrative tribunal, advises the cabinet with regard to the form and legality of executive decrees and must be consulted whenever the Assembly grants the government "special powers" for one year to issue decrees. Such powers under article 38 of the constitution were granted in 1960, after de Gaulle had suppressed the revolt of the French settlers in Algeria. Under article 16, which has never been used, the president himself can proclaim an emergency and take all steps he deems necessary upon consultation with the Constitutional Council. His power would undoubtedly include the issuing of executive decrees, but the article specifies also that Parliament shall be in session and cannot be dissolved during the duration of the state of emergency.

Regarding the filling-in of legislation, the National Assembly has long been in the habit of regulating certain matters by *loi-cadre,* or framework law, delegating an unsually large part of its legislative authority to administrative discretion. The reason for this extraordinary confidence in administrative wisdom and integrity lies in the long tradition of the French administrative state and in the high caliber of the civil service, which is recruited from the best schools and specially trained. Administrative discretion also includes broad departmental powers to issue rules and regulations, which are considered an exercise of the police power of the state. The ubiquitous Conseil d'État checks the more important rules and regulations for conflict with the laws or the citizen's constitutional liberties. Complaints by injured parties are not addressed to the courts, as in Britain and the United States, but to the Conseil d'État, which operates also in the capacity of a high tribunal of administrative law.

German practice   In the German executive tradition, executive decree-making power and administrative discretion also play a very prominent role. The executive was strong before 1945, because autocratic monarchy was abandoned only in 1918. Administrative discretion still is all-pervasive because, as in France, the tradition of the administrative state, especially in Prussia, goes back much further than that of any other modern governmental institution. After the fall of the monarchy in 1918, the constitution of the democratic Republic of Weimar established a strong, popularly elected president, not unlike the constitution of the Fifth Republic after 1962. To this president the constitution in its article 48 entrusted largely undefined emergency powers as an "emergency brake," in case responsible politicians were to lose control over the as yet untried democratic institutions of the young republic.

As it developed, the crises of the Weimar Republic occurred with such frequency that a veritable flood of presidential emergency decrees was issued under article 48. During the last years before Hitler came to power, these decrees finally became the only legislative output of the federal government, as the Reichstag (Federal Diet) was stalemated by a combined majority of uncooperative Nazi and Communist deputies. Among these emergency decrees were some suspending certain civil rights and fundamental freedoms of the citizens, others alternately forbidding and allowing the Nazi storm troopers and other paramilitary groups to parade in the streets, and some replacing the legal (and staunchly democratic) government of the state of Prussia with federal (and pro-Nazi) authority. After Hitler was appointed chancellor, moreover, the Reichstag passed an Enabling Act granting him full powers to suspend parts of the constitution and to rule by executive decree.

After these experiences with executive power, the framers

of the present West German Basic Law of 1949 understandably shied away from granting any such decree-making powers to their federal president, who was weakened also in other ways. The Basic Law of the Bonn Republic also provides for a "legislative emergency"—a state in which the Bundestag may be unwilling or unable to pass urgent government legislation—but it is carefully hedged about: the cabinet, the federal president, and the Bundesrat must agree on the emergency legislation passed in this manner over the heads of the elected representatives of the people in the Bundestag, and there is a time limit of six months.

The cabinet and each ministry also have sweeping powers to issue orders for the purpose of carrying out the laws and running the administrative apparatus, both of the federation and the state governments. German practice distinguishes between orders of law (*Rechtsverordnungen*) and administrative rules (*Verwaltungsverordnungen*). The orders of law are generally based on a specific legislative authorization of the cabinet or a minister to regulate or to fill in the details of a law; they have the force of law. The administrative rules pertain more to the organization and procedures of administrative agencies and their personnel. In the majority of cases, and especially when the administration of federal laws by the state governments is involved, the Bundesrat has to give its approval to both orders of law and administrative rules. The public can have recourse to administrative or to constitutional courts.

POLICY IMPLEMENTATION AND APPLICATION

Presumably, the lawmaking and rule-making activities of executive and legislative bodies set into motion a mechanism of administration to implement the decisions made. Neither legislators nor executive and top administrative policy makers can do more than issue the relevant commands and observe their execution. It is up to the administrative role structures, and sometimes to nonadministrative structures such as churches or social and economic organizations,[7] to embark on a pattern of activities that will carry out the policy goals decided upon.

[7] See, for example, the remarks on southern Italy by Joseph La Palombara, *Bureaucracy and Political Development*. Princeton, N.J.: Princeton University Press, 1963, p. 42.

The dividing line between policy and administration is difficult to draw, considering the presence of such factors as lobbying in administration, and its precise location varies considerably among different systems and over time. Its basic significance, however, is as crucial to comparative analysis as the distinction between tradition and modernity. Administration does not include the setting of policy goals, except within such goals as may have been laid down by the policy makers. The policy makers, of course, may well include heads of administrative agencies or technical specialists on the subject under consideration. There are also policy implications in the manner of implementation. Administrative policies for the maintenance of the administrative organization, however, are part of administration, separate from the making of public policies as the term has been used here.

We are dealing, then, primarily with *how* administrators pursue predetermined and well-understood goals and how, in so doing, they behave toward one another and toward their environment. Some of the relevant aspects were implied in Chapter 7 in our discussion of recruitment and socialization for civil service systems as well as in Max Weber's definition of bureaucracy. What remains to be discussed is the range of administrative behavior from advanced to developing countries and from democracies to totalitarian regimes.

Basic attitudes toward administration

How administrators pursue the goals decided upon by policy makers is determined, among other factors, by basic attitudes, which differ considerably between advanced and developing countries. Although public administration is prima facie a rather modern phenomenon, a mostly traditional environment together with a shortage of urbane, modernly educated persons gives developing administrative systems certain distinctive behavioral features of traditionalism or transitionalism. Often there is an insufficiently developed functional specificity about administrative actions and policies, complemented by the relative lack of functionally specific associations among the public. In their decisions the policy makers themselves often tend to be more expressive than instrumental, preferring the grand gesture or symbol to the pragmatic attack on the nearly insoluble problems their countries face. Their administrators understand this expressive intent all too well and may, if anything, contribute further expressive gestures or symbols, rather than attempting to carry out a policy that was not meant to be carried out in the first place. This is a major source of the gap between theory and practice in developing administration, which so often manifests itself in such forms as unfinished major building projects, unfunded or insufficiently funded projects of regional development, or politically motivated highway projects in countries without automobiles.

Social bases of administrators

Another major variable in administrative development relates to the system of social stratification. In traditional autocracies, the administrators are closely and obviously subservient to a small, privileged class of oligarchs and not to any reasonable definition of the "public" interest. During the transitional phase, especially in bureaucratic elite systems, the administrators become considerably more independent, except that, as in France [8] before 1945, a new upper class of well-educated civil service families may develop and monopolize that "public interest" with a generous admixture of self-interest. This phenomenon is a matter of general experience in many transitional and even rather advanced administrative systems from Germany to Thailand. As Joseph La Palombara explains, American efforts to bring scientific management to public administration from Bangkok to Bologna are often stymied by the social elitist consciousness of many a foreign bureaucracy, which balks at the egalitarian and democratic overtones of American scientific management. In a bureaucratic elite system, the word "public" in public administration may merely denote a paternalistic benevolence toward the masses on the part of the self-perpetuating bureaucratic elite.

Corruption and patronage

A third problem relates to the role of corruption and patronage in developing administrations. During the early stages of nation building, a developing national party system often requires

[8] See, for example, the remarks of Maurice Duverger in Martin Kriesberg, ed., *Public Administration in Developing Countries.* Washington, D.C.: Brookings, 1965, pp. 8–10.

spoils and patronage in order to maintain large, far-flung organizations. Rapid economic development likewise has been quite compatible with public venality and corruption among government officials, at least in the early stages. The alternative—a strong bureaucracy during this phase—may present a major threat to the development of parties and political responsibility. A well-established bureaucratic elite has been a most successful rival to the parties, for example, of Imperial Germany and Japan. Developing private enterprise likewise is likely to suffer from the constant interference of an incorruptible, meddlesome bureaucracy, whose concern for economic development and planning is more often hostile rather than sympathetic to private initiative. The implicit sense of rivalry of the developing central bureaucracy toward autonomous political or economic structures applies also to the development of local self-government at the periphery.[9] A modernizing central elite is not anxious to develop local power unless the latter is either under central control or at least motivated by the same modernizing zeal. The perfect system in France and elsewhere is a good example of central bureaucratic control over local government resulting from bureaucratic elitism.

The social setting of developing administration can, for several reasons, also contribute to the prevalence of corruption. One is the need of many an African head of state or Latin-American *presidente* for absolute personal loyalty of his staff. Surrounded by rivals plotting *coups d'état* or even assassination, these chief executives and their ministers are too preoccupied with their personal and political security to worry much about their staff's administrative competence, training, or attitude toward public service. The loyalty of family members, for example, or of the lifelong clique is better insurance against hostile coups than a nonnepotistic or graftproof service. The low salaries and limited or graft-ridden promotion system similarly may make corruption a way of life for civil servants who have to feed a family and maintain dignified appearances.[10]

The problem of corruption raises questions also of recruit-

[9] See especially Fred Riggs in La Palombara, *Bureaucracy and Political Development*, pp. 127–135.

[10] See especially Frank Tannenbaum in Kriesberg, *Public Administration in Developing Countries*, pp. 36–42.

ment, training, and socialization.[11] Graft and bribery are not likely to be cured by raising salaries, even though low salaries may well have been a contributing factor. To break the entrenched custom of the *mordida* or any kind of "tipping expectation" of public servants, only a career civil service as described in the last chapter will suffice. Once there is a broad and well-trained manpower base from which persons can be recruited at an early age for a lifetime career, proper socialization within the service can also instill in them an appreciation for the values and integrity desirable in a career service. Control mechanisms, such as auditing and investigating cases of possible corruption, have only a limited deterrence value, although they are widely used in all administrative systems including the most advanced. The best disciplinary controls are the subtle inducements of promotion, morale, and career satisfaction, provided that a setting of career ethos and service solidarity makes these rewards meaningful.

TOTALITARIAN ADMINISTRATION

Development of a loyal bureaucracy

Both the haphazard control mechanisms of developing administrations and the relatively superfluous disciplinary controls of advanced civil service systems are a far cry from the vast systems of political control that direct and supervise the administrative leviathan in totalitarian countries. In communist countries, the transition from developing administration to totalitarian control presents problems of its own; Lenin, for example, lamented that five years after the revolution of 1917 the party had good political control only over the few thousand state officials at the very top of the vast transitional bureaucracy: "Down below, however, there are hundreds of thousands of old officials who came to us from the Tsar and from bourgeois society and who, sometimes consciously and sometimes unconsciously, work against us." [12]

---

[11] See also the contributions of E. Eliot Kaplan and Roy W. Crawley in Kriesberg, *Public Administration in Developing Countries,* pp. 124–138 and 162–176.

[12] Quoted by Merle Fainsod in La Palombara, *Bureaucracy and Political Development,* p. 250. Earlier, the local councils (soviets) of

Only massive training and public education programs over a long period allowed the Soviet state eventually to build up a new and loyal bureaucracy, ending the cumbersome task of police and party supervision over the bureaucrats and the military inherited from the old regime.

The early problems of communist administration in Eastern Europe, China, and North Korea very likely resembled the first decade of the Soviet Union. At first—and sometimes, as in Red China, again and again—party control would assert itself with a vast political purge of the bureaucracy and the placement of trusted party members into the key positions of the administration at all levels. Such measures, however, could not make up for the lack of reliable manpower nor screen out the gathering swarms of opportunists. At the local and regional levels, therefore, party-guided soviets or people's congresses (China) would intervene and exercise control over the bureaucrats. The object of control in this case was not so much corruption, bungling, and laxity as political disloyalty.

The early days of the Nazi dictatorship were another case in point. Here the takeover of the German career service was effected by means of a special civil service act, passed within a few months of Hitler's appointment as chancellor. First, the previous prohibition of Nazi membership for civil servants in the largest state, Prussia, was revoked, allowing large numbers of Nazi recruits in the service to jump on the bandwagon. Then the civil service act provided the incentive for a purge by allowing for denunciation and dismissal of civil servants on grounds of "political unreliability," an open invitation to Nazis old and new to denounce their bosses and take over their jobs. It is fair to say that this measure broke the moral fiber of the German career service at the same time that it established effective party control over the bureaucracy.

Administrative control and responsibility

Once the full-fledged totalitarian administration has evolved, it occupies a very important position in the totalitarian system.

---

workers, peasants, and soldiers of 1917 wielded administrative as well as legislative powers. See Herbert McClosky and John E. Turner, *The Soviet Dictatorship*. New York: McGraw-Hill, 1960, pp. 318–319.

In the Soviet Union, for example, policy making occurs largely within the Council of Ministers, administrative agencies, and planning commissions, whose legislative proposals are given to the soviets for official enactment. To be sure, the Communist party makes basic policy decisions in these agencies and then has them enacted in the Supreme Soviet or at lower levels. Many party-made policies, of course, are never laid down in legislation. In practice the Council of Ministers is never overruled by the courts or by the Supreme Soviet, to which it is supposed to be responsible. The administration is closely intertwined at the top with the party, whereas at the bottom of the vast structure the control mechanisms rather than the bureaucracy itself are in the hands of the party. Recruitment and placement of party members throughout the bureaucracy are under party supervision, and the party insists also on ideological commitment by all civil servants.

Official communist theory, according to A. Y. Vyshinsky, claims that there is *no bureaucracy* in the Soviet Union but only "servants of society," who administer the far-flung social and economic activities of the state in the "socialist interest." Owing to Marx's anarchistic bias, the official attitude toward administration is indeed highly ambiguous and encourages the periodic purges that threaten Soviet administrators.[13] Even government ministers are often swept away by shifts in the party line or minor "errors." China's "great proletarian cultural revolution" was also aimed in large part against "bureaucratism" and a presumably bourgeoisified bureaucratic establishment in party and administration. Given the millions of administrators needed to carry on the communist vision of government and economy, the reality of an overblown bureaucracy and of a bureaucratic caste is nearly unavoidable.[14]

Soviet administrative practice is also highly centralized, although a few recent concessions have been made to the need to decentralize economic management. As with the Nazi "leader-

---

[13] In the early days, Lenin also experimented with an unskilled "mass administration" without salaried ranks or differentiation by skill and competence. Since those days, administrative salaries at the top have become ten and fifteen times as high as at the bottom.

[14] Administrative overstaffing, red tape, and unwieldiness are constant complaints in communist countries.

ship principle," Soviet ministers and agency heads are given sweeping authority and responsibility for practically everything that goes on within their bailiwicks. By the same token, they are also blamed and dismissed for the smallest infractions by underlings. This "democratic centralism" is presumably balanced by organized public participation in administration, consultation with the local volunteer *aktivs,* and the political responsibility of the councils of ministers to their respective soviets, which also elect them. Thus vertical responsibility toward the top is coupled with "horizontal responsibility" toward the soviets.[15]

Other controls are the financial audit, familiar from Western practices, and the ubiquitous agents of the Committee of State Security (KGB) in nearly each administrative office and factory. The KGB also guards against all kinds of malfeasance, corruption, and disloyalty and has the power to intervene in administrative action at any time. For a secret political police with a net of informers and undercover agents, the KGB presence in the administration is surprisingly overt. The *aktivs* mentioned above and mass organizations such as the Communist Youth League (*Komsomol*) also make it their business to watch and, if necessary, publicly to denounce administrative laxness and waste, as does the party press. The police-state surveillance over the private lives of administrators, which they share with all soviet citizens, rounds out the picture of control.

Administration and ideology

To put the role of totalitarian administration into proper perspective, it is necessary to recall the character and thrust of totalitarian ideologies. When the Bolsheviks took over Russia —and the same goes for the communist revolutions elsewhere— they were already a movement of people fanatically obsessed by their ideology, which was a modernizing ideology. Under the impact of circumstances such as foreign intervention and civil war, peculiar Russian underground traditions such as a passion for unanimity, and the internal dynamics of fanaticism and ambition, the Communist party took hold of Russian society with a never-flagging determination to instill in it a new political

[15] See McClosky and Turner, *The Soviet Dictatorship,* chap. 12. According to manpower studies cited there, the number of administrative and technical personnel in 1936 already approached ten million.

culture. This political culture of communism, including the zig-zagging party line, has supplied the major cohesive force behind the extraordinary effort to modernize Russia overnight. Administration was the indispensable tool of the sustained effort of forced modernization, even though the spirit of totalitarian ideology and utopia is inherently antibureaucratic. German and Italian fascism were also modernization ideologies of an idiosyncratic sort, as are other ideologies of revolutionary nationalism, and they too were inherently destructive to bureaucracy despite protestations to the contrary.

Once the totalitarian ideology has been established by propaganda, education, and terror as the consuming passion of an entire people, the party and its leader become its executors and the administration their long arm. Party and leaders can adapt themselves constantly to the exigencies of the moment, since they are the originators and interpreters of that consuming faith. The administration, however, can survive only if its structure and bureaucratic standards remain flexible almost beyond recognition. Thus it is either destroyed and replaced at an early point, or else its well-indoctrinated administrators become nearly indistinguishable from the ideologically mobilized masses or from their partisan manipulators. The spirit of professionalism typical of a well-developed bureaucracy is anathema to the ideological populism of totalitarian movements. As the Chinese "cultural revolution" seems to demonstrate, in a country seized by totalitarian fervor it is far more important to be "red" than to be "expert," and anyone convinced of the contrary must be humbled in his pride.[16]

[16] See also Carl J. Friedrich and Zbigniew Brzezinski, *Totalitarian Dictatorship and Autocracy,* 2d ed. New York: Praeger, 1965, chap. 16.

CONSTITUTIONS AND COURTS
Legal systems and the judicial process

If the study of policy-making institutions such as legislatures and executive branches can be called the stepchild of some modern approaches to comparative politics, then the study of law, constitutions, and courts may well be the orphan. A reaction to an overemphasis on legalism is understandable, but we are clearly going too far if we ignore the legal fabric and processes behind such a large part of political life.

In Western nations, in particular, legalism and the propensity for constructing legal institutions are so prominent that a political observer simply cannot ignore them without doing violence to the facts. In communist countries and developing nations, too, the attempted legalism of constitutions and legal processes should not be disregarded, even if the law is not observed with Western literalness. The notions of "socialist legality" or of nationalistic legitimacy are still highly ideological, to be sure. But they are legal notions *in statu nascendi* and will mature into stable legal systems if given enough time. Except for transient revolutionary periods, organized social life simply cannot go on without norms and a lawlike system of order of one kind or another.

LAW AND THE POLITICAL CULTURE

All law is derived from and based on sets of values and beliefs, deep-seated attitudes, political style, and evaluative processes, such as those we examined in discussing political cultures. Law is related to a given political culture somewhat as tools or artifacts are related to a given cultural system. Law is at once a product of the culture and an autonomous factor helping to mold and change it along evolutionary lines. Law also tends to become a focus of institutionalization, both as a public repository of societal values and style and as a functional instrumentality. Thus, the law or the constitution is a showcase of the norms and symbols of a given society. And it also becomes the focus for the evolution of lawmaking, law-changing, law-adjudicating, and law-enforcing institutions. These institutions and their manner of operating, again, are colored by the political culture that in the last analysis created them, and they become autonomous factors of the culture and the political system as well.

There is a dynamic relationship between the political culture and the subcultures of a given society on the one hand and its law and government on the other. This relationship ranges from slow-changing (traditional) societies, where law and government merely reflect the political culture, to fast-changing societies (transitional and modern), where law and government try to initiate and steer the social and economic changes. In a traditional society, for example, mores and beliefs are embodied in customary law, which in turn sanctions them and, by threatening punishment for nonobservance, helps to socialize youth into membership and participation in the society. A judicial system that encourages judges to apply the mores and norms of the community in their decisions, as is the custom in common-law countries, likewise makes the law reflect the society.

With modern *statutory laws,* however, the norms and beliefs may stem from one small group, such as a modernizing elite, and be imposed upon a majority that have rather different or varying mores and values. Although new laws may encounter resistance at first, a reasonably well-integrated political system will soon incorporate them into the community norms and beliefs. The making and enforcement of new laws by government thus become a smooth mechanism for changing a society's belief system itself. It also helps to replace the polycommunal, particularistic belief and value systems with uniform universal norms, thereby helping to build homogeneous modern nations from culturally pluralistic antecedents.

Influence of religion

Among the ideological elements, the belief systems that often make up the "spirit of the laws," religion is among the most profound. Ancient ancestral cults and polytheistic religions played a dominant role in the foundation of Greek city-states and of Rome, not to mention the ancient empires. Those old religions supplied the mores and norms of society, as well as lending legitimate authority to governments. Without medieval Catholicism, the notions of medieval law and hierarchic authority are as hard to understand as are the early Huguenot or English ideas of sixteenth- and seventeenth-century constitutionalism without reference to various Protestant religions. There is also, then, no reason to underestimate the contemporary effect of Islam on the legal and constitutional traditions of the Arab world.[1] The impact of Islam, like that of other traditional religions, has many aspects and derives from varying schools, ranging from traditional Islamic notions of legitimacy and community to the reformist Islamic legislation that has changed the ethics of the *Shari'a* in a modern direction. There are totalitarian ideologies on the neo-Islamic or ultranationalist right, and there are curious similarities, if not affinities, between Islam and communism.[2] Similar relationships between Russian

[1] See, for example, Richard H. Nolte, ed., *The Modern Middle East.* New York: Atherton Press, 1963, chaps. 9–11, and Manfred Halpern, *The Politics of Social Change in the Middle East and North Africa.* Princeton, N.J.: Princeton University Press, 1963, chaps. 1–2, 7–9, 11.

[2] See the discussion in Dankwart Rustow, *The Appeal of Communism to Islamic Peoples.* Washington, D.C.: Brookings, 1965; Halpern, *The Politics of Social Change in the Middle East and North Africa,* pp. 156–159; and Leonard Binder, *The Ideological Revolution in the Middle East.* New York: Wiley, 1964, chaps. 2–5. Also, Majid Khadduri, "From Religions to National Law," in J. H. Thompson and R. D. Reischauer, *Modernization of the Arab World.* New York: Van Nostrand-Reinhold, 1966, chap. 4.

communism and the Orthodox faith and between all totalitarian ideologies and religious millenarian movements have been noted on many occasions.

Totalitarian legal order

Totalitarianism by definition involves deep-seated negative attitudes toward existing law and legal institutions that may indeed resemble religious zealotry and fanaticism. This is not to deny that totalitarian ideologies involve strongly held ethical and normative convictions, which may indeed produce a whole new legal order in communist or fascist states. In particular, they include new notions of legitimate authority and of the role and the rights of the individual in a totalitarian society. It is very revealing, for example, to reflect upon the phenomenon of "revolutionary justice" and the persuasive enforcement of conformity at the grass-roots level in Communist China and other communist states. Partly in reaction to the earlier tyranny of class law and class justice and partly out of a populistic urge to make everyone equal, the revolutionary tribunals of the Chinese Peasant Associations of the early years worked harsh justice on the landlords and other "class enemies." While the poor and deserving could expect leniency from the illiterate peasants and workers sitting on the tribunals, moreover, counterrevolutionary elements were executed or sentenced to "reform by manual labor" under politic supervision. For breaches of labor discipline and minor disputes, the Chinese still use People's Arbitration and Conciliation Committees similar to the Soviet volunteer police brigades (*druzhiny*) and comrade courts, which bring peer and neighborhood pressure to conform on the minor deviant cases. Such volunteer activity legitimizes peer-group pressures present in all societies and elevates them to the status of enforceable community norms—in other words, law.[3]

Politics and Law These differences from Western notions of law become even clearer when we examine the conventional borderline between politics and matters of law and judicial ad-

---

[3] See Robert G. Wesson, "Volunteers and Soviets," *Soviet Studies,* 15 (January 1964). The sentences often provide for a public apology, a published reprimand, and restitution or minor fines—in other words, persuasion rather than punishment. See especially the discussion in Wil-

ministration. In the broadest sense, of course, all law and adjudication is political. Popular usage in Western countries, however, prefers to separate existing law and judicial administration from the processes of partisan political controversy and lawmaking. With the exception of special-interest or class interpretations, a legislative bill is no longer "political" from the moment of its enactment. Judges and court procedures, furthermore, must be as free as possible from partisan "political" ties and influences, so as not to taint the law they administer. By way of contrast, the judiciary of totalitarian countries, whether communist or fascist, is emphatically political, as is the intent of the law. Not only are many judges loyal members of the totalitarian party, but they affect an activist style of ideological crusading disdainful of any formalism or the law codes. They are very much intent on creating new law from the fullness of their ideological certainty. The special courts and new legal interpretations of Nazi justice, for example, also exuded this politicized spirit while evading the rigidity of the inherited structures and codes.[4] No greater contrast in trial practice is imaginable than between the use of common-law barristers to represent their clients in adversary proceedings and the new lawyers of Red China, who are not meant to be their clients' agents but the servants of "the people's law."

Totalitarian crime and punishment   The Chinese have always been suspicious of the motives of the go-between, but this totalitarian practice goes even beyond the widespread naïve popular hostility toward the defender of presumed criminals. It goes to the heart of the rationale of totalitarianism, to its conception of crime and punishment. Today we can smile about the naïve faith of the old Bolshevik leaders that crime was merely the product of capitalist society and would disappear the moment a true socialist system was introduced. Russians convicted of "economic crimes" and sentenced most harshly for what would be rather minor offenses in most Western countries are less inclined to smile. The real crimes in the totalitarian view, whether

liam G. Andrews, *Soviet Institutions and Policies, Inside Views*. New York: Van Nostrand-Reinhold, 1966, pp. 201–204.

[4] On this subject, see especially Otto Kirchheimer, *Political Justice*. Princeton, N.J.: Princeton University Press, 1961.

Communist or National Socialist, neoreligious zealot or anti-colonialist fanatic, are historical and ontological in nature, and only the historical end of their perpetrators or representatives can satisfy the totalitarian wrath. Contrary to all logic, charity, and even to the totalitarians' own authoritative writings such as those of Marx, bourgeois capitalists and "imperialists," Jews, competing religionists and secularizers, and former colonialists bear such an enormous historical burden of "objective guilt" as only their blood can wash away. It is on the same insane rationale that totalitarian regimes extend their persecution also to all political antagonists, "unreliables" in their own ranks, and any further categories of "objective enemies" that occur to the paranoid minds of their leaders. The great proletarian revolution in China, the Moscow purge trials, and the routine presumption of guilt in Soviet trials, which was reversed only after Stalin's death, evidenced an ever-widening circle of victims of the homicidal urge of the totalitarian mania.

Western legal tradition

In the constitutional democracies of the West, by comparison, the conceptions of the nature of law and of crime and punishment have followed a predemocratic legal tradition of centuries, even millennia. There are well-trained professionals of bar and bench to tend it, long-established legal institutions and procedures, and many kinds of formalized law, all of them carefully isolated from political pressure and ideological passions.

Private and public law   The distinction between *private law* and *public law* is as old as the Roman-law tradition and remains an important division between large substantive areas of modern law. Private law concerns the relationships among private individuals and corporations, including, for example, conflicting claims to the same property, contractual provisions, and obligations arising from marriage or divorce. Public law defines and regulates rights and duties, of which the state is either the subject (the holder of a right) or the object of a duty to perform. Public law would include, for example, the right of the state to collect fees, customs duties, and taxes from individuals, and condemnation proceedings to acquire private land for public use. Public law would also include individual claims for social welfare under legislation that obliges the public authorities to disburse certain amounts in case of certain kinds of disability, unemployment, or accident. The distinction between private and public law is particularly important in Roman-law countries such as France, where a different supreme court is provided for private cases, the *Cour de Cassation*. Cases of public law are handled by the Conseil d'État.

Civil and criminal law   Another significant distinction rooted in Western political cultures is that between *civil law* and *criminal law,* for which some systems provide different codes and different courts. A civil-law case is normally a dispute brought by two or more private persons or corporations for decision by a court, say for breach of contract, defamation of character, or divorce. Civil-law suits can also be brought by a governmental agency against a private party, such as a contractor. The French *droit civil,* for example, embraces the law of persons, including the protection of the interests of minors, family law, property law, contracts and torts, community property, and estates. Cases under criminal law are invariably brought by the state, though often upon a complaint by an aggrieved party. The public prosecutor or district attorney then levels accusation at the defendant "in the name of the people." Criminal law defines crimes against the public order, such as homicide, rape, or illegal use of drugs, and provides the appropriate punishment. The verdict is one of guilty or not guilty, and a jury is often employed, as befits the one governmental function that can most deeply affect the lives of citizens by taking away their property, liberty, or even their lives.

Other categories of law   In some countries other categories of law have been given to separate courts. *Commercial law* is the body of usages and statutes that have been developed in centuries of business transactions and commerce, often transcending the boundaries of legal systems and even nation-states. *International law,* public and private, similarly grew from custom, usage, general notions of law, and treaties among states. Unlike most kinds of law, international law lacks the iron hand of enforcement, except by the hand of the aggrieved party or of an international organization, although there is an International

Court of Justice and there have long been arbitral tribunals called for special cases.

Constitutional law is the law of the constitution, including implementing legislation, such as organic laws setting up governmental institutions or defining the relations between them. By its very nature, it is presumed to be of a higher order than ordinary law and on conflict overrides the validity of the latter. Constitutional law in the form of cases and court rulings is likely to be more highly developed in the few countries practicing *judicial review,* such as the United States. This is not to say that no elaborate constitutional law is to be found in a country like France. On the contrary, French constitutional law is spelled out in the legal treatises and textbooks of French law faculties, and occasional rulings of the Conseil d'État are part of it. In Great Britain, where no court can invalidate parliamentary legislation, the courts can still interpret the laws and their constitutional context in *quo warranto* proceedings, which do produce some case law on the constitution.

Constitutional law is a part of public law and not always clearly separated from *administrative law.* Administrative law consists of the rules and regulations governing the organization and procedures of administrative agencies. It is generally promulgated by higher administrative agencies for the lower levels, and its passage often involves some legislative action or review. To the extent that administrative law defines the form and organization of governmental agencies, it may coincide with parts of constitutional law.

Labor law is the outgrowth of less than a century of collective contracts and legislation governing the relations between employers and employees. The complexity of modern tax legislation and the thicket of social security laws in some countries have also led to the growth of *internal revenue* or *fiscal law,* and *social insurance law,* with appropriate tribunals to consider complaints and challenges to state action.

ROMAN-LAW AND COMMON-LAW SYSTEMS

Coextensive with the French and the British patterns of modernization, the two most widely used legal systems in the Western world are derived from the Roman-law tradition or from the

English common law. The differences between the two are fundamental and manifest themselves in many ways. Historical in their roots, perhaps even a matter of different temperaments, each has often been described by legal experts belonging to one system in terms most unfavorable to the other. Some of the distinguishing labels have borne overtones of bias, as when common-law writers contrasted the "inquisitorial" procedure of Roman-law courts with the "accusatorial" procedure of their own. Sometimes demonstrably false principles are attributed to Roman-law systems, such as that "the accused is considered guilty until proven innocent." Sometimes, also, the comparison has merely averred, rather erroneously, that Roman law was purely statutory and common law strictly judge-made law. An attempt will be made here to present an unbiased comparison.

A look at the historical backgrounds of both Roman law and common law may help to clarify the comparison.

History of Roman law

Roman law during the first six centuries of ancient Rome (from the origin of the Twelve Tables in about the middle of the fifth century B.C. until the second century after Christ) was a system very much like the idealized image of the common law two thousand years later: it relied chiefly on judicial decisions and well-established, but unwritten, legal customs. In those days, it owed its vitality and flexibility as much to its closeness to the facts of each case as to its reluctance to theorize and to commit its legal notions to verbal formulas. The Roman *ius civile,* after which present-day Roman law is sometimes misleadingly called "civil law," was perhaps the proudest monument to the genius of the Roman republic. But it was not until Rome had become an autocratic empire and its civilization had passed through centuries of decline that Roman law was codified in the famous Justinian Code of A.D. 533.

While further centuries of anarchy and chaos filled the void left by the fall of the Roman Empire, Roman law survived in the form of the canon law of the Catholic church until its rediscovery by the new French and Italian universities of the twelfth century. By this time, far more primitive tribal and feudal systems of law had established themselves in most of the new feudal monarchies of Europe. The rediscovered Roman law, annotated by learned jurists, seemed very advantageous to the educated and mercantile classes in the newly arising cities and also to many a feudal monarch, who would have preferred the absolute authority of the Roman emperor to dependence on the vagaries in loyalty of his feudal lords. In the centuries to come, therefore, Roman law was revived and to varying degrees imposed upon the prevailing political cultures. At least it became an influential source of legal method and concepts, even where it was not formally introduced. Areas that were once an integral part of the Roman Empire, such as southern France and Italy, naturally went farthest in this direction, while many Slavic and German states tended to mix local customary law in various ways with the Roman tradition. Its influence reached as far as Scotland and the Scandinavian countries, and even England was several times on the verge of adopting Roman law. There is no denying the influence of Roman-law thinking on the development of the common law and equity.

The present Roman-law countries, having different historical backgrounds and having received Roman law at different times, offer a considerable variety of legal customs and practices. At the same time, they are more alike today than they were two hundred years ago. In 1804, Napoleon I promulgated the French *code civil,* soon to be followed by further law codes. The *code civil* became the model for the legal systems of Portugal, Spain, and the Latin-American republics, as well as for Quebec and Louisiana; for Switzerland, Germany, Austria, Belgium, the Netherlands, and Italy; for countries such as Turkey and Japan who chose it in their quest for modernization, and also for the African and Asian colonies and dependencies of the foregoing countries, such as the Eastern European territories of Hapsburg.

Origin of English common law

The English common law originated at about the same time as the medieval rediscovery of Roman law. It was the result of the efforts of English kings such as Henry II to centralize judicial authority by means of traveling judges, who rode from local court to local court, hearing cases and fashioning a "common law" from regionally diverse legal customs. With the help of court records, a legal profession of high caliber, and great jurists such as Henry of Bracton, the common law soon became a complete and stable system built on the *rule of precedent* (*stare decisis*), which meant that all principles used in judicial decisions have to be deduced from earlier cases. Such a rule was not as restrictive as it may appear, since precedents can be construed narrowly or liberally, and the facts of two cases are hardly ever alike. It provided uniformity and certainty without depriving the judges of a creative role.

Still, there evidently was enough rigidity and dearth of remedies in the common law to give rise to a second strand in the development of English law, cases at *equity,* by definition a source of judicial remedies dictated by natural law and reason. Where common law, for example, would only grant damages after the fact, equity might force a defendant to live up to his contractual obligations or to abstain from conduct injurious to the plaintiff. Writs of equity originally were granted by the king's chancellor rather than the courts, but in time they also gave rise to a large body of judge-made case law governed by the rule of precedent.

While equity merely complements or mitigates the common law, the needs of changing society for exceptions to the rules led to increasing legislative activity on the part of "the High Court of Parliament." The resulting statutes soon began to govern most of English criminal law and other areas as well. In the United States, likewise, statutes have long occupied vast areas of the law, superseding a large part of what was once exclusively governed by common law and equity. Common-law jurists still insist that theirs is a *judge-made, bench-made,* or *case law,* but they are evidently speaking of a mode of treating and looking at legal problems, a "mode of judicial and juristic thinking" (according to Roscoe Pound), and a way of teaching the law rather than a pure case law without statutory, "legislative" definitions. In this form, common-law systems spread from England and Wales to Ireland, to the American colonies, and finally to English-speaking Canada, New Zealand, and Australia. It also exerted considerable influence on the legal systems of India, English-speaking Africa, the Scandinavian countries, and Israel.

Comparison of the two systems

It should be evident from the historical backgrounds of Roman-law and common-law systems that they have a great deal in common. The real differences can hardly be stated in terms of the slightly varying mixtures of statutes, judicial interpretation, and case law. Common-law countries have plenty of statutes and even some codification; they also have their great jurists and legal commentaries. Roman-law countries cannot enforce statutes without some judicial interpretation, and there is a rule of precedent binding lower courts to the decisions of higher courts, thus creating considerable bodies of case law wherever the law codes have gaps. Often recent statutes and older codes form a patchwork rather than the harmonious and comprehensive edifice of a *code civil*. The real difference lies far more in the approach of judges, lawyers, and laymen to the law than in the elements and sources used.

The different attitude of a Roman-law judge can be glimpsed especially from decisions in cases where the statutory law is silent, obscure, or insufficient. In such a case, a common-law judge might boldly proceed to state a new rule, perhaps with reference to obscure and distant precedent. Or he could refuse to accept the case for one reason or another, or decide the case on narrow technical grounds without venturing an opinion on issues that he feels insufficiently confident to judge. A Roman-law judge, by comparison, is very reluctant to take on the role of creating a new rule. The law specifically compels him to decide the case brought before him in the broadest of terms, a refusal being considered a denial of justice to the parties before him. He would very likely seek to relate his decision to the existing code, either by interpolating the intent of the legislators as expressed on other matters, or by analogy from the logic of other parts of the code. He might argue from the context in the code or from the theories in the legal textbooks written by university professors of law. The training of a Roman-law judge, his role of conception, and his idea of the nature of the law and of the judicial process evidently differ a great deal from those of his common-law counterpart.

There are also considerable national differences among

Roman-law systems and between different schools of jurisprudence that put varying stress on sociological understanding, legal positivism, or formalism. In any case the fundamental underlying concept of the law is profoundly rationalistic and aesthetic in nature. Roman-law jurists see their own law as *ratio scripta* (written reason)—perfectly rational, harmonious, natural, elegant, even beautiful. There is very little of the typical common-law emphasis on experience, pragmatism, or the profound respect for the stubborn facts of judicial practice, or much concern for the social relationships outside of the courtroom. A Roman-law jurist would be shocked at the statement of Justice Oliver Wendell Holmes that "the life of the law has not been logic; it has been experience." He sets his trust in logic and hence looks for guidance to the lawgivers and the law professors rather than to courtroom experience with actual cases. In this sense, then, common law is indeed judge-made, litigation-born, and a "trial-lawyer's law." Roman law is a "professor's law," the law of the great codifications, which have sought to draw the whole life of civil society, of crime and punishment, or of commercial transactions, each into a comprehensive, perfect code of law.

Law-court procedures   These profound differences in attitude and concept cannot help fashioning decisively the procedure of law courts in Roman-law and common-law countries, not to mention the differences in judicial procedure among these countries and even among various states of the United States. The role of the judge in either system varies with the kind of law at issue. In a civil-law suit, where two private parties face each other, the differences are not as great and not as controversial as in criminal-law proceedings. It is in the latter only that common-law observers have criticized Roman-law procedures as "inquisitorial." In ancient Rome as well as in pre-revolutionary France, the role of a Roman-law judge was associated and sometimes combined with that of the examining magistrate or the public prosecutor, which often meant that provincial judges would initiate the proceedings against an alleged lawbreaker and try the case in the first instance. From this precedent grew a concept of the activist role of the judge in criminal trials, which has lasted even after the functions of public prosecutors and the judges were separated more carefully.[5]

Before the trial can begin in a French criminal court today, an investigating judge (*juge d'instruction*) carries out a careful preliminary examination (*enquête*) of the case, including an interrogation of the accused and the chief witnesses and an examination of the evidence. If the *enquête* yields insufficient evidence, the case is dropped. At the trial, the judges (generally more than one) actively participate in the courtroom questioning of witnesses and of the defendant. A French criminal trial thus becomes the public repetition of the preceding investigation with the apparent objective on the part not only of the public prosecutor, but of the judges as well, of proving the defendant guilty according to the definition of the law. Behind this "inquisitorial" conduct of the judges lies a deep belief in the objective nature of the crime committed and the court's duty to get at this objective truth. Investigating judges regularly confront witnesses whose accounts differ in order to force them to come up with "the true story" of what happened. This search for truth places comparatively little emphasis on procedural safeguards or rules regarding the admissibility of evidence in the trial, in large part because it is the judge rather than an opposing party that conducts the cross-examination.

A different conception of the law and of crime and punishment is evident in common-law procedure in criminal trials, in which the preliminary investigation is conducted before the *grand jury*. This body of laymen decide whether the evidence against a person warrants an indictment—that is, whether he should be called into court. A negative finding by the grand jury means usually that the case is dropped. An indictment, on the other hand, leads to the great courtroom battle between the two opposing lawyers that characterizes the Anglo-American *adversary method*. While the two teams struggle either to prove the case of the prosecution or to rebut it, the judge does not participate actively in the questioning of defendants and witnesses or in the weighing of evidence. He is rather the referee of the match who guards the observance of the large body of

[5] Even today French judges occasionally transfer to prosecuting functions and back again with an ease that shocks common-law observers.

rules of combat—procedural safeguards and rules of evidence that have been developed over centuries of courtroom practice. In the end, the judge charges the jury with the fateful decision between *guilty* or *not guilty.* Here, too, the common-law jury deliberates alone, whereas French juries in the courts of assize deliberate together with the judges, who are likely to dominate the deliberations. Behind the great concern of common-law criminal procedure for the rights of the accused there lies a deep awareness of the likelihood of judicial error and of the inherent limitations of the human quest for truth.

There can be little doubt that common-law procedure gives the defendant in criminal trials a better chance to clear himself. But this is not to say that it must be inherently more likely to procure justice. The adversary method can be credited with a great many historical contributions to individual freedom, such as the right to confront witnesses, the right to counsel and to reasonable bail, the privilege not to have to incriminate oneself, the protection against cruel and unusual punishment, and many others. But judicial systems must stand other tests as well, such as the speedy and inexpensive availability of judicial remedies, the easy and equal access to counsel even for indigents, or the freedom of criminal trials from community pressures. The present common-law systems have not always compared favorably on some of these counts with French judicial practice. There is no statistical evidence that would indicate which of the two systems of criminal trial leads more often to wrongful convictions, but there can be little doubt that common-law courts and juries more often let a guilty person go unpunished than is likely to happen, say, in France. If the guilty go free, this is also a serious diminution of the rights of the aggrieved or the community. On the other hand, Roman-law systems can rarely point to anything even resembling the independence of common-law judiciaries from their administrations or ministries of justice.

Organization of judiciary systems

The organization of modern judiciaries varies according to differences in political cultures, national historical traditions, and other circumstances. All court systems are hierarchically organized, with *trial courts,* or *courts of original jurisdiction,* forming the lowest level of the pyramid. Hearings of different kinds of cases often start at varying levels, depending on the seriousness of the matter as determined by law. A trial court renders a complete decision on the facts of a case, as well as on the law pertaining to it. But if the losing party in proceedings before a trial court believes it can demonstrate errors in law, adverse community pressures, or gross prejudice on the part of the trial court, it can make an appeal to the next higher court. An *appellate court* then reconsiders the points at issue and has the power to overrule the lower court if it so desires. In common-law systems, the appellate courts generally accept the findings of a trial court as to the facts. Since there may be several levels of appeal, a case can be appealed all the way to the highest tribunal, provided the higher appellate courts accept it. The highest courts often limit their jurisdiction to cases raising fundamental issues of legal interpretation. Most courts with appellate jurisdiction in some matters also have original jurisdiction in others. Even the United States Supreme Court has, in addition to its appellate jurisdiction over cases considered by the lower federal courts, original jurisdiction to hear cases involving ambassadors and other foreign agents and cases to which a state government is a party.

Federal court systems   If a country has a federal form of government, this may complicate the organization and course of appeals of its judiciary. American federalism has two separate court systems, federal and state, each confined chiefly to cases involving the laws made by its particular level of government. By contrast, German and Swiss federalism, and with some modification Canada as well, give their *Länder,* cantonal, or provincial courts jurisdiction over both state and federal law. The federal courts serve only on appeal to maintain uniformity in legal interpretation, though they may also have original jurisdiction over such subjects as disputes among the states or between the federal and state governments. Soviet federalism has a unified, centrally controlled judiciary, whose public prosecutors on all levels are responsible to the procurator general, while the judges are elected by the soviets of each level under the guidance of the Communist party.

Functional divisions of court systems Finally, there are considerable differences between court systems characterized by functional divisions and those that prefer a single court hierarchy for all or almost all cases at law. In practice, the difference is more one of degree than a basic dichotomy. Among the United States federal courts, for example, a pyramid of general courts composed of the district courts, courts of appeal, and the Supreme Court have been the dominant pattern from the very beginning of the American republic, when the Judiciary Act of 1789 merged courts of law and courts of equity. The only specialized tribunals, apart from military courts and the independent regulatory commissions, are the Customs Court, the Court of Customs and Patent Appeals, and the Court of Claims. The purpose of the first two is obvious from their names. The Court of Claims decides suits against the federal government within the narrow limits allowed. Most disputes accepted for a ruling of this court have involved claims arising from federal contracts. In contrast to the simplicity of the organization of the federal courts, American state courts present a picture of confusing complexity. There are probate courts, police courts, domestic relations courts, juvenile courts, magistrates courts, and regulatory boards of every description that vie by sheer number with the general courts.

English courts English courts, to which American practices owe so much, used to be a maze of functional divisions and separate courts until the Judicature Acts of the 1870s. At that time the distinction between common law and equity was eliminated and the various central courts of civil jurisdiction were combined into the *High Court of Justice,* whose divisions still bear names telling of their earlier separation: *Chancery* (equity cases); *Queen's Bench* (all civil cases); and *Probate, Divorce,* and *Admiralty Division.* The Consolidation Act of 1925 completed the judicial reorganization, juxtaposing the course of civil law appeals from the High Court and a *Court of Appeals* to the course of criminal appeals from the *courts of quarter sessions* and the *courts of assize* to the *Court of Criminal Appeal.* The highest appellate tribunal for England and Wales is the *House of Lords,* where the *legal peers* and nine *lords of appeal in ordinary* hear both civil and criminal appeals under the chairmanship of the *lord chancellor* if a fundamental issue of legal interpretation seems to be involved. The separation between courts of criminal and of civil jurisdiction reaches down to the *county courts* (civil) and *justices of the peace* or, in cities, *stipendiary magistrates* (criminal). There are also various regulatory tribunals setting rates and handling complaints.

French courts   The French courts have also been divided into a three-step civil-law hierarchy, composed of *courts of instance* and of *grand instance* (*superior courts*) and *courts of appeal;* and a criminal-law hierarchy ranging from the criminal sections of the *courts of instance* and the *courts of correction* to the *assize courts.* The *Court of Cassation,* at the apex of the system of ordinary courts, furnishes authoritative interpretations of the law in its civil, criminal, or petitions sections and can order a case retried by another court of the same level as the one from which the case was appealed. There are also separate *commercial tribunals, councils on labor disputes, children's, farm lease,* and *social security courts.* Serious cases before these specialized courts may be appealed to the civil-law appeal courts. West Germany has a similar proliferation of specialized social insurance, labor-management, finance, and administrative courts in addition to the hierarchy of ordinary courts.

In France the largest rival to the predominance of the ordinary courts is the hierarchy of administrative courts, which exercises considerable control over the bureaucracy in the absence of American-style judicial review. In Anglo-American practice the state still cannot be sued without its consent for the actions of its servants in the course of discharging their duties. France, Germany, and other Roman-law countries have established these administrative tribunals to hear complaints and lawsuits of the public involving administrative actions. The defendant in these cases is the state itself, not the state official in charge of the action, as is generally assumed in common-law suits of this nature in England or the United States. Malfeasance in office, if present, is tried separately by disciplinary courts, who can punish or dismiss a public employee if he is found guilty. In France, each of twenty-four regions has its *administrative tribunal* for this purpose. And the litigation section of the Conseil d'État can decide appeals from the administrative tribunals. The French as well as the West German administrative courts enjoy the same guarantees of judicial independence as the ordinary civil and criminal courts.

Quality and training of judges and lawyers

The quality and training of lawyers and judges also tells much about the basic differences among legal systems. The political judges and the non-client-oriented lawyers of Red China and other totalitarian regimes form an extreme contrast to the abundant lawyers in the politics of many a former British colony, such as India or Ghana. Lawyers and civil servants with a legal education are also prominent in the politics of such bureaucratic elitist systems as France, Germany, and Japan. And in the United States, the dominant role of lawyers in politics (and everything) has led to the jocular assertion that this is a "dictatorship of attorneys." Alexis de Tocqueville called American lawyers a substitute for aristocracy, and the whole style of American politics probably owes a great deal to them.

Quite generally speaking, the judiciary's role and the quality of the justice meted out depend ultimately on the quality and training of the judges and lawyers, who are the main factors of the judicial process. When we speak of courts that are a check upon legislative or executive power, for example, we assume that the judges and other judicial personnel are so carefully selected and well trained that we can safely entrust them with the power to overrule legislative or executive decisions. This is all the more important, since it is generally easier to remove or fail to reelect a legislator or executive figure than a judge. With the exception of state court judges in some American states, judges never have to stand for popular election or reelection at all. Election for a fixed term by a legislature is frequently used.[6] Since it is suspected of tying the judiciary to the political alignments in the legislature, this mode of appointment may also be of questionable merit. The most popular method of appointment and reappointment is by the executive branch according to

[6] It is used in the Soviet Union for all but the lowest courts. In Switzerland, the federal legislature elects the Federal Tribunal for a six-year term, and in the Bonn Republic the two houses alternately fill vacancies on the Federal Constitutional Court.

established standards and procedures and in many cases "during good behavior"—that is, for life. Thus there must be well-established methods of training, selection, and outside supervision to assure the integrity and impartiality, not to mention the knowledge and intelligence, expected of such a powerful office.

Anglo-American practices   In the Anglo-American countries judges are recruited chiefly from among the practicing lawyers, and the bond between bench and bar continues in many respects after they have been appointed. In England a distinction is drawn, moreover, between *barristers* and *solicitors,* and judges are selected solely from among the former. The *barristers* are the small but highly qualified elite of court lawyers who are authorized to plead cases in the higher courts. They belong to the historic four *Inns of Court*—centuries-old, voluntary organizations that are half law school and half professional association. The Inns of Court train and examine the future barristers and enforce the professional standards of the bar during their entire career. Although it draws its recruits almost exclusively from the upper classes, the scholarly, self-effacing background of the bar has ensured a level of judicial ability and integrity that has few rivals in the world. All higher judges are appointed by the crown in consultation with the prime minister and the lord chancellor, who also selects the lesser judges. By the time they become judges, they generally have years of successful practice and experience behind them. The *solicitors* are office lawyers who accept and prepare cases but cannot plead them except in the lowest courts.

In the United States and the older Dominions, no distinction is made between barristers and solicitors. Judges are recruited chiefly from the bar, which also polices the profession, its formal training in the law schools, and the admission of attorneys to the bar. Bar associations in the United Sates are a powerful influence maintaining and improving the quality of judicial practice and organization. The upper-middle-class composition typical of the British judiciary is far less pronounced in the United States and the Commonwealth. As in England and Wales, the *justices of the peace* and other minor court justices often need not possess any formal legal training. Judges of higher courts generally have had broad practical experience in the practice of the law, and often in politics, before they win office. Their background of experience tends to give them an independence of mind undiminished by the partisan ties to which they may owe their office. Common-law judges everywhere have also developed a remarkable sense of independence from the executive authority, almost a bias against it, even when they have been appointed by it.

Practices in Roman-law countries In a Roman-law country such as France, being a judge generally implies membership in a judicial career service patterned after and often associated with the general civil-service system. The average French judge enters judicial service at the lower levels directly upon leaving law school and passing an appropriate state examination. Far from being an experienced, independent-minded attorney, the typical young Roman-law judge still reflects the uniformity of approach and the concern with the form of his presentation of his human-istic secondary education as well as the theoretical bent of mind of his law-school professors. He starts out in a provincial town and, always sharing the bench with two other judges (except on the lowest level), is quickly absorbed by the *esprit de corps* of the judiciary, its traditional approach to law, and the formal constraint on the three judges on the bench to hand down a unanimous, *per curiam* decision without dissenting opinions. The French judicial career is a haven of lifetime security with frequent promotions for the deserving. It cannot but attract persons seeking tranquillity rather than the competition of the market-place, and those rather inclined to support the powers that be. At the same time, the highest French courts can boast persons of outstanding ability and a sense of professional perfection that is a source of stability for the entire judicial and civil service. The professionalism and civil-service mentality of the French judiciary also shield it from such political pressures as lie heavily at times upon the higher common-law courts. The expectation of frequent promotion by one's superiors, on the other hand, may make some French judges more obsequious than one can expect an Anglo-American judge to be, whose judicial career is only to a small degree based on such hopes.

A considerable contrast in attitude and temperament separates the French judge from the *avocat* and *avoué,* the

French equivalents of barrister and solicitor. The *avocat* ranks in social prestige with the magistrate and the law professors. But unlike the police magistrate (*magistrature assise*) and other judges, the *avocat* is a man of the "free professions" who seeks his fortune in the marketplace. He is responsible for his conduct primarily to his bar association (*ordre des avocats*). In contrast to British barristers, the *avocat* specializes chiefly in the oral development of his case, the *plaidoyer,* which can be compared to a common-law trial lawyer's final summation of the arguments to the jury. French trial practice gives the *avocat* no opportunity to cross-examine witnesses or to employ the procedural maneuvers for which common-law practice is famous. The *avoué* is an office lawyer with certain official functions who usually acts as the agent of the litigants. French law also permits persons to plead their own case and to offer legal advice and services without any formal training.

The close link between the French judiciary and administration is also evident in the relations between the judges and the judicial administration (*ministère public*) from the procurators of the lowest to the highest level. The French *procureur* is the equivalent of the American district attorney and attorney general and follows the same course of formal training as the French judge. There is also a certain amount of interchange of personnel between judiciary and procuracy. The personnel of the five-member administrative courts, for example, is recruited from among able, experienced civil servants who have had years of firsthand experience with administrative practices without necessarily acquiring a bias on the side of the administration. The more than eighty members of the Litigation Section of the Conseil d'État,[7] which hears appeals from the administrative courts, are selected from two sources: (1) from among the products of the prestigious postgraduate École Nationale d'Administration, which trains the cream of the French top civil service in a highly competitive three-year course from which fewer than 150 graduate each year, and (2) from the top-echelon civil servants of the ministries and the regional prefectures, or

---

[7] The other four sections are smaller and exercise functions such as the drafting of cabinet bills, rendering advisory opinions, and reviewing administrative rules. Their members are recruited in the same fashion as those of the litigation section.

by special appointments from outside or from the ranks. The *conseillers* are a body of extraordinary qualifications and prestige.

West German practices   The West German judiciary and legal profession greatly resemble their French equivalents. The similarities used to be even greater before 1933. The most significant exception is that members of the Federal Constitutional Court are elected by Parliament and mostly from outside the career judiciary. Both the lifetime career judges selected from other federal courts and the lawyers and professors serving eight-year terms on the court must have formal legal training. The diversity of backgrounds, the selection by the political parties and *Land* delegations in Parliament, and the functions of judicial review and guardianship over the constitutional life of West Germany have combined to create a group of high judges unlike any to be found in a Roman-law country. Their independence of mind reminds observers of the judges of the United States Supreme Court, which may have served as a model for the framers of the West German constitution and the organic law on the court.

CONSTITUTIONALISM IN THE WEST

The deep-seated legalism and institutionalism of Western political cultures found supreme expression in the idea that the entire political system should be subjected to a "higher law," the law of the constitution.[8] With the benefit of hindsight today, it is possible to trace the antecedents of constitutionalism all the way back to ancient Greece and Rome and the Judeo-Christian tradition. The idea of restraining rulers with laws, procedural safeguards, and covenants, or of limiting their power, dividing it, or checking it with countervailing power, is an ancient one indeed.[9] The committing of these devices and guarantees to a solemnly proclaimed, popular document whose force is above the authority of the policy-making institutions of government is not much older than the American and French revolu-

[8] See especially Edward S. Corwin, *The "Higher Law" Background of American Constitutional Law.* Ithaca, N.Y.: Cornell University Press, 1955 (first published in *Harvard Law Review,* 1928).

[9] See Charles M. McIlwain, *Constitutionalism Ancient and Modern,* 2d ed. Ithaca, N.Y.: Cornell University Press, 1947, chaps. 2–5.

tions.[10] And it is only from that age on that written constitutions are popularly conceived as major autonomous factors of government, independent of the negotiating or contracting parties who originated them. True, constitutions come to life and remain alive only to the extent that individuals, groups, and parties take on the political roles they provide. But the "living constitution" in most Western countries commands enough legitimacy to overcome most attempts to disregard it.

From its antecedents, the constitutional tradition of Western countries acquired a number of characteristic features that deserve detailed discussion. As Carl J. Friedrich has demonstrated conclusively, the integration and unification of national territories and the growth and centralization of bureaucracies immediately preceded and could be taken for granted by the early attempts at constitutionalizing governmental power.[11] Constitutionalism, in other words, brought well-organized political power under control, rather than brought order to chaos or anarchy. Furthermore, and chiefly because of the circumstances and traditions of British history, an extraordinarily important role fell to the common-law judges and their law in restraining monarchic power, while in many other European countries monarchy had made itself the absolute sovereign over courts and representative assemblies. Finally, there was the ancient notion of popular sovereignty, which long before the beginning of our democratic age brought forth an intense concern with a popular "right of revolution" and a "constituent power" residing in the people, a right to dissolve and reorganize unsatisfactory government.[12]

Link with revolution

Upon this foundation, then, the great (and also some minor) revolutions of the age of popular government began to exercise

[10] The background, to be sure, included more than a century of theories of social contract and division of power, ranging from the Huguenots to Montesquieu, in addition to the British enactments and practices emerging from the civil wars of the 1640s. But the serious and popularly based attempts at written constitutions began with the revolutions named.

[11] See especially Carl J. Friedrich, *Constitutional Government and Democracy,* 4th ed. Waltham, Mass.: Blaisdell, 1967, chaps. 1 and 2.

[12] Friedrich, *Constitutional Government and Democracy,* pp. 129–133 and chap. 8.

the constituent power to bring forth one after the other of the modern written constitutions. The link with revolution not only is theoretically important, but it lent a new constitution the legitimacy needed after the bonds of the old order were destroyed. There has always been something awesome about the use of the constituent power, a kind of "myth of founding" a new social order. And constitutions in well-established constitutional states have often been regarded with sentiments otherwise reserved for religious observances.[13]

Not every state owes it existence to such an act of foundation. The monarchies of England and France evolved without such an abrupt break with the past. The current British system, the result of three centuries of nonrevolutionary development, never even adopted a formal constitution. In France, by contrast, the revolutionary mystique of 1789 cast its spell over French politics for a century and a half, while new upheavals lent legitimacy to several later acts of constitutional foundation.

The adoption of written constitutions in Europe did not signify the arrival of egalitarian democracy, even though the masses of the people played a major role in the revolutionary upheavals. The adoption of the early constitutions generally was the triumph of the liberal bourgeoisie, which was not above excluding the lower classes from power by means of suffrage laws with property qualifications. It was not until the twentieth century in most cases [14] that adult manhood suffrage, not to mention female suffrage, was introduced in most European countries. The progressive enfranchisement of all adults, signifying the arrival of egalitarian democracy, eventually removed what had hitherto been a continual enticement to a revolution of the masses against a small oligarchy. The processes of liberal

[13] See also Carl J. Friedrich, *Man and His Government* (New York: McGraw-Hill, 1963), chap. 22, on the significance of the act of foundation.

[14] Apart from the United States, and except for the attempts of Bonapartists such as Bismarck to mobilize the lower-class vote against the liberal bourgeoisie, universal and equal manhood suffrage in the major European countries was not introduced until 1918 or, in France and Great Britain, 1945 and 1948, respectively. See especially the table comparing the progressive broadening of the suffrage by Stein Rokkan in Austin Ranney, *The Study of Political Behavior*. Urbana, Ill.: University of Illinois Press, 1962, p. 75.

democracy, by allowing the majority to have the final word, would presumably obviate the need for revolutions. If "the people" were dissatisfied with their government, they could presumably change it by ballots rather than bullets.

The faith in progress

Underlying this theory of democracy-instead-of-revolution was a deep European faith in progress, which permeated especially the seventeenth, eighteenth, and nineteenth centuries. The faith in progress underwent a number of distinctive phases, varying in their emphasis on reason, the emancipation of a supposedly "natural order" of society from traditional restraints, political reconstruction, and economic growth. Except for brief glimpses in the 1640s, only the latter half of this period began to concern itself with political means of facilitating progress. Progress-minded liberals in the French revolution, for instance, and even more in the nineteenth century, did not have an entirely positive image of democracy. Liberals from de Tocqueville to John Stuart Mill always preferred to qualify their faith in the democratic process or to impose on it various kinds of restraints. The conservative answer to classical liberalism, of course, at first rejected in principle both the idea of progress and democracy. Only the socialist movements and ideologies fully endorsed both progress and democracy, although with strong emphasis on economic conditions and equality. Since the liberals had attempted to use constitutional government to modify and restrain democracy, moveover, the socialists felt consderable suspicion toward many of the contrivances of constitutional democracy until the middle of the twentieth century. However varied the views on democratic constitutionalism, the Western faith in progress is the closest analogy to the developing countries' "ideology of development."

Western political thinking

As Western constitutions stand today, and in the form in which they have been copied widely both among and outside the Western nations, they embody several distinctive and not entirely complementary strains of political thinking. One is the tradition of limited government, including such devices as individual rights and checks and balances. The other is the doctrine of political responsibility, which progressively made executive authority more and more accountable to the people, within the limits set by the practical difficulties of such responsibility. The tradition of limited governmental authority goes back to such venerable ancient and medieval sources as the omnipresent law and the "mixed constitution." [15] This older tradition was predominant before the rise of popular government, at a time when the best hope of taming governmental power appeared to lie in dividing power and in subjecting government to the law. In the American system of government, this older tradition is still dominant, although the tradition of responsibility has asserted itself at significant points, such as the evolution of the American presidency to popular and legislative leadership, or the expansion of the suffrage. In Great Britain, on the Continent, and in the Commonwealth countries, however, the older tradition has had to yield the center of the stage to governmental responsibility.

English traditions

An understanding in depth of the older tradition of law and other checks on governmental authority requires a brief reexamination of the development of English law and constitutional theory in the twelfth and thirteenth centuries. In this era the common law began to evolve as a body of case law, beginning with the decisions of the traveling judges of Henry II. Both this body of law and the royal judiciary subsequently grew into major factors of constitutional development. This period also saw the origin of the Magna Charta, that extraordinary charter of baronial rights and liberties, which soon were expanded to include commoners and even the despised peasants. Its celebrated thirty-ninth clause originally referred only to nobles: "No free man shall be taken, or imprisoned, or disseised [expropriated], or outlawed, or exiled, or in any way destroyed, nor will we go against him, or send against him, except by lawful judgment of his peers or by the laws of the land." But eventually it applied to every man. Another factor was the self-assertion of the early English parliaments, which for two hundred years insisted that English

---

[15] The ancient theory of constitutional government owed much to the belief that "mixing" monarchic, oligarchic, and democratic elements would tend to forestall the inevitable decay believed inherent in any purely monarchic, oligarchic, or democratic regime.

kings reissue similar charters, some thirty in all, and forced two kings to leave the throne.

Equally significant for the earlier constitutional traditions were the writings of the English jurist Henry de Bracton (died 1268), perhaps the first writer to systematize the medieval and ancient heritage of law for constitutional purposes. Bracton distinguished between a proper sphere of royal powers within which a king was legally supreme and a sphere of recognized rights and privileges of subjects that was solely under the law and therefore removed from arbitrary action by the sovereign. This concept in effect reconciled the Roman idea of absolute sovereignty with the contractual notion of the feudal relationship between lord and vassal. It thereby showed the way toward the granting in perpetuity of rights, liberties, and privileges to noblemen and corporate bodies. Bills of rights and solemn guarantees in written constitutions were the final outcome of this development.[16]

Coke's challenge to absolutism   One of the most dramatic moments of the unfolding of this constitutional tradition occurred at the beginning of the English constitutional struggles of the seventeenth century. By this time, the historic liberties of freedmen, their representative estates, and the *parlements* (courts) in France were already giving way to royal absolutism. The princes of German states had adopted imperial Roman law to suit their hankering for absolute power over their subjects. And in England a century of Tudor absolutism had led to the elaborate theory of King James I (1566–1625) that kings rule by divine right rather than by consent or by law. But King James's claim to absolute authority was contested by Sir Edward Coke, the chief justice of England, who threw into the balance the whole common law, the independence of the learned judges, and a revived and expansively interpreted Magna Charta, which had been forgotten for several generations. Coke and his colleagues insisted that the common law was a substantially unchangeable constitution setting down both the structure of government and the basic liberties of the subjects. Neither king

[16] See especially McIlwain, *Constitutionalism Ancient and Modern,* chaps. 1, 4–6.

nor parliament had any authority to change the fundamental law from which their own rights and duties derived.

James dismissed Coke upon this challenge to royal supremacy. But this historical incident reaffirmed the tradition of the *rule of law* in its purest form, as government subject to an overriding law. For the ancients and for later modern theorists, this was the law of nature, a part of the cosmic order from which specific natural rights, the rights of man, could be deduced. For Coke and the English tradition, however, it was the historic common law from which "the historic rights of Englishmen" were derived. At first glance the net effect on constitutional government appears to be the same. But in practice the historic common law turned out to be stronger and better suited to endure.

One important factor for the enduring qualities of the historic law has been that it is judge-made and judge-interpreted, and consequently tied to the highly trained legal knowledge of an elite, the "artificial reason" of the learned men of the law, as Sir Edward Coke called it in order to distinguish it from the "natural reason" of King James I, who wanted to render his own justice after principles of his own devising. An independent judiciary has therefore become one of the most important features of modern constitutional government. In some countries, such as the United States, judicial independence and the guardianship of the fundamental law of the constitution have even led to a mild *judicial supremacy,* a system in which the "high priests" of the constitution generally have the last word on constitutional questions.[17]

Evolution of individual rights and liberties

Another landmark of modern constitutionalism has been the evolution of *individual rights and liberties,* a trend highlighted by the increasing emancipation of the individual over the centuries. Here the course of development follows two main lines— that of *procedural safeguards,* especially regarding the rights of the accused in criminal trials, and that of guaranteeing substantive human rights and liberties against governmental interference.

[17] See especially Corwin, *The "Higher Law" Background of American Constitutional Law,* pp. 38–57, and Friedrich, *Constitutional Government and Democracy,* chap. 4.

Procedural safeguards   In common-law countries, the procedural safeguards were in time subsumed under the phrase "due process of law," without which no person shall be deprived of life, liberty, property, or the pursuit of happiness. Among the safeguards are also substantive limitations upon the police powers of the state, the presumption of innocence until proven guilty, the freedom from unreasonable search and seizure, from excessive bail, and from cruel and unusual punishments, the right to a grand jury indictment, the right to a writ of habeas corpus and to a trial by jury, the right to counsel and a reasonable opportunity to defend oneself, the right to judicial appeal, and the freedom from double jeopardy and self-incrimination. This complex system of procedural protection is by no means accepted in its entirety throughout the Western world. In France, for example, habeas corpus is not recognized, and class distinctions at times color the practices of courts and police. In West Germany the principle that the accused shall be considered innocent until proven guilty was explicitly recognized only rather recently in a reform of criminal law. The procedure in criminal trials in Roman-law countries generally tends to weight the scales against the accused. In the United States, there are also frequent controversies about such matters as the admissibility of certain kinds of evidence, jury selection practices, the rights of indigents, and community pressures upon the jury. In all countries of the Western world, even where procedural safeguards are highly developed, there are occasional breakdowns in the system in the form of cases of police brutality, miscarriage of justice, or discriminatory practices of one sort or another. Procedural devices can be only as reliable and perfect as the persons who administer them: requiring trial by jury, for example, cannot prevent juries from rendering wrong verdicts.

Substantive rights and liberties   The attempts to guarantee substantive rights and liberties to individuals are the hard core of modern constitutionalism, and the procedural safeguards form an integral part of it. The most important substantive freedom was described by John Locke in his *Two Treatises of Government:* "Every man has a property in his own person. This nobody has any right to but himself." This *freedom of the body* that one takes for granted today must be contrasted with such institutions as slavery, serfdom, forced labor, and other kinds of involuntary servitude that were prevalent not so long ago and can still be found in some parts of the world. Other typical forms in which this freedom has been claimed in Western countries are the free choice of job or occupation, of a spouse, and of movement throughout the country and across its borders unhindered by iron curtains, armed guards, and walls.

Persons duly convicted of crimes and people committed to mental institutions are exempt from the protection against physical restraint. Hence, the security offered by this guarantee depends also on the integrity of the whole judicial system. To prevent the abuse of judicial power, there are the procedural safeguards named above and also such protections as the freedom from bills of attainder, ex post facto laws, special courts, and other breaches in the formal system of law. The law should be general and equal in its application to everyone, with due notice to the persons affected by it, and with known and impartial procedures of adjudication and enforcement.

A second substantive *freedom* is that *of mind and conscience,* which should be contrasted with practices of religious intolerance, the zealotry of moral or patriotic righteousness, or the enormous social pressures toward conformity. In England, a citadel of civil liberties, the last of the legislative acts discriminating against nonconformist Protestants, Jews, and Catholics were not rescinded until the second half of the nineteenth century. Religious intolerance is still rampant in many Western countries, especially where no separation has been brought about between church and state. Even in the United States, despite the constitutional guarantee of freedom to worship, there are occasional encroachments on the liberties of small sects and religious minorities, as well as frequent debates over the fine line dividing political heresy from conspiracy.

A corollary of the freedom of thought and conscience is the freedom of expressing one's convictions without fear of reprisal, governmental or otherwise. *Freedom of speech, of the press, of debate and discussion* imply also the freedom to criticize, to question, to challenge, and to say unpopular things. These freedoms are important regulatives of political democracy. But in most Western countries there are also limitations on this complex of freedoms. As soon as the freedom of thought turns from the privacy of the mind to the publicity of a thought expressed, there arises also the possibility of injury to others or to the community at large, which may call for legal restraints and remedies. In times of war or national emergency, moreover, such possible injury to the community is construed more expansively than in peacetime and is linked to such imponderables of national self-preservation as the fighting morale of the troops or the readiness of the people at large to sacrifice. Like the previously mentioned liberties, the guarantees of freedom of speech and of the press do not extend very far into the past of most Western countries. Its landmarks include the failure of the British Parliament in 1695 to renew the Licensing Act, moving pleas for free speech such as John Milton's *Areopagitica* (1644) and John Stuart Mill's *Essay on Liberty* (1859), and contemporary debates on such matters as the thin line between pornography and literature, or between seditious propaganda and legitimate protest.[18]

The third substantive freedom is that of *equal access* to the advantages and opportunities available in a free society. John Locke, for example, spoke of the right of every man, by "the labour of his body and the work of his hands," to acquire land and other property not already owned by someone else. Eighteenth- and nineteenth-century liberals asserted a freedom to use their property for purposes of capitalistic production, a right to buy and sell, and a freedom to enter contracts with no restraints whatever. Today, people are more concerned about their equal access to jobs, educational opportunities, or housing, and about restrictions of this access on grounds of race, sex, or other arbitrary criteria. While the specific threats to equal opportunity may have changed with the economic setting, the individual's basic desire to pursue his own economic advancement remains the same. It has always been difficult to guarantee these rights by constitutional law, beyond such things as the protection of contracts, the maintenance of equal justice under the law, and the guaranteeing of property rights so long as they do not injure the rights of others or the welfare of the com-

[18] See the survey by Freda Castberg, *Freedom of Speech in the West: A Comparative Study of Public Law in France, the United States and Germany*. London: G. Allen, 1961.

munity. Making access a reality often requires special legislation and easier adjudication of wrongs.

A fourth substantive freedom evolved by modern constitutionalism is in some ways perhaps the most important, because its possession provides the means for the enforcement and expansion of other freedoms. This *freedom of political activity* includes such more specific liberties as the right to petition the government for a redress of grievances, the right of association for political or economic purposes, and the right to assemble peacefully and to discuss and criticize the authorities that be.

These liberties, too, are limited in many Western constitutions in anticipation of possible injury to third parties or to the public.

These four freedoms, together with the procedural safeguards and with voting rights and representative government, have been the vital core of modern constitutionalism as it has evolved in the West, passing such landmarks as the Magna Charta, the common law, the Petition of Right of 1628, the Habeas Corpus Act of 1679, the Bill of Rights of 1689, and numerous bills and declarations of human rights, most notably those of the Virginia Constitution of 1776, the first ten amendments to the United States Constitution, and the French Declaration of the Rights of Man. No respectable national constitution today is without such a guarantee of civil rights and liberties, and no Western government should be regarded as respectable that does not allow at least a major part of these guarantees to become an enforceable reality. The central importance of guaranteeing civil rights led some European political thinkers and statesmen to refer to constitutional government as *garantisme*. It is the determination to make these guarantees real that distinguishes Western-style democracy from the totalitarian regimes and dictatorships of the twentieth century, as well as from the traditional autocracies of earlier days.

Governmental responsibility

Hardly less important than the constitutional tradition of limited government and guaranteed rights is the tradition of *governmental responsibility*. The development of representative institutions on the one hand, and the desire for democracy on the other, constitute the vital two-way linkage of representation and responsibility between the people and their rulers. Representation proceeds from the bottom up, and responsibility from the governmental agencies downward to the people.

The ancient principle of popular sovereignty was incapable of realization in a large state until representative assemblies arose side by side with the hereditary monarch and his princes. The British Parliament, for example, began with a Great Council called in the thirteenth century and traveled a long way to become a permanent institution during the Restoration of the seventeenth century. During this period it wielded some power over the royal purse and occasionally called the monarch to account for matters of general policy. It was generally unable, short of violent revolution, to hold kings responsible for their day-to-day actions. In a second phase, beginning with the Glorious Revolution of 1688 and the Act of Settlement of 1701, Parliament established the principle of *parliamentary sovereignty* and that the monarchy only ruled at its sufferance. Even that step soon relapsed into the *status quo ante* of autocracy. In a third phase, starting in the eighteenth century, however, the bulk of executive authority passed from the hands of the hereditary monarch to the hands of a prime minister and his cabinet, who could be overthrown by Parliament at any time without a large-scale revolution. Simultaneously, the development of parliamentary parties allowed Parliament to keep the running dispute between the executive authority and popular opinion inside its own halls.

In this manner, the more subtle and in the long run far more effective harness of political responsibility replaced crude control by threat of revolution. Parliaments and legislative assemblies elsewhere in Europe followed the British example of how to tame executive authority. Even in the United States, where the special problems of monarchy ceased along with that institution in 1776, there was for a while a tradition of legislative supremacy (but not parliamentary government) founded on the Congress' monopoly over legislation and finances, which as late as the end of the nineteenth century caused Woodrow Wilson to describe American government as "congressional government."

After this victory of Parliament over executive authority,

however, there remained the question of how representative Parliament really was. It was quite conceivable, as such famous philosophers as Rousseau suggested, that the people had only exchanged one set of irresponsible rulers for another. And so there set in the long process of legislative reorganization and electoral reform that has characterized the last century and a half in most Western countries, as well as the growth of modern party systems in these legislatures. In this connection one could also mention the many reorganization schemes that attempted to make legislatures more responsible, such as the drive for legislative salaries that would enable people from the lower classes to serve in Parliament, the shortening of terms of office, and attempts to reorganize a legislative assembly's internal structure to eliminate strongholds of organized interests.[19]

The full development of these structural devices to hold executive power responsible to the elected representatives of the people, and the representatives responsible to those who elect them, still left the people in a rather ineffective position vis-à-vis their government. As long as the people were not organized, as long as they faced their government as separate, unrelated individuals, they were unable to oppose specific governmental policies, much less to develop any policy of their own for the government to follow. What the tradition of governmental responsibility now required was the development of broadly based political parties, which could organize the likeminded for purposes of making public policy proposals, selecting candidates for public office, and seeking mass support for both. Only when political parties established a link reaching from the formation of popular opinion all the way to the formation of public policy by governmental agencies could popular control of government be said to have become possible on a day-by-day basis. Since the formation of an intelligent popular opinion also requires a steady flow of reliable information from many independent sources, a free press and other mass media responsible to the public complete the system of responsible government.

This brief resumé of the evolution of the structures and

---

[19] On this subject see also Sydney Bailey, *British Parliamentary Democracy,* 2d ed. Boston: Houghton Mifflin, 1962, and Karl Loewenstein, *British Cabinet Government.* New York: Oxford, 1967, especially chaps. 3–5.

concepts of Western constitutionalism has demonstrated the slow, groping process by which the desired relationships were made possible. The process of improvement must go on as long as there are still major shortcomings and lapses in the real constitutional life of Western democracies. To be sure, constitutional government never promised to deliver salvation or even substantive justice, as many political ideologies do. But it is capable of providing *procedural justice* and rational and orderly processes of political change if properly developed and guarded against abuse.[20]

CONSTITUTIONAL PROBLEMS IN THE DEVELOPING NATIONS

At the same time that students of comparative politics have tended to pay less attention to written constitutions, the number of new constitutions adopted by old and new states has sharply increased. The new nations, in particular, have adopted constitutions as if they were the required certificates of their birth. Federal unions have laid down their basic compacts in written constitutions specifying the privileges and duties of the member states and of the union government. And in all these cases, the Western tradition of limited government, individual or group rights, and political responsibility has been the model and precedent.

The desire on the part of new nations to acquire this mark of status in the world of nations is genuine, even if it outruns their capacity, and at times their willingness, to adhere closely to the letter of the legalistic documents they adopt. Adopting constitutions is part and parcel of the spreading *world culture* that has given certain Western overtones to political modernization everywhere. Its cultural values, such as democracy and nationhood, are increasingly becoming amalgamated with the native cultural and subcultural patterns in most developing countries.[21] This process of acculturation, of course, involves conflicts, survivals of the native patterns, and breakdowns of

[20] See also Karl Loewenstein, "Reflections on the Value of Constitutions in Our Revolutionary Age," in Arnold J. Zurcher, ed., *Constitutions and Constitutional Trends since World War Two*. New York: New York University Press, 1951, pp. 191–224.

[21] See the description of the process of cultural diffusion in political modernization in Lucian W. Pye, *Aspects of Political Development*. Boston: Little, Brown, 1966, pp. 9–11.

the adopted mode as well. And these cultural conflicts explain, better than any condescending theory of imperfect constitutional "imitation," why developing constitutionalism often differs from the Western models.

Within the area of diffusion of the cosmopolitan political culture there are also recognizable national patterns. It is hardly surprising to find, for example, that the communist satellites in Eastern Europe and Asia incorporated many clauses and provisions of the Soviet constitution into their own constitutional documents, undoubtedly along with the Soviet interpretation of their practical meaning. This applies in particular to their ambitious and totally unenforceable bills of rights. An extraordinary amount of faithful copying also has carried parts of the original French Declaration of Human Rights (1789) for nearly two centuries all over the globe. More recently, the influence of French political culture on its former West African colonies encouraged the adoption of the presidential-parliamentary system and the economic council of the Fifth Republic by the latter, for better or for worse. The classic area for the cross-currents of this diffusion process is still Latin America, whose twenty countries have had among them nearly 200 constitutions of American, French, and British derivation since reaching independence. The frequency of constitutional change, and the general patterns of nonobservance and outright violation of these constitutions by successive dictatorships, led many an observer to conclude that Latin-American constitutionalism was largely a sham.[22]

Problems of political stability

Perhaps, however, many of the common negative observations on the constitutional life of developing countries are a little too facile and shallow. An analysis in depth of Latin-American constitutionalism, for example, would seem to require an awareness of the nature of political stability in an unbalanced, transitional "conflict society." It is supercilious for more developed societies to look down on the propensity for dictatorship of

[22] See especially J. Lloyd Mecham, "Latin American Constitutions: Nominal and Real," *Journal of Politics,* May 1959, pp. 258–275, and the literature cited there, as well as the standard literature on Latin-American governments, such as William Stokes, *Latin American Politics.* New York: Crowell, 1959, chap. 19.

transitional politics, when in fact authoritarian regimes were common in the early days of most currently advanced countries. The great internal contradictions of transitionalism all too often present only a choice between self-destructive anarchy and development dictatorships of a charismatic, partisan, or military type. Where the maintenance and survival of governmental authority becomes such a predominant concern of the incumbents of high office, much of the usefulness of constitutional government to facilitate nonviolent political change becomes inoperative. The incumbent power structure will tend to do everything, including violating or appropriately "revising" the constitution, to remain in control, while their opposition will turn to revolutions as the only means of effecting political change.[23]

Limitation of governmental authority

If developing constitutionalism, then, appears to fall short of the goal of facilitating nonviolent change, the question should be raised whether its record is any better in limiting governmental authority by checks and balances or with guarantees of individual or group rights. The answer is flatly negative. Political authority, for the reasons mentioned earlier, tends to be either unlimited or nonexistent. Whenever it establishes itself in a developing country, it centralizes power in the hands of the executive, regardless of how the constitution attempts to divide and check governmental authority. Again, Latin-American practices provide a particularly clear example because their record covers a much longer period, and a propensity toward legalism in politics is by no means absent. In spite of a few attempts to break the pattern of executive omnipotence,[24] however, there is no denying the endemic weakness of any legislative check on the presidential dictator typical of Latin-American constitutional history. And the feeble assertion of the *recurso de inconstitucionalidad* (judicial review) has likewise been a far cry from the checking power of the American Supreme Court, the model

---

[23] See also Merle Kling, "Towards a Theory of Power and Political Instability in Latin America," *Western Political Quarterly,* March 1956, pp. 21–35, and Michael Brecher, *The New States of Asia.* New York: Oxford, 1966, chap. 2.

[24] The Uruguayan plural executive has been the only significant exception to the rule of presidential dictatorship.

for the practice.[25] The only organized group capable of exercising any real check on the chief executive in most of the developing countries today is the military, if indeed it is not in control itself.

Guarantees of rights and liberties

As for guarantees of individual or group liberty, it must be remembered that individualism and individual rights are not at all a part of most traditional cultures and are only gradually being recognized as desirable by the more modernized parts of the population of many developing countries. There are exceptions, to be sure, such as among the more European countries of Latin America, where a determined, anarchic kind of individualism flourishes that makes the United States and Great Britain look like regimented societies of conformists.[26] Elsewhere, however, "individualism" occurs mostly by default of society or governmental action—an alienated, selfish, or isolated individualism growing from the breakup of local and family structures. Unless the self-conscious individual is willing to cooperate with others in common social, economic, and political efforts, neither democracy nor even planned development is likely to result. Individualist democracy, Western-style, is therefore mostly a slogan and rallying cry to help assimilate the upwardly mobile of other social classes into the small political elite. It expresses a desire for social advancement on the part of individuals in the mobilized masses rather than a well-understood conception of the role of individuals in an organized commonwealth.[27] Given these conditions, a "guided democracy" along paternalistic lines as in Sukarno's Indonesia or Ayub

[25] Stokes, *Latin American Politics,* chaps. 16, 17, and 19. A conspicuous exception to what appears to be the typical state of constitutional divisions of power has been India, where the judiciary has remained independent, the army under civilian control, and the elections honest and distinguished by a minimum of repression of opposition parties.

[26] See, for instance, the remarks of Kalman Silvert, *The Conflict Society* (New York: American Universities Field Staff, 1966), chap. 10, on Argentine conceptions of personal freedom.

[27] On this question, see especially Manfred Halpern, *The Politics of Social Change.* Princeton, N.J.: Princeton University Press, 1963, pp. 214–223. At this point, it should also be noted that the freedom of economic pursuit is not always concomitant with other individual liberties. It may well be severely restricted in social democratic countries that secure all other liberties of the individual, and it may be the only freedom in brutal dictatorships.

Khan's Pakistan may find genuine popular acceptance, just as the totalitarian people's democracies of communist countries look far less fraudulent to the transitional populations inside than to the Western outsider.

As for specific individual and group rights, the story of the practices of developing countries is far more complex than a juxtaposition of constitutional promise and actual performance can ever suggest. In all organized communities, the community has certain rights to restrict the conduct of individuals, and police and regulatory powers cut deeply into the rights of individual autonomy. Many developing constitutions expressly sanction, for example, such measures as exile, geographical confinement, or "preventive detention" for political opponents, practices common also in some totalitarian regimes for this purpose. Preventive detention, in particular, as a kind of prior restraint in anticipation of unlawful conduct, is in gross conflict with Western notions of constitutional and criminal law. It also places an amount of confidence in the integrity of police and correctional institutions that these rarely deserve in developing countries.[28] Frequently, emergency clauses enable governments to suspend all individual rights, including that against arrest and detention without judicial sanction, and the result may be the same. However, a balanced assessment of these practices will have to concede that the internal turmoil, civil unrest, and revolutionary violence present in some developing nations is in any case a rather unlikely setting for the perfection of the slow and subtle processes of constitutional protection of personal liberties.

Lack of political consensus

The endemic weakness of governments amid this turmoil and against a noncooperative public, furthermore, also raises the question of the lacking political consensus in most developing countries. The rapid transition from traditionalism to modernity is likely to destroy the consensus on law and moral values of the old society without replacing it effectively with a new faith. Traditional remainders and modernizing elites or ideological

[28] See especially the detailed discussion by David M. Bayley, *Public Liberties in the New States*. Skokie, Ill.: Rand McNally, 1964, pp. 23–53.

movements face each other in a hostile fashion, unable to come to a new consensus, as has happened on occasion in most Western countries as well. Lucky is the nation with a successful revolution and a lasting revolutionary myth that sets forth the details of individual and group rights for incorporation into a constitution. Far more typical is a confusion between the old and the new values, an uncertainty of authority and governmental legitimacy, and, therefore, a low regard for personal liberties and the procedures to safeguard them. Quite often, also, individual rights are threatened more by anarchy than by despotic authority.

The potential for conflict and anarchy is particularly great at the Achilles heel of most developing countries, cultural pluralism in its various forms. Given a number of distinct tribal, ethnic, religious, and cultural communities loosely held together by political bonds of new nationhood, and given also inherited and perhaps disintegrating systems of ethnic or other cultural stratification, the role of such political rights as a free and equal ballot or freedom of the press and of assembly and association can be explosive. Whereas in a homogeneous society in transition no better vehicle for democratization can be imagined than the introduction and vigorous exercise of these political rights by all adult citizens, their effect on polycommunal societies is quite different. Electoral competition between culturebound parties may degenerate into head-on cultural conflict. Freedom of the press may become a freedom to inflame cultural prejudices, which with the help of free assembly and association can then be organized for control or combat between cultures. Based on the "cultural census" of elections or any other means of counting, nearly all common institutions can become a bone of contention in a polycommunal society—public education, governmental personnel, official languages, or the adopted national flag or symbols. Worst of all, majority rule may well be used to justify oppressive rule by a cultural majority over a minority. If modern constitutions are indeed birth certificates of nationhood, apparently a people must first become a fairly homogeneous nation to enjoy their full benefits.[29]

[29] See the excellent survey in Charles W. Anderson *et al., Issues of Political Development.* Englewood Cliffs, N.J.: Prentice-Hall, 1967, chaps. 1–4.

Constitutional arrangements, it should be emphasized, can offer fair and equitable safeguards for cultural defense wherever the majority will permit them to be established. Special religious immunities and injunctions can be solemnly incorporated, from the protection of the holy cows of India to the Moslem injunction against the use of intoxicants. Even-handed or neutral cultural policies with regard to the schools, public personnel, and the designation of official languages and symbols can be laid down in constitutions and, hopefully, followed from then on. There are even cases of bi- or tricultural sharing in governmental authority, as in Lebanon, by constitutional agreement. Other schemes for allocating representation to minorities in legislatures and executive organs have been quite successful in many states, although they tend to perpetuate by cultural census and rewards what may be divisions of rather temporary identification over the long run of nation building. The question arises whether the rewards should go for successful integration or segregation.

Going one step further, there are various possibilities in setting up minorities in locally self-governing units, as member states of a federation, or as separate, sovereign countries. India, Malaysia, Nigeria, and many other developing countries have taken the federal road with varying results. On the other hand, secession, expulsion, cultural encapsulation, civil war, and genocide are the grim alternatives to what could be a rational and mutually beneficial constitutional bargain. Unfortunately, many people can learn only by first making major mistakes. This, too, is hardly an exclusive feature of the politics of development.[30]

Essential values of constitutionalism

In the last analysis, the enduring value of constitutionalism, East or West, advanced or developing, realized or merely attempted, is found far beyond its most obvious devices and mechanisms. It lies in the moral purposes of the social order it is supposed to protect, the values of the ideology it enshrines, and the quality of the governing elite to which it lends stability. Rather than quibbling over how effectively the well-known devices work in the Third World or whether the development con-

[30] See especially Anderson *et al., Issues of Political Development,* pp. 67–71 and 76–79.

stitutions really mean what they say, students of developing constitutionalism should perhaps be studying the nature of various transitional societies, each according to its own moral values, its ideologies of development, and the quality of its development leadership. Only when these three elements have been ascertained beyond reasonable doubt is it proper to ask what kind of a constitutional order might best serve a given society.

It may well be that the revolutionary changes going on in a particular transitional society had better not be arrested at this point and that turmoil and violence for the sake of a better future are preferable to constitutionally ordered stalemate or regression. Nor should the sincerity with which various ideologies of development are held, from communism and "development socialism" [31] to all kinds of nativist or religious authoritarianisms, deter anyone from judging them on their merits and by the practices of their movements. Ideology and revolution are by their very nature so closely related to the intent and content of constitutions that the latter simply cannot be understood without an intimate knowledge of the former. The legitimate authority behind the government and its monopoly of violence, moreover, cannot just be ordered by the fiat of a constituent assembly. Neither can a nonexistent political and moral consensus be created by the adoption of a constitution. On the contrary, a truly "living" constitution must grow from legitimizing processes at hand and from an existing consensus that embodies at least some substantive and most procedural concerns of government.[32]

As for the quality of the leadership, there is little indication that the developing nations of today share the distrust and contempt for political rulers and leaders that motivated much of the Western constitutional attempt at limiting governmental authority. They may, of course, be misled by well-managed cults of personality, or perhaps they are deceiving themselves about the integrity of their leadership. The fact remains that the cur-

---

[31] See especially the discussion of development socialism in Anderson *et al., Issues of Political Development,* chaps. 10 and 11, and Aristide Zolberg, *Creating Political Order.* Skokie, Ill.: Rand McNally, 1966, chap. 2.

[32] See also Spiro, *Government by Constitution.* New York: Random House, Inc., 1959, *passim.*

rent leadership in many new nations enjoys a goodly measure of lasting popularity and, even in Latin America, appears to have more to fear from assassins and small bands of rivals than from their people at large. The same can be said about the one-party systems of many developing countries whose monopoly of power, once successfully imposed by a self-conscious modernizing elite, acquired broad popular acceptance as a rationale of popular government in the spirit of the revolutionary-centralizing movement itself. Constitutional government in the Western image presupposes an acceptance of social and corporate pluralism, which has always been obnoxious to the minds of radicals and socialists from Robespierre to Auguste Bebel. Their equivalents in West Africa likewise preferred to eliminate all institutional checks on the authority of the party. Thus, the West-African party states created their own institutional order, which reflected both the nature of their societies and the purposes of their development ideologies and needs. In spite of the treatment of opposition in these states, one-party monopoly and the avoidance of dissension on fundamental goals and policies can hardly be said to be dysfunctional to development there, provided, of course, that the leadership acts in good faith.[33]

[33] See especially Zolberg, *Creating Political Order,* chaps. 4 and 5.

10
THE POLITICAL SYSTEM AND THE WORLD

The debate over applying systems theory to the internal politics of a nation-state is still relatively new. By the time theories of the national system began to be more widely accepted, numerous theories of the international system had been in vogue for many years.[1] Systemic conceptualization, indeed, appears to be easier among clearly separable and lasting political entities, such as sovereign states, than within a single body politic, where the boundaries among identifiable entities are doubtful and changing and the entities themselves change and fade away with astonishing rapidity. The greater simplicity of applying systemic models is noticeable at all levels of analysis, including those linking particular countries to the international system however defined. While the international system as such and even the bilateral interaction system of two countries is less pertinent here, a systems approach can also be used for the lowest level of

[1] See, for example, K. J. Holsti, *International Politics.* Englewood Cliffs, N.J.: Prentice-Hall, 1967, chaps. 2 and 3, and the literature cited there, or E. Raymond Platig, *International Relations Research: Problems of Evaluation and Advancement.* Santa Barbara, Calif.: Clio Press, 1967, pp. 10–13, and the bibliographical references there.

international systems analysis [2]—namely, the *linkage between national and international politics.*

A national political system interacts with others and with the international system in many ways, all of which deserve detailed attention on the part of a student of comparative politics. The present discussion cannot do justice to all the relevant aspects without turning into a full-length treatise on foreign relations. Instead, the topics closest to the emphasis in this book will be stressed. The political-culture approach to the making of foreign policy will take up the bulk of this concluding chapter.

One can study the attitudes underlying a political culture and its subcultures in terms of the subjective orientations of political actors toward the international system, toward other actors and their conduct, and toward the "self," individual or collective, and, of course, also in terms of subjective notions such as national mission and identity. Beginning with these subterranean layers of opinion formation, we can also distinguish the channels of the flow of opinions and juxtapose them to the channels of influence on the actual making of foreign policy by national governments. Finally, the cohesion and boundary maintenance of these nation-state entities deserves some discussion. We live in an age of cross-national organizations and movements, whose emergence and triumph can spell the penetration or end of the bodies politic that are the subject of this volume.

POLITICAL CULTURE AND THE INTERNATIONAL SYSTEM

In the context of domestic politics, as we have seen, political culture is the total of subjective orientations toward government and its activities, toward other actors, and toward oneself as political actor. It includes prerational beliefs and attitudes, such as the presence or absence of a sense of social trust or a deeply felt identity crisis. Rational belief systems, such as ideologies, religious creeds, or moral convictions, may also play a major role, as do unstated beliefs about the role of coercion and

[2] On the "levels of analysis," see Platig, *International Relations Research,* pp. 34–41, and David J. Singer, "The Level-of-Analysis Problem in International Relations," reprinted in James N. Rosenau, ed., *International Politics and Foreign Policy,* rev. ed. New York: Free Press, 1969.

violence in political life. And there are tried and proven ways of studying cultural systems that suggest satisfactory methods of approach to any given political culture. Let us examine the bearing of a political-culture approach on the linkage between a national and the international political system.

The level of knowledge

There is, first of all, the question of the level of knowledge among the system's adult population about the outside world. How large a percentage of Americans have a reasonably accurate cognitive map of the international system? How many do so today as compared to a generation or two ago, when higher education and even the completion of high school was still limited to a small section of the population? It stands to reason that people whose knowledge of international affairs is slight and hazy will feel little involvement and little willingness to undergo great sacrifices for exigencies they fail to understand. This applies especially to distant wars or warlike activities of their government. It is even more true of entanglement in international alliances and organizations such as the United Nations, as long as the benefits of participation are not readily linked to a threatened attack on one's own country.

The same questions can be raised about Western European countries, which a mere generation ago were still considered best informed on international affairs and therefore best equipped to cope politically with this shrinking world. The question of the level of knowledge and interest particularly serves to distinguish modern, newspaper-reading publics from traditional illiterate and ignorant populations, such as Daniel Lerner described in *The Passing of Traditional Society*.[3] A traditional

[3] Daniel Lerner, *The Passing of Traditional Society*. New York: Free Press, 1957, pp. 24–28 and *passim*. A recent article by Daniel H. Willick, "Public Interest in International Affairs: A Cross-National Study," *Social Science Quarterly*, 50 (September 1969), 272–285, compared "attentive foreign policy publics" in several modern countries and arrived at 17 percent of the adult population in Great Britain, 27 percent in West Germany, 12 percent in France, 9 percent in Japan, and 4 percent in Italy, with education, social class, and sex usually the characteristics setting off the well-informed from the rest. On the concept of "attentive foreign policy publics," see also Gabriel A. Almond, *The American People and Foreign Policy*. New York: Harcourt, Brace, 1950.

peasant village is so unaware of, if not hostile toward, the out-side world that its place could well be on the moon rather than in a developing country. Socially more mobilized people, such as urban migrants in the *barrios* or *favelas* of Latin America, are more aware of the existence of other countries, although their cognitive map is likely to be grossly distorted.

The problems of analyzing the level of knowledge in de-veloping countries pose further problems, which may also be of interest in advanced societies. One such problem is the differ-entiation of cognitive levels among the subcultures of a country, ranging from the most isolated and traditional to the well-informed political elite. Another problem deals with the meas-urement of knowledge of international affairs along a continuum rather than in dichotomous terms. After all, the adequacy of information is always an open question. Even the best-informed specialists on a particular area are in constant pursuit of the ultimate truth about conditions and problems there. As for a general understanding of the outside world, surely there are many degrees of knowledge, ranging between total ignorance and the savvy of a "man of the world," that have a bearing on the formation of the opinions of the masses of people.

It is also most likely that the level of knowledge about the international system will vary according to the proximity to the observer. A person can be a parochial in his awareness of situations in far-off Asia while being comparatively well-informed about countries immediately adjacent to his own or especially involved with his own country. To the extent that personal familiarity, or the awareness of friendly or hostile relations, may be the spur to higher levels of knowledge, proximity will make for better information. Thus, most people's cognitive maps of the international world may well be made up of regional circles of awareness beyond which everything recedes into the haze and distortion of unfamiliarity.[4] To the extent that international relations today are characterized by an international, world political system rather than self-contained regional systems, then, most people simply do not fully comprehend what is going on.

[4] With nations known for isolationist tendencies, their size and the respondents' subjective distance to the borders also encourage indifference to foreign affairs.

Affective relationships

The question of individuals' affective relationship toward the international system and their country's role in it takes up the largest area of systematic study in the political-culture approach to international relations. Some of its aspects need not detain us long, since they relate to the national government, which has been discussed earlier. People who trust their government in domestic politics are rather likely to do so in foreign policy as well, perhaps more so or less so depending on their level of international knowledge. Subcultural affinities for neighboring states, such as among the overseas Chinese of South East Asia for Red China, may of course tend to negate trust in their governments' foreign policy, especially if patterns of ethnic discrimination are present. At the extreme of irredentism, again, a minority's total distrust toward the national government draws no distinction between foreign and domestic policy.[5] This subcultural differential is one of the major exceptions to the general rule that conationals will regard their own government as their main agent toward the outside world. Another exception is ideology, which will be discussed below.

Sense of agency   This sense of agency with regard to the government's role toward other countries and the international scene usually involves thinking of one's government *as an instrument* as well as important reinforcing mechanisms of identification and the collective sense of identity. It goes considerably beyond the sense of agency underlying a person's relation to his legislator or lawyer, even though both of them may represent him toward a potentially hostile world of national politics or civil relations. A person is far more likely to argue with his lawyer or to distrust his congressman, because he can do so within what looks like an orderly, civilized world in which a disloyal agent cannot do much harm to the person he represents. The international world, by contrast, is one of violent anarchy in which might makes right and an individual needs his government to protect him from coming to grief. For this reason, and also

[5] See especially the extensive literature on Eastern Europe between the two world wars.

because the outside world seems so alien and incomprehensible, people are likely to identify very strongly with their government and whatever it does toward the strangers outside the national borders. Real and imagined torts to the agencies of the national government by other countries are experienced as personal injuries or as insults to one's personal honor. A sense of collective identity crystallizes in confrontation with a presumably hostile or spiteful world, and the individuals of a nation identify with the national community.

Attitudes toward the international system   The perception of one's country's role in world politics raises further dimensions of individual attitudes toward the international system. For many years, for example, the Gallup Poll and cooperating public opinion institutes in foreign countries have asked representative samples of the populations of Great Britain, France, the United States, West Germany, Italy, and some other countries whether they were satisfied with their country's position in the world. The unfavorable responses were highest in Great Britain and the United States, rising to the neighborhood of 50 percent in critical years. It is not entirely clear what these responses imply, beyond a sense of declining empire or uneasiness with worldwide obligations. It is not even clear, except from supplementary questions in some countries, whether the dissatisfied respondents would like their countries to possess more or less power, and precisely what they understand by "position." We can conjecture from this dissatisfaction a measure of disaffection toward the international system as such, a system that has accorded the particular nation a lesser position than it "deserves." The difficulties in interpretation arise mostly from the way affective attitudes and evaluation processes are interrelated, almost inseparable.

The clearest cases of disaffection with the international system, perhaps, can be found in the sets of national and irredentist attitudes that arose from the cataclysmic consequences of World War I. The agony and disappointment of the dominant peoples of the disintegrating Ottoman, Hapsburg, and German empires merged with awakening appetites for modern democratic participation to produce virulent mass movements, including, among other things, a consuming hatred for the new international order laid down in peace settlements by the victors. The victorious nations, on the other hand, quickly clothed the hard-won new order with the mantle of righteousness and universal international organization. With the victorious status quo thus sanctified, the challengers and their respective causes as well as many irredentist minorities, who found themselves still unliberated by the peace settlement, were made to appear as criminal aggressors, bent on breaking international law and order. The prevailing international system, consequently, was viewed by these "outlaws" as illegitimate—a settlement imposed by force and against their consent. And they could hardly wait for the next violent upheaval against "the system" that might allow them to right the alleged wrongs.

Disaffection with the international system also springs from a large range of attitudes toward the role of one's country in the world. The scale from isolationism to international involvement, for example, is full of ambiguities hinging upon the perception of the international environment. An isolationist may prefer withdrawal because he is repelled by the nature of the international system or because he is confident that it will take care of itself and poses no threats to his country or to friendly nations. An internationalist, by the same token, may favor involvement because he views the international system as a jungle requiring immediate intervention or because he would like to see his country a part of a well-organized international order. Neither isolationism nor interventionism per se, in other words, clearly shows the presence of trust or disaffection toward the international system.[6] The propensity of new nations toward neutralism also is often really a desire for isolation or "nonintervention" while they are working out their internal problems. In their case, also, distinctions between different parts of the international system become salient. Like most smaller or weaker countries, the new nations—with some notable exceptions—have a rather positive attitude toward international organizations, such as the specialized agencies of the United Nations, and a rather negative opinion of the major powers and their wars and manipulations.

[6] See, for example, Selig Adler, *The Isolationist Impulse* (New York: Collier, 1961), or the literature on Afro-Asian neutralism.

National "mission" Individual perception of a country's role may also be preoccupied with the historic "mission" or "purpose" of a nation in a particular region or in the world at large. Much of the literature on such subjects has tended either toward unabashed advocacy or toward tongue-clucking at such a foolish and potentially disastrous notion. But the task of the analyst is not to praise or to condemn, but to find out how large a proportion of the people believe in such a mission and what sort of action they would support in carrying it out. Recent world history is full of such notions of national purpose, which deserve to be called the great myths of world politics. They mobilize great nations in pursuit of empire or in the defense or recapturing of ancient or lost empires. They often lead nations into confrontations with one another, even holy wars fueled by visions of righteousness on both sides. Most of the time these notions of historic purpose have been limited, owing perhaps to the predominantly regional character of international politics. But there have always been myths of universal empire, crusades to spread a religious faith to all mankind, or delusions of a nation's being the universal defender of freedom or democracy in the world, especially against the challenge of universal crusades such as communism.

IDEOLOGY AND VIOLENCE IN INTERNATIONAL AFFAIRS

Political ideologies and the making of foreign policy do not bear a necessary and cogent relation to one another except in the minds of some ideologues. Even highly ideological regimes have frequently set their preferences aside and allied themselves strictly according to their national interest—the Soviet Union with Nazi Germany or the United States with Franco Spain. In some international situations, undoubtedly, an ideologically doctrinaire foreign policy might be a stupid foreign policy or even suicidal, given the dog-eat-dog nature of international politics.[7] But here, as with all clashes between subjective opinion and the hard facts of international reality, most of the time only hindsight makes the reality clear. Foreign-policy makers and the

[7] See at this point especially the literature contrasting "realism" and "idealism" in American foreign policy, such as the writings of John H. Herz, or see Louis J. Halle, "Strategy versus Ideology," *Yale Review,* 44 (September 1956).

public at large can never have all the naked facts before them when they have to make a decision, only competing interpretations of reality. And among these interpretations, those impelled by a strong ideological faith generally vary only by degree from nonideological views in their distortion of reality.

This is not to say that ideologically committed foreign-policy makers would not conduct foreign relations very differently from pragmatists. While their view of international reality may differ only by degree, their personal involvement hinges also on personality characteristics such as their assertiveness or aggressiveness, their desire to manipulate, and their skill at using what means for manipulation are available to them. The *process of evaluation,* in other words, is likely to produce far more different political action than the cognitive patterns might suggest. It is a well-known fact, for example, that ideologically committed statesmen are especially selective in weighing the facts and circumstances before them, discarding or making light of whatever seems to clash with their ideology. One extreme example was Adolf Hitler's propensity in the 1930s to dismiss or muzzle any German diplomat abroad who reported international opinions or circumstances unfavorable to the Nazi plans of war and Hitler's own visions of grandeur.[8]

Communist foreign policy

The most notable instance of ideological perception of international affairs in our age has been the communist view of international politics. Both Marx and Lenin regarded foreign policy as the continuation of domestic policy and, hence, determined by the class character of the various states in the international system. Capitalistic states are the instrument of the oppression of the proletariat by the bourgeoisie, the argument goes, and therefore their domestic and foreign policies are necessarily capitalistic and "imperialistic." According to Lenin,[9] imperialism and colonialism are the natural outgrowth of the

[8] See especially Gordon A. Craig, *From Bismarck to Adenauer: Aspects of German Statecraft.* Washington, D.C.: The Johns Hopkins Press, 1958, pp. 112–123.

[9] This theory in Lenin's book on imperialism (1917) was not original, but had already appeared in writings of J. A. Hobson and Franz Hilferding.

"highest stage of capitalism"—that is, a stage characterized by domestic monopolies and the export of finance capital to backward countries, whose unstable politics require the exporting country to protect its investments by taking over political control. Even where it does not aim at the establishment of colonies or dependencies, in the communist view, the foreign policy of capitalistic states is bound to be hostile to the interests of the "socialist" (that is, communist) countries and exploitative toward the working classes everywhere—especially to the "external proletariat," the ex-colonial peoples of the Third World.

The communist states, by contrast, are viewed as following a foreign policy friendly to the working classes of all countries, because they are governed "in the interest of the toiling masses." In the light of this claim, the failure of the international trade-union movement and socialist or social democratic parties to recognize the championship of their cause by the communist states raises difficulties. Official doctrine responds simply by accusing the anticommunist socialists and trade unions—the vast majority of workingmen in most Western countries—of having sold out to the capitalistic system. Before 1945 the Soviet Union, being the only communist state in existence, imposed on all faithful followers and communist parties abroad the obligatory defense of the "socialist motherland" against all threats and rivals. This was accomplished by means of the Communist International (Comintern) and by a special pledge contained in the twenty-one points every bona fide Communist party had to adopt. The pledge obliged each Communist in case of conflict to uphold the interests of the "socialist motherland" over those of his own country, thus making foreign communist parties tools of Soviet foreign policy.

Since the establishment of many more communist states and their relative drifting apart, this question of loyalty to the communist movement has become highly ambiguous. To give a concrete example, where does the primary obligation of an Italian Communist lie, when the interests and foreign policies of the Soviet Union clash with those of Communist Yugoslavia, Roumania, Czechoslovakia, or Red China? Even more dismaying to the Soviet Communists, they have found themselves lumped together with capitalistic and "revisionist" nations by the Chinese Communists, who are calling upon all African,

Asian, and Latin-American peoples to follow them and to defend their interests against all enemies, including the Soviet Union.[10]

Soviet foreign policy

The Soviet Union offers us a historical record of how ideology and actual foreign policies have corresponded for more than half a century. The making of Soviet foreign policy has always been accompanied by heavy, obsessive ideologization disseminated by well-planned propaganda throughout the masses in the country and through foreign communist parties abroad. Yet the visions conjured up by this steady drone of communist propaganda changed rapidly from one phase of Soviet foreign policy to the next. In the early years, when world revolution was expected to break out everywhere, the emphasis was on organizing communist parties in all the countries in upheaval to be ready for that day. With Stalin's advent to power, the strategy changed to securing the "socialist motherland" before anything else, and the official foreign policy entered a phase of seeking international guarantees and protection from the League of Nations and the Western powers. World War II saw the Soviet Union gyrate wildly from the cynical Nazi-Soviet pact, aggression against Finland, and the annexation of Polish and other territories into the antifascist wartime alliance with the Western powers and back again to unabashed aggression by means of communist coups throughout Eastern Europe and parts of Asia and the Middle East.

Only after the death of Stalin was the Soviet Union, now a superpower, prepared to speak tentatively of peaceful coexistence and competition with the West. The evident desire for consolidation and maintenance of the communist empire, in any case, failed to keep the Soviet Union from such aggressive policies as culminated in the Cuban missile adventure or in the attempts to promote communist revolutions in the developing countries. Neither did the professed pacifism of communist parties around the world detain the Soviet Union from intervention with massive force against intracommunist revolutions in

[10] See, for example, Vernon V. Aspaturian, "Internal Politics and the Soviet System," in R. Barry Farrell, ed., *Approaches to Comparative and International Politics*. Evanston, Ill.: Northwestern University Press, 1966, p. 212.

Hungary, Poland, and East Germany, and even against mild reforms in Czechoslovakia. As Lenin wrote in an oft-quoted passage, the championing of nonviolence and international peace by communists never for a moment was meant to deny communist support to violent insurrection against reactionary oppressors nor to wars against "imperialism." Thus, the world revolution is evidently continuing in spite of professed ideological pacifism.[11]

As regards the impact of ideology on Soviet foreign policy, then, it is not a simple, direct relationship of thought and action. It rather seems to be a swirling of forethought, doublethink, and afterthought about a fairly continuous thread of self-interested actions. Few would deny that communist ideology is a meaningful guide to Soviet foreign-policy makers, and one that an outsider must understand thoroughly. But obviously other potent considerations are also at work, such as the self-preservation of the communist elite and the national interest of the Soviet Union.

Other strongly held ideologies, too, have been imperfectly applied to national foreign policies. The German Nazi regime, for example, was not deterred by its anti-Semitic ideology from making friends with Arab leaders, nor by its race worship from concluding a pact with the Japanese. Neither did its championing of the cause of German irredentist minorities keep it from selling out the German minority of South Tyrol in Hitler's quest for Mussolini's support. These compromises of virulent ideology with narrow visions of self-interest make the illiberal lapses of Western liberal democracies appear minor.

Peace, war, and pacifism

One reason for attaching great importance to the role of ideologies and belief systems in international relations is the perennial problem of peace and war. Noble as the striving for universal peace has always been, most pacifistic lines of argument are flawed by an excessive simplemindedness about the

---

[11] See also the pertinent selections in G. A. Lanyi and W. C. McWilliams, *Crisis and Continuity in World Politics.* New York: Random House, Inc., 1966, pp. 185–213; see also R. Barry Farrell's discussion of ideology in "closed societies," *Approaches to Comparative and International Politics,* p. 170.

human motives for violence and war. There are, of course, several strains of pacifism, especially the gentle-minded and tough-minded schools, which make it hard to generalize. Nearly all of them assume falsely, however, that most individuals and nations strongly desire peace for its own sake and are willing to make considerable sacrifices for it, except perhaps for a few "greedy or sick bullies."

Gentle-minded pacifists, who are often less perceptive than the others about politics, are likely to be sadly resigned when confronted with warlike sentiment or political action. Tough-minded pacifists often show a sharp edge of hatred and belligerence directly under their dedication to nonviolence and peace, a discongruity that earned them the nickname "switch-blade pacifists" as early as the 1920s. Their hostility is directed especially against alleged warmongers in industry or the military, or whatever other culprits their particular demonology happens to single out. Some German pacifists during and after World Wars I and II were convinced that their ruling class was the cause of all the evil wars and oppression in the world just as some American pacifists today, sharing a curiously reversed vision of American omnipotence, attribute all international wars and oppression to their own government.

Unfortunately, it is only the pacifists who want peace at any price. Other people, whole nations and their governments, invariably give peace and nonviolence merely a conditional role, and one of lower priority than their national interests as they perceive them or than the beliefs and way of life they hold dear. Once a country's prevalent interpretation of the national interest or ideological significance has identified the object or issue that is so important to it, the question of war and peace seems to hinge chiefly on the *intensity* of its desire to have its way. At this point, pragmatic nations in stable circumstances may indeed prefer to pursue their objectives by means short of force, unless they feel threatened, while movements, leaders, and governments obsessed with an ideological crusade more readily go to war when they feel thwarted or deprived. Aggravating circumstances, such as an unstable international situation, major recent crises, or a record of continual friction among the contending parties, may lower the boiling point with both pragmatic and doctrinaire regimes. Escalation from action to reaction may also help trigger the violent response that seems to be always possible, with even the most civilized or modern countries responding like two snarling beasts.[12]

Greater likelihood of aggressiveness in foreign policy may stem also from internal instability. As Michael Haas has reminded us, nineteenth-century sociology still believed military aggression to be characteristic of poor, agrarian societies, whereas modern industrial societies would favor stable international relations that did not interfere with trade and economic development.[13] Lewis F. Richardson's statistics of wars, however, have clearly demonstrated twentieth-century wars to be more prevalent and destructive than ever. Haas therefore undertook to relate the incidence of military clashes to other indicators of stresses and tensions typical of industrial societies, hoping to show the correlation between social change and national aggressiveness in the twentieth century.[14] Rudolph J. Rummel in his Dimensionality of Nations (DON) project related the "foreign conflict behavior" of eighty-two nations to various dimensions, including their economic development, international contacts and cooperativeness, internal instability and heterogeneity, and the values and psychological motivations of their peoples.[15] Neither one of these studies, though, appears to have sufficiently emphasized what was a major reason for wars in modern Europe and is once more increasingly virulent in many countries of Asia, Africa, and Latin America—namely, nationalism.

[12] The mechanisms of action and reaction also involve the sense of agency in confrontations and, most of all, in war, when regression to animal ferocity or infantile rage replaces the semblance of rationality otherwise characteristic of human behavior. See also Joseph H. de Rivera, *The Psychological Dimension of Foreign Policy.* Columbus, Ohio: Merrill, 1968, chaps. 2–4.

[13] See David J. Singer, ed., *Quantitative International Politics,* pp. 216–217. Joseph A. Schumpeter in *Imperialism and Social Classes* (ed. and with an introduction by Paul M. Sweezy. New York: A. M. Kelley, 1951) skillfully motivated aggressiveness with political atavism and the urge of traditional ruling classes to deflect domestic unrest by engaging in international conflict.

[14] See his article in Singer, *Quantitative International Politics,* p. 215.

[15] See Rudolph J. Rummel, "The Relationship between National Attributes and Foreign Conflict Behavior," in Singer, *Quantitative International Politics,* p. 187.

Nationalism

Nationalism has been the driving ideological force of the age of modernization everywhere, often scarcely overshadowed by communism or fascism.[16] The same underlying processes of social mobilization or the stimulus of foreign conquest, war, and revolution appear to be behind all the ideological mass movements of our time. Nationalism in the modern sense of the word is not just solidarity among people sharing a common language, faith, or history, and not the same as loyalty to one's ruler and homeland. In the Middle Ages and the Renaissance, ascribed social status was still far more important than being English or French, except to a few nationalist intellectuals such as Dante or Machiavelli. On a mass level, identification with the national community arose only with the great historic revolutions.

Liberal nationalism   The French Revolution gave the word *nation* its modern meaning as the new source of legitimacy, replacing the monarchy, the church, and the nobility. The French bourgeoisie, the third estate, claimed to represent the whole nation and seized power on its behalf. This revolutionary nationalism became wedded to revolutionary liberalism and eventually turned into liberal nationalism. For the next fifty years and longer, liberal nationalism was the fighting creed of middle-class movements among such peoples as the Germans, Danes, Poles, and Italians, striving to liberalize their social order and to achieve national unification or emancipation.

From the beginning, liberal nationalism harbored profound ambiguities, if not irreconcilable contradictions. Despite nationalistic overtones, the creed of the French and American revolutionaries had been cosmopolitan. As the armies of Napoleon carried the gospel of the French Revolution over the battlefields of Europe, they professed to bring national and individual liberty to the peoples whose governments they defeated. While the liberal-national creed fell on willing ears, the defeated nations

[16] See especially John H. Kautsky's essay in his *Political Change in Underdeveloped Countries: Nationalism and Communism* (New York: Wiley, 1962), where nationalism and communism in developing nations are linked so closely with one another as to be almost interchangeable.

could not help but see in the French armies alien conquerors establishing a self-serving empire. Thus French nationalism engendered a German and Italian nationalist reaction and similar movements everywhere, whose antagonism to French imperialism often outweighed their liberal inspiration.

To be sure, the liberal nationalism of the American Revolution had also been greatly enhanced by hostility to British imperialism, and the French revolutionaries never received more mass support than when the armies of foreign monarchs invaded France to snuff out the revolutionary challenge to the old order. But the process of social and political modernization in America, Great Britain, the Low Countries, and France was sufficiently advanced at the time to give liberalism a broad and lasting base, which it did not enjoy in Italy, Germany, on the Iberian peninsula, or among the Slavic peoples. Where national unity still had to be achieved against the resistance of princes and sovereign states, as in Italy and Germany, the strength of the traditional forces exacted crucial compromises from the liberal-national movements. National unification could be attained only with the cooperation of such forces as the kings and aristocratic establishments of the strongest states—such as Prussia in Germany or Savoy in Italy—who were most unlikely to be won over by appeals to democratic sentiment. And so the weakness of liberalism and the expediencies of unification combined to permit the survival of strong authoritarian elements and to lend a halo to such brute military force as was necessary to overcome the resistance to unification. None of the prominent figures of the struggles for Italian or German national unification in the 1860s, in fact, could be called a liberal democrat. Many of them were rather conservative diplomats or strident nationalists.

Liberal nationalism among such peoples as the Poles or the modern Greeks, whose nationhood required liberation from the Russian, German, Hapsburg, or Ottoman empires, was similarly far more nationalistic than liberal. They thought of liberty more in terms of liberation from an alien yoke than as a new internal social order. Like many prominent Italian and German nationalists, they put collective liberty above individual liberty, although their quasi-colonial status tended to imbue them with a pervasive antiauthoritarian affect. In this, the "unredeemed" nationalisms of nineteenth-century Eastern Europe resembled the nationalism of the new nations of today, except that the aspirations for social, economic, and political modernization of the latter are rather more concrete and purposeful than were the quasi-religious dreams of national salvation of nineteenth- and twentieth-century *Europa irredenta*. The *modernizing nationalism* of former colonial peoples in Africa, Asia, the Middle East, and Latin America is clearly oriented toward the universal "world culture" that has challenged the survivals of traditionalism. By comparison, then, the contemporary "new nationalism" is more liberal than that of nineteenth-century central, southern, or eastern Europe.[17]

Problems of defining nations and nationality   The deepest ambiguity of liberal nationalism lay in the definition of the term *nation* and in the nature of the attitudes to be inculcated toward it. Nations, like individuals, are products of heredity and environment, although the heredity is clearly cultural rather than biological. Where a people had experienced a common fate under a common government for centuries and within clearly defined boundaries, as in France or England, it seemed easy to assume that national communities were among the "givens" of the human condition, eternal verities only now uncovered. But what about the identity of a nation of people who, like the Germans, had for centuries existed in many different states and even under different flags, including those of neighboring countries? What if some parts of what one nationalist movement claimed to be one great nation wanted to be little nations unto themselves? The larger Pan-Arab nation promoted by President Nasser of Egypt includes several smaller nations, such as Morocco, Tunisia, and Iraq, that each have their own, less inclusive, nationalist movements and, in some cases, smaller nationalities within, such as the Kurds of Iraq. Or what if large areas, as in Eastern Europe, are populated by such a mixture of awakening Magyar, Slavic, Teutonic, and other nationalities as to make the drawing of ethnic boundaries impossible? What if the imposition of such borders leads to the Balkan-

[17] See, for example, Paul Sigmund, ed., *Ideologies of the Developing Nations,* rev. ed. New York: Praeger, 1967, and George I. Blanksten and Pablo Gonzalez Casanova in Farrell, *Approaches to Comparative and International Politics,* pp. 131, 220.

ization of whole regions into states so small they cannot survive?

Nationalist ideologies having nationality as a principle of political organization may be useful to a large, contiguous community united by consciousness of national identity and loyalty. Under such optimal conditions, nationalism can direct the enormous energies released by the massive social mobilization taking place on the way from traditionalism to modernity into constructive channels for building a nation-state and reorganizing society. In particular, nationalism can serve to marshal the forces necessary to achieve national unity or independence from alien control as prerequisites to development. Where national identity is doubtful or controversial, however, nationalism can become a destructive force. Young nations, like young individuals, can suffer identity crises so severe that they are led into extremely asocial, aggressive behavior. When several ethnic communities inhabit the same area, for example, nationalism among them may awaken appetites for power that increase ethnic friction to the point of discrimination, persecution, even genocide, unless violence can be restrained and a more inclusive political faith takes the place of ethnic nationalism.

Imperialistic nationalism The ominous development of European nationalism in an imperialistic direction in the late nineteenth and early twentieth centuries bears further testimony to the ambiguities and dangers inherent in nationalism. As middle-class movements became increasingly conservative in reaction to the rise of socialist movements, the uglier aspects of nationalism came to the fore in both domestic and foreign policy. Movements and spokesmen for "integral nationalism" arose, such as the French *Action Française*. Integral nationalists were obsessed with the integrity or "purity" of the nation, an obsession that implied a desire to purge it of "alien" elements in culture and population. There were ugly scandals, such as the Dreyfus affair, and other anti-Semitic manifestations. Carried to an extreme in biological terms, integral nationalism amounted to racism, demanding, as it were, the establishment of a "pure French race" or an "Anglo-Saxon race" or a "German race." In this form, its theories and sentiments were picked up after World War I by fascist writers and movements.

Even more significant, nationalism became the aggressive assertion of one's national interest or national rights, regardless of the conflicting rights of other nations. The wounded pride of a nation defeated in war, such as the French at Sedan (1870) and the Germans in 1918, became a powerful spur to aggressive action. Competition for colonies or foreign markets or for a proper place among the great powers stirred up nations, arousing their desire to use force against one another. Worship of one's own nation was all too often accompanied by loathing for the "inferior breeds." Nations who had minorities living in neighboring countries demanded large cessions of territory, regardless of what other ethnic stocks might be living there or what other nations might claim the same territory. Latecomers to the race for colonies, such as Germany and Italy, also claimed to be inhibited in their development by a lack of "living space," which they demanded from neighboring countries or from the established colonial powers. Such were the crass national egotisms of both the "have" and "have-not" nations among whom World War I broke out.

Although the principle of national self-determination played an important role in the peace settlement of 1919, at least on the side of the victorious Allies, a few years later the defeated powers and some others who felt cheated went on a new rampage of aggressive nationalism. Japan plunged into Manchuria (1931) and later into China (1937); Italy seized Fiume (1921) and, under Mussolini, grabbed Ethiopia (1936) and Albania (1939); Hitler's Germany remilitarized the Rhineland (1936) and seized Austria (1938), Czechoslovakia (1938–1939), and West Poland (1939); and the Soviet Union helped itself to East Poland (1939), the Baltic countries, and parts of Finland and Roumania (1940). The League of Nations proved unable to stop the resurgence of nationalist power politics. Finally a second great alliance of powers in World War II beat down what had become an unabashed drive for empire by the three Axis powers, Italy, Germany, and Japan.[18]

With World War II the fury of European nationalisms seemed to have run its course. The postwar leaders of conti-

[18] See especially Richard N. Rosecrance, *Action and Reaction in World Politics.* Boston: Little, Brown, 1963, chaps. 8 and 9, on "imperialist nationalism" and its consequences.

nental Europe have tried to bury the ghost of nationalism underneath the idea of an economic and political union of European states. Attempts by President de Gaulle of France to shore up his country's national grandeur in the traditional manner have had about them a curious air of anachronism. The revival of national feeling in Eastern Europe, on the other hand, still spells liberalization and national emancipation from the Soviet empire in the original tradition of liberal nationalism, although evidently without the full ramifications of the liberal faith.

New nationalisms The national independence movements of Asia, Africa, the Middle East, and Latin America also are motivated by the desire for liberty from foreign domination. But with many of them the nationalism also tends to get bogged down in ethnic antagonisms that pit Africans against Africans or Arabs or Indians, or Malays and Javanese against Chinese in South East Asia, with results no better than those of integral nationalism in Europe.

As national leaders face the usual drab postindependence problems, and their newly born nations experience the postindependence letdown, the temptation is great to turn on neighboring countries. An awakening nation, after all, is one of the largest and most excited in-groups imaginable, and it is not surprising that the intense in-group feeling should feed on hostility against out-groups, or at least against the colonial powers of yesterday. In this unstable situation, causes for conquest or empire building are easily found. Indonesia claimed distant ethnic kinship and Malay collaboration with "the colonialists" for its war on Malaysia. President Nasser of Egypt has promoted his Pan-Arab union by pouring out vast torrents of radio propaganda and by exporting Egyptian schoolteachers and other trained personnel to the less-developed new nations of Africa. Some African nationalist leaders similarly sought to build up their own power by intervention in the troubles and insurrections of other countries, such as the former Belgian Congo.

The plans and manipulations of foreign-policy makers in both the West and the East have been disarrayed in many a critical area, as by a spectacular and dramatic process the new nationalisms have asserted themselves. Where perhaps villages or tribes had been quiescent for centuries under various foreign overlords, as in South East Asia, there are suddenly masses of people identifying with new national communities and rising up against outside manipulation whatever the label or justification. These peoples have stood up and now want to determine their own destiny according to their own sense of collective identity. They want to participate in world affairs and world history and of their own free will. Never again, they say, do they want to be the object of a foreign will or foreign control. This sense of pride and identification with the national community, like other attitudes surveyed here, is subjective in nature and has little to do with a sophisticated awareness of the complexity of most issues of international politics or economics. Consequently, politicians, parties, and other groups in the new nations often capitalize on the nationalistic sentiments of the masses of the people with all kinds of appeals or special pleadings of little relevance to the substance of nationalism.

Political-culture approach to nationalism

The basic attitudes of nationalism and national identification are not beyond the grasp of political-culture research, and neither are most of the other ideologies or belief systems discussed here with regard to international politics. It is worth repeating here an earlier response to certain criticisms of the political-culture approach.[19] Knowing the subjective orientations of a people and its subcultural groups toward the international system is *a necessary but not a sufficient step* toward understanding their behavior and policy. Ignoring the psychocultural dimension, as many political scientists have indeed done in the past, would mean remaining in ignorance of mass opinion and the opinions of such elite groups as make foreign policy even in the most dictatorial or oligarchical systems. To make the connection between the micro and macro levels of political analysis, however, the findings of political-culture research indeed require integration with a model of the political system in question and its decision-making process. The model allocates roles and influence to each opinion group and accounts for the processing of inputs from the outside. To claim more ex-

[19] See especially Robert T. Holt and John E. Turner, *The Political Basis of Economic Development.* New York: Van Nostrand-Reinhold, 1966, pp. 27–32.

planatory power for psychocultural findings by themselves would be unrealistic.

Another frequent criticism of psychocultural study refers to the distinction between orientation and attitudes on the one hand and actual behavior on the other. As it applies to the set of orientations to the international system, here too (as in Chap. 3) the analytical distinction is a misleading one. To begin with, behavior relates to specific, active, foreign-policy roles, which are occupied only by a very small portion of adults with opinions on the subject. Second, the line dividing political culture and behavior artificially divides a complex whole, in which behavior acts on 'the process of opinion formation and the latter in turn acts on behavior by means of its evaluative processes. The issue is an old one, and it is usually argued from rare and spectacular cases of dissonance between what people say and what they actually do. Generally speaking, however, there is a substantial consonance between opinion and behavior with frequent adjustments on both sides. Such spectacular cases of dissonance as involve options of violent action or readiness to go to war, for example, usually stem from the unsophisticated or overly rationalistic treatment of the many dimensions of political culture, including attitudes toward violence, and do not in fact show dissonance between thought and action.

THE MAKING OF FOREIGN POLICY

The making of foreign policy is not substantially different from domestic-policy making, in that it also requires a concrete model of how a given political system works, how its groups and formal roles interact in the making of decisions, and how the political subcultures of all these groups of persons come to bear on the outcome. What is different about foreign policy is that through it, governments deal with equals who are generally beyond their control and often rival their own capability for enforcement. There are also considerable barriers to information and communication with foreign partners and potential enemies, so that foreign policy often is marked by extreme caution, if not paranoia, and violent, irredeemable misperceptions. Major mistakes can snowball into major wars or, in the nuclear age, mutual annihilation between great powers.

Role of mass opinion

The role of mass opinion in foreign-policy making varies widely from country to country, depending on the size of the "attentive public," [20] the presence of democracy, and the integrity and capacity of the information processes.[21] A totalitarian country with a party-controlled press has such complete monopoly control over what its people can know about the outside world that it could even afford to allow the people to influence what the government does. In autocratic regimes, the low level of literacy keeps people from knowing and caring enough about international affairs to exert pressure upon the government. Even then, as czarist Russia experienced in 1905 and 1917, major wars and defeat can help the masses experience the realities of the international situation so violently as to trigger massive revolutions. Even in a democracy, a jingoistic press and government censorship can mislead the public on major issues of foreign policy. In most developing countries the attentive public on foreign affairs is likely to be very small and the press captive or limited to a small, literate audience. Thus mass opinion on foreign affairs is either nonexistent or artificially created by propaganda and indoctrination. In a communist or fascist state, manipulated mass opinion on foreign-policy issues, such as hatred for the "paper tiger U.S.A." or the "Soviet revisionists," can be used for internal purges and the manipulation of attitudes on other issues as well, thus serving for internal consolidation rather than external aggression.

Interest groups

Interest groups and their political subcultures play a considerable role in all political systems, with some differential according to the stage of development. From the prominence of nonassociational and institutional groups, especially the military, in developing countries, the spectrum runs to a heavy role for

[20] Discussed previously on p. 471, fn. 3.

[21] See also the theories underlying Bernard C. Cohen, *The Political Process and Foreign Policy: The Making of the Japanese Peace Settlement*. Princeton, N.J.: Princeton University Press, 1957, and Bernard C. Cohen, *The Press and Foreign Policy*. Princeton, N.J.: Princeton University Press, 1963. Also Gabriel A. Almond, *The American People and Foreign Policy*. New York: Harcourt, 1950.

associational groups such as labor unions or organized agriculture in the more advanced countries. Actually though, as may be recalled, organized labor is likely to be more politically and ideologically engaged during the transitional stage than later, when greater functional specificity presses it to stay out of partisan politics. The ubiquitous military, on the other hand, is always sufficiently important to throw its weight around in foreign policy whether the country concerned is the Sudan, the Soviet Union, contemporary China, or the United States. The formal role of the military as defense-policy makers may greatly fortify the military influence on official foreign policy. And when the military takes over by coup, of course, its leading *junta* may become the government itself.[22]

Foreign-policy elites

Political parties as decision makers have a policy content, shaped by their political subculture, as well as a role assigned by the system. One-party systems and ideological parties may be cohesive enough to make policy as a body. In most parties in government or opposition, however, the design of foreign policy is developed as oligarchically as possible. Foreign-policy studies in Great Britain, France, and other countries have suggested that there is some kind of foreign-policy elite within the upper echelons of the ruling party that excludes even other parts of the party elite.

The search for a foreign-policy elite of influential men naturally leads us beyond the ideology or subculture of a particular party to other influential groups in more or less formal roles. Comprising one such group are the opinion makers and

[22] Outstanding in their analysis of the role and opinions of interest groups in foreign-policy making have been, for instance, Hans Speier and W. Phillips Davison, eds., *West German Leadership and Foreign Policy*. New York: Harper & Row, 1957, and Karl W. Deutsch and Lewis J. Edinger, *Germany Rejoins the Powers: Mass Opinion, Interest Groups, and Elites in Contemporary German Foreign Policy*. Stanford, Calif.: Stanford University Press, 1959. See also James N. Rosenau, *National Leadership and Foreign Policy: A Case Study in the Mobilization of Public Support*. Princeton, N.J.: Princeton University Press, 1963, and Lester Milbrath in Rosenau, *Domestic Sources of Foreign Policy*. New York: Free Press, 1967.

opinion leaders in press, radio, and television, and perhaps also academic figures with a reputation for foreign-policy analysis. Knowing the international scene well and being able to give sound advice on foreign policy is a rare skill indeed. And considering that theirs is a kind of science of survival, their counsel is so sought after that they often find themselves coopted into the power structure of great states.

Formal foreign-policy roles   The most obvious way to locate the foreign-policy elite of a country is to analyze the formal role structure of foreign-policy making. Constitutions and parliamentary or ministerial rules of order are not a bad place to start, at least in a constitutional system, since they lay down the basic distribution of roles and functions of foreign-policy making among the various agencies. According to the Western constitutional tradition, parliaments or rather their foreign-policy and defense committees are given a substantial role in such matters as declaring war, ratifying treaties, or worrying about the nation's military preparedness.[23] But most functions relating to the day-to-day conduct of foreign policy, such as sending, instructing, and receiving reports from ambassadors and spies, as well as receiving envoys and negotiating agreements, have always been with the executive. In communist states, the foreign-policy elite is largely identical with the other policy-making elites at the very top of party and state, and increasingly identical with the military, as in China.[24]

Real versus formal roles   Whatever the formal distribution of roles among government agencies may be, the real distribution still has to be ascertained, and it is often somewhat different from the blueprint. From the constitution of the Fifth Republic, for example, no one could have guessed that President de Gaulle would invade the province of the foreign minister so continually and decisively as to make the latter his errand boy, a distribution

[23] See also studies of legislative foreign-policy making such as James A. Robinson, *Congress and Foreign Policy-Making.* Homewood, Ill.: Dorsey Press, 1962, and Theodore Lowi in Rosenau, *Domestic Sources of Foreign Policy.*

[24] See again Farrell, *Approaches to Comparative and International Politics,* pp. 189–194, and the writings of Edgar Furniss.

of roles not intended in the constitution. Unplanned relationships among decision-making bodies in foreign policy often replace equality with dominance and subordination or vice versa. Extra-constitutional arrangements, too, such as kitchen cabinets or personal advisers to chief executives, may overshadow the legitimate advisory bodies. The search for the true system of influence in foreign-policy making, in fact, gets our discussion back to the foreign-policy elite.

A recent study of foreign-policy elites in France and Germany by Karl W. Deutsch, Lewis J. Edinger, Roy C. Macridis, and Richard L. Merritt drew from each country elite samples composed roughly (the final sample deviated from the original quotas) of thirty each of political opinion, business, and civil-service leaders, fifteen military leaders, and another thirty prominent members of other professions. These men were asked a series of questions about the foreign-policy issues facing their countries in the mid-sixties, especially their views on European unification, disarmament, NATO and de Gaulle's foreign and defense policies, and the nature of the evolving regional and international systems.[25] Attempts have been made to expand this research to other NATO member states and to increase its depth by studying mass communications in connection with it. There is also an increasing amount of sophisticated comparative public-opinion research on foreign-policy views among more specific elites.

BEYOND THE POLITICAL SYSTEM

Our earlier discussion of ideologies and belief systems exposed the inherent limitations of an approach based on the study of national political systems. The system with which governments interact when they make foreign policy is international, as some of the organizations and ideologies at work may be also. The great ideological crusades of our age have shown no respect for national boundaries, often dedicating themselves to world revo-

---

[25] Karl W. Deutsch, Lewis J. Edinger, and others, *France, Germany and the Western Alliance*. New York: Scribner, 1967. This study was commissioned by the U.S. Arms Control and Disarmament Agency, which published all the original reports resulting from it.

lution or world conquest. In the wake of major wars and tottering old empires, in particular, new nationalisms create new national communities, and new utopian faiths forge new supranational empires. Subversion of the nation-state by internationally organized groups or by defecting natives is so common as to require no examples today.

In an age of regional and international organizations, also, most citizens of nation-states have become quite aware of the limits of national capabilities in peace and war. Instead of the sovereign state, great alliances take care of their defense. Regional organizations unify markets and pool economic and labor resources beyond the capacity of the individual political system. And many new nations, however proud of their hard-won independence, are glad to share their autonomy in planning and development with the aid and technical assistance agencies of the United Nations, regional organizations, or a major power. The proliferation of such interrelationships of national and international political systems in some functional areas has led James N. Rosenau to speak of *penetrated systems*,[26] an apt phrase to denote the obliteration of the boundary among national or between national and international systems. It bears witness, among other things, to the state of the international system, and it highlights the quasi-domestic political wrangling between, say, Russians and Poles or Americans and Italians in the foreign- and defense-policy areas of nearly all international powers today.

These limitations of the political system, of course, also reflect back upon our ways of studying them and our understanding of the nature of politics. After all, politics has never been completely encompassed by what we call the political system today. International entanglements aside, it has nearly always been set off from other social concerns, which, depending on the particular political culture, were viewed as being exempt from it or carefully protected against its grasping hands. Just as many people in different lands deny the legitimate authority of their nation-states to limit or define their interaction with other nations and their nationals, so the Western tradition and

[26] James N. Rosenau, "Pre-theories and Theories of Foreign Policy," in Farrell, *Approaches to Cooperative and International Politics*, p. 53.

other cultural traditions as well have denied their government's legitimate right to interfere with people's social lives and beliefs. The nature of politics itself, indeed, has always tended to point beyond politics and beyond political systems to matters of belief, of values, and of human purpose.

SELECTED BIBLIOGRAPHY

(Books listed for one chapter are not repeated elsewhere.)

General

Banks, Arthur S., and Robert B. Textor. *Cross-Polity Survey*. Cambridge, Mass.: M.I.T. Press, 1963.

Buckley, Walter. *Sociology and Modern Systems Theory*. Englewood Cliffs, N.J.: Prentice-Hall, 1963.

Easton, David. *A Systems Analysis of Political Life*. New York: Wiley, 1966.

Eckstein, Harry, and David E. Apter, eds., *Comparative Politics: A Reader*. New York: Free Press, 1963.

Eisenstadt, S. N. *The Political Systems of Empires*. New York: Free Press, 1963.

Finer, Herman. *Theory and Practice of Modern Government*. London: Methuen, 1969.

Functionalism in the Social Sciences. Monograph No. 5. Annals of the American Academy of Political and Social Science, February 1965.

Kling, Merle. "Area Studies and Comparative Politics," *American Behavioral Scientist,* September 1964, pp. 7–10.

Macridis, Roy C. *The Study of Comparative Government*. New York: Doubleday, 1955,

———, and Bernard E. Brown, *Comparative Politics*. 3d ed. Homewood, Ill.; Dorsey Press, 1968.

Merritt, Richard L., and Stein Rokkan, eds. *Comparing Nations*. New Haven, Conn.: Yale University Press, 1966.

Parsons, Talcott. *The Social System,* New York: Free Press, 1967.

Przeworski, Adam, and Henry Teune. *The Logic of Comparative Social Inquiry*. New York: Wiley, 1970.

Ranney, Austin, ed. *Essays on the Behavioral Study of Politics*. Urbana, Ill.: University of Illinois Press, 1962.

Russett, Bruce M., *et al. The World Handbook of Political and Social Indicators*. New Haven, Conn.: Yale University Press, 1964.

Scarrow, Howard A. *Comparative Political Analysis*. New York: Harper & Row, 1969.

Chapter One

Almond, Gabriel A., and James S. Coleman. *The Politics of the Developing Areas*. Princeton, N.J.: Princeton University Press, 1960.

Almond, Gabriel A., and G. Bingham Powell, Jr. *Comparative Politics: A Developmental Approach*. Boston: Little, Brown, 1966.

Apter, David E., *The Political Kingdom of Uganda*. Princeton, N.J.: Princeton University Press, 1961.

————. *The Politics of Modernization.* Chicago: University of Chicago Press, 1965.

Black, Cyril E. *The Dynamics of Modernization.* New York: Harper & Row, 1967.

————. *The Transformation of Russian Society: Aspects of Social Change since 1861.* Cambridge, Mass.: Harvard University Press, 1960.

Eisenstadt, S. N. *Modernization: Protest and Change.* Englewood Cliffs, N.J.: Prentice-Hall, 1966.

Finkle, Jason, and Richard W. Gable, eds. *Political Development and Social Change.* New York: Wiley, 1966.

Hagen, Everett E. *On the Theory of Social Change.* Homewood, Ill.: Dorsey Press, 1962.

Holt, Robert T., and John E. Turner. *The Political Basis of Economic Development.* Princeton, N.J.: Van Nostrand-Reinhold, 1966.

Huntington, Samuel P. *Political Order in Changing Societies.* New Haven, Conn.: Yale University Press, 1968.

Kautsky, John H., ed. *Political Change in Underdeveloped Countries.* New York: Wiley, 1962.

Lerner, Daniel. *The Passing of Traditional Society.* New York: Free Press, 1958.

Millikan, Max F., and Donald L. M. Blackmer, eds. *The Emerging Nations.* Boston: Little, Brown, 1961.

New Nations and Political Development. Annals of the American Academy of Political and Social Science, March 1965.

Rustow, Dankwart. *A World of Nations: Problems of Political Modernization.* Washington, D.C.: Brookings, 1967.

Scott, Andrew M., William A., and Trudi M. Lucas. *Simulation and National Development.* New York: Wiley, 1966.

Shils, Edward. *Political Development in the New States.* The Hague: Mouton, 1962.

Silvert, Kalman H., ed. *Discussion at Bellagio.* New York: American Universities Field Staff, 1964.

Sinai, L. Robert. *The Challenge of Modernization.* New York: Norton, 1964.

Von der Mehden, Fred. *Politics of the Developing Nations.* Englewood Cliffs, N.J.: Prentice-Hall, 1964.

Wallerstein, Immanuel, ed. *Social Change: The Colonial Situation.* New York: Wiley, 1966.

Ward, Barbara. *The Rich Nations and the Poor Nations.* New York: Norton, 1962.

Ward, Robert E. *Studying Politics Abroad: Field Research in the Developing Areas.* Boston: Little, Brown, 1964.

Zolberg, Aristide. *Creating Political Order: The Party-States of West Africa.* Chicago: Rand McNally, 1966.

Chapter Two

Almond, Gabriel A. *The Appeals of Communism.* Princeton, N.J.: Princeton University Press, 1954.

Barber, James D. *The Lawmakers: Recruitment and Adaptation to Legislative Life.* New Haven, Conn.: Yale University Press, 1965.

Brzezinski, Zbigniew, and Samuel P. Huntington. *Political Power: USA/USSR.* New York: Viking, 1963.

Califano, Joseph A. *The Student Revolution: A Global Confrontation.* New York: Norton, 1970.

Coleman, James S. *Education and Political Development.* Princeton, N.J.: Princeton University Press, 1965.

Converse, Philip, and Georges Dupeux. "Politicalization of the Electorate in France and the U. S.," *Public Opinion Quarterly,* 26 (1962), 1–23.

Cowan, L. Gray, James O'Connell, and David G. Scanlon, eds. *Education and Nation-Building in Africa.* New York: Praeger, 1966.

Davies, James C. *Human Nature in Politics.* New York: Wiley, 1963.

Dawson, Richard E., and Kenneth Prewitt. *Political Socialization.* Boston: Little, Brown, 1969.

Dennis, Jack. *A Survey and Bibliography of Contemporary Research on Political Learning and Socialization.* Madison, Wisc.: Center for Cognitive Learning, University of Wisconsin, 1967.

Easton, David, and Jack Dennis. *Children in the Political System: Origins of Political Legitimacy.* New York: McGraw-Hill, 1969.

Edinger, Lewis. *Political Leadership in Industrial Societies.* New York: Wiley, 1967.

Eisenstadt, S. N. *From Generation to Generation.* New York: Free Press, 1956.

Erikson, Erik. *Childhood and Society.* New York: Norton, 1950.

———. *Young Man Luther.* New York: Norton, 1958.

Feuer, Lewis. *The Conflict of Generations.* New York: Basic Books, 1968.

Goldrich, Daniel. *Sons of the Establishment: Elite Youth in Panama and Costa Rica.* Skokie, Ill.: Rand McNally, 1966.

Greenstein, Fred. *Personality and Politics.* Chicago: Markham, 1969.

Frey, Frederick W. *The Turkish Political Elite.* Cambridge, Mass.: M.I.T. Press, 1965.

Hoffman, Stanley, ed. *In Search of France.* New York: Harper & Row, 1965.

Hyman, Herbert. *Political Socialization.* New York: Free Press, 1959.

Langton, Kenneth P. *Political Socialization.* New York: Oxford, 1969.

Laqueur, Walter Z. *Young Germany.* New York: Basic Books, 1963.

Lasswell, Harold D., and Daniel Lerner. *World Revolutionary Elites.* Cambridge, Mass.: M.I.T. Press, 1965.

Lipset, Seymour M., ed. *Student Politics.* New York: Basic Books, 1967.

———, and Leo Lowenthal, eds. *Culture and Social Character.* New York: Free Press, 1961.

———, and Aldo Solari, eds. *Elites in Latin America.* New York: Oxford, 1967.

Marvick, Dwaine, *et al.,* eds. *Political Decision-Makers.* New York: Free Press, 1961.

Milbrath, Lester. *Political Participation.* Skokie, Ill.: Rand McNally, 1965.

Political Socialization: Its Role in the Political Process. Annals of the American Academy of Political and Social Science, September 1965.

Roig, Charles, and F. Billon-Grand. *La Socialization Politique des Enfants.* Paris: Colin, 1968.

Seligman, Lester. *Leadership in a New Nation.* New York: Atherton Press, 1964.

Wylie, Laurance. *Village in the Vaucluse.* Cambridge, Mass.: Harvard University Press, 1951.

Chapter Three

Aguilar, Luis A., ed. *Marxism in Latin America.* New York: Knopf, 1968.

Almond, Gabriel A., and Sidney Verba. *The Civic Culture.* Princeton, N.J.: Princeton University Press, 1963.

Apter, David E., ed. *Ideology and Discontent.* New York: Free Press, 1964.

Arendt, Hannah. *The Origins of Totalitarianism.* New ed. New York: Harcourt, 1966.

Aron, Raymond. *The Opium of the Intellectuals.* New York: Norton, 1957.

Banfield, Edward and Laura. *The Moral Basis of a Backward Society.* New York: Free Press, 1967.

Bellak, Robert N. *Religion and Progress in Modern Asia.* New York: Free Press, 1965.

Binder, Leonard. *The Ideological Revolution in the Middle East.* New York: Wiley, 1964.

Ebenstein, William. *Today's Isms.* 5th ed. Englewood Cliffs, N.J.: Prentice-Hall, 1967.

Eckstein, Harry, ed. *Internal War.* New York: Free Press, 1964.

Eisenstadt, S. N. *Religious Transformation and Modernity.* New York: Basic Books, 1967.

Finer, Samuel E. *The Man on Horseback.* New York: Praeger, 1962.

Friedland, William H., and Carl G. Rosberg, eds. *African Socialism.* Stanford, Calif.: Stanford University Press, 1964.

Geertz, Clifford, ed. *Old Societies and New States.* New York: Free Press, 1963.

Halpern, Manfred. *The Politics of Social Change in the Middle East and North Africa.* Princeton, N.J.: Princeton University Press, 1963.

Hobsbawm, E. J. *Social Bandits and Primitive Rebels.* New York: Free Press, 1959.

Johnson, Chalmers. *Revolutionary Change.* Boston: Little, Brown, 1966.

Landauer, Carl. *European Socialism.* 2 vols. Berkeley, Calif.: University of California Press, 1959.

Lane, Robert E. *Political Ideology.* New York: Free Press, 1962.

Lopreato, Joseph. *Peasants No More.* San Francisco: Chandler, 1967.

McClelland, David C. *The Achieving Society.* New York: Van Nostrand-Reinhold, 1961.

Mead, Margaret. *Soviet Attitudes toward Authority.* New York: McGraw-Hill, 1951.

————, and Roda Metraux. *Themes in French Culture.* Stanford, Calif.: Stanford University Press, 1954.

Moore, Barrington, Jr. *Social Origins of Dictatorship and Democracy.* Boston: Beacon, 1966.

Moore, Frank W. *Reading in Cross-Cultural Methodology.* Princeton, N. J.: Human Relations Area Files Press, 1961.

National Character in the Perspective of the Social Sciences. Annals of the American Academy of Political and Social Science, March 1967.

Nolte, Ernst. *The Three Faces of Fascism.* New York: Holt, Rinehart and Winston, Inc., 1966.

Parson, Talcott. *Essays in Sociological Theory.* Rev. ed. New York: Free Press, 1954.

Pye, Lucian W. *Politics, Personality, and Nation-Building.* New Haven, Conn.: Yale University Press, 1962.

————. *The Spirit of Chinese Politics.* Cambridge, Mass.: M.I.T. Press, 1968.

————, and Sidney Verba, eds. *Political Culture and Political Development.* Princeton, N.J.: Princeton University Press, 1966.

Rose, Richard. *Politics in England.* Boston: Little, Brown, 1966.

Schwartz, Frederick R. O. *Nigeria: The Tribes, the Nation, or the Race.* Cambridge, Mass.: M.I.T. Press, 1965.

Sigmund, Paul E. *Ideologies of the Developing Nations.* New York: Praeger, 1962.

Silvert, Kalman H., ed. *Churches and States: The Religious Institution and Modernization.* New York: American Universities Field Staff, 1967.

Von der Mehden, Fred. *Religion and Nationalism in South East Asia.* Madison, Wisc.: University of Wisconsin Press, 1963.

Ward, Robert E., and Dankwart A. Rustow, eds. *Political Modernization in Japan and Turkey.* Princeton, N. J.: Princeton University Press, 1966.

Weber, Eugene, and Hans Rogger. *The European Right.* Berkeley, Calif.: University of California Press, 1965.

Women Around the World. Annals of the American Academy of Political and Social Science, January 1968.

Chapter Four

Ake, Claude, *A Theory of Political Integration.* Homewood, Ill.: Dorsey Press, 1967.

Alderfer, Harold. *Local Government in Developing Countries.* New York: McGraw-Hill, 1964.

Anderson, Charles W., Fred von der Mehden, and Crawford Young. *Issues of Political Development.* Englewood Cliffs, N.J.: Prentice-Hall, 1967.

Bendix, Reinhard. *Nation-Building and Citizenship.* New York: Wiley, 1964.

Chapman, Brian. *French Local Government.* London: G. Allen, 1953.

Cowan, L. Gray. *Local Government in West Africa.* New York: Columbia University Press, 1958.

Cox, Richard. *Pan-Africanism in Practice.* New York: Oxford, 1964.

Deutsch, Karl W. *Nationalism and Social Communication.* Cambridge, Mass.: M.I.T. Press, 1953.

————. *The Nerves of Government.* New York: Free Press, 1966.

————. "Social Mobilization and Political Development," *American Political Science Review,* 55 (September 1961), 493–514.

————, and William Foltz, eds. *Nation-Building.* New York: Atherton Press, 1963.

Duchacek, Ivo D. *Comparative Federalism* New York: Holt, Rinehart and Winston, Inc., 1970.

Earle, Valerie. *Federalism: Infinite Variety in Theory and Practice.* Itasca, Ill.: F. E. Peacock, 1968.

Emerson, Rupert. *From Empire to Nation.* Boston: Beacon Press, 1962.

Fagen, Richard R. *Politics and Communication.* Boston: Little, Brown, 1966.

Finer, Herman. *English Local Government.* New York: Columbia University Press, 1934.

Friedrich, Carl J. *Constitutional Government and Democracy*. 4th ed. Boston: Ginn and Blaisdell, 1968.
————. *Man and His Government*. New York: McGraw-Hill, 1963.
————. *Trends of Federalism in Theory and Practice*. New York: Praeger, 1968.
Griffith, J. A. G. *Central Departments and Local Authorities*. London: G. Allen, 1966.
Hicks, W. K., *et al*. *Federalism and Economic Growth in Underdeveloped Countries*. London: G. Allen, 1961.
Hodgkin, Thomas. *Nationalism in Colonial Africa*. New York: New York University Press, 1957.
Lerner, Daniel. *The Passing of Traditional Society*. New York: Free Press, 1958.
Livingston, William. *Federalism in the Commonwealth*. London: Cassell, 1963.
Mair, Lucy. *Primitive Government*. New York: Oxford, 1962.
McCord, William. *The Springtime of Freedom*. New York: Oxford, 1965.
Pye, Lucian W., ed. *Communications and Political Development*. Princeton, N.J.: Princeton University Press, 1963.
Riker, William. *Federalism: Origin, Operation, Significance*. Boston Little, Brown, 1964.
Robson, William A. *Local Government in Crisis*. London: G. Allen, 1966.
Silvert, Kalman H. *The Conflict Society: Reaction and Revolution in Latin America*. New York: American Universities Field Staff, 1966.
Swartz, Marc J. *Local Level Politics*. Chicago: University of Chicago Press, 1968.
————. *Political Anthropology*. Chicago: University of Chicago Press, 1966.
Ward, Barbara. *Nationalism and Ideology*. New York: Norton, 1966.
Wheare, Kenneth C. *Federal Government*. 4th ed. New York: Oxford, 1964.

Chapter Five
Allardt, Erik, and Yrjö Littunen, eds. *Cleavages, Ideologies and Party Systems*. Helsinki: Academic Bookstore, 1964.
Alford, Robert R. *Party and Society*. Chicago: Rand McNally, 1963.
Barnes, Samuel H. *Party Democracy: Politics in an Italian Socialist Federation*. New Haven, Conn.: Yale University Press, 1967.
Beer, Samuel H. *British Politics in the Collectivist Age*. New York: Knopf, 1965.
Black, Cyril E., and Thomas P. Thornton, eds. *Communism and Revolution: The Strategic Uses of Political Violence*. Princeton, N.J.: Princeton University Press, 1964.
Burks, R. V. *The Dynamics of Communism in Eastern Europe*. Princeton, N.J.: Princeton University Press, 1961.
Coleman, James S., and Carl G. Rosberg, Jr., eds. *Political Parties and National Integration in Tropical Africa*. Berkeley, Calif.: University of California Press, 1964.
Crotty, William J., ed. *Approaches to the Study of Party Organization*. Boston: Allyn & Bacon, 1968.
———— *et al.*, eds. *Political Parties and Political Behavior*. Boston: Allyn & Bacon, 1966.

Dahl, Robert A., ed. *Political Oppositions in Western Democracies.* New Haven, Conn.: Yale University Press, 1966.

Duverger, Maurice. *Political Parties.* London: Methuen, 1954.

Eldersveld, Samuel J. *Political Parties: A Behavioral Analysis.* Chicago: Rand McNally, 1962.

Epstein, Leon D. *Political Parties in Western Democracies.* New York: Praeger, 1967.

Friedrich, Carl J., and Zbigniew K. Brzezinski. *Totalitarian Dictatorship and Autocracy.* 2d ed. New York: Praeger, 1965.

Hodgkin, Thomas. *African Political Parties.* Baltimore: Penguin, 1962.

Johnson, Chalmers A. *Peasant Nationalism and Communist Power.* Stanford, Calif.: Stanford University Press, 1962.

Lakeman, Enid, and James D. Lambert. *Voting in Democracies.* London: Faber, 1955.

La Palombara, Joseph, and Myron Weiner, eds. *Political Parties and Political Development.* Princeton, N. J.: Princeton University Press, 1966.

Leiserson, Avery. *Parties and Politics: An Institutional and Behavioral Approach.* New York: Knopf, 1958.

Lipset, Seymour M. *Political Man.* New York: Doubleday, 1960.

———, and Stein Rokkan, eds. *Party Systems and Voter Alignments.* New York: Free Press, 1967.

McKenzie, Robert T. *British Political Parties.* Rev. ed. New York: Praeger, 1963.

Maier, Joseph, and Richard W. Wheatherhead, eds. *The Politics of Change in Latin America.* New York: Praeger, 1964.

Milnor, Andrew J., ed. *Comparative Political Parties: Selected Readings.* New York: Crowell, 1969.

———. *Elections and Political Stability.* Boston: Little, Brown, 1969.

Neumann, Sigmund. *Modern Political Parties.* Chicago: University of Chicago Press, 1954.

Olson, Mancur, Jr. *The Logic of Collective Action.* Cambridge, Mass.: Harvard University Press, 1965.

Riker, William. *The Theory of Political Coalitions.* New Haven, Conn.: Yale University Press, 1962.

Scalapino, Robert A., ed. *The Communist Revolution in Asia.* Englewood Cliffs, N.J.: Prentice-Hall, 1965.

Schapiro, Leonard. *The Communist Party of the Soviet Union.* New York: Random House, 1959.

Stammer, Otto, ed. *Party Systems, Party Organization and the Politics of the New Masses.* Berlin: Institute for Political Science, 1968.

Tarrow, Sidney. *Peasant Communism in Southern Italy.* New Haven, Conn.: Yale University Press, 1968.

Tucker, Robert C. "Toward a Comparative Politics of Movement Regimes," *American Political Science Review,* 55 (June 1961), 281–289.

Weber, Eugene. *Varieties of Fascism.* Princeton, N.J.: Van Nostrand, 1964.

Weiner, Myron. *The Politics of Scarcity.* Chicago: Chicago University Press, 1962.

Chapter Six

Braunthal, Gerald. *The Federation of German Industry in Politics.* Ithaca, N.Y.: Cornell University Press, 1965.

Downs, Anthony. *An Economic Theory of Democracy*. New York: Harper & Row, 1959.

Eckstein, Harry. *Pressure Group Politics*. Stanford, Calif.: Stanford University Press, 1960.

Ehrmann, Henry. *Organized Business in France*. Princeton, N.J.: Princeton University Press, 1957.

————, ed. *Interest Groups on Four Continents*. Pittsburgh, Pa.: University of Pittsburgh Press, 1958.

Finer, Samuel E. *Anonymous Empire*. London: G. Allen, 1958.

Frye, Charles. "Parties and Pressure Groups in Weimar and Bonn," *World Politics,* 17 (July 1965), 635–655.

Galenson, Walter. *Trade Union Democracy in Western Europe*. Berkeley, Calif.: University of California Press, 1961.

————, ed. *Comparative Labor Movements*. Englewood Cliffs, N.J.: Prentice-Hall, 1952.

————. *Labor and Economic Development*. New York: Wiley, 1959.

Gutteridge, William. *Armed Forces in New States*. New York: Oxford, 1962.

Huntington, Samuel P. *The Soldier and the State*. New York: Random House, 1964.

Janowitz, Morris. *The Military in the Political Development of New Nations*. Chicago: University of Chicago Press, 1964.

Johnson, John J. *Political Change in Latin America: The Emergence of the Middle Sectors*. Stanford: Stanford University Press, 1958.

————, ed. *The Role of the Military in Underdeveloped Countries,* Princeton, N.J.: Princeton University Press, 1962.

La Palombara, Joseph. *Interest Groups in Italian Politics*. Princeton, N.J.: Princeton University Press, 1964.

Lipset, Seymour M. *Political Man*. New York: Doubleday, 1960.

Meynaud, Jean. *Nouvelles Études sur les Groupes de Pression en France*. Paris: Colin, 1962.

Millen, Bruce M. *The Political Role of Labor in Developing Countries*. Washington, D.C.: Brookings, 1963.

Potter, Allen. *Organized Groups in British National Politics*. London: Faber, 1961.

Pye, Lucian W. *Aspects of Political Development*. Boston: Little, Brown, 1966.

Ralston, David B. *Soldiers and States: Civil-Military Relations in Modern Europe*. Boston: Heath, 1966.

Rose, Richard, ed. *Studies in British Politics*. New York: St. Martin's Press, 1966.

————, and Arnold J. Heidenheimer, eds. *Comparative Political Finance,* special issue of *Journal of Politics* (August 1962).

Rothman, Stanley. *European Society and Politics*. Indianapolis, Ind.: Bobbs-Merrill, 1970.

Rustow, Dankwart. *The Politics of Compromise*. Princeton, N.J.: Princeton University Press, 1955.

Shell, Kurt L., ed. *The Democratic Political Process: A Cross-National Reader*. Boston: Ginn & Blaisdell, 1969.

Snow, Peter G. *Government and Politics in Latin America: A Reader*. New York: Holt, Rinehart and Winston, Inc., 1962.

Spiro, Herbert J. *The Politics of German Codetermination*. Cambridge, Mass.: Harvard University Press, 1958.

Sturmthal, Adolf. *The Tragedy of European Labor.* New York: Free Press, 1957.

———, ed. *White Collar Trade Unions.* Urbana, Ill.: University of Illinois Press, 1966.

Weiner, Myron. *Party Politics in India.* Princeton, N.J.: Princeton University Press, 1957.

Chapter Seven

Bailey, Sydney D. *British Parliamentary Democracy.* 2d ed. Boston: Houghton Mifflin, 1962.

———, ed. *Parliamentary Government in the Commonwealth.* New York: Philosophical Library, 1952.

Binder, Leonard. *Iran: Political Development in a Changing Society.* Berkeley, Calif.: University of California Press, 1962.

Bodet, Gerald P. *Early English Parliaments: High Courts, Royal Councils or Representative Assemblies?* Boston: Heath, 1966.

Brogan, Denis W., and Douglas V. Verney. *Political Patterns in Today's World.* New York: Harcourt, 1963.

Carter, Gwendolen M., and John Herz. *Major Foreign Powers.* 4th ed. New York: Harcourt, 1962.

Chapman, Brian. *The Profession of Government.* London: G. Allen, 1959.

Crozier, Michael. *The Bureaucratic Phenomenon.* Chicago: University of Chicago Press, 1964.

Eisenstadt, S. N. *Essays on Comparative Institutions.* New York: Wiley, 1965.

Finer, Herman. *Theory and Practice of Modern Government.* London: Methuen, 1961.

Frank, Elke, ed. *Lawmakers in a Changing World.* Englewood Cliffs, N.J.: Prentice-Hall, 1966.

Freedeman, Charles E. *The Conseil d'État in Modern France.* New York: Columbia University Press, 1961.

Fried, Robert C. *Comparative Political Institutions.* New York: Crowell-Collier-Macmillan, 1966.

Heidenheimer, Arnold J. *The Governments of Germany.* 2d ed. New York: Crowell, 1966.

Loewenstein, Karl. *Political Power and the Governmental Process.* Chicago: University of Chicago Press, 1957.

———. *British Cabinet Government.* New York: Oxford, 1967.

Macridis, Roy C., and Bernard E. Brown. *The DeGaulle Republic: Quest for Unity.* 2d ed., Homewood, Ill.: Dorsey Press, 1970.

Macridis, Roy C., and Robert E. Ward. *Modern Political Systems: Europe, and Asia.* 2d ed. Englewood Cliffs, N.J.: Prentice-Hall, 1968.

Marx, Fritz Morstein. *The Administrative State.* Chicago: University of Chicago Press, 1957.

Meyer, Paul. *Administrative Organization: A Comparative Study of the Organization of Public Administration.* London: Stevens, 1957.

Pisanelli, Codacci, ed. *Parliaments.* London: Cassell, 1962.

Riggs, Fred. *Administration in Developing Countries.* Boston: Little, Brown, 1964.

Sampson, Anthony. *Anatomy of Britain Today.* New York: Harper & Row, Colophon, 1965.

Spiro, Herbert J. *Government by Constitution*. New York: Random House, 1959.
Waldo, Dwight. *Comparative Public Administration: Prologue, Problems and Promise*. Chicago: ASPA, 1964.
Wheare, Kenneth C. *Legislatures*. New York: Oxford, 1963.
Zurcher, Arnold J., ed. *Constitutions and Constitutional Trends since World War II*. 2d ed. New York: New York University Press, 1955.

Chapter Eight
Andrews, William G., ed. *European Politics I: The Restless Search*. Princeton, N.J.: Van Nostrand, 1966.
————. *European Politics II: The Dynamics of Change*. Princeton, N.J.: Van Nostrand, 1969.
Beer, Samuel H., and Adam B. Ulam. *Patterns of Government*. 3d ed. New York: Random House, 1967.
Brown, Bernard E. *New Directions in Comparative Politics*. New Delhi: Asia Publishing House, 1962.
Carter, Gwendolen M., and Alan F. Westin, eds. *Politics in Europe*. New York: Harcourt, 1965.
Christoph, James B., and Bernard E. Brown, eds. *Cases in Comparative Politics*. 2d ed. Boston: Little, Brown, 1969.
Cole, R. Taylor, ed. *European Political Systems*. 2d ed. New York: Knopf, 1959.
Daalder, Hans. *Cabinet Reform in Britain 1914–1963*. Stanford, Calif.: Stanford University Press, 1963.
Dallin, Alexander, and Alan F. Westin, eds. *Politics in the Soviet Union: Seven Cases*. New York: Harcourt, 1966.
Edinger, Lewis J. *Politics in Germany*. Boston: Little, Brown, 1968.
Ehrmann, Henry W. *Politics in France*. Boston: Little, Brown, 1968.
————, ed. *Democracy in a Changing Society*. New York: Praeger, 1964.
Fainsod, Merle. *How Russia Is Ruled*. Rev. ed. Cambridge, Mass.: Harvard University Press, 1964.
Germino, Dante, and Stefano Passigli. *The Government and Politics of Contemporary Italy*. New York: Harper & Row, 1968.
Groennings, Sven, Michael Leiserson, and E. W. Kelley, eds. *The Study of Coalition Behavior: Theoretical Perspectives and Cases from Four Continents*. New York: Holt, Rinehart and Winston, Inc., 1970.
Heady, Ferrell. *Public Administration: A Comparative Perspective*. Englewood Cliffs, N.J.: Prentice-Hall, 1966.
————, and Sybil L. Stokes, eds. *Papers in Comparative Public Administration*. Ann Arbor, Mich., University of Michigan Institute of Public Administration, 1962.
Kriesberg, Martin, ed. *Public Administration in Developing Countries*. Washington, D.C.: Brookings, 1965.
La Palombara, Joseph. *Italy: The Politics of Planning*. Syracuse, N.Y.: Syracuse University Press, 1966.
————, ed. *Bureaucracy and Political Development*. Princeton, N.J.: Princeton University Press, 1963.
Lasswell, Harold, and Daniel Lerner, eds. *The Policy Sciences*. Stanford, Calif.: Stanford University Press, 1950.
McCloskey, Herbert, and John E. Turner. *The Soviet Dictatorship*. New York: McGraw-Hill, 1960.
Montgomery, John D., and William J. Siffin, eds. *Approaches to De-*

velopment: Politics, Administration and Change. New York: Mc-Graw-Hill, 1966.

Pennock, J. Roland. *Self-Government in Modernizing Nations.* Englewood Cliffs, N.J.: Prentice-Hall, 1964.

Pfiffner, John M., and Robert V. Presthus. *Public Administration.* New York: Ronald, 1960.

Pye, Lucian W., ed. *Cases in Comparative Politics: Asia.* Boston: Little, Brown, 1970.

Strauss, Eric. *The Ruling Servants.* New York: Praeger, 1960.

Wraith, Ronald, and Edgar Simpkins. *Corruption in Developing Countries.* New York: Norton, 1964.

Chapter Nine

Abraham, Henry J. *Courts and Judges.* New York: Oxford, 1959.

———. *Judicial Process: An Introductory Analysis of the Courts of the United States, England, and France.* New York: Oxford, 1962.

Andrews, William G. *Constitutions and Constitutionalism.* Princeton, N.J.: Van Nostrand, 1961.

———. *Soviet Institutions and Policies: Inside Views.* Princeton, N.J.: Van Nostrand, 1966.

Bayley, David M. *Public Liberties in the New States.* Chicago: Rand McNally, 1964.

Castberg, Freda. *Freedom of Speech in the West: A Comparative Study of Public Law in France, the United States, and Germany.* London: G. Allen, 1961.

Corwin, Edward S. *The Higher Law Background of American Constitutional Law.* Ithaca, N. Y.: Cornell University Press, 1955.

David, Rene, and Henry de Vries. *The French Legal System.* N.Y.: Oceana, 1958.

Jackson, Richard M. *The Machinery of Justice in England.* 3d ed. New York: St. Martin's, 1960.

Kelsen, Hans. *The Communist Theory of Law.* New York: Praeger, 1955.

Kirchheimer, Otto. *Political Justice.* Princeton, N.J.: Princeton University Press, 1961.

McIlwain, Charles H. *Constitutionalism, Ancient and Modern.* 2d ed. Ithaca, N.Y.: Cornell University Press, 1947.

Mecham, J. Lloyd. "Latin American Constitutionalism: Nominal and Real," *Journal of Politics,* May 1959, pp. 258–275.

Nolte, Richard M., ed. *The Modern Middle East.* New York: Atherton Press, 1963.

Schwartz, Bernard. *French Administrative Law and the Common Law World.* New York: New York University Press, 1954.

———, ed. *The Code Napoleon and the Common Law World.* New York University Press, 1956.

Stokes, William. *Latin American Politics.* New York: Crowell, 1959.

Thompson, J. M., and R. D. Reischauer. *Modernization of the Arab World.* Princeton, N.J.: Van Nostrand, 1966.

Chapter Ten

Adler, Selig. *The Isolationist Impulse.* New York: Collier, 1961.

Almond, Gabriel A. *The American People and Foreign Policy.* New York, Harcourt, 1950.

Brecher, Michael. *The New States of Asia: A Political Analysis.* New York: Oxford, 1966.

Carter, Gwendolen. *Independence for Africa.* New York: Praeger, 1960.

Cohen, Bernard C. *The Political Process and Foreign Policy: The Making of the Japanese Peace Settlement.* Princeton, N.J.: Princeton University Press, 1957.

————. *The Press and Foreign Policy,* Princeton, N.J.: Princeton University Press, 1963.

Deutsch, Karl W., and Lewis J. Edinger. *Germany Rejoins the Powers: Mass Opinion, Interest Groups, and Elites in Contemporary German Foreign Policy,* Stanford: Stanford University Press, 1959.

————, Roy C. Macridis, and Richard L. Merritt. *France, Germany and the Western Alliance.* New York: Scribner, 1967.

Farrell, R. Barry, ed. *Approaches to Comparative and International Politics.* Evanston, Ill.: Northwestern University Press, 1966.

Grosser, Alfred. *French Foreign Policy under De Gaulle.* Boston: Little, Brown, 1965.

Hanrieder, Wolfram. *West German Foreign Policy: International Pressure and Domestic Response.* Stanford, Calif.: Stanford University Press, 1967.

Holsti, K. J. *International Politics.* Englewood Cliffs, N.J.: Prentice-Hall, 1967.

Horowitz, Irving Louis. *Three Worlds of Development.* New York: Oxford, 1966.

Lanyi, George A., and W. C. McWilliams. *Crisis and Continuity in World Politics.* New York: Random House, 1966.

Macridis, Roy C., ed. *Foreign Policy in World Politics.* 3d ed. Englewood Cliffs, N.J.: Prentice-Hall, 1967.

————. *Modern European Governments: Cases in Comparative Policy-Making.* Englewood Cliffs, N.J.: Prentice-Hall, 1968.

North, Robert C. *The Foreign Relations of China.* Belmont, Calif.: Dickenson, 1969.

Power, Paul F. *Neutralism and Disengagement.* New York: Scribner, 1964.

Robinson, James A. *Congress and Foreign Policy-Making.* Homewood, Ill.: Dorsey, 1962.

Rosecrance, Richard N. *Action and Reaction in World Politics.* Boston: Little, Brown, 1963.

Rosenau, James N. *Domestic Sources of Foreign Policy.* New York: Free Press, 1967.

————. *International Politics and Foreign Policy.* Rev. ed. New York: Free Press, 1969.

Silvert, Kalman H., ed. *Expectant Peoples: Nationalism and Development.* New York: Random House, 1963.

Speier, Hans, and W. Phillips Davison, eds. *German Leadership and Foreign Policy.* New York: Harper & Row, 1957.

Waltz, Kenneth N. *Foreign Policy and Democratic Politics.* Boston: Little, Brown, 1967.

Wesson, Robert G. *The Imperial Order.* Berkeley, Calif.: University of California Press, 1967.

————. *Soviet Foreign Policy in Perspective.* Homewood, Ill.: Dorsey, 1969.

Wilkinson, David O. *Comparative Foreign Relations: Framework and Methods.* Belmont, Calif.: Dickenson, 1969.

INDEX